thelightningpress.com

MW00652787

# SMARTBOOK

# Counterterrorism, WMD & HYBRID THREAT

## Guide to Terrorism, Hybrid and Emerging Threats

**The Lightning Press**
Norman M Wade

# The Lightning Press

2227 Arrowhead Blvd.
Lakeland, FL 33813
**24-hour Voicemail/Fax/Order:** 1-800-997-8827
**E-mail:** SMARTbooks@TheLightningPress.com
**www.TheLightningPress.com**

# (CTS1) The Counterterrorism, WMD & Hybrid Threat SMARTbook
## Guide to Terrorism, Hybrid and Emerging Threats

*\* This is the second printing of CTS1 (Jul 2017), incorporating an updated DNI World Threat Assessment and additional materials from START/GTD. An asterisk marks changed pages.*

# [CTS1]
# Notes to Reader

## Guide to Terrorism, Hybrid and Emerging Threats

**Terrorism** has evolved as a preferred tactic for ideological extremists around the world, directly or indirectly affecting millions of people. Terrorists use many forms of unlawful violence or threats of violence to instill fear and coerce governments or societies to further a variety of political, social, criminal, economic, and religious ideologies.

A **hybrid threat** is the diverse and dynamic combination of regular forces, irregular forces, and/or criminal elements all unified to achieve mutually-benefiting effects. They can operate conventionally and unconventionally, employing adaptive and asymmetric combinations of traditional, irregular, and criminal tactics and using traditional military capabilities in old and new ways.

**Counterterrorism** activities and operations are taken to neutralize terrorists, their organizations, and networks in order to render them incapable of using violence to instill fear and coerce governments or societies to achieve their goals. The purpose of CT is to disrupt, isolate, and dismantle terrorist organizations and networks to render them incapable of striking the homeland, US facilities and personnel, or US interests abroad.

**Weapons of mass destruction (WMD)** are chemical, biological, radiological, or nuclear (CBRN) weapons or devices capable of a high order of destruction and/or causing mass casualties. The terrorist threat is amplified by the proliferation of WMD and their potential use by terrorists. The existence of these materials and the potential for use by actors of concern precipitates the need to plan, prepare for, and counter their use.

**Critical infrastructure** is a term used by governments to describe assets that are essential for the functioning of a society and economy - the infrastructure. **Protection** is the preservation of the effectiveness and survivability of mission-related military and nonmilitary personnel, equipment, facilities, information, and infrastructure deployed or located within or outside the boundaries of a given operational area.

**Consequence management** refers to measures to protect public health and safety, restore essential government services, and provide emergency relief to governments, businesses, and individuals affected by the consequences of terrorism.

## SMARTbooks - DIME is our DOMAIN!

SMARTbooks: Reference Essentials for the Instruments of National Power (D-I-M-E: Diplomatic, Informational, Military, Economic)! Recognized as a "whole of government" doctrinal reference standard by military, national security and government professionals around the world, SMARTbooks comprise a comprehensive professional library designed with all levels of Service in mind.

SMARTbooks can be used as quick reference guides during actual operations, as study guides at education and professional development courses, and as lesson plans and checklists in support of training. Visit **www.TheLightningPress.com**!

# [CTS1]
# References

The following primary references were used to compile *CTS1: The Counterterrorism, WMD & Hybrid Threat SMARTbook*. All references are open-source, public domain, available to the general public, and/or designated as "approved for public release; distribution is unlimited." *CTS1: The Counterterrorism, WMD & Hybrid Threat SMARTbook* does not contain classified or sensitive material restricted from public release.

## Joint Publications (JPs)

| | | |
|---|---|---|
| JP 3-12(R) | Feb 2013 | Cyberspace Operations (Redacted) |
| JP 3-26 | Oct 2014 | Counterterrorism |
| JP 3-26* | Nov 2009 | Counterterrorism |
| JP 3-28 | Jul 2014 | Defense Support to Civil Authority |
| JP 3-40 | Oct 2014 | Countering Weapons of Mass Destruction |
| JP 3-41 | Jun 2012 | Chemical, Biological, Radiological, and Nuclear Consequence Management |

## Army Doctrine Publication (ADP), Army Doctrine Reference Publications (ADRPs), Army Techniques Publications (ATPs), and Training Circulars (TCs)

| | | |
|---|---|---|
| ADP/ADRP 3-37 | Aug 2012 | Protection |
| ATP 3-11.41 | Jul 2015 | Multi-Service TTPs for CBRN Consequence Management Operations |
| TC 7-100 | Nov 2010 | Hybrid Threat |

## Other Publications and Manuals

U.S. Army TRADOC G2 Handbook No. 1 (Version 5.0), A Military Guide to Terrorism in the Twenty-First Century, Aug 2007.

DCSINT Handbook No. 1.02, Critical Infrastructure, Aug 2006.

TRADOC Pamphlet 525-3-1, The U.S. Army Operating Concept: Win in a Complex World 2020-2040, Oct 2014.

NIPP 2013, National Infrastructure Protection Plan: Partnering for Critical Infrastructure Security and Resilience, Dept of Homeland Security, 2013.

## Additional Reference Sources

Combating Terrorism Center at West Point

Federal Bureau of Investigation

National Consortium for the Study of Terrorism and Responses to Terrorism (START). Global Terrorism Database [Data file]. Retrieved from http://www.start.umd.edu/gtd

National Counterterrorism Center (NCTC)

U.S. Department of State, Bureau of Counterterrorism

*\* Editor's Note: Chapter one on "The Terrorist Threat" from the 2009 edition of JP 3-26 was not carried forward or updated to the 2014 edition. Because the chapter contained valuable doctrinal reference material on the terrorist threat, it is referenced extensively in this book.*

# [CTS1]
# Foreword

The terrorist attacks of September 11, 2001, fundamentally transformed the United States national security establishment. In the years following, the United States government renounced its Cold War posture and embraced an entirely new security stance. The landmark changes put terrorism on the mind of all Americans- from government officials, to new immigrants, business travelers, school children, and ordinary citizens.

One of the most significant security threats to the people of the United States comes from international terrorism. Recent events have shown, tragically, that the treat from terrorism is likely to be with us for some time. Terrorists seek to inflict mass casualties without warning and are often motivated through extremist ideologies.

The terrorist threat is always evolving; therefore, it is important that we, as counterterrorism students and practitioners, stay as prepared and informed as possible on how to meet this threat.

I am very pleased to work with The Lightning Press on this *Counterterrorism, WMD & Hybrid Threat SMARTbook*. This SMARTbook sets out a comprehensive approach towards understanding the nature of domestic and international terrorism, state-sponsored terrorism, and the behaviors and characteristics of terrorists. It then explains the nature of hybrid threats, counterterrorism strategies, and counterterrorism tactics. The fundamentals of command and control, risk management, cyber threats, weapons of mass destruction, protection planning, consequence management, and workplace violence are all outlined and discussed in detail.

In publishing this SMARTbook, we aim to provide a single resource for a basic understanding of contemporary terrorism. It is written for the audience of citizens, students, and counterterrorism practitioners -- military and civilian. This timely volume provides a clear framework for understanding today's complex security threats. More importantly, it gives students a firm baseline for continuing terrorism and counterterrorism studies, and it gives practitioners a reference for how the U.S. government has organized to meet the threat from terrorist activity.

We at Henley-Putnam University, and our colleagues at Lightning Press, hope that through this SMARTbook, we will have the opportunity to make a unique contribution to the field of terrorism and counterterrorism, as well as open up new dialogue on this multifaceted topic.

Diane L. Maye, Ph.D.
Dean, Terrorism and Counterterrorism Studies
Henley-Putnam University

# (CTS1)
# Acknowledgements

**SMARTbooks: Reference Essentials for the Instruments of National Power (D-I-M-E: Diplomatic, Informational, Military, Economic)!**

Recognized as a "whole of government" doctrinal reference standard by military, national security and government professionals around the world, SMARTbooks comprise a comprehensive professional library designed with all levels of Soldiers, Sailors, Airmen, Marines and Civilians in mind. Applying informational art to doctrinal science, SMARTbooks make reference as easy as 1-2-3!

Our new "National Power" series is a nested collection of supporting and related titles, but with a different focus and "Whole of Government" domain scope (D-I-M-E: Diplomatic,Informational, Military, Economic). Authored by established subject matter experts and industry thought leaders, National Power SMARTbooks are in-depth, single-topic, multi-volume specialty books across multiple reference categories, coupled with the same unique SMARTbook series approach to reference/technical writing and informational art.

The author and publisher would like to thank and acknowledge the following individuals who contributed subject matter expert and thought-leader research, review and materials to this book (listed in order of appearance):

Dr. Diane Maye
Dr. Troy Mitchell
Dr. Tamara A. Mouras
Paul Beach
Jay Martin
Dr. Thomas Hennefer

Norman M. Wade
Author/Publisher
The Lightning Press SMARTbooks

*\* This is the second printing of CTS1 (Jul 2017), incorporating an updated DNI World Threat Assessment and additional materials from START/GTD. An asterisk marks changed pages.*

# (CTS1)
# Table of Contents

**Chap 1**

# The Terrorist Threat

**2-Table of Contents**

# Hybrid & Future Threats

Chap 2

# Chap 3
# Forms of Terrorism (Tactics & Techniques)

# Counterterrorism

# Chap 5 — Critical Infrastructure

# Chap 6

# Protection Planning & Preparation

# Countering Weapons of Mass Destruction

# IV. CWMD Execution

**Chap 8**

# Consequence Management (CM)

# I. Terrorism (Overview/Introduction)

*Ref: JP 3-26, Counterterrorism (Nov '09), chap 2 and JP 3-26 (2014), chap. 1.*

America is at war with extremists who advocate and use violence to gain control over others and threaten our way of life. Violent extremists find it useful to mischaracterize the war as a religious or cultural clash (e.g., between Islam and the West). These violent extremists see the United States and other western societies as primary obstacles to achieving their political ends. The greatest strength of our society is its freedom and openness. The extremist networks will continue to exploit the seams in open societies around the globe, and consequently, the United States and partner nations remain vulnerable to terrorist violence designed to undermine those relationships and cause some members to abandon the struggle.

*(Dan Howell / Shutterstock.com)*

Terrorists use many forms of unlawful violence or threats of violence to instill fear and coerce governments or societies to further a variety of political, social, criminal, economic, and religious ideologies. Terrorists threaten the national power, sovereignty, and interests of the United States and our allies. Terrorists organize and operate in a number of ways. Some operate within transnational networks, others operate as small independent groups, and others operate alone. The terrorist threat is amplified by the proliferation of weapons of mass destruction (WMD) and their potential use by terrorists. The United States strives to enlist the support of the international community, adapts alliances, and creates new partnerships to facilitate regional solutions that contain and defeat terrorists, their organizations, and networks.

## I. What is Terrorism?

Terrorism has been described as both a tactic and strategy; a crime and a holy duty; a justified reaction to oppression and an inexcusable action. Definition may depend on whose point of view is being represented. Terrorism has often been an effective tactic for the weaker side in a conflict. As an asymmetric form of conflict, terrorism projects coercive power with many of the advantages of military force at a fraction of the cost to the terrorist. Terrorism is a means -- a method -- to an objective.

# Defining Terrorism

*Ref: U.S. Army TRADOC G2 Handbook No. 1 (Version 5.0), A Military Guide to Terrorism in the Twenty-First Century (Aug '07), pp. 1-2 to 1-6 and FBI.GOV.*

The U.S. Department of Defense (DOD) approved definition of terrorism is: "The calculated use of unlawful violence or threat of unlawful violence to inculcate fear; intended to coerce or to intimidate governments or societies in the pursuit of goals that are generally political, religious, or ideological."

For the purposes of this SMARTbook, this will be the standard definition. However, this is one of many definitions. A sampling of definitions by the Federal Bureau of Investigation (FBI) and the Department of State (DOS) illustrate the different perspectives of categorizing and analyzing terrorism.

The FBI uses this: "Terrorism is the unlawful use of force and violence against persons or property to intimidate or coerce a government, the civilian population, or any segment thereof, in furtherance of political or social objectives." The U.S. Department of State uses the definition contained in Title 22 U.S.C. Section 2656f(d). According to this section, "terrorism" means "premeditated politically-motivated violence perpetrated against non-combatant targets by sub-national groups or clandestine agents."

The National Counterterrorism Center (NCTC) uses this Title 22 definition of terrorism also in its annual reports of terrorism incidents around the world. These definitions stress the respective institutional concerns of the organizations using them. The FBI concentrates on the unlawful aspect in keeping with its law enforcement mission.

The Department of State concerns itself with politically motivated actions by sub-national or clandestine actors as functions affect international relations and diplomacy. Terrorism is "...fundamentally political so the political significance of major events is vital to determining meaningful responses."

## Related Definitions

### Terrorist
An individual who uses violence, terror, and intimidation to achieve a result. (JP 1-02)

### Antiterrorism (AT)
Defensive measures used to reduce the vulnerability of individuals and property to terrorist acts, to include limited response and containment by local military forces. (JP 1-02)

### Combating Terrorism (CbT)
Actions, including antiterrorism and counterterrorism, taken to oppose terrorism throughout the entire threat spectrum. Also called CbT. (JP 1-02. Source: JP 3-26)

### Counterterrorism (CT)
Activities and operations taken to neutralize terrorists and their organizations and networks in order to render them incapable of using violence to instill fear and coerce governments or societies to achieve their goals. Also called CT. (Approved for incorporation into JP 1-02. Source: JP 3-26)

### Transnational Threat
Any activity, individual, or group not tied to a particular country or region that operates across international boundaries and threatens United States national security or interests. (JP 1-02. Source: JP 3-26)

Outside the United States Government, there are greater variations in what features of terrorism are emphasized in definitions. One comment used often is, "One state's terrorist is another state's freedom fighter." There is clearly a wide array of definitions for terrorism. Despite this, several common elements may assist in defining terrorism: political, psychological, violent, dynamic, and deliberate. The United Nations produced this description in 1992; "An anxiety inspiring method of repeated violent action, employed by semi-clandestine individual, group or state actors, for idiosyncratic, criminal or political reasons, whereby - in contrast to assassination - the direct targets of violence are not the main targets." The UN has no internationally-agreed definition of terrorism. Yet in September 2006, the United Nations and its Member States demonstrated signs of collective progress in agreement to a global strategy to counter terrorism.

Terrorism, like a theatrical play, can be viewed as a deliberate presentation to a large audience in order to gain attention, spotlight a particular message, and seek a response favorable to the actor. The purpose of such actions can have sinister impact on national, regional, and global populations. Global communications provide a stage for near instantaneous media exploitation. Anxiety can increase as random or deliberate acts of terror often target civilians as victims. Similar to a play, the objective of the experience is to affect the feelings and attitudes of the audience.

# Definitions of Terrorism in the U.S. Code

*https://www.fbi.gov/about-us/investigate/terrorism/terrorism-definition (accessed Mar '16)*

18 U.S.C. § 2331 defines "international terrorism" and "domestic terrorism" for purposes of Chapter 113B of the Code, entitled "Terrorism":

## International Terrorism

"International terrorism" means activities with the following three characteristics:

- Involve violent acts or acts dangerous to human life that violate federal or state law;
- Appear to be intended (i) to intimidate or coerce a civilian population; (ii) to influence the policy of a government by intimidation or coercion; or (iii) to affect the conduct of a government by mass destruction, assassination, or kidnapping; and
- Occur primarily outside the territorial jurisdiction of the U.S., or transcend national boundaries in terms of the means by which they are accomplished, the persons they appear intended to intimidate or coerce, or the locale in which their perpetrators operate or seek asylum.*

*\* FISA defines "international terrorism" in a nearly identical way, replacing "primarily" outside the U.S. with "totally" outside the U.S. 50 U.S.C. § 1801(c).*

## Domestic Terrorism

"Domestic terrorism" means activities with the following three characteristics:

- Involve acts dangerous to human life that violate federal or state law;
- Appear intended (i) to intimidate or coerce a civilian population; (ii) to influence the policy of a government by intimidation or coercion; or (iii) to affect the conduct of a government by mass destruction, assassination, or kidnapping; and
- Occur primarily within the territorial jurisdiction of the U.S.

## Federal Crime of Terrorism

18 U.S.C. § 2332b defines the term "federal crime of terrorism" as an offense that:

- Is calculated to influence or affect the conduct of government by intimidation or • coercion, or to retaliate against government conduct; and
- Is a violation of one of several listed statutes, including § 930(c) (relating to killing or attempted killing during an attack on a federal facility with a dangerous weapon); and § 1114 (relating to killing or attempted killing of officers and employees of the U.S.).

# II. Nature of the Enemy

*Ref: JP 3-26, Counterterrorism (Nov '09), pp. II-2 to II-3.*

Terrorist groups, regardless of ideology, origin, location, or organizational structure have some common basic needs to survive and remain credible to their followers: funding, security, an ability to produce and distribute propaganda, a support infrastructure, an ability to recruit, and the means to conduct violent acts against selected targets.

*(Combating Terrorism Center)*

The principal enemy is a transnational movement, consisting of extremist organizations, networks, and individuals – and their state and non-state supporters – which uses terrorism for ideological ends. For example, the brand of terrorism used by Islamic terrorist groups has included the use of children and the mentally challenged as unknowing participants in suicide-bombing attacks against both fellow civilians and government personnel alike. Unlike traditional military adversaries, these transnational terrorists have shown no tendency to be deterred, adding significantly to the complexity of countering them. This enemy is often educated, absolutely dedicated, highly motivated, and shows little restraint. Terrorists find freedom of action within physical and virtual safe havens by exploiting modern technology, the population, the civil liberties of the societies they attack, and their extreme ideology. A common extremist ideology is what links some often disparate organizations into terrorist networks. Although they may have differing local goals or objectives, ideological extremism is the foundation of this movement's overall success. It is the key to motivation, recruitment, and direct and indirect support, and serves as the basis for justifying terrorist actions no matter how abhorrent.

Our secondary enemy is the other collective VEOs that interfere with our CT efforts and which may transition to overt sponsorship of or active participation in direct action against the United States, our PNs, and our interests.

There are a variety of state and non-state actors identified with terrorism that have been generally categorized as opportunists, extremists, and terrorists. Often, the three may be indistinguishable.

## Opportunists

Opportunists are members of criminal organizations (e.g., narcoterrorists), weapon proliferators, or state sponsors, who undercut the rule of law and governmental legitimacy, contributing to an environment of corruption and violence. Opportunists take advantage of opportunities as they arise. They often allow the existence of terrorist safe havens and sanctuaries in various regions of the world or provide mutual support to satisfy other interests. The United States is just beginning to understand the collusive nature of this criminal-extremist nexus—a convergence of opportunists' and extremists' interests. A key danger of the association are terrorists/extremists seeking to obtain and use, or threaten to use, WMD, may find their efforts assisted by those opportunists who might not endorse the extremists' views or methods but who are merely seeking financial gain.

## Extremists

Extremists are those who seek to force their ideological beliefs on others. They oppose—in principle and practice — the right of people to choose how to live and how to organize their societies; and support the murder of ordinary people to advance their extremist ideological objectives. Many violent extremists, because of the degree to which they carry their violence, are best described as terrorists. VEO is a characterization of organized extremists who may not be part of a transnational terrorist network, the primary enemy, but are organized and dangerous enough to be the secondary enemy in the long war on terrorism.

## Terrorist

The term terrorist refers to those who commit acts of terrorism. Terrorist acts or the threat of terrorism have been in existence for thousands of years. Despite a history longer than the modern nation-state, the use of terror by governments and those that contest their power appears poorly understood. When terror is applied to acts and actors in the real world of today, meaning and intent can point in many directions. Part of this dilemma is due to use of terror tactics by actors at all levels of social and political interaction. Is the "Unabomber" with his solo campaign of terror a criminal, terrorist, or revolutionary? How does a Timothy McVeigh differ from a Theodore Kaczynski? Can either of them be compared to a revolutionary government who coined the word terrorism by instituting systematic state terror against its population in the 1790s? What differs in radicalized American-based Islamic terrorists with no direct links to transnational networks such as al-Qaida? How does a domestic or "home grown" terrorist differ from an insurgent in Iraq or Afghanistan or other regions of the world? What is the face of terrorism today?

# III. Nature of the Conflict

In the years preceding the 9/11 attacks, the United States countered terrorism primarily through diplomacy and law enforcement. The President of the United States declared those attacks acts of war by an enemy that threatens to destroy our freedoms and way of life. Since that time, the DOD's understanding of the nature of the war and the nature of the enemy continues to mature and evolve.

Our future efforts will often be executed in the urban areas of various nation states. As a result, the nature of military operations will be limited by issues of national sovereignty and political risk, all significantly influenced by public opinion at home and abroad.

The employment of military and other instruments of national power against terrorist organizations is complicated by their secretive nature, widely dispersed resources, support by some populations and governments, often decentralized control, and an almost seamless integration into diverse communities worldwide. The easy availability, speed, and simplicity of global communications, financial transfers, and inter-continental movement of people enable the terrorists' global reach and their capacity to rapidly adapt their tactics and techniques to breach security measures and elude capture.

The conditions that extremist networks exploit to operate and survive have developed over the years, and those conditions must be altered through long-term, sustained operations using both direct and indirect approaches. Success against transnational terrorism will not occur in a single, defining moment but through a sustained effort to compress the scope and capabilities of terrorist organizations/VEOs, isolating them regionally and individually, and then destroying them within state borders.

Terrorist networks, such as al-Qaeda, may employ irregular, catastrophic, or disruptive methods to challenge US security interests. Irregular threats involve the employment of "unconventional" methods and tactics to counter the traditional advantages of stronger opponents. Catastrophic threats involve the acquisition, possession, and potential use of WMD or methods and material producing WMD-like effects. Disruptive threats may come from terrorist organizations that develop and use breakthrough technologies to negate current US advantages.

# IV. What Defines a Terrorist/Terrorist Group?

The term terrorist refers to those who commit acts of terrorism. Goals and objectives of terrorists and terrorist organizations differ throughout the world and range from regional single-issue terrorists to the aims of transnational radicalism and terrorism.

Terrorism is primarily a psychological act that communicates through violence or the threat of violence.

Common motivational categories include separatism, ethnocentrism, nationalism, and revolution. Ideological categories can be framed by political, religious, or social purpose. Domestic or indigenous terrorists are "home-grown," that is, they can be native born or naturalized citizens of a nation. They operate normally within and against their own country of residence. International or transnational terrorists can be visualized as operating primarily between two nations and their geographic region. International groups may operate in multiple countries, but retain a regional geographic focus for their activities. Terrorism is becoming more violent as terrorist organizations realize the value of notoriety due to spectacular attacks and the mass media exploitation that results.

## Terrorist Behaviors, Characteristics, & Motivations

Terrorism is a rationally selected tactic usually employed in the pursuit of ideological aims. However, some individuals or small violent organizations that employ terrorist means may not always be concerned with particular causes or an avowed ideology. These terrorists may be motivated purely by a desire to commit violent acts. From a psychological behavioral perspective, terrorism may fulfill a compelling need and this form of terrorism treats avowed ideology and political causes as after the fact justification. Another behavioral perspective is one based on rational choice. Terrorism is a tactic selected after rational consideration of the costs and benefits in order to achieve an objective.

Singular personality profiles of terrorists do not exist. In general, terrorists often feel alienated from society, have a perceived grievance, or regard themselves as victims of an injustice. An examination of characteristics of terrorists include aspects of status, education and intellect, age, gender, and appearance.

Motivation categories describe terrorist groups in terms of their goals or objectives. Some of common motivational categories are separatist, ethnocentric, nationalistic, and revolutionary. Goals and objectives of terrorist organizations differ throughout the world and range from regional single-issue terrorists to the aims of transnational radicalism and terrorism. As the most prominent democracy and significant economic, military, and political power in the world, the U.S. is a convenient and appealing target for extremists.

*See pp. 1-11 to 1-18 for further discussion.*

## Terrorist Organizational Models

A terrorist organization's structure, membership, resources, and security determine its capabilities, influence, and reach. A general knowledge of the prevalent models of terrorist organizations helps to understand their overall capabilities. A terrorist organization is characterized by its levels of commitment, the tactical level cellular organization, group organizational structure, and its primary motivation.

Terrorists are now increasingly part of a far broader but indistinct system of networks than previously experienced. Groups based on religious or single-issue motives lack a specific political or nationalistic agenda and therefore have less need for a hierarchical structure to coordinate their actions. Instead, they can depend on loose affiliation with like-minded groups or individuals from a variety of locations. General goals and targets are announced, and individuals or cells are expected to use flexibility and initiative to conduct the necessary actions.

*See pp. 1-19 to 1-24 for further discussion.*

# V. Terrorism Threat Model

*Ref: JP 3-26, Counterterrorism (Nov '09), fig. III-2, p. III-8.*

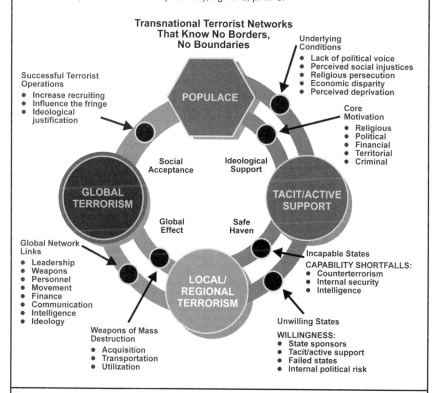

This representative model from JP 3-26 (2009) shows how violent extremist organizations (VEOs) can use terrorism as a circle that operates around four critical components:

- **A populace** from which extremists have the potential to draw support
- **Tacit and/or active support** given to the extremist by some of the sympathetic populace
- **Local/regional terrorism** as a result of states unwilling or incapable of countering violent extremists
- **Global terrorism** that results from global networks built upon popular support and the inability of states to control local and regional extremist networks

The cycle is completed when successful terrorist operations (at the global or local/regional level) reinforce their ideological justification, and influence that portion of the populace that is susceptible to the extremist ideology.

# VI. Irregular Warfare (IW) & Insurgencies

*Ref: JP 3-26, Counterterrorism (Nov '09), pp. 1-11 to 1-2, and JP 3-26 (2014), p. I-5.*

Warfare is the mechanism, method, or modality of armed conflict against an enemy. It is the "how" of waging war. The US military recognizes two basic forms of warfare: traditional and irregular. Terrorism is principally a tool of irregular warfare, but it is seen in unlawful actions of state and non-state actors during traditional warfare.

IW is a violent struggle among state and non-state actors for legitimacy and influence over the relevant populations. IW favors indirect approaches and asymmetric means, though it may involve the full range of military and other capabilities, in order to erode an adversary's power, influence, and will.

IW involves a variety of operations and activities that occur in isolation or combined with conventional force operations. An adversary using irregular methods typically will endeavor to wage protracted operations in an attempt to break the will of their opponent and influence relevant populations.

Activities applicable to IW include, but are not limited to: foreign internal defense (FID), security force assistance (SFA), COIN, CT, unconventional warfare (UW), stability operations, strategic communication (SC), psychological operations (PSYOP), IO, civil-military operations (CMO), intelligence and counterintelligence, and law enforcement.

The focus of IW is on the relevant population and not military platforms or armed forces, as it is in traditional war. IW is a struggle for legitimacy and influence over a population from which its authority to act originates, and is conferred upon either its government or leadership. IW depends not just on military prowess, but also an understanding of such social dynamics as tribal politics, social networks, religious influences, and cultural mores. Therefore, the key to success in IW comes from the ability of a group or organization to influence populations to gain or enhance political authority. Governance is the mechanism through which those political authorities serve the needs of the population. Terrorist and insurgent organizations may seek to attack and disrupt governments and their supporting ideology as a means to erode legitimacy. Hence, all parties seek to undermine their adversaries' legitimacy in order to isolate them physically and psychologically from the relevant populations. At the same time, terrorist and insurgents also seek to bolster their own legitimacy and credibility with those same populations. However, defeating terrorist organizations usually requires maintaining the legitimacy and enhancing the credibility of a political authority to support and govern the relevant population. These actions serve as a means to eliminate terrorist safe havens and set favorable conditions in which direct action can more effectively dismantle or neutralize the terrorist organizations.

Successful CT requires stable, long-term engagement to develop comprehensive knowledge of the global and regional environments and provide security and stability for key populations. However, security and stability cannot be provided by military operations alone. As a major IW activity, CT efforts should include all instruments of national power to undermine an adversary's power and will, and its credibility and legitimacy to influence the relevant population. Terrorists use physical or psychological violence to disrupt the capabilities of political authorities to govern. Terrorists seek safe haven within un-governed or under-governed areas. These areas can be decisive points in the CT effort — especially if the terrorist organization migrates towards insurgency tactics and seeks to fulfill governance functions as a means of gaining legitimacy from the population. Security, then, becomes a critical element of any plan to defeat a terrorist network; because without it, a terrorist can gain significant influence by inducing and/or exploiting a population's grievances.

IW activities such as CT often will be led by a USG agency other than the DOD. The complex nature of terrorist organizations and their focus on population coercion require joint force commanders (JFCs) to synchronize operations with the activities of the interagency and PN teams to achieve a unity of effort beyond that traditionally associated with direct action CT missions. CT operations require JFCs and their staffs to work closely with interagency and multinational counterparts during all stages of planning and execution to achieve unified action and ensure that actions taken by one organization complement the actions of others.

For long-term CT campaigns/operations, an indirect approach for continual shaping and stabilizing should be synchronized with direct approach actions. All US efforts should be integrated with those of the PN in a global and regional context. These efforts require patience, coupled with consistent and persistent messages describing the USG focus on and support of the relevant populations and their legitimate government. Paramount to success in planning CT is an appreciation for the basic human physiological, safety, and security needs as motivating factors common to all populations. The extent to which the USG and other regional and global partners can provide the basis for the relevant population to meet these human needs will affect the degree of popular support of and/or noninterference with joint force CT operations.

# Links between Terrorism and Insurgencies/ Guerilla Warfare

Terrorism is a violent act outside the normal bounds of civil law and conventional military conduct. Terrorism is often linked to an insurgency or guerrilla warfare, but is not necessarily a tactic or technique required of an insurgency or guerrilla campaign. Insurgency and guerilla warfare can overlap in execution. Although these forms of conflict may often have similar goals,differences exist among insurgency, guerilla warfare, and terrorism. An insurgency is a political effort with a specific aim to overthrow a constituted government. Guerrilla warfare is military and paramilitary operations conducted in enemy held or hostile territory by irregular, predominantly indigenous forces. An insurgency and guerrilla warfare can use terrorism as a means to shape an environment. Adapting to counter superior military forces or technological capabilities, an insurgent or guerrilla can create conditions that persuade or coerce a target audience to directly or indirectly support an insurgent or guerrilla agenda.

The goal of an insurgency is to challenge the existing government for control of all or a portion of its territory, or force political concessions in sharing political power. The key element in insurgent strategy is effective control or influence over a relevant population. A supportive population provides security, intelligence, logistical support, and a recruiting base for each side in an insurgency and counterinsurgency struggle. If the insurgency gains control over an increasing percentage of the population, the government will correspondingly lose effective control over a larger percentage of the population.

Terrorism normally does not contend for actual control of territory. Actors in an operational environment intend for violent acts to force their will on their targets. Insurgencies require the active or tacit support of some portion of the involved population. A terror group rarely has the active support of a large percentage of the population. While insurgents may describe themselves as insurgents or guerrillas, terrorists will not usually refer to themselves as terrorists. They may describe themselves using military or political terminology such as freedom fighters, soldiers, or activists.

*Refer to TAA2: Military Engagement, Security Cooperation & Stability SMARTbook (Foreign Train, Advise, & Assist) for further discussion. Topics include Security Cooperation & Security Assistance (Train, Advise, & Assist), Stability Operations (ADRP 3-07), Peace Operations (JP 3-07.3), Counterinsurgency Operations (JP & FM 3-24), Civil-Military Operations (JP 3-57), Multinational Operations (JP 3-16), Interorganizational Coordination (JP 3-08), and more.*

# VII. Forms of Terrorism

Terrorism is one of the oldest forms of human conflict. Before societies organized to wage war against each other, individuals and small bands engaged in terror tactics to achieve limited goals–to overthrow existing leaders, toward off potential rivals, or to frighten opposing groups from lands they wished to claim for themselves.

Forms of terrorism threats range non-state transnational networks with global reach capability such as al-Qaida, terrorist cells affiliated with regional or international aims, or individual self-radicalized and unaffiliated terrorists with single issue agendas. Yet, each type of network or terrorist cell has criminal intentions limited by finite capability. Terrorists exist as a foreign and domestic threat of the United States in the U.S. Homeland and in United States presence throughout the world.

Although the means and ends have evolved throughout history, the central elements of terrorism–fear, panic, violence, and disruption–have changed little through time. As the world enters the 21st Century, terrorism remains a vexing problem–an anachronistic fixture of human relations as paradoxically human and inhuman in the third Millennium as it was before the dawn of recorded history.

*See chap. 3, "Forms of Terrorism", for further discussion.*

## A. State-Sponsored Terrorism

Some nations and states often resort to violence to influence segments of their population, or rely on coercive aspects of state institutions. National governments can become involved in terrorism or utilize terror to accomplish the objectives of governments or individual rulers. Most often, terrorism is equated with non-state actors or groups that are not responsible to a sovereign government. However, internal security forces can use terror to aid in repressing dissent, and intelligence or military organizations can perform acts of terror designed to further a state's policy or diplomatic efforts abroad.

*See pp. 1-25 to 1-30 for further discussion.*

## B. International Terrorism

International terrorism involves violent acts or acts dangerous to human life that are a violation of the criminal laws of the United States or any state, or that would be a criminal violation if committed within the jurisdiction of the United States or any state. These acts appear to be intended to intimidate or coerce a civilian population, influence the policy of a government by intimidation or coercion, or affect the conduct of a government by assassination or kidnapping. International terrorist acts occur outside the United States or transcend national boundaries in terms of the means by which they are accomplished, the persons they appear intended to coerce or intimidate, or the locale in which their perpetrators operate or seek asylum.

*See pp. 1-31 to 1-74 for further discussion.*

## C. Domestic Terrorism

Domestic terrorism is the unlawful use, or threatened use, of force or violence by a group or individual based and operating entirely within the United States or Puerto Rico without foreign direction committed against persons or property to intimidate or coerce a government, the civilian population, or any segment thereof in furtherance of political or social objectives.

*See pp. 1-75 to 1-84 for further discussion.*

# II. Terrorist Behavior, Characteristics, Motivations

Ref: JP 3-26, Counterterrorism (Nov '09), pp. II-4 to II-8, and U.S. Army TRADOC G2 Handbook No. 1 (Version 5.0), A Military Guide to Terrorism in the Twenty-First Century (Aug '07), chap. 2.

The following discussion provides an insight into terrorist behaviors at both the individual and group levels, examines the impact of group goals and motivations on terrorist planning and operations, and provides observations of general terrorist characteristics. Goals and objectives of terrorist organizations differ throughout the world and range from regional single-issue terrorists to the aims of transnational radicalism and terrorism.

(FBI.GOV)

Terrorism is primarily a psychological act that communicates through violence or the threat of violence. Common motivational categories include separatism, ethnocentrism, nationalism, and revolution. Ideological categories can be framed by political, religious, or social purpose.

Domestic or indigenous terrorists are "home-grown," that is, they can be native born or naturalized citizens of a nation. They operate normally within and against their own country of residence. International or transnational terrorists can be visualized as operating primarily between two nations and their geographic region. International groups may operate in multiple countries, but retain a regional geographic focus for their activities. Terrorism is becoming more violent as terrorist organizations realize the value of notoriety due to spectacular attacks and the mass media exploitation that results.

# I. Terrorist Behavior

Terrorism is a rationally selected tactic usually employed in the pursuit of ideological aims. However, some individuals or small violent organizations that employ terrorist means may not always be concerned with particular causes or an avowed ideology. These terrorists may be motivated purely by a desire to commit violent acts. From a psychological behavioral perspective, terrorism may fulfill a compelling need and this form of terrorism treats avowed ideology and political causes as after the fact justification. Another behavioral perspective is one based on rational choice. Terrorism is a tactic selected after rational consideration of the costs and benefits in order to achieve an objective.

## A. Individual Terrorist Behaviors

### Utopian View

Some terrorists have utopian goals regardless of their aims. This utopianism expresses itself forcefully as an extreme degree of impatience with the "status quo" of the rest of the world that validates the terrorists' extreme methods. This view commonly perceives a crisis too urgent to be solved other than by the most extreme methods. Alternately, the perception is of a system too corrupt or ineffective to see or adopt the "solution" the terrorist espouses. This sense of desperate impatience with opposition is central to the terrorist world view. This is true of both the secular and religiously motivated terrorist, although with slightly different perspectives as to how to impose their solutions. There is also a significant impractical element associated with this utopian mind-set. Although their goals often involve the transformation of society or a significant reordering of the status quo, individual terrorists, even philosophical or intellectual leaders, are often vague or uncaring as to what the future order of things will look like or how their ideas will be implemented. Change, and the destructive method by which change is brought about, may be much more important than the end result.

### Interaction with Others

Terrorists interact within their groups at both the member and leadership levels. Individuals forming or joining groups normally adopt the "leader principle" which amounts to unquestioning submission to the group's authority figure. This explains the prevalence of individual leaders with great charisma in many terrorist organizations. Such leaders can demand tremendous sacrifices from subordinates. This type of obedience can cause internal dissension when a leader is at odds with the group or factions arise in the organization. Another adaptation of the individual is accepting an "in-group" (us against the world) mentality. This results in a presumption of automatic morality on the part of the other members of the group, and purity of their cause and goals. Thus, violence is necessary and morally justified and the use of violence becomes a defining characteristic.

### Dehumanization of Nonmembers

There is a dehumanization of all "out-group" individuals. This dehumanization permits violence to be directed indiscriminately at any target outside the group. Dehumanization also removes some of the stigma regarding the killing of innocents. Another aspect is that by making the oppressed people an abstract concept, it permits the individual terrorist to claim to act on their behalf.

### Lifestyle Attractions

A terrorist may choose violence as a lifestyle. It can provide emotional, physical, perceived religious, and sometimes social rewards. Emotionally, the intense sense of belonging generated by membership in an illegal group can be satisfying. Physical rewards can include such things as money, authority, and adventure. This lure often can subvert other motives. Social rewards may be a perceived increase in social status or power.

# II. Terrorist Characteristics

*Ref: JP 3-26, Counterterrorism (Nov '09), pp. II-7 to II-8 (chap 2).*

Singular personality profiles of terrorists do not exist. In general, terrorists often feel alienated from society, have a perceived grievance, or regard themselves as victims of an injustice. The following provides some general characteristics:

## Status

Contrary to a belief that terrorism is a product of poverty and despair, terrorists most commonly originate from middle class backgrounds, with some coming from extreme wealth and privilege. While guerilla fighters and gang members often come from poor and disadvantaged backgrounds, and may adopt terrorism as a tactic, terrorist groups that specifically organize as such generally come from middle and upper social and economic strata. The leadership may use less educated and socially dispossessed people to conduct acts of terrorism. Even within terrorist groups that espouse the virtues of "the people" or "the proletariat," leadership consists of those of middle class backgrounds.

## Education and Intellect

In general, terrorists, especially their leaders, are usually of average or better intelligence and have been exposed to advanced education. Very few terrorists are uneducated or illiterate. Some leaders of larger terrorist organizations may have minimal education, but that is not the norm. Terrorist groups increasingly are recruiting members with expertise in areas such as communications, computer programming, engineering, finance, and the sciences. Among terrorists that have had exposure to higher learning, many are not highly intellectual and are frequently dropouts or possess poor academic records. However, this is subject to the norms of the society from which they originate. Societies where religious fundamentalism is prevalent, the focus of advanced studies may have been in religion or theology.

## Age

Terrorists tend to be young. Leadership, support, and training cadres can range into the 40- to 50-year-old age groups, but most operational members of terrorist organizations are in the 20- to 35-year-old age group. The amount of practical experience and training that contributes to making an effective operative is not usually present in individuals younger than the early 20s. Individuals in their teens have been employed as soldiers in guerilla groups, but terrorist organizations tend to not accept extremely young members, although they will use them as nonoperational supporters. Groups that utilize suicide operations often employ very young individuals as suicide assets, but they likely are not actual members of the organization and are simply coerced or exploited into an operational role.

## Gender

The terrorists' gender is predominately male, but not exclusively male, even in groups that are rigorously Islamic. Females in these groups are used to support operations or assist in intelligence gathering. Some fundamentalist Islamic groups, however, may use females in the actual conduct of terrorist operations. In groups where religious constraints do not affect women's roles, female membership may be high and leadership roles within the group are not uncommon. Female suicide bombers have been employed with a growing frequency.

## Appearance

Terrorists are often unremarkable in individual characteristics and attempts to "profile" likely terrorist groups' members may not be productive. They may not appear out of the ordinary and are capable of normal social behavior and appearance. Over the long term, elements of fanatical behavior or ruthlessness may become evident, but they are typically not immediately obvious to casual observation.

## B. Behaviors within Groups

Terrorists within groups usually have different behaviors collectively than individually. Groups are collectively more daring and ruthless than the individual members. The individual terrorist does not want to appear less committed than the others, and will not object to proposals within the group that they would not consider as an individual. Peer pressure is the norm. Group commitment stresses secrecy and loyalty to the group and ideological intensity abounds. However, this same peer pressure and intensity can sometimes result in the forming of splinter groups or dissenting individual members, and run the risk of compromising the original group's purpose. New causes may evolve as a result.

# III. Motivations and Goals

Motivation categories describe terrorist groups in terms of their goals or objectives. Some of common motivational categories are separatist, ethnocentric, nationalistic, and revolutionary.

*See the following pages (pp. 1-16 to 1-18) for an overview and discussion of terrorist motivations categories (goals and objectives).*

Understanding the goals of the enemy promotes an active approach to analyzing the transfer of goals to objectives, and objectives into operational plans and actions. While prediction is conditional, a terrorist will consider target value and cost required of the terrorist organization to successfully attack. Goals and objectives of terrorist organizations differ throughout the world and range from regional single-issue terrorists to the aims of transnational radicalism and terrorism. As the most prominent democracy and significant economic, military, and political power in the world, the U.S. is a convenient and appealing target for extremists.

Transnational political movements that use unlawful violence to advance their objectives are referred to as Violent Extremist Organizations (VEOs) and are de facto terrorists. VEOs may initially start as adherents of a localized or transnational political movement, bound together by ethnicity, religious belief, caste affiliation, or common goal. While these groups tend to be motivated by real or imagined unjust treatment from a government (or governments), these VEOs may turn to transnational organized crime to provide financial, material, or personnel support, despite a purported abhorrence for criminal or immoral activity. The al-Qa'ida reliance on the Haqqani criminal network in Afghanistan and Pakistan is an example. Additionally, many criminal and terrorist organizations have developed political branches to offer legal protection, obfuscation, and a means to develop the trappings of a state, e.g., Lebanese Hezbollah.

Other terrorists and insurgent groups will continue to exploit weak governance, insecurity, and economic and political fragility in an effort to expand their areas of influence and provide safe havens for violent extremists, particularly in conflict zones. Sunni violent extremist groups are increasingly joining or initiating insurgencies to advance their local and transnational objectives. Many of these groups are increasingly capable of conducting effective insurgent campaigns, given their membership growth and accumulation of large financial and materiel caches. This trend increasingly blurs the lines between insurgent and terrorist groups as both aid local fighters, leverage safe havens, and pursue attacks against US and other Western interests.

No single paradigm explains how terrorists become involved in insurgencies. Some groups like ISIL in Syria and al-Qa'ida in the Islamic Maghreb (AQIM) in Mali have worked with local militants to incite insurgencies. Others, like Boko Haram, are the sole instigators and represent the primary threat to their respective homeland's security. Still others, including al-Shabaab, are the primary beneficiaries of an insurgency started by others. Finally, other groups, such as core al-Qa'ida, have taken advantage of the relative safe haven in areas controlled by insurgent groups to build capabilities and alliances without taking a primary leadership role in the local conflict.

# Impact of Terrorist Goals and Motivations on Planning

*Ref: JP 3-26, Counterterrorism (Nov '09), pp. II-6 to II-7.*

Strategies against terrorists require understanding their point of view. Understanding and knowledge of VEO's preferences and capabilities provides a baseline to conduct successful CT operations and promotes the use of active approaches, both direct and indirect, to counter the threat.

## Terrorist Asset Cost Versus Target Value

Terrorist groups require recruitment, preparation, and integration into the operational structure of the group. Recruits also require extensive vetting to ensure that they are not infiltrators. A group's leadership will not employ assets without weighing the value of the asset, the probability of success, and the potential benefits to the group. For example, suicide bombings are on the increase. This type of terrorist attack provides effective target results for relatively low cost. Normally in a terrorist operation, extensive preoperational surveillance and reconnaissance, exhaustive planning, and sufficient resources will be committed to the operation.

## Operational Intent of Terrorism

At the fundamental level, terrorism is a psychological act that communicates through the medium of violence or the threat of violence. Terrorist strategies are aimed at publicly causing damage to symbols or inspiring fear. Timing, location, and method of attacks accommodate media dissemination and ensure wide-spread reporting to maximize impact. In its purest form, a terrorist operation often will have the goal of manipulating popular perceptions, and strives to achieve this by controlling or dictating media coverage. This control need not be overt, as terrorists analyze and exploit the dynamics of major media outlets and the pressure of the "news cycle." In considering possible terrorist targets, a massive destructive attack launched against a target that does not attract media coverage may not be a suitable target for the intended effect and targeted population.

## Ideological and Motivational Influences on Operations

Ideology and motivation are the primary characteristics that influence the objectives of terrorist operations. Groups with secular ideologies and nonreligious goals often will attempt highly selective and discriminate acts of violence to achieve a specific political aim. This often requires the terrorist group to keep casualties to the minimum amount necessary to attain the objective. This is both to avoid a backlash that might severely damage the organization and to also maintain the appearance of a rational group that has legitimate grievances. By limiting their attacks, the group reduces the risk of undermining external political and economic support. Groups that comprise a "wing" of an insurgency, or are affiliated with sometimes legitimate political organizations often operate under these constraints. The tensions caused by balancing these considerations are often a prime factor in the development of splinter groups and internal factions within these organizations. In contrast, religiously oriented groups typically attempt to inflict as many casualties as possible. An apocalyptic frame of reference may deem loss of life as irrelevant and encourage mass casualty producing incidents. Losses among this group are of little account because such casualties will reap the benefits of the afterlife. Likewise, nonbelievers, whether they are the intended target or collateral damage, deserve death, because their killing may be considered a moral duty. Another common form of symbolism in terrorist targeting is striking on particular anniversaries or commemorative dates.

# Motivations of Terrorist Organizations (Goals and Objectives)
*Ref: JP 3-26, Counterterrorism (Nov '09), pp. II-13 to II-17.*

There are many different categories of terrorism and terrorist groups. These categories serve to differentiate terrorist organizations according to specific criteria, which are usually related to the field or specialty of whoever is selecting the categories. Also, some categories are simply labels appended arbitrarily, often by the media. For example, every terrorist organization is by definition "radical," as terrorist tactics are not the norm for the mainstream of any group.

## A. Government Affiliation Categories

Categorizing terrorist groups by their affiliation with governments provides indications of their means for intelligence, operations, and access to types of weapons. Joint doctrine identifies three affiliations: non-state supported, state-supported, and state-directed terrorist groups.

### Non-state supported
These are terrorist groups that operate autonomously, receiving no significant support from any government.

### State-supported
These are groups that generally operate independently but receive support from one or more governments. Sometimes the support is passive or submissive as the government allows the terrorist group a safe haven within the country.

### State-directed
These groups operate as an agent of a government and receive substantial intelligence, logistic, and operational support from the sponsoring government.

## B. Motivation Categories

Motivation categories describe terrorist groups in terms of their ultimate goals or objectives. While political or religious ideologies will determine the "how" of the conflict, and the sort of society that will arise from a successful conclusion, motivation is the "what" in terms of end state or measure of success. Some of the common motivation categories are:

### Separatist
Separatist groups desire separation from existing entities through independence, political autonomy, or religious freedom or domination. The ideologies separatists subscribe to include social justice or equity, anti-imperialism, as well as the resistance to conquest or occupation by a foreign power.

### Ethnocentric
Groups of this persuasion view race as the defining characteristic of a society and a select group is often perceived superior because of its inherent racial characteristics. Ethnicity, therefore, becomes a basis of cohesion.

### Nationalistic
The loyalty and devotion to a nation, and the national consciousness derived from placing one nation's culture and interests above those of other nations or groups is the motivating factor behind these groups. This can find expression in the creation of a new nation, or in splitting away part of an existing state to join with another that shares the perceived "national" identity.

## Revolutionary

These groups are dedicated to the overthrow of an established order and replacing it with a new political or social structure. Although often associated with communist political ideologies, this is not always the case, and other political movements can advocate revolutionary methods to achieve their goals.

# C. Ideological Categories

Ideological categories describe the political, religious, or social orientation of the group. While some groups will be seriously committed to their avowed ideologies, for others, ideology is poorly understood, and primarily a justification for their actions to outsiders or sympathizers. It is a common misperception to believe that ideological considerations will prevent terrorists from accepting assistance or coordinating activities with terrorists or states on the opposite side of the religious or political spectrum. Common ideological categories include:

## Political

Political ideologies are concerned with the structure and organization of the forms of government and communities. While observers outside terrorist organizations may stress differences in political ideology, the activities of groups that are diametrically opposed on the political spectrum are similar to each other in practice.

- **Right-wing.** These groups are associated with the reactionary or conservative side of the political spectrum, and often, but not exclusively, are associated with fascism or neo-Nazism. Despite this, right-wing extremists can be every bit as revolutionary in intent as other groups, the difference being that their intent is to replace existing forms of government with a particular brand of authoritarian rule.

- **Left-wing**. These groups are usually associated with revolutionary socialism or variants of communism (e.g., Maoist, Marxist-Leninist). With the demise of many communist regimes, and the gradual liberalization of the remainder towards capitalism, left-wing rhetoric can often move towards and merge with anarchistic thought.

- **Anarchist**. Anarchist groups are anti authority or antigovernment, and strongly support individual liberty and voluntary association of cooperative groups. Often blending anti capitalism and populist or communist-like messages, modern anarchists tend to neglect the issue of what will replace the current form of government. They generally promote small communities as the highest form of political organization necessary or desirable. Currently, anarchism is the ideology of choice for many individuals and small groups that have no particular dedication to any ideology, and are looking for a convenient philosophy to justify their actions.

## Religious

Religiously inspired terrorism is on the rise, with over a forty percent increase of total international terrorist groups espousing religious motivation since 1980. While Islamic terrorists and organizations have been the most active, and the greatest recent threat to the United States, all of the major world religions have extremists that have taken up violence to further their perceived religious goals. Religiously motivated terrorists seek justification of their objectives from religious authorities to promote their cause as infallible and nonnegotiable.

Religious motivations can also be tied to ethnic and nationalist identities, such as Kashmiri separatists who combine their desire to break away from India with the religious conflict between Islam and Hinduism. Numerous religious denominations have either seen activists commit terrorism in their name, or spawned cults professing adherence to the larger religion while following unique interpretations of that particular religion's dogma. Cults that adopt terrorism are often apocalyptic in their worldview, and are extremely dangerous and unpredictable. Of note, religiously inspired cults executed the first confirmed uses of biological and chemical nerve agents by terrorists.

*Continued on next page*

# Motivations of Terrorist Organizations: Goals & Objectives (Cont.)

Continued from previous page

Religious motivations can also be tied to ethnic and nationalist identities, such as Kashmiri separatists who combine their desire to break away from India with the religious conflict between Islam and Hinduism. Numerous religious denominations have either seen activists commit terrorism in their name, or spawned cults professing adherence to the larger religion while following unique interpretations of that particular religion's dogma. Cults that adopt terrorism are often apocalyptic in their worldview, and are extremely dangerous and unpredictable. Of note, religiously inspired cults executed the first confirmed uses of biological and chemical nerve agents by terrorists.

## Social

Often particular social policies or issues will be so contentious that they will incite extremist behavior and terrorism. Frequently this is referred to as "single issue" or "special interest" terrorism.

# D. Location or Geographic Categories

Geographic designations have been used in the past, and although they are often confusing, and even irrelevant when referring to international and transnational terrorism, they still appear. Often, a geographical association to the area with which the group is primarily concerned will be made. "Mid-Eastern" is an example of this category and came into use as a popular shorthand label for Palestinian and Arab groups in the 1970s and early 1980s. Frequently, these designations are only relevant to the government or state that uses them. However, when tied to particular regions or states, the concepts of domestic and international terrorism can be useful.

## Domestic or Indigenous

These terrorists are "home-grown" and operate within and against their home country. They are frequently tied to extreme social or political factions within a particular society, and focus their efforts specifically on their nation's sociopolitical arena.

## International

Often describing the support and operational reach of a group, "international" and "transnational" are often loosely defined. International groups typically operate in multiple countries, but retain a geographic focus for their activities. For example, Hezbollah has cells worldwide, and has conducted operations in multiple countries, but is primarily focused on influencing the outcome of events in Lebanon and Israel. An insurgency-linked terrorist group that routinely crosses an international border to conduct attacks, and then flees to safe haven in a neighboring country, is "international" in the strict sense of the word, but does not compare to groups that habitually operate across regions and continents.

Continued from previous page

## Transnational

Transnational groups operate internationally, but are not tied to a particular country, or even region. Al-Qaeda is transnational; being made up of many nationalities, having been based out of multiple countries simultaneously, and conducting operations throughout the world. Their objectives affect dozens of countries with differing political systems, religions, ethnic compositions, and national interests.

# III. Terrorist Organizational Models

Ref: JP 3-26, Counterterrorism (Nov '09), chap. 2, and U.S. Army TRADOC G2 Handbook No. 1 (Version 5.0), A Military Guide to Terrorism in the Twenty-First Century (Aug '07), chap. 3.

A terrorist organization's structure, membership, resources, and security determine its capabilities, influence, and reach. A general knowledge of the prevalent models of terrorist organizations helps to understand their overall capabilities. A terrorist organization is characterized by its levels of commitment, the tactical level cellular organization, group organizational structure, and its primary motivation.

## Terrorist Organizational Characteristics

| I | Terrorist Levels of Commitment |

| II | Tactical-level Cellular Organization |

| III | Group Organizational Structure |

| IV | Primary Motivations |

Ref: JP 3-26, Counterterrorism (Nov '09), chap. 2.

## I. Terrorist Levels of Commitment

Typically, there are four different levels of commitment within a terrorist organization: passive supporters, active supporters, cadre, and leadership. The ratio of people characterizing each successive level of commitment within terrorist organizations is astounding.

See following page (p. 1-21).

## II. Tactical-level Cellular Organization

The smallest elements of terrorist organizations are the cells at the tactical level — the building blocks for the terrorist organization. One of the primary reasons for a cellular or compartmental structure is security. A cellular structure makes it difficult for an adversary to penetrate the entire organization, and the compromise or loss of one cell does not compromise the identity, location, or actions of other cells. Personnel within one cell may not be aware of the existence of other cells or their personnel and, therefore, cannot divulge sensitive information to infiltrators or captors. Terrorists may organize cells based on tribal, family, or employment relationships, on a geographic basis, or by specific functions such as direct action or intelligence.

Some cells may be multifunctional. The terrorist group uses the cells to control its members. Cell members remain in close contact with each other in order to provide emotional support and to prevent desertion or breach of security procedures. The cell leader is normally the only person who communicates and coordinates with higher levels and other cells. Thus, a local terrorist group could, unwittingly, be part of a larger transnational or international network.

# III. Group Organizational Structure

There are two typical organizational structures used by terrorist groups: networked and hierarchical. Newer groups tend to organize or adapt to the network model. Terrorist groups associated with political organizations and activities prefer the more structured and centralized control of the hierarchical structure to coordinate their violent action with political action (e.g., traditional Leninist or Maoist groups) because strict control of activities can be difficult to enforce in a networked organization. Within either of those two larger organizational structures, however, virtually all terrorist groups use variants of "cellular organizations" (i.e., compartmentalization) at the tactical level to enhance security and to organize for operations.

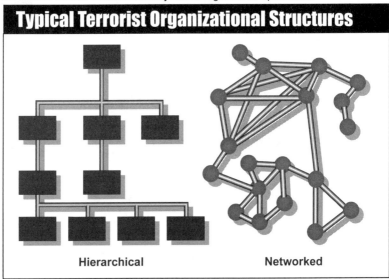

**Typical Terrorist Organizational Structures**

Hierarchical          Networked

*Ref: JP 3-26, Counterterrorism (Nov '09), fig. II-2, p II-11.*

## A. Hierarchical Structure

These organizations have a well-defined vertical chain of command and responsibility. Information flows up and down organizational channels that correspond to these vertical chains, but may not move horizontally through the organization. This is more traditional, and is common of groups that are well established with a command and support structure. Hierarchical organizations feature greater specialization of functions in their subordinate cells (support, operations, intelligence). Normally, only the cell leader has knowledge of other cells or contacts, and only senior leadership has visibility of the entire organization. In the past, some significant "traditional" terrorist organizations influenced by revolutionary theory or ideology used this structure: Japanese Red Army, the Red Army Faction in Germany, the Red Brigades in Italy, as well as ethno-nationalist terrorist movements such as the Palestine Liberation Organization, and the Provisional Irish Republican Army (IRA). These organizations had a clearly defined set of political, social or economic objectives, and tailored aspects

# Terrorist Levels of Commitment

*Ref: JP 3-26, Counterterrorism (Nov '09), chap. 2, pp. 2-8 to 2-10 (fig. 2-1, p. 2-9).*

Typically, there are four different levels of commitment within a terrorist organization: passive supporters, active supporters, cadre, and leadership.

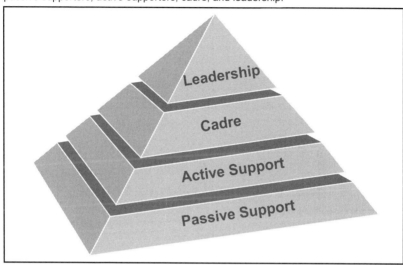

## Leaders

Leaders provide direction and policy; approve goals and objectives; and provide overarching guidance for operations. Usually leaders rise from within the ranks of any given organization, or create their own organization, and are ruthless, driven, and very operationally oriented in order to accomplish their objectives.

## Cadre

Cadre is the nucleus of "active" members, the zealots, who comprise the core of a terrorist organization. This echelon plans and conducts not only operations, but also manages areas of intelligence, finance, logistics, IO, and communications. Mid-level cadres tend to be trainers and technicians such as bomb makers, financiers, and surveillance experts. Low-level cadres are the bombers and foot soldiers for other types of attacks.

## Active Supporters

Active supporters participate in the political, fund-raising, and information activities of the group. Acting as an ally or tacit partner, they may also conduct initial intelligence and surveillance activities, and provide safe houses, financial contributions, medical assistance, and transportation assistance for cadre members. Usually, they are fully aware of their relationship to the terrorist group but do not commit violent acts.

## Passive Supporters

Passive supporters are typically individuals or groups that are sympathetic to the announced goals and intentions of the terrorist organization or its ideology, but are not committed enough to take action. Passive supporters may interact with a front group that hides the overt connection to the terrorist group, or passive supporters may intermingle with active supporters without being aware of what their actual relationship is to the organization. Sometimes fear of reprisal from terrorists compels passive support. Sympathizers can be useful for political activities, fund-raising, and unwitting or coerced assistance in intelligence gathering or other nonviolent activities.

# Basic Network Concepts

Ref: JP 3-26, Counterterrorism (Nov '09), chap. 2, pp. 2-12 to 2-13.

Terrorists are now increasingly part of a far broader but indistinct system of networks than previously experienced. Groups based on religious or single-issue motives lack a specific political or nationalistic agenda and therefore have less need for a hierarchical structure to coordinate their actions. Instead, they can depend on loose affiliation with like-minded groups or individuals from a variety of locations. General goals and targets are announced, and individuals or cells are expected to use flexibility and initiative to conduct the necessary actions.

## Tactical Concepts

 **Chain Network**

 **Hub or Star and Wheel Network**

 **All-Channel Network**

A network structure may be a variation of several basic nodal concepts, a node being an individual, a cell, another networked organization, or even a hierarchical organization. A terrorist network may consist of parts of other organizations (even governments), which are acting in ways that can be exploited to achieve the network's organizational goals. The effectiveness of a networked organization is dependent on several things.

- Network effectiveness requires a unifying idea, concern, goal, or ideology. Without that unifier, networks can take actions or pursue objectives that are counterproductive, and independent nodes may not develop the necessary synergism for success of the network.

- Networks can distribute the responsibility for operations while providing redundancies for key functions. The various cells need not contact or coordinate with other cells except for those essential to a particular operation or function. The avoidance of unnecessary coordination or command approval for action provides deniability to the leadership and enhances operations security.

- Networks need not be dependent on the latest information technology to be effective. The organizational structure and the flow of information inside the organization (i.e., their information management plan) are the defining aspects of networks. While information technology can make networks more effective, low-technology means such as couriers and landline telephones can enable networks to operate effectively.

- Changes in terrorist leadership, whether through generational transition or as a response to enhanced security operations, may signal significant adjustments to terrorist group organizational priorities and its means of conducting terrorism

# Basic Types of Networks

There are three basic types of network structures, depending on the ways in which elements (nodes) are linked to other elements of the structure: the chain, hub (or star and wheel), and all-channel. A terrorist group may also employ a hybrid structure that combines elements of more than one network type. For example, a transnational terrorist organization might use chain networks for its money laundering activities, tied to a hub network handling financial matters, tied, in turn, to an all channel leadership network to direct the use of the funds into the operational activities of a hub network conducting pre-targeting surveillance and reconnaissance. Organizational structure that may appear very complex during initial assessments of terrorist groups may be more understandable when viewed in the context of chain, hub variants, or all channel networks.

## Chain

Each node links to the node next in sequence and communication between the nodes is by passing information along the line. This organization is typical among networks that have a common function such as smuggling goods and people or laundering money.

## Hub or Star and Wheel

Outer nodes communicate with one central node, which may not be the leader or decision maker for the network. A variation of the hub is a wheel design where the outer nodes communicate with one or two other outer nodes in addition to the hub. A wheel configuration is common for a financial or economic network.

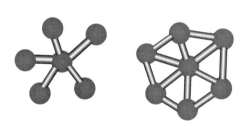

## All-Channel

All nodes are connected to each other. The network is organizationally "flat," meaning there is no hierarchical command structure above it. Command and control is distributed within the network. This is communication intensive and can be a security problem if the linkages can be identified or reconstructed. However, the lack of an identifiable "head" confounds the targeting and disrupting efforts normally effective against hierarchies.

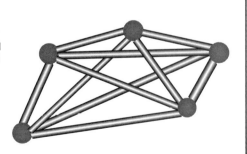

of their organizations (such as a "political" wing or "social welfare" group) to facilitate their success. The necessity to coordinate actions between various "fronts," some political and allegedly nonviolent, and the use of violence by terrorists and some insurgents, favored a strong hierarchical structure.

## B. Networked Structure

Terrorists are now increasingly part of a far broader but indistinct system of networks than previously experienced. Groups based on religious or single-issue motives lack a specific political or nationalistic agenda and therefore have less need for a hierarchical structure to coordinate their actions. Instead, they can depend on loose affiliation with like-minded groups or individuals from a variety of locations. General goals and targets are announced, and individuals or cells are expected to use flexibility and initiative to conduct the necessary actions.

*See previous pages (pp. 1-22 to 1-23) for further discussion of basic network concepts.*

# IV. Primary Motivations (Goals & Objectives)

Motivation categories describe terrorist groups in terms of their goals or objectives. Some of common motivational categories are separatist, ethnocentric, nationalistic, and revolutionary.

*(The Pan Am 103 Bombing / FBI.GOV)*

There are many different categories of terrorism and terrorist groups. These categories serve to differentiate terrorist organizations according to specific criteria, which are usually related to the field or specialty of whoever is selecting the categories. Also, some categories are simply labels appended arbitrarily, often by the media. For example, every terrorist organization is by definition "radical," as terrorist tactics are not the norm for the mainstream of any group.

*See pages (pp. 1-16 to 1-18) for an overview and discussion of terrorist motivations categories (goals and objectives).*

# IV(a). State-Sponsored Terrorism

*Ref: U.S. Department of State; and the National Counterterrorism Center (NCTC); and U.S. Army TRADOC G2 Handbook No. 1 (Version 5.0), A Military Guide to Terrorism in the Twenty-First Century (Aug '07), pp. 1-9 to 1-11.*

Some nations and states often resort to violence to influence segments of their population, or rely on coercive aspects of state institutions. National governments can become involved in terrorism or utilize terror to accomplish the objectives of governments or individual rulers. Most often, terrorism is equated with non-state actors or groups that are not responsible to a sovereign government. However, internal security forces can use terror to aid in repressing dissent, and intelligence or military organizations can perform acts of terror designed to further a state's policy or diplomatic efforts abroad.

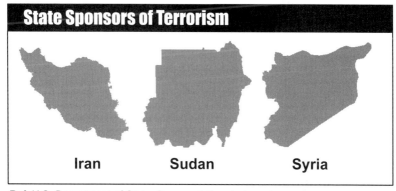

**State Sponsors of Terrorism**

| Iran | Sudan | Syria |

*Ref: U.S. Department of State, Bureau of Counterterrorism.*

Countries determined by the Secretary of State to have repeatedly provided support for acts of international terrorism are designated pursuant to three laws: section 6(j) of the Export Administration Act, section 40 of the Arms Export Control Act, and section 620A of the Foreign Assistance Act. Taken together, the four main categories of sanctions resulting from designation under these authorities include restrictions on US foreign assistance; a ban on defense exports and sales; certain controls over exports of dual use items; and miscellaneous financial and other restrictions.

Designation under the above-referenced authorities also implicates other sanctions laws that penalize persons and countries engaging in certain trade with state sponsors.

To designate a country as a State Sponsor of Terrorism, the Secretary of State must determine that the government of such country has repeatedly provided support for acts of international terrorism. Once a country is designated, it remains a State Sponsor of Terrorism until the designation is rescinded in accordance with statutory criteria.

A wide range of sanctions are imposed as a result of a State Sponsor of Terrorism designation, including:

- A ban on arms-related exports and sales
- Controls over exports of dual-use items, requiring 30-day Congressional notification for goods or services that could significantly enhance the terrorist-list country's military capability or ability to support terrorism
- Prohibitions on economic assistance
- Imposition of miscellaneous financial and other restrictions

The list began on December 29, 1979, with Libya, Iraq, South Yemen, and Syria. Cuba was added to the list on March 1, 1982 and Iran on January 19, 1984. Later North Korea in 1988 and Sudan on August 12, 1993 were added. South Yemen was removed from the list in 1990, Iraq was removed in 2004, Libya was removed in 2006, North Korea was removed in 2008, and Cuba was removed in 2015.

# I. State Terror

This form of terror is sometimes referred to as "terror from above" where a government terrorizes its own population to control and repress them. These actions are acknowledged policy of the government and apply official institutions such as the judiciary, police, military, and other government agencies. Changes to legal codes can permit or encourage torture, killing, or property destruction in pursuit of government policy.

Examples in recent decades include Stalin's purges of the 1930s that terrorized an entire Soviets population. Nazi Germany during the 1930s-1940s aimed at the deliberate destruction of state enemies and intimidation of nations and regional states. Methods included demonstration trials with predetermined verdicts on political opponents, punishing family or friends of suspected enemies of the regime, and extralegal use of police or military force against the population. More recent examples are Amin's policies of mayhem and murder in Uganda, and Saddam Hussein's use of chemical weapons on his own Kurdish population in Iraq.

Other types of state terror can include death squads as unofficial actions taken by officials or functionaries of a regime to repress or intimidate their own population. While these officials will not claim responsibility for such activities, information often indicates that these acts are sponsored by the state. Several programs in South and Central American regimes during the 1970s terrorized their populations with death squads.

States may employ terrorist networks with no formal recognition. Terror activities may be directed against the governmental interests of other nations or private groups or individuals viewed as dangerous to the state.

# II. State Sponsors of Terror

Some governments provide supplies, training, and other forms of support to non-state terrorist organizations. This support can be provided without intending any specified governing authority by the state. Provision can be safe haven or physical basing for a terrorist network. Another crucial service a state sponsor can provide is false documentation for personal identification such as passports or internal identity documents. Other means of support can include access to training facilities and expertise not readily available to terrorists, extension of diplomatic protections and services such as immunity from extradition, use of embassies and other protected grounds, or diplomatic pouches to transport weapons or explosives.

## Government Affiliation Categories

*Ref: JP 3-26, Counterterrorism (Nov '09), pp. II-4 to II-8.*

Categorizing terrorist groups by their affiliation with governments provides indications of their means for intelligence, operations, and access to types of weapons. Joint doctrine identifies three affiliations: non-state supported, state-supported, and state-directed terrorist groups.

*See p. 1-16 for further discussion.*

# A. Iran
http://www.state.gov/j/ct/rls/crt/2014/239410.htm (Accessed Mar 2016)

Designated as a State Sponsor of Terrorism in 1984, Iran continued its terrorist-related activity in 2014, including support for Palestinian terrorist groups in Gaza, Lebanese Hizballah, and various groups in Iraq and throughout the Middle East. This year, Iran increased its assistance to Iraqi Shia militias, one of which is a designated Foreign Terrorist Organization (FTO), in response to the Islamic State in Iraq and the Levant (ISIL) incursion into Iraq, and has continued to support other militia groups in the region. Iran also attempted to smuggle weapons to Palestinian terrorist groups in Gaza. While its main effort focused on supporting goals in the Middle East, particularly in Syria, Iran and its proxies also continued subtle efforts at growing influence elsewhere including in Africa, Asia, and, to a lesser extent, Latin America. Iran used the Islamic Revolutionary Guard Corps-Qods Force (IRGC-QF) to implement foreign policy goals, provide cover for intelligence operations, and create instability in the Middle East. The IRGC-QF is the regime's primary mechanism for cultivating and supporting terrorists abroad.

Iran views Syria as a crucial causeway in its weapons supply route to Lebanese Hizballah, its primary beneficiary, and as a key pillar in its "resistance" front. In 2014, Iran continued to provide arms, financing, training, and the facilitation of primarily Iraqi Shia and Afghan fighters to support the Asad regime's brutal crackdown that has resulted in the deaths of at least 191,000 people in Syria, according to August UN estimates. Iran publicly admits to sending members of the IRGC to Syria in an advisory role.

Likewise in Iraq, despite its pledge to support Iraq's stabilization, Iran increased training and funding to Iraqi Shia militia groups in response to ISIL's advance into Iraq. Many of these groups, such as Kata'ib Hizballah (KH), have exacerbated sectarian tensions in Iraq and have committed serious human rights abuses against primarily Sunni civilians. The IRGC-QF, in concert with Lebanese Hizballah, provided training outside of Iraq as well as advisors inside Iraq for Shia militants in the construction and use of sophisticated improvised explosive device (IED) technology and other advanced weaponry. Similar to Hizballah fighters, many of these trained Shia militants have used these skills to fight for the Asad regime in Syria or against ISIL in Iraq.

Iran has historically provided weapons, training, and funding to Hamas and other Palestinian terrorist groups, including Palestine Islamic Jihad (PIJ) and the Popular Front for the Liberation of Palestine-General Command (PFLP-GC).

Since the end of the 2006 Israeli-Hizballah conflict, Iran has also assisted in rearming Lebanese Hizballah, in direct violation of UNSCR 1701. General Amir Ali Hajizadeh, head of the IRGC Aerospace Force stated in November that "The IRGC and Hezbollah are a single apparatus jointed together," and Lebanese Hizballah Deputy Secretary General Naim Qassem boasted that Iran had provided his organization with missiles that had "pinpoint accuracy" in separate November public remarks. Iran has provided hundreds of millions of dollars in support of Lebanese Hizballah in Lebanon and has trained thousands of its fighters at camps in Iran. These trained fighters have used these skills in direct support of the Asad regime in Syria and, to a lesser extent, in support of operations against ISIL in Iraq. They have also continued to carry out attacks along the Lebanese border with Israel.

Iran remained unwilling to bring to justice senior al-Qa'ida (AQ) members it continued to detain, and refused to publicly identify those senior members in its custody. Iran previously allowed AQ facilitators to operate a core facilitation pipeline through Iran since at least 2009, enabling AQ to move funds and fighters to South Asia and Syria.

Iran remains a state of proliferation concern. Despite multiple UNSCRs requiring Iran to suspend its sensitive nuclear proliferation activities, Iran continued to be in noncompliance with its international obligations regarding its nuclear program.

# B. Sudan

*http://www.state.gov/j/ct/rls/crt/2014/239410.htm (Accessed Mar 2016)*

Sudan was designated as a State Sponsor of Terrorism in 1993 due to concerns about support to international terrorist groups. Sudan remained a generally cooperative partner of the United States on counterterrorism. During the past year, the Government of Sudan continued to support counterterrorism operations to counter threats to U.S. interests and personnel in Sudan.

Elements of al-Qa'ida-inspired terrorist groups remained in Sudan. The Government of Sudan has taken steps to limit the activities of these elements and has worked to disrupt foreign fighters' use of Sudan as a logistics base and transit point for terrorists going to Syria and Iraq. However, groups continued to operate in Sudan in 2014 and there continued to be reports of Sudanese nationals participating in terrorist organizations.

In 2014, Sudan continued to allow members of Hamas to travel, fundraise, and live in Sudan.

In June 2010, four Sudanese men sentenced to death for the January 1, 2008 killing of two U.S. Embassy staff members escaped from Khartoum's maximum security Kober prison. That same month Sudanese authorities confirmed that they recaptured one of the four convicts and a second escapee was reported killed in Somalia in May 2011. The recaptured murderer is being held in Kober Prison, and as of December 2014, appeals of his pending death sentence were still ongoing. The whereabouts of the other two convicts are unknown.

In February 2013, one of five men convicted of aiding the 2010 escape attempt by the four convicted killers received a presidential commutation of his remaining sentence. Sudanese authorities explained his release was part of a broad administrative parole affecting 200 other prisoners who had served some portion of their sentences with good behavior. U.S. government officials protested the commutation and urged Sudanese authorities to imprison the convicted accomplice for the full 12 years of his sentence. The individual remained free on parole at year's end.

Sudanese authorities this year released most of the 25 individuals detained in a December 2012 raid on what the Government of Sudan described as a terrorist training camp operating in Dinder National Park. Members of the so-called "Dinder cell" were charged with terrorism and murder stemming from the deaths of several police involved in the December 2012 raid. One trial judge from the country's terrorism court remanded several cases back to the attorney general for additional interrogations and those accused continued to be held in prison. The remaining Dinder detainees have had sessions with Dr. Essam Ahmed al-Basher, who helps lead the Government of Sudan's "extremist rehabilitation program."

In general, the Government of Sudan appeared to oppose the financing of extremist elements. Sudanese officials have welcomed Hamas members to Khartoum, however, and its members are permitted to conduct fundraising in Sudan. The Central Bank of Sudan and its financial intelligence unit, renamed the Financial Information Unit in late 2014, circulated to financial institutions a list of individuals and entities that have been included on the UN 1267 sanctions committee's consolidated list, as well as the U.S. government's lists of terrorist organizations/financiers. The financing of terrorism per UN Resolution 1373 was criminalized in Sudan pursuant to Sudan's Money Laundering Act of 2003.

Additionally, Sudan has yet to take concrete steps to resolve the crisis in the Two Areas of Southern Kordofan and Blue Nile, to include ending aerial bombardments, allowing sufficient and sustained humanitarian access, and resuming political dialogue to resolve the conflicts.

# C. Syria

*http://www.state.gov/j/ct/rls/crt/2014/239410.htm (Accessed Mar 2016)*

Designated in 1979 as a State Sponsor of Terrorism, the Asad regime continued its political support to a variety of terrorist groups affecting the stability of the region and beyond, even amid significant internal unrest. The regime continued to provide political and weapons support to Lebanese Hizballah and continued to allow Iran to rearm the terrorist organization. The Asad regime's relationship with Hizballah and Iran continued to grow stronger in 2014 as the conflict in Syria continued. President Bashar al-Asad remained a staunch defender of Iran's policies, while Iran has exhibited equally energetic support for Syrian regime efforts to defeat the Syrian opposition. Statements supporting terrorist groups, particularly Hizballah, were often in Syrian government speeches and press statements.

The Syrian government had an important role in the growth of terrorist networks in Syria through the permissive attitude the Asad regime took towards al-Qa'ida's foreign fighter facilitation efforts during the Iraq conflict. Syrian government awareness and encouragement for many years of violent extremists' transit through Syria to enter Iraq, for the purpose of fighting Coalition Troops, is well documented. Syria was a key hub for foreign fighters en route to Iraq. Those very networks were the seedbed for the violent extremist elements, including ISIL, which terrorized the Syrian and Iraqi population in 2014 and – in addition to other terrorist organizations within Syria – continued to attract thousands of foreign terrorist fighters to Syria in 2014.

As part of a broader strategy during the year, the regime still attempted to portray Syria itself as a victim of terrorism, characterizing all of its armed opponents as "terrorists."

Asad's government has continued to generate significant concern regarding the role it plays in terrorist financing. Industry experts reported that 60 percent of all business transactions were conducted in cash and that nearly 80 percent of all Syrians did not use formal banking services. Despite Syrian legislation that required money changers to be licensed by the end of 2007, many continued to operate illegally in Syria's vast black market, estimated to be as large as Syria's formal economy. Regional hawala networks (an informal value transfer system based on the performance and honor of a large network of money brokers operating outside traditional western financial systems) remained intertwined with smuggling and trade-based money laundering, and were facilitated by notoriously corrupt customs and immigration officials. This raised significant concerns that some members of the Syrian government and the business elite were complicit in terrorist finance schemes conducted through these institutions.

Despite the progress made through the Organization for the Prohibition of Chemical Weapon's Executive Council and UNSCR 2118 (2013) to dismantle and destroy Syria's chemical weapons program, there continued to be significant concern, given ongoing instability in Syria, that these materials could find their way to terrorist organizations. Additionally, Syria continued to use toxic chemicals, including chlorine, as a weapon against its citizens. Syria's behavior raises serious questions about the regime's willingness to comply with its Chemical Weapons Convention and UNSCR 2118 obligations.

# III. Countries That Have Been Removed from the State Sponsors of Terror List

*Ref: https://en.wikipedia.org/wiki/State_Sponsors_of_Terrorism (accessed Mar '16)*

The list began on December 29, 1979, with Libya, Iraq, South Yemen, and Syria. Cuba was added to the list on March 1, 1982 and Iran on January 19, 1984. Later North Korea in 1988 and Sudan on August 12, 1993 were added. South Yemen was removed from the list in 1990, Iraq was removed in 2004, Libya was removed in 2006, North Korea was removed in 2008, and Cuba was removed in 2015.

## Cuba

Cuba was added to the list on March 1, 1982. As a result of the December 17, 2014 agreement to restore relations with Cuba, the President has instructed the Secretary of State to immediately launch a review of Cuba's inclusion on the list, and provide a report to the President within six months regarding Cuba's alleged support for international terrorism. Obama announced on April 14, 2015, that Cuba was being removed from the list. Cuba would not come off the list until after a 45-day review period, during which the US Congress could try blocking Cuba's removal via a joint resolution. Congress did not act, and Cuba was officially removed from the list on May 29, 2015.

## Iraq

Iraq was added to the list on December 29, 1979 and removed in 1982 to allow US companies to sell arms to it while it was fighting Iran in the Iran–Iraq War; it was re-added following its 1990 invasion of Kuwait. The State Department's reason for including Iraq was that it provided bases to the Mujahedin-e-Khalq (MEK), the Kurdistan Workers Party (PKK), the Palestine Liberation Front (PLF), and the Abu Nidal organization (ANO). It was again removed following the 2003 invasion and the overthrow of the government of Saddam Hussein. Following the invasion, US sanctions applicable to "state sponsors of terrorism" against Iraq were suspended on May 7, 2003 and President Bush announced the removal of Iraq from the list on September 25, 2004.

## Libya

Libya was added on December 29, 1979. On May 15, 2006, the United States announced that Libya would be removed from the list after a 45-day wait period. Secretary of State Condoleezza Rice explained that this was due to "...Libya's continued commitment to its renunciation of terrorism".

## North Korea

North Korea was added in 1988. On June 26, 2008, President George W. Bush announced that he would remove North Korea from the list. On October 11, the country was officially removed from the list for meeting all nuclear inspection requirements. The U.S State Department said it made the decision as Pyongyang had agreed to verification of all of its nuclear programs, etc. As of 2011, North Korea, unlike the other countries removed and the designated state sponsor of terrorism Sudan, is still listed as not fully cooperating with the United States to reduce terrorism.

## South Yemen

South Yemen was added to the list on December 29, 1979. It had been branded a sponsor of terrorism due to its support for several left-wing terrorist groups. South Yemen was dropped from the list in 1990 after it merged with the Yemen Arab Republic (North Yemen), to become Yemen.

# IV(b). International Terrorism

*Ref: U.S. Department of State, Bureau of Counterterrorism; and the National Counterterrorism Center (NCTC).*

A number of resources available to assess the current terrorist threat. The following sections are provided as an overview to several of these resources.

# I. Country Reports on Terrorism and Patterns of Global Terrorism

*Ref: http://www.state.gov/j/ct/rls/crt/132196.htm*

U.S. law requires the Secretary of State to provide Congress, by April 30 of each year, a full and complete report on terrorism with regard to those countries and groups meeting criteria set forth in the legislation. This annual report is entitled Country Reports on Terrorism. Beginning with the report for 2004, it replaced the previously published Patterns of Global Terrorism.

The report covers developments in countries in which acts of terrorism occurred, countries that are state sponsors of terrorism, and countries determined by the Secretary to be of particular interest in the global war on terror. As provided in the legislation, the report reviews major developments in bilateral and multilateral counterterrorism cooperation as well.

The report also provides information on terrorist groups responsible for the death, kidnapping, or injury of Americans, any umbrella groups to which they might belong, groups financed by state sponsors of terrorism, reports on all terrorist organizations on the Foreign Terrorist Organization (FTO) list, and other terrorist groups determined by the Secretary to be relevant to the report.

Beginning with the report for 2005, Country Reports on Terrorism will also address terrorist sanctuaries and terrorist attempts to acquire weapons of mass destruction. It will also include statistical information provided by the National Counterterrorism Center (NCTC) on the number of individuals killed, injured, or kidnapped by terrorist groups.

## Replacing Patterns of Global Terrorism with Country Reports on Terrorism

Since September 11, 2001, changes in organization and responsibilities in the intelligence community, combined with the dynamic pace of the global war on terrorism, prompted the Department of State to take a fresh look at Patterns of Global Terrorism, its contents and its governing legislation.

In July 2004, the 9/11 Commission recommended creation of a National Counterterrorism Center (NCTC) to provide an authoritative agency for all-source analysis of global terrorism. The President implemented the recommendation by executive order in August 2004, and the agency was created via the Intelligence Reform and Terrorism Prevention Act the following December.

That law designates the NCTC as the primary organization for analysis and integration of "all intelligence possessed or acquired by the United States government pertaining to terrorism or counterterrorism." It further states that the NCTC would be the government's "shared knowledge bank on known and suspected terrorists and international terror groups, as well as their goals, strategies, capabilities, and networks of contact and support."

# II. DNI Worldwide Threat Assessment (2017)

*Ref: Daniel R. Coats, Director of National Intelligence, Statement for the Record, Worldwide Threat Assessment of the US Intelligence Community (May 23, 2017).*

*Note: This is an abbreviated extract of the terrorism and WMD portion from the Director of National Intelligence's Worldwide Threat Assessment (dated May 23, 2017).*

The worldwide threat from terrorism will remain geographically diverse and multifaceted—a continuing challenge for the United States, our allies, and partners who seek to counter it. Sunni violent extremists will remain the primary terrorist threat. These extremists will continue to embroil conflict zones in the Middle East, Africa, and South Asia. Some will also seek to attempt attacks outside their operating areas.

Iran continues to be the foremost state sponsor of terrorism and, with its primary terrorism partner, Lebanese Hizballah, will pose a continuing threat to US interests and partners worldwide. The Syrian, Iraqi, and Yemeni conflicts will continue to aggravate the rising Sunni-Shia sectarian conflict, threatening regional stability.

## Terrorist Threat to the United States

US-based homegrown violent extremists (HVEs) will remain the most frequent and unpredictable Sunni violent extremist threat to the US homeland. They will be spurred on by terrorist groups' public calls to carry out attacks in the West. The threat of HVE attacks will persist, and some attacks will probably occur with little or no warning. In 2016, 16 HVEs were arrested, and three died in attacks against civilian soft targets. Those detained were arrested for a variety of reasons, including attempting travel overseas for jihad and plotting attacks in the United States. In addition to the HVE threat, a small number of foreign-based Sunni violent extremist groups will also pose a threat to the US homeland and continue publishing multilingual propaganda that calls for attacks against US and Western interests in the US homeland and abroad.

## Dynamic Overseas Threat Environment

The Islamic State of Iraq and ash-Sham (ISIS) continues to pose an active terrorist threat to the United States and its allies because of its ideological appeal, media presence, control of territory in Iraq and Syria, its branches and networks in other countries, and its proven ability to direct and inspire attacks against a wide range of targets around the world. However, territorial losses in Iraq and Syria and persistent counterterrorism operations against parts of its global network are degrading its strength and ability to exploit instability and societal discontent. ISIS is unlikely to announce that it is ending its self-declared caliphate even if it loses overt control of its de facto capitals in Mosul, Iraq and Ar Raqqah, Syria and the majority of the populated areas it once controlled in Iraq and Syria.

Outside Iraq and Syria, ISIS is seeking to foster interconnectedness among its global branches and networks, align their efforts to ISIS's strategy, and withstand counter-ISIS efforts. We assess that ISIS maintains the intent and capability to direct, enable, assist, and inspire transnational attacks. The number of foreign fighters traveling to join ISIS in Iraq and Syria will probably continue to decline as potential recruits face increasing difficulties attempting to travel there. The number of ISIS foreign fighters leaving Iraq and Syria might increase. Increasing departures would very likely prompt additional would-be fighters to look for new battlefields or return to their home countries to conduct or support external operations.

During the past 16 years, US and global counterterrorism (CT) partners have significantly reduced al-Qa'ida's ability to carry out large-scale, mass casualty attacks, particularly against the US homeland. However, al-Qa'ida and its affiliates remain a significant CT threat overseas as they remain focused on exploiting local and regional conflicts. In 2016, al-Nusrah Front and al-Qa'ida in the Arabian Peninsula (AQAP) faced CT pressure in Syria and Yemen, respectively, but have preserved the resources, manpower, safe haven, local influence, and operational capabilities to continue to pose a threat. In Somalia, al-Shabaab sustained a high pace of attacks in Somalia and continued to threaten the northeast and coastal areas of Kenya. Its operations elsewhere in East Africa have diminished after the deaths of many external plotters since 2015, but al-Shabaab retains the resources, manpower, influence, and operational capabilities to pose a real threat to the region, especially Kenya. In North and West Africa, al-Qa'ida in the Lands of the Islamic Maghreb (AQIM) escalated its attacks on Westerners in 2016 with two high-profile attacks in Burkina Faso and Cote d'Ivoire. It merged with allies in 2017 to form a new group intended to promote unity among Mali-based jihadists, extend the jihad beyond the Sahara and Sahel region, increase military action, and speed up recruitment of fighters. In Afghanistan and Pakistan, remaining members of al-Qa'ida and its regional affiliate, al-Qa'ida in the Indian Subcontinent (AQIS), continued to suffer personnel losses and disruptions to safe havens in 2016 due to CT operations. However, both groups maintain the intent to conduct attacks against the United States and the West.

# Weapons of Mass Destruction and Proliferation

State efforts to modernize, develop, or acquire weapons of mass destruction (WMD), their delivery systems, or their underlying technologies constitute a major threat to the security of the United States, its deployed troops, and allies. Both state and non-state actors have already demonstrated the use of chemical weapons in the Levant. Biological and chemical materials and technologies—almost always dual use—move easily in the globalized economy, as do personnel with the scientific expertise to design and use them for legitimate and illegitimate purposes. Information about the latest discoveries in the life sciences also diffuses rapidly around the globe, widening the accessibility of knowledge and tools for beneficial purposes and for potentially nefarious applications.

- Russia Pressing Forward With Cruise Missile That Violates the INF Treaty. Russia has developed a ground-launched cruise missile (GLCM) that the United States has declared is in violation of the Intermediate-Range Nuclear Forces (INF) Treaty.

- China Modernizing its Nuclear Forces. The Chinese People's Liberation Army (PLA) has established a Rocket Force—replacing the longstanding Second Artillery Corps—and continues to modernize its nuclear missile force by adding more survivable road-mobile systems and enhancing its silo-based systems.

- Iran and JCPOA. Tehran's public statements suggest that it wants to preserve the Joint Comprehensive Plan of Action (JCPOA)—because it views the JCPOA as a means to remove sanctions while preserving some nuclear capabilities. It expects the P5+1 members to adhere to their obligations, although Iran clearly recognizes the new US Administration is concerned with the deal. Iran's implementation of the JCPOA has extended the amount of time Iran would need to produce enough fissile material for a nuclear weapon from a few months to about a year.

- Iran is pursuing capabilities to meet its nuclear energy and technology goals and to give it the capability to build missile-deliverable nuclear weapons, if it chooses to do so. Its pursuit of these goals will influence its level of adherence to the JCPOA. We do not know whether Iran will eventually decide to build nuclear weapons.

- North Korea Continues To Expand WMD-Applicable Capabilities. North Korea's nuclear weapons and missile programs will continue to pose a serious threat to US interests and to the security environment in East Asia in 2017.

- Chemical Weapons in Iraq and Syria. We assess the Syrian regime used the nerve agent sarin in an attack against the opposition in Khan Shaykhun on 4 April 2017 in what is probably the largest chemical weapons attack since August 2013. We continue to assess that Syria has not declared all the elements of its chemical weapons program to the Chemical Weapons Convention (CWC) and has the capability to conduct further attacks.

Given NCTC's mandate to be the U.S. Government's "shared knowledge bank" for data on global terrorism, and the statutory requirements for the Department of State's annual report to focus primarily on policy issues, it was appropriate to transfer the responsibilities for accumulating statistical information to NCTC. NCTC is already charged with compiling data on terrorist incidents and is the source of any data used to respond to the new statutory requirements.

To reflect the inclusion of NCTC statistical data in the Department of State's annual report and to avoid any confusion resulting from comparing current data with that generated before NCTC's participation, the name of the annual report was changed to Country Reports on Terrorism beginning with the 2004 document.

# III. National Counterterrorism Center (NCTC)

*http://nctc.gov*

NCTC serves as the primary organization in the U.S. government for integrating and analyzing all intelligence pertaining to terrorism possessed or acquired by the U.S. government (except purely domestic terrorism); serves as the central and shared knowledge bank on terrorism information; provides all-source intelligence support to government-wide counterterrorism activities; establishes the information technology (IT) systems and architectures within the NCTC and between the NCTC and other agencies that enable access to, as well as integration, dissemination, and use of, terrorism information.

NCTC serves as the principal advisor to the Director of National Intelligence (DNI) on intelligence operations and analysis relating to counterterrorism, advising the DNI on how well US intelligence activities, programs, and budget proposals for counterterrorism conform to priorities established by the President.

Unique among US agencies, NCTC also serves as the primary organization for strategic operational planning for counterterrorism. Operating under the policy direction of the President of the United States and the National Security Council NCTC provides a full-time interagency forum and process to plan, integrate, assign lead operational roles and responsibilities, and measure the effectiveness of strategic operational counterterrorism activities of the U.S. government, applying all instruments of national power to the counterterrorism mission.

Under US law, NCTC focuses exclusively on international terrorism. There are other organized groups that engage in violent acts—some are criminal organizations with no political or social agenda, and some are domestic terrorist groups; however, this guide reflects NCTC's international focus. Senior Intelligence Community officials assess the greatest international terrorist threats currently facing the United States come from violent extremists inspired by al-Qa'ida, including its allies and affiliates, who are committed to conducting attacks inside the United States and abroad. These groups promote an ideology that presents a radical vision of Islam that is not followed or endorsed by the vast majority of Muslims.

# IV. Foreign Terrorist Organizations
*Ref: http://www.state.gov/j/ct/rls/other/des/123085.htm (accessed March 2016).*

Foreign Terrorist Organizations (FTOs) are foreign organizations that are designated by the Secretary of State in accordance with section 219 of the Immigration and Nationality Act (INA), as amended. When reviewing potential targets, CT looks not only at the actual terrorist attacks that a group has carried out, but also at whether the group has engaged in planning and preparations for possible future acts of terrorism or retains the capability and intent to carry out such acts.

*Listed in order of date designation on list.*

Abu Nidal Organization (ANO)
Abu Sayyaf Group (ASG)
Aum Shinrikyo (AUM)
Basque Fatherland and Liberty (ETA)
Gama'a al-Islamiyya (Islamic Group) (IG)
HAMAS
Harakat ul-Mujahidin (HUM)
Hizballah
Kahane Chai (Kach)
Kurdistan Workers Party (PKK) (Kongra-Gel)
Liberation Tigers of Tamil Eelam (LTTE)
National Liberation Army (ELN)
Palestine Liberation Front (PLF)
Palestinian Islamic Jihad (PIJ)
Popular Front for the Liberation of Palestine (PFLP)
PFLP-General Command (PFLP-GC)
Revolutionary Armed Forces of Colombia (FARC)
Revolutionary People's Liberation Party/Front (DHKP/C)
Shining Path (SL)
al-Qa'ida (AQ)
Islamic Movement of Uzbekistan (IMU)
Real Irish Republican Army (RIRA)
Jaish-e-Mohammed (JEM)
Lashkar-e Tayyiba (LeT)
Al-Aqsa Martyrs Brigade (AAMB)
Asbat al-Ansar (AAA)
al-Qaida in the Islamic Maghreb (AQIM)
Communist Party of the Philippines/New People's Army (CPP/NPA)
Jemaah Islamiya (JI)
Lashkar i Jhangvi (LJ)

Ansar al-Islam (AAI)
Continuity Irish Republican Army (CIRA)
Islamic State of Iraq and the Levant (formerly al-Qa'ida in Iraq)
Islamic Jihad Union (IJU)
Harakat ul-Jihad-i-Islami/Bangladesh (HUJI-B)
al-Shabaab
Revolutionary Struggle (RS)
Kata'ib Hizballah (KH)
al-Qa'ida in the Arabian Peninsula (AQAP)
Harakat ul-Jihad-i-Islami (HUJI)
Tehrik-e Taliban Pakistan (TTP)
Jundallah
Army of Islam (AOI)
Indian Mujahedeen (IM)
Jemaah Anshorut Tauhid (JAT)
Abdallah Azzam Brigades (AAB)
Haqqani Network (HQN)
Ansar al-Dine (AAD)
Boko Haram
Ansaru
al-Mulathamun Battalion
Ansar al-Shari'a in Benghazi
Ansar al-Shari'a in Darnah
Ansar al-Shari'a in Tunisia
ISIL Sinai Province (formally Ansar Bayt al-Maqdis)
al-Nusrah Front
Mujahidin Shura Council in the Environs of Jerusalem (MSC)
Jaysh Rijal al-Tariq al Naqshabandi (JRTN)
ISIL-Khorasan (ISIL-K)

Legal Criteria for Designation under Section 219 of the INA as amended:
- It must be a foreign organization.
- The organization must engage in terrorist activity, or terrorism, or retain the capability and intent to engage in terrorist activity or terrorism.
- The organization's terrorist activity or terrorism must threaten the security of U.S. nationals or the national security (national defense, foreign relations, or the economic interests) of the United States.

# V. Combating Terrorism Center at West Point

*https://www.ctc.usma.edu/*

The Combating Terrorism Center is an independent, privately funded, research and educational institution situated at West Point that contributes to the academic body of knowledge and informs counterterrorism policy and strategy.

## Mission

Situated at the nexus of theory and practice, the Combating Terrorism Center serves as an important national resource that rigorously studies the terrorist threat and provides policy-relevant research while moving the boundaries of academic knowledge. The CTC's distinguished scholars, international network of experts, and access to senior U.S. government leadership set it apart from any other like enterprise.

## A. Counterterrorism Practitioner Education

The Combating Terrorism Center is the largest provider of counterterrorism and countering violent extremism (CVE) education to federal, state, and local government in the United States. From assisting FDNY leadership with an 11 week graduate seminar, to educating every new special agent at the FBI, to providing seminars to the Intelligence Community; the Combating Terrorism Center remains committed to an educational model that promotes interagency, multi-jurisdictional educational events. Since defeating terrorist threats depends on a unity of effort, it is imperative that our programs not only provide relevant information but also strengthen professional networks and collaboration between multiple stakeholders. Partner institutions include:

- FBI-CTC Collaboration
- FDNY Counterterrorism Leadership Program
- Department Of Justice Education
- Department Of Homeland Security Education

## B. Research Philosophy & Publications

The Combating Terrorism Center is one of the leading academic institutions devoted to the study of terrorism. The four topical programs outlined below comprise the core of our research agenda, and reflect our understanding of the key contemporary terrorism issues sets facing academics and government officials.

Research areas and sample featured publications include:

## Terrorist Ideology

Understanding the ideological underpinnings of violent groups is crucial to countering and defeating terrorist entities. This research program examines the ideas driving modern terrorism, the transmission of those ideas, and the doctrinal schisms within violent movements.

## Terrorist Strategy And Structure

The landscape of terrorist actors and the strategies they employ are consistently evolving. The strategy and structure program examines the actors, organizational platforms, and violent methods that terrorists use in pursuit of their goals.

## South Asia

South Asia faces unique and complex challenges stemming from growing anti-Western sentiment, nuclear armed regional rivals, and a complex blend of militant actors. This research program contextualizes the nature of the terrorist threat emanating from and developing within Pakistan, Afghanistan, India, and Bangladesh.

## Emerging Threats

The Emerging Threats research program informs the academic and policy communities on nascent and underappreciated terrorist threats. This program looks across the phenomenon of terrorism and focuses on the evolution, innovation among existing terrorist actors, and the emergence of new threats.

# C. Advising Philosophy & Value

The Center's advisory mission is to provide unique insights into the terrorism problem set in order to inform policy discussions. Due to the Center's deep subject matter expertise and independence, the Combating Terrorism Center is consistently called upon to serve as a trusted, independent analytical voice for senior policymakers as well as practitioners in the field. The policy advising portion of the Center's mission is solely a by-product of the CTC's focus on rigorous research and education. The Center does not advocate for specific policy positions and provides advice only on matters that are situated within their subject matter expertise.

# ISIL, Syria & Iraq Resources

*https://www.ctc.usma.edu/isil-resources*

The Combating Terrorism Center at West Point provides a gateway to resources, research, and analysis the Combating Terrorism Center has produced over the last decade about the Islamic State in Iraq and the Levant (ISIL), also referred to as the Islamic State of Iraq and al Sham (ISIS), the Islamic State (IS) or Da`ish, and its predecessors (al-Tawhid wa-al-Jihad, al-Qa`ida in Mesopotamia (AQI), Majlis Shura al-Mujahidin, Hilf al-Muttayibin and the Islamic State of Iraq (ISI)). Additional CTC research and analysis about factors shaping the conflict in Iraq and Syria is also included. These resources contextualize the development of ISIL. Resources are organized into six categories: major reports, CTC Sentinel articles, CTC Perspectives, CTC commentary about the early development of AQI, declassified primary sources produced by AQI, ISI and other militant groups in Iraq, and media coverage of the CTC's research.

# VI. Global Terrorism Database (GTD) by START

*Ref: National Consortium for the Study of Terrorism and Responses to Terrorism (START). Global Terrorism Database [Data file]. Retrieved from http://www.start.umd.edu/gtd*

The Global Terrorism Database (GTD) contains information on over 140,000 terrorist attacks is currently the most comprehensive unclassified terrorism database in the world, with information on more than 27,000 bombings, 13,000 assassinations, and 2,800 kidnappings.

It consists of two distinct databases: GTD1, which covers 1970-1997, and GTD2, which covers 1998-2004. Unlike many other event databases, the GTD includes systematic data on international as well as domestic terrorist incidents that have occurred during this time period. For each GTD incident, information is available on the date and location of the incident, the weapons used and nature of the target, the number of casualties, and -- when identifiable -- the identity of the perpetrator. This data has been used by a number of studies that explore the relationship between religion and terrorism, most often those focusing on Islamist organizations.

Unlike many other event databases, the GTD includes systematic data on domestic as well as transnational and international terrorist incidents that have occurred during this time period and now includes more than 140,000 cases. For each GTD incident, information is available on the date and location of the incident, the weapons used and nature of the target, the number of casualties, and--when identifiable--the group or individual responsible.

Statistical information contained in the Global Terrorism Database is based on reports from a variety of open media sources. Information is not added to the GTD unless and until we have determined the sources are credible. Users should not infer any additional actions or results beyond what is presented in a GTD entry and specifically, users should not infer an individual associated with a particular incident was tried and convicted of terrorism or any other criminal offense. If new documentation about an event becomes available, an entry may be modified, as necessary and appropriate.

## Characteristics of the GTD

- Contains information on over 140,000 terrorist attacks
- Currently the most comprehensive unclassified data base on terrorist events in the world
- Includes information on more than 58,000 bombings, 15,000 assassinations, and 6,000 kidnappings since 1970
- Includes information on at least 45 variables for each case, with more recent incidents including information on more than 120 variables
- Supervised by an advisory panel of 12 terrorism research experts
- Over 4,000,000 news articles and 25,000 news sources were reviewed to collect incident data from 1998 to 2014 alone

In sum, the Global Terrorism Database is a compilation of distinct data collection efforts from 1970 to the present. From 1970 to 1997 the data were constructed primarily from incidents recorded in real-time by PGIS using a broad-based definition of terrorism. Data from this period are updated and corrected on an ongoing basis. The data from 1998 through 2007 were primarily collected retrospectively, while data on more recent events are being collected in real-time and with the benefit of more robust media archives and improved collection methodology. Users should note that differences in levels of attacks and casualties before and after 1997, 2008, and 2012 may be at least partially explained by differences in data collection.

# About START

*https://www.start.umd.edu*

## Overview

The National Consortium for the Study of Terrorism and Responses to Terrorism—better known as START—is a university-based research and education center comprised of an international network of scholars committed to the scientific study of the causes and human consequences of terrorism in the United States and around the world.

A Department of Homeland Security Center of Excellence headquartered at the University of Maryland, START supports the research efforts of leading social scientists at more than 50 academic and research institutions, each of whom is conducting original investigations into fundamental questions about terrorism, including:

- What is the nature of terrorism in the world today? How has terrorist activity evolved over time? How does terrorism vary across geographies? And what do these trends indicate about likely future terrorism?
- Under what conditions does an individual or a group turn to terrorism to pursue its goals? What is the nature of the radicalization process?
- How does terrorism end? What are the processes of deradicalization and disengagement from terrorism for groups and individuals?
- What actions can governments take to counter the threat of terrorism?
- What impact does terrorism and the threat of terrorism have on communities, and how can societies enhance their resilience to minimize the potential impacts of future attacks?

START experts apply a range of research methods to the exploration of these questions in order to deliver findings based on the best available open-source evidence and data. At the heart of START's work are the principles that the research it is conducting must be both scientifically rigorous and directly relevant to homeland security professionals.

START is a part of the collection of Centers of Excellence supported by the U.S. Department of Homeland Security's Science and Technology Directorate and also receives funding and support from a variety of Federal agencies, private foundations, and universities. All of START's research is conducted using non-classified materials and its findings are those of individual researchers and do not reflect the official position of any START funders.

## START's Mission

To advance science-based knowledge about the human causes and consequences of terrorism and serve as a leading resource for homeland security policymakers and practitioners.

## START's Vision

START will provide homeland security policy-makers and practitioners with the highest quality, data-driven research findings on the human causes and consequences of terrorism in an effort to ensure that homeland security policies and operations reflect these understandings about human behaviors.

## Research Areas and Publications

Research areas and related publications include:

- Terrorism and Violent Extremism
- Counterterrorism and Countering Violent Extremism
- Radicalization and Deradicalization
- Risk Communication and Resilience
- Unconventional Weapons and Technology

# Overview: Terrorism in 2014 (GTD Data)

*Ref: Miller, Erin. "Overview: Terrorism in 2014." Background Report, START (Aug 2015).*

*Editor's Note: This section provides an overview from START's Background Report on patterns of terrorism in 2014, highlighting trends from the Global Terrorism Database (GTD). This is START's most current published annual terrorism report, released in August, 2015. GTD collection is ongoing and is updated annually. The 2015 data and annual terrorism reports is projected to be released late-Summer 2016 (after this book's production).*

## Overview

In 2014, more than 16,800 terrorist attacks took place worldwide, causing more than 43,500 deaths and more than 40,900 injuries, including perpetrator casualties. More than 11,800 people were taken hostage in terrorist attacks in 2014.

Worldwide patterns of terrorism in 2014 were heavily influenced by conflicts in key locations. Although terrorist attacks took place in 99 countries, nearly half of all attacks (47%) took place in Iraq, Pakistan, and Afghanistan. Likewise, more than half (60%) of all fatalities took place in Iraq, Nigeria, and Afghanistan.

In addition, worldwide trends in casualties caused by terrorist attacks reveal several noteworthy developments. First, nearly one quarter (24%) of all fatalities that resulted from terrorist attacks in 2014 were perpetrator fatalities. This is by far the highest proportion of perpetrator fatalities recorded in the GTD, compared to an annual average of 5 percent of all fatalities between 1970 and 2013. Second, 28 attacks in 2014 caused more than 100 total fatalities, compared to an average of 3.7 such mass-fatality attacks each year between 1970 and 2013.

Several of the most active perpetrator organizations, including the Islamic State of Iraq and the Levant (ISIL), al- Shabaab, Boko Haram, and al-Qa'ida in the Arabian Peninsula (AQAP) experienced extreme increases in frequency and lethality of terrorist attacks in 2014. New perpetrator organizations—including the Donetsk People's Republic and the Luhansk People's Republic—emerged in Ukraine, carrying out hundreds of deadly attacks against both combatant and non-combatant targets.

Finally, patterns of terrorism in 2014 were marked by a dramatic increase in the number of hostages taken—11,821--more than four times as many as the annual average from 1970 to 2013. The analysis below describes these trends in greater detail.

## Location

Consistent with patterns from 2013 and 2012, Iraq, Pakistan, and Afghanistan experienced the most terrorist attacks by a wide margin. However, while the frequency and lethality of terrorism increased in Iraq and Afghanistan in 2014, in Pakistan both the number of terrorist attacks (-3%) and the total number of fatalities (-16%) decreased.

Continued on next page

| Country | Total Attacks 2014 | Total Fatalities 2014 | % Perpetrator Fatalities 2014 | % Change Attacks 2013-2014 | % Change Total Fatalities 2013-2014 | % Change Perpetrator Fatalities 2013-2014 |
|---|---|---|---|---|---|---|
| Iraq | 3925 | 13076 | 13% | 38% | 86% | 248% |
| Pakistan | 2146 | 2409 | 22% | -3% | -16% | 34% |
| Afghanistan | 1820 | 5411 | 46% | 26% | 46% | 106% |
| Ukraine | 889 | 1396 | 30% | 17680% | 139500% | 42300% |
| Somalia | 862 | 1582 | 27% | 158% | 145% | 171% |
| India | 859 | 488 | 12% | 24% | 4% | 82% |
| Yemen | 760 | 1349 | 23% | 79% | 116% | 183% |
| Libya | 729 | 690 | 6% | 149% | 196% | 207% |
| Nigeria | 713 | 7774 | 20% | 107% | 286% | 241% |
| Philippines | 597 | 472 | 33% | -8% | 9% | 212% |
| Thailand | 423 | 192 | 6% | -11% | -24% | -31% |
| Egypt | 346 | 338 | 22% | 9% | 39% | 85% |
| Syria[2] | 326 | 3301 | 27% | 17% | 112% | 908% |
| Israel | 293 | 49 | 33% | 692% | 2350% | - |
| Colombia | 230 | 143 | 11% | 56% | 6% | 167% |
| Lebanon | 204 | 115 | 13% | 69% | -39% | -57% |
| Sudan | 157 | 546 | 40% | 241% | 148% | 76% |
| West Bank / Gaza Strip | 135 | 67 | 30% | 111% | 458% | 233% |
| Bangladesh | 129 | 37 | 5% | -7% | 270% | - |
| Kenya | 115 | 315 | 8% | 46% | 53% | 39% |

Among the 20 countries that experienced the most terrorist attacks in 2014, three were not among the top 20 in 2013. Most notably, while Ukraine experienced relatively few terrorist attacks in 2013, a growing conflict in the region involved hundreds of terrorist attacks in 2014. Violent attacks in Ukraine in 2014 primarily targeted the military (55%), private citizens and property (15%), government buildings and personnel (6%), police (5%), businesses (4%), transportation infrastructure (4%), and journalists and media targets (4%). These attacks resulted in more than 1,300 fatalities, including more than 400 perpetrator fatalities, and nearly 300 passengers who were killed when members of the Donetsk People's Republic purportedly launched a surface-to-air missile at a Malaysia Airlines commercial flight.

In addition, both Israel and Sudan experienced very large relative increases in number and lethality of terrorist attacks between 2013 and 2014. In Israel, one-third (33%) of all fatalities from terrorist attacks were perpetrator fatalities, and 61 percent of all fatalities were caused by attacks targeting the military. The most active perpetrator organizations in Israel were Hamas (51%), Ansar Bayt al-Maqdis (10%), and Palestinian Islamic Jihad (9%).

In Sudan, violence primarily targeted private citizens and property (39%) and refugee camps (15%), and military targets (7%). Nearly two-thirds (65%) of the attacks in Sudan were attributed to the Janjaweed militia. A particularly large proportion (40%) of the fatalities caused by terrorist attacks in Sudan were perpetrator fatalities. This is in part due to a single attack in which members of the Sudan People's Liberation Movement-North attacked Sudanese Armed Forces (SAF) in Alatmur, resulting in the deaths of more than 100 assailants.

Countries that were ranked among those with the most terrorist attacks in 2013, but not in 2014 include Russia (which saw a 68% decrease in attacks and a 55% decrease in fatalities), Nepal (93% decrease in attacks; 100% decrease in fatalities), and the United Kingdom (25% decrease in attacks; 100% decrease in fatalities.

Continued on next page

# Overview: Terrorism in 2014 (Cont.)

## Casualties

Several new trends emerged with respect to casualties of terrorist attacks in 2014. In particular, the proportion of total fatalities that were perpetrator fatalities (24%) is the highest recorded since collection of the GTD began in 1970. Perpetrator fatalities are a result of several different scenarios: suicide attacks in which the perpetrators intend to kill themselves; accidental deaths of perpetrators killed while attempting to carry out an attack; or attacks, targeting either combatants or non-combatants, in which security forces respond and a clash ensues.

In 2014, 39 percent of the attacks in which perpetrators were killed were suicide attacks, compared to 51 percent in 2013 and 42 percent in 2012. Of the remaining attacks, 45 percent targeted the military, and 30 percent targeted police. Among countries that experienced at least 50 fatalities from terrorist attacks in 2014, those with the highest proportion of perpetrator fatalities were Uganda (77% of 98 fatalities), Cameroon (73% of 788 fatalities), China (50% of 322 fatalities), and Afghanistan (46% of 5,411 fatalities).

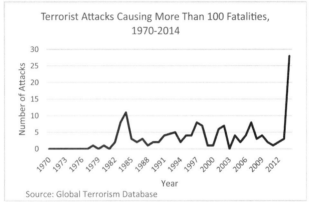

Terrorist Attacks Causing More Than 100 Fatalities, 1970-2014

Source: Global Terrorism Database

A second trend regarding casualties in 2014 pertains to the frequency of extreme mass-fatality terrorist attacks. Worldwide, the number of attacks involving more than 100 fatalities increased to 28, from three in 2013. These attacks took place in Nigeria (9 attacks), Iraq (7), Syria (4), Cameroon (3), Ukraine (2), South Sudan (1), Sudan (1), and Pakistan (1). The most common perpetrator organizations were Boko Haram (11 attacks) and the Islamic State of Iraq and the Levant (ISIL; 11). Combined, these 28 attacks caused more than 7,300 fatalities (17% of all fatalities worldwide throughout 2014), including more than 2,000 perpetrator fatalities (20% of all perpetrator fatalities worldwide throughout 2014).

Several attacks in 2014 were the deadliest attacks in recent history. For example, in June, ISIL claimed responsibility for an attack in which assailants seized a prison in Badush, Iraq, and killed 670 Shi'a prisoners, while freeing Sunni prisoners. Also in June, members of ISIL abducted and killed at least 1,500 Iraqi soldiers at Camp Speicher in Tikrit, Iraq. In August, ISIL assailants attacked Yazidi civilians in Sinjar, Iraq, killing at least 500 and abducting 300 others, many of whom were ultimately released in 2015.

## Perpetrators

ISIL and the Taliban were responsible for the most terrorist attacks in 2014, with 28 percent of all attacks for which a perpetrator organization was identified. These organizations, along with Boko Haram, were also responsible for an increasingly disproportionate number of fatalities—59 percent of all fatalities caused by attacks in which a perpetrator organization was identified, compared to 46 percent in 2013.

| Perpetrator Organization | Total Attacks 2014 | Total Fatalities 2014 | % Change Total Attacks 2013-2014 | % Change Total Fatalities 2013-2014 |
|---|---|---|---|---|
| Islamic State of Iraq and the Levant (ISIL) / AQI | 1263 | 9596 | 179% | 411% |
| Taliban | 1038 | 4194 | 34% | 53% |
| Al-Shabaab | 865 | 1783 | 170% | 141% |
| Boko Haram | 493 | 7112 | 111% | 311% |
| Donetsk People's Republic | 325 | 1005 | - | - |
| New People's Army (NPA) | 291 | 190 | 36% | 22% |
| Al-Qa'ida in the Arabian Peninsula (AQAP) | 285 | 889 | 99% | 140% |
| Communist Party of India - Maoist / Maoists | 324 | 204 | 52% | -1% |
| Tehrik-i-Taliban Pakistan (TTP) | 179 | 974 | 13% | 30% |
| Revolutionary Armed Forces of Colombia (FARC) | 163 | 88 | 54% | -19% |
| Huthis | 134 | 234 | 538% | 284% |
| Luhansk People's Republic | 110 | 173 | - | - |
| Baloch Republican Army (BRA) | 103 | 52 | 312% | 79% |
| Bangsamoro Islamic Freedom Movement (BIFM) | 88 | 98 | 31% | 72% |
| Al-Nusrah Front | 82 | 838 | 82% | 19% |
| Communist Party of India - Maoist (CPI-Maoist) | 70 | 88 | 49% | 1% |
| Hamas (Islamic Resistance Movement) | 66 | 71 | 6500% | 3450% |
| Kurdistan Workers' Party (PKK) | 61 | 21 | 190% | 50% |
| National Liberation Army of Colombia (ELN) | 60 | 57 | 200% | 50% |
| Ansar Bayt al-Maqdis (Ansar Jerusalem) | 60 | 157 | 329% | 214% |

All of the top-ranked perpetrator organizations underwent substantial increases in terms of frequency of terrorist violence between 2013 and 2014. Although responsible for relatively fewer attacks, Hamas was attributed responsibility for 66 attacks in 2014, compared to only one in 2013. Only two organizations decreased the lethality of their terrorist activity: the Communist Party of India- Maoist (1% decrease in total fatalities) and the Revolutionary Armed Forces of Colombia (FARC; 19% decrease in total fatalities).

While many of these organizations, including the New People's Army (NPA), FARC, and the Kurdistan Workers' Party (PKK) have been active for many years, if not decades, two new perpetrator organizations emerged in 2014 and immediately became highly active. The Donetsk People's Republic and the Luhansk People's Republic, both active in Ukraine, carried out bombings (38%), armed assaults (31%), kidnappings (15%), and facility/infrastructure attacks (9%) beginning in April 2014. The Donetsk People's Republic was attributed responsibility for more than 1,000 total fatalities, including the deaths of nearly 300 passengers killed by a surface-to-air missile launched at a Malaysia Airlines commercial flight.

# Hostages

The past decade witnessed the continued, and at times rapid, increase in the number of terrorist attacks involving hostages or kidnap victims. From 1970 to 2004, there were on average 149 attacks per year that involved hostages. From 2005-2014, that number rose to an average of 485 hostage-taking events per year, a 225% increase. 2014 in particular was a watershed year for attacks involving hostages. There were more than 1,400 such incidents during the year, in which more than 11,800 people were kidnapped or held hostage. This represents a 121% increase in hostage-taking events between 2013 and 2014, and a 253% increase in the total number of hostages during this time period.

Despite the increase in the number of kidnappings and hostage taking events since 2005, the average fatality per attack of incidents involving hostages remained relatively stable between 2005 and 2013. This pattern changed significantly in 2014, however, when the average number of individuals killed in attacks involving hostages rose to more than 7 per attack. This increase was driven by a number of mass-fatality events involving hostages that took place during the year,

# Overview: ISIL-Related Terrorsim (2002-2015)

*Ref: Miller, Erin. "Patterns of Islamic State-Related Terrorism, 2002--2015" Background Report, START (Aug 2016). Access the full report at: http://www.start.umd.edu/publications*

For more than a decade, the organization now known as the Islamic State of Iraq and the Levant (ISIL), or simply the Islamic State, has carried out deadly terrorist attacks. Beginning as a small network led by Jordanian Abu Musab al-Zarqawi, the first terrorist attack attributed to this group was the assassination of American diplomat Laurence Foley in Amman, Jordan in October 2002. Since then, the group initially known as Tawhid and Jihad (Jama'at al-Tawhid w'al-Jihad (the Party of Monotheism and Jihad)) has undergone a complex evolution, including name changes, leadership changes, and shifts in allegiance to other Salafi-jihadist organizations, most notably al-Qaida. In addition, the reach of ISIL's violence surpasses its own membership, to include attacks carried out by other groups and individuals who have pledged allegiance to ISIL regardless of whether or not formal ties exist.

## ISIL-Related Terrorism: Overview

Between 2002 and 2015, more than 4,900 terrorist attacks were carried out by groups or organizations affiliated with the organization now known as the Islamic State. These attacks caused more than 33,000 deaths and 41,000 injuries (including perpetrator casualties), and involved more than 11,000 individuals held hostage or kidnapped. Excluding incidents where the perpetrator group was not identified, these attacks represented 13 percent of all terrorist attacks worldwide, 26 percent of all deaths, 28 percent of all injuries, and 24 percent of all kidnap victims or hostages due to terrorism during the same time period.

Among ISIL-related perpetrators of terrorism, "core" ISIL was responsible for the majority of attacks (58%), deaths (58%), and especially hostages (88%), compared to ISIL predecessor groups, ISIL-affiliated groups, and individuals inspired by ISIL. Attacks carried out by ISIL and ISIL predecessor groups each comprised 42 percent of all injuries caused in ISIL-related terrorist attacks.

Although attacks carried out by individuals who claimed allegiance to ISIL have drawn considerable media attention in recent months, these perpetrators were responsible for less than 1 percent of all ISIL-related attacks and casualties between 2002 and 2015. In addition, attacks carried out by individuals inspired by ISIL were 74 percent less deadly on average than ISIL-related attacks in general (1.9 deaths per attack on average, compared to 7.3).

## Patterns Of ISIL-Related Terrorism Over Time and Location

The graph below illustrates patterns of ISIL-related terrorist attacks over time, highlighting the perpetrators' relationship to ISIL:

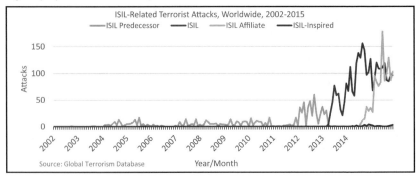

ISIL-Related Terrorist Attacks, Worldwide, 2002-2015
— ISIL Predecessor — ISIL — ISIL Affiliate — ISIL-Inspired

Source: Global Terrorism Database

Year/Month

Between October 2002 and April 2013, ISIL predecessors (primarily known as al-Qaida in Iraq (AQI) and the Islamic State of Iraq (ISI)) carried out attacks almost exclusively in Iraq (95%). An additional 5 percent of attacks carried out by the perpetrator organizations that would become ISIL took place in Syria beginning in December 2011. Initially sources attributed responsibility for the attacks in Syria to AQI, and in 2012 al-Nusrah Front began claiming responsibility for attacks in Syria. In addition, four attacks were carried out in Jordan—one in 2002 (by Tawhid and Jihad) and three in 2005 (by AQI). Two men reportedly linked to AQI carried out an attack in the United Kingdom in 2007.

From May 2013 through the end of the year, ISIL carried out an average of 46 attacks per month. In 2014, the frequency of attacks more than doubled to 106 attacks per month, and in 2015, ISIL carried out 102 terrorist attacks per month. In mid-2014, increasing numbers of attacks were carried out by new and existing organizations that pledged allegiance to ISIL, loosely described here as ISIL affiliates. Among the first of these organizations to declare allegiance to ISIL was the Bangsamoro Islamic Freedom Movement (BIFM), active in the Philippines.

The first attack carried out by an individual who was reportedly inspired by ISIL, though not directly linked to the organization, took place in April 2014 in the United States. In Seattle, an assailant shot and killed a civilian and later claimed he had done so in response to U.S. military involvement in Iraq and Afghanistan.

A total of 26 attacks were carried out in 2014 and 2015 by individuals inspired by ISIL. These attacks killed 50 people, including 13 perpetrators, and took place primarily in the United States (8 attacks), France (6), Australia (4), Denmark (2), and Canada (2).

## Terrorist Attacks by ISIL

As ISI evolved into ISIL, the group's tactics remained extraordinarily destructive. Between 2013 and 2015, there were 32 occasions on which ISIL carried out more than 10 attacks in a single day, all in Iraq. Furthermore, the number of cases in which ISIL attacks resulted in more than 100 deaths increased from six to 16 between 2013 and 2015. These attacks targeted private citizens (6 attacks), military (5), police (3), business (1), and government (1) targets.

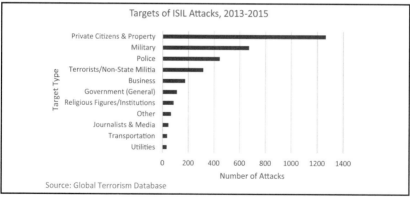

The deadliest attacks attributed to ISIL took place in Iraq in June 2014, when assailants abducted more than 1,600 Iraqi Air Force recruits at Camp Speicher in Tikrit and ultimately killed most, if not all of them. In a separate attack earlier that month, ISIL operatives killed more than 600 Shia prisoners at Badush prison in Nineveh.

The most frequent targets of ISIL attacks between April 2013 and the end of 2015 were private citizens and property (39%). Perhaps most notably, attacks primarily targeting private citizens resulted in more than 6,100 people held hostage or kidnapped. Available sources indicate that approximately 1,200 of these victims were subsequently released. The remaining victims were either killed or their status is unknown.

# VII. Terrorist Leader Profiles (2016 Snapshot)

*Individuals profiled here are a sampling of lhose listed on the US Government's Rewards for Justice site or on FBI sites devoted to terrorism. These individuals have been either indicted or are being sought for their involvement in international terrorism.*

### Ayman Al-Zawahiri ($25 Million Reward)

Ayman al-Zawahiri is a physician and the founder of the Egyptian Islamic Jihad. This organization opposes the secular Egyptian Government and seeks its overthrow through violent means. Al-Zawahiri is believed to have served as an advisor and doctor to Usama Bin Ladin. He has been indicted for his alleged role in the 7 August 1998 bombings of the US embassies in Dar es Salaam, Tanzania, and Nairobi, Kenya, attacks that killed 224 civilians and wounded over 5,000 others.

### Abu Bakr Al-Baghdadi ($10 Million Reward)

Abu Bakr al-Baghdadi, also known as Abu Du'a, is the senior leader of the terrorist organization Islamic State of Iraq and the Levant (ISIL). Abu Du'a is in charge of overseeing all operations and is currently based in Syria. Abu Bakr al-Baghdadi has taken personal credit for a series of terrorist attacks in Iraq since 2011. He has claimed responsibility for the June 2013 operations against the Abu Ghraib prison outside Baghdad and the March 2013 suicide-bombing assault on the Ministry of Justice, among other attacks against Iraqi Security Forces and Iraqi citizens going about their daily lives.

### Hafiz Mohammad Saeed ($10 Million Reward)

Hafiz Mohammad Saeed is a former professor of Arabic and Engineering, as well as the founding member of Jamaat-ud-Dawa, a radical Ahl-e-Hadith Islamist organization dedicated to installing Islamist rule over parts of India and Pakistan, and its military branch, Lashkar-e-Tayyiba. Saeed is suspected of masterminding numerous terrorist attacks, including the 2008 Mumbai attacks, which resulted in the deaths of 166 people, including six American citizens. The Republic of India has issued an Interpol Red Corner Notice against Saeed for his role in the 2008 Mumbai terror attacks.

### Mullah Omar ($10 Million Reward)

Mullah Omar's Taliban regime in Afghanistan sheltered Usama Bin Ladin and his Al-Qa'ida network in the years prior to the September 11 attacks.

Although Operation Enduring Freedom removed the Taliban regime from power, Mullah Omar remains at large and represents a continuing threat to the United States and its allies.

## Yasin Al-Suri ($10 Million Reward)

Ezedin Abdel Aziz Khalil, more commonly known as Yasin al-Suri, is a senior al-Qa'ida facilitator based in Iran. Yasin al-Suri was arrested by Iranian authorities in December 2011 after the announcement of the $10 million Rewards for Justice offer, but he has resumed leadership of al-Qa'ida's Iran-based network. As head al-Qa'ida facilitator in Iran, Yasin al-Suri is responsible for overseeing al-Qa'ida efforts to transfer experienced operatives and leaders from Pakistan to Syria, organizing and maintaining routes by which new recruits can travel to Syria via Turkey, and assisting in the movement of al-Qa'ida external operatives to the West.

## Abubakar Shekau ($7 Million Reward)

Abubakar Shekau is the leader of Jama'atu Ahl as-Sunnah li-Da'awati wal-Jihad, more commonly known as Boko Haram. Boko Haram, which means "Western education is forbidden," is a Nigeria-based terrorist organization that seeks to overthrow the current Nigerian government and replace it with a regime based on Islamic law. The group has existed in various forms since the late 1990s.

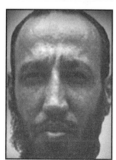

## Hamad El Khairy ($5 Million Reward)

Hamad el Khairy is the leader and a founding member of the terrorist group Movement for Unity and Jihad in West Africa (MUJWA, also known as MUJAO and TWJWA). Under Khairy's leadership, MUJWA members have carried out kidnapping operations, terrorist attacks, and abductions of foreign diplomats. Khairy has claimed responsibility for the April 2012 kidnapping of seven Algerian diplomats in Mali, and has appeared in MUJWA videos making threats against those who oppose the organization. In January 2012, Khairy stated that MUJWA's goal was to "impose sharia law across the whole of West Africa."

## Abdelkarim Hussein Mohamed al-Nasser ($5 Million Reward)

On 25 June 1996, members of Saudi Hizballah carried out a terrorist attack on the Khobar Towers housing complex near Dhahran, Saudi Arabia. At the time, the complex was used to house US military personnel. The terrorists drove a tanker filled with plastic explosives into the parking lot and detonated it, all but destroying the nearest building. The attack killed 19 US servicemen and one Saudi citizen, and wounded 372 others. Abdelkarim Hussein Mohamed al-Nasser was indicted in the Eastern District of Virginia for the 25 June 1990.

# VIII. Terrorist Group Profiles

Representative profiles of terrorist groups from the NCTC and the Department of State's Foreign Terrorist Organization list are provided on the following pages:

*Under US law, NCTC focuses exclusively on international terrorism. There are other organized groups that engage in violent acts—some are criminal organizations with no political or social agenda, and some are domestic terrorist groups; however, this guide reflects NCTC's international focus. Senior Intelligence Community officials assess the greatest international terrorist threats currently facing the United States come from violent extremists inspired by al-Qa'ida, including its allies and affiliates, who are committed to conducting attacks inside the United States and abroad.*

# Abu Sayyaf Group (ASG)

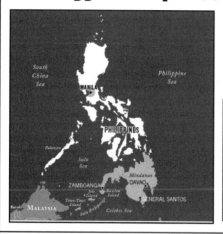

*ASG flag*

The Abu Sayyaf Group (ASG) is the most violent of the Islamic separatist groups oper-ating in the southern Philippines and claims to promote an independent Islamic state in western Mindanao and the Sulu Archipelago. Split from the Moro National Libera-tion Front in the early 1990s, the group currently engages in kidnappings for ransom, bombings, assassinations, and extortion, and has had ties to Jemaah Islamiyah (JI). The ASG operates mainly in Basilan, Sulu, and Tawi-Tawi Provinces in the Sulu Archi-pelago and has a presence on Mindanao. Members also occasionally travel to Manila.

The ASG has used terror both for financial profit and to promote its jihadist agenda. In April 2000, an ASG faction kidnapped 21 persons—including 10 Westerners—from a Malaysian resort, and, in May 2001, the ASG kidnapped three US citizens and 17 Filipinos from a resort in Palawan, Philippines, later murdering several of the hostages, including one US citizen. In June 2002, one of the two remaining hostages was killed in a crossfire between Philippine soldiers and the ASG. On 27 February 2004, mem-bers of ASG leader Khadafi Janjalani's faction bombed a ferry in Manila Bay, killing 116, and on 14 February 2005 they perpetrated simultaneous bombings in the cities of Manila, General Santos, and Davao, killing at least eight and injuring about 150. In 2006, Janjalani's faction relocated to Sulu, where it joined forces with local ASG sup-porters who are providing shelter to fugitive JI members from Indonesia.

In July 2007, members of the ASG and the Moro Islamic Liberation Front engaged a force of Philippine marines on Basilan Island, killing 14. In November 2007, a motorcycle bomb exploded outside the Philippine Congress, killing a Congressman and three staff members. While there was no definitive claim of responsibility, three suspected ASG members were arrested during a subsequent raid on a safe house. In January 2009, the ASG kidnapped three International Red Cross workers in Sulu prov-ince, holding one of the hostages for six months. Philippine marines in February 2010 killed Albader Parad, one of the ASG's most violent sub-commanders, on Jolo Island. In 2011, the ASG kidnapped several individuals and held them for ransom. In February 2012, a Philippine military airstrike against a terrorist encampment on Jolo Island killed senior ASG leader Gumbahali Jumdail, also known as Dr. Abu. In March 2013, the ASG released an Australian citizen the group had held hostage for fifteen months. In June 2014, Philippine authorities arrested senior ASG figure ASG Khair Mundos in metro Manila.

# Afghan Taliban

*Mullah Mohammad Oma*

*Afghan Taliban flag*

The Taliban is a Sunni Islamist nationalist and pro-Pashtun movement founded in the early 1990s that ruled most of Afghanistan from 1996 until October 2001. The movement's founding nucleus—the word "Taliban" is Pashto for "students"—was composed of peasant farmers and men studying Islam in Afghan and Pakistani madrasas, or religious schools. The Taliban found a foothold and consolidated their strength in southern Afghanistan.

By 1994, the Taliban had moved their way through the south, capturing several provinces from various armed factions who had been fighting a civil war after the Soviet-backed Afghan government fell in 1992. The Taliban's first move was to institute a strict interpretation of Qur'anic instruction and jurisprudence. In practice, this meant often merciless policies on the treatment of women, political opponents of any type, and religious minorities.

In the years leading up to the 11 September 2001 attacks in the United States, the Taliban provided a safe haven for al-Qa'ida. This gave al-Qa'ida a base in which it could freely recruit, train, and deploy terrorists to other countries. The Taliban held sway in Afghanistan until October 2001, when they were routed from power by the US-led campaign against al-Qa'ida.

The Afghan Taliban's leader is Mullah Mohammad Omar, who was the president of Afghanistan during the Taliban's rule. The US Government is offering a $10 million reward for information leading to his capture.

The Afghan Taliban are responsible for most insurgent attacks in Afghanistan. In January 2014, the group staged a suicide and small-arms attack on the popular Lebanese Taverna restaurant in Kabul, killing 21 people, including three Americans, marking one of the deadliest attacks against Western civilians in Kabul since 2001. In a one-week span in March 2014, the Taliban conducted four high-profile attacks in Kabul city, culminating in a 28 March attack on a heavily guarded guesthouse in Kabul for employees of a US aid group. The targeted guesthouse was next to a Christian charity and day-care center that may have been the intended target. The next day, the Taliban conducted an attack on the headquarters of Afghanistan's election commission with rockets and automatic rifles, following an attack on the provincial election office earlier that week. On 20 March, the Taliban attacked Kabul's luxurious Serena Hotel, killing nine civilians who were all shot at point-blank range by four insurgents armed with small pistols smuggled inside.

# Al-Nusrah Front

*Al-Nusrah Front flag*

Al-Nusrah Front is one of the most capable al-Qaʻida-affiliated groups operating in Syria during the ongoing conflict. The group in January 2012 announced its intention to overthrow Syrian President Bashar al-Asad's regime, and since then has mounted hundreds of insurgent-style and suicide attacks against regime and security service targets across the country. The group is committed not only to ousting the regime, but also seeks to expand its reach regionally and globally. Initially, al-Nusrah Front did not publicize its links to al-Qaʻida in Iraq or Pakistan.

The Islamic State of Iraq and the Levant (ISIL) played a significant role in founding the group. ISIL predecessor organizations used Syria as a facilitation hub and transformed this facilitation and logistics network into an organization capable of conducting sophisticated explosives and firearms attacks. ISIL leaders since the beginning of al-Nusrah Front's participation in the conflict provided their facilitation hub with personnel and resources, including money and weapons.

During 2013, al-Nusrah Front and ISIL were consumed by a public rift stemming from ISIL leader Abu Bakr al-Baghdadi's April 2013 statement announcing the creation of ISIL and claiming the merger of both groups. Al-Nusrah Front and ISIL have strategies for Syria, and a public merger between them probably would have undermined al-Nusrah Front's autonomy in the country. In April 2013, al-Nusrah Front's leader, Abu Muhammad al-Jawlani, pledged allegiance to al-Qaʻida leader Ayman al-Zawahiri.

During early 2014, the rift between al-Nusrah Front and ISIL—in which ISIL has openly accused al-Qaʻida senior leaders of deviating from what it perceives as the correct jihadist path—has taken place not just on the ground but in social media as well. Al-Nusrah Front's leaders probably have learned lessons from members' previous experiences in Iraq and have sought to win over the Syrian populace by providing parts of the country with humanitarian assistance and basic civil services. Several Syria-based armed opposition groups cooperate and fight alongside Sunni extremist groups, including al-Nusrah Front, and are dependent upon them for expertise, training, and weapons. Al-Nusrah Front has managed to seize territory, including military bases and infrastructure in northern Syria.

The group's cadre is predominately composed of Syrian nationals, many of whom are veterans of previous conflicts, including the Iraq war. Thousands of fighters from around the world have traveled to Syria since early 2012 to support oppositionist groups, and some fighters aspire to connect with al-Nusrah Front and other extremist groups.

# Al-Qa'ida

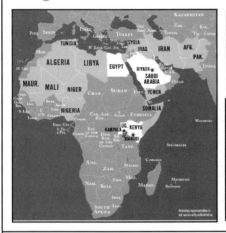

*Ayman al-Zawahiri*

*Al-Qa'ida flag*

Established by Usama Bin Ladin in 1988 with Arabs who fought in Afghanistan against the Soviet Union, al-Qa'ida's declared goal is the establishment of a pan-Islamic caliphate throughout the Muslim world. Toward this end, al-Qa'ida seeks to unite Muslims to fight the West, especially the United States, as a means of overthrowing Muslim regimes al-Qa'ida deems "apostate," expelling Western influence from Muslim countries, and defeating Israel. Al-Qa'ida issued a statement in February 1998 under the banner of "the World Islamic Front for Jihad Against the Jews and Crusaders" saying it was the duty of all Muslims to kill US citizens—civilian and military—and their allies everywhere. The group merged with the Egyptian Islamic Jihad (al-Jihad) in June 2001.

On 11 September 2001, 19 al-Qa'ida suicide attackers hijacked and crashed four US commercial jets—two into the World Trade Center in New York City, one into the Pentagon near Washington, D.C., and a fourth into a field in Shanksville, Pennsylvania—leaving nearly 3,000 people dead. Al-Qa'ida also directed the 12 October 2000 attack on the USS Cole in the port of Aden, Yemen, which killed 17 US sailors and injured another 39, and conducted the bombings in August 1998 of the US embassies in Nairobi, Kenya, and Dar es Salaam, Tanzania, killing 224 people and injuring more than 5,000. Since 2002, al-Qa'ida and affiliated groups have conducted attacks worldwide, including in Europe, North Africa, South Asia, Southeast Asia, and the Middle East.

In 2005, Ayman al-Zawahiri, then Bin Ladin's deputy and now the leader of al-Qa'ida, publicly claimed al-Qa'ida's involvement in the 7 July 2005 bus bombings in the United Kingdom. In 2006, British security services foiled an al-Qa'ida plot to detonate explosives on up to 10 transatlantic flights originating from London's Heathrow airport. During that same time period, numbers of al-Qa'ida-affiliated groups increased.

Following the 2011 death of Bin Ladin, al-Qa'ida leaders moved quickly to name al-Zawahiri as his successor. The group remains a cohesive organization and what is widely called al-Qa'ida's Core leadership continues to be important to the global movement despite leadership losses. Other jihadist groups, however, like the Islamic State of Iraq and the Levant (ISIL), have gained prominence and challenged the Core's global leadership.

Al-Qa'ida remains committed to conducting attacks in the United States and against American interests abroad. The group has advanced a number of unsuccessful plots in the past several years, including against the United States and Europe. This highlights al-Qa'ida's ability to continue some attack preparations while under sustained counterterrorism pressure and suggests it may be plotting additional attacks against the United States at home or overseas.

# Al-Qa'ida in the Arabian Peninsula (AQAP)

*Nasir al-Wahishi*

*AQAP flag*

Al-Qa'ida in the Arabian Peninsula (AQAP) is a Sunni extremist group based in Yemen that has orchestrated numerous high-profile terrorist attacks. One of the most notable of these operations occurred when AQAP dispatched Nigerian-born Umar Farouk Abdulmutallab, who attempted to detonate an explosive device aboard a Northwest Airlines flight on 25 December 2009—the first attack inside the United States by an al-Qa'ida affiliate since 11 September 2001. That was followed by an attempted attack in which explosive-laden packages were sent to the United States on 27 October 2010. The year 2010 also saw the launch of Inspire magazine, an AQAP-branded, English-language publication that first appeared in July, followed by the establishment of AQAP's Arabic-language al-Madad News Agency in 2011. Dual US-Yemeni citizen Anwar al-Aulaqi, who had a worldwide following as a radical ideologue and propagandist, was the most prominent member of AQAP; he was killed in an explosion in September 2011.

In August 2013, the US State Department temporarily closed several embassies in response to a threat associated with AQAP. Since then, AQAP has conducted a number of high-profile attacks inside Yemen targeting the Yemeni Government, including a complex, multistage attack in December 2013 against Yemen's Ministry of Defense that killed at least 52 people, and in February 2014 the group freed over two dozen prisoners after attacking Sanaa's central prison. Shortly thereafter the group released a video entitled "Drops of Rain," which depicted a large gathering of AQAP members operating openly while their leader threatened the United States. In May 2014, the US Embassy in Sanaa closed for a month due to a heightened threat from the group.

AQAP's predecessor, al-Qa'ida in Yemen (AQY), came into existence after the escape of 23 al-Qa'ida members from prison in Sanaa, in February 2006. Several escapees helped reestablish the group and later identified fellow escapee al-Wahishi as the group's new amir.

AQAP emerged in January 2009 following an announcement that Yemeni and Saudi terrorists were unifying under a common banner. The leadership of this new organization was composed of the group's amir, Nasir al-Wahishi; now-deceased deputy amir Sa'id al-Shahri; and military commander Qasim al Rimi, all veteran extremist leaders. The group has targeted local, US, and Western interests in the Arabian Peninsula, but is now pursuing a global strategy. AQAP elements withdrew from their southern Yemen strongholds in June 2012, when Yemeni military forces under new President Abdu Rabbo Mansour Hadi—with the support of local tribesmen—regained control of cities in Abyan and Shabwah that had served as AQAP strongholds since 2011.

# Al-Qa'ida in the Lands of the Islamic Maghreb

Abdelmalek Droukdal

## (AQIM)

AQIM flag

Al-Qa'ida in the Lands of the Islamic Maghreb (AQIM) is an Algeria-based Sunni Muslim jihadist group. It originally formed in 1998 as the Salafist Group for Preaching and Combat (GSPC), a faction of the Armed Islamic Group, which was the largest and most active terrorist group in Algeria. The GSPC was renamed in January 2007 after the group officially joined al-Qa'ida in September 2006. The group had close to 30,000 members at its height, but the Algerian Government's counterterrorism efforts have reduced GSPC's ranks to fewer than 1,000. The current leader of AQIM is Abdelmalek Droukdal, who has been in charge of AQIM since it was founded in 1998 as the GSPC.

AQIM historically has operated primarily in the northern coastal areas of Algeria and in parts of the desert regions of southern Algeria and the Sahel. Since the French-led military intervention in early 2013, however, the group has reduced its presence in northern Mali and expanded into Libya and Tunisia. AQIM mainly employs conventional terrorist tactics, including guerrilla-style ambushes, mortar, rocket, and IED attacks. The group's principal sources of revenue include extortion, kidnapping for ransom, and donations. In May 2009, AQIM announced it had killed a British hostage after months of failed negotiations. In June of the same year, the group publicly claimed responsibility for killing US citizen Christopher Leggett in Mauritania because of his missionary activities. In 2011, a Mauritanian court sentenced a suspected AQIM member to death and two others to prison for the American's murder.

AQIM since 2010 has failed to conduct the high-casualty attacks in Algeria that it had in previous years. Multinational counterterrorism efforts—including a joint French-Mauritanian raid in July 2010 against an AQIM camp—resulted in the death of some AQIM members and possibly disrupted some AQIM activity.

In 2012, AQIM took advantage of political chaos in northern Mali to consolidate its control there and worked with the secular Azawad National Liberation Movement (MNLA) to secure independence in Kidal, Gao, and Timbuktu for ethnic Tuaregs. The Islamic militant group Ansar al-Dine was formed to support the creation of an Islamic state in Mali ruled by sharia.

Since 2011, dissident groups of AQIM members broke away to form Movement for Unity and Jihad in West Africa (MUJAO) and al-Mulathamun Battalion and its subordinate unit al-Muwaqi'un Bil-Dima ("Those Who Sign With Blood") led by former AQIM battalion leader Mokhtar Belmokhtar. In August 2013 these groups merged to form al-Murabitun, ("The Sentinels"), and officially formalized the groups' ties; their stated goals are to "unite all Muslims from the Nile to the Atlantic in jihad against Westerners" and to curb French influence in the region.

# Boko Haram

*Abubakar Shekau*

Boko Haram, which refers to itself as "Jama'atu Ahl as-Sunnah li-Da'awati wal-Jihad" (JASDJ; Group of the Sunni People for the Calling and Jihad) and "Nigerian Taliban"—other translations and variants are used—is a Nigeria-based group that seeks to overthrow the current Nigerian Government and replace it with a regime based on Islamic law. It is popularly known in Nigerian and Western media as "Boko Haram," which means "Western education is forbidden" (the word boko is a holdover from the colonial English word for book). The group, which has existed in various forms since the late 1990s, suffered setbacks in July 2009 when clashes with Nigerian Government forces led to the deaths of hundreds of its members, including former leader Muhammad Yusuf.

In July 2010, Boko Haram's former second-in-command, Abubakar Shekau, appeared in a video claiming leadership of the group and threatening attacks on Western influences in Nigeria. Later that month, Shekau issued a second statement expressing solidarity with al-Qa'ida and threatening the United States. Under Shekau's leadership, the group has continued to demonstrate growing operational capabilities, with an increasing use of improvised explosive device (IED) attacks against soft targets. The group set off its first vehicle-borne IED in June 2011. On 26 August 2011, Boko Haram conducted its first attack against a Western interest—a vehicle-bomb attack on UN headquarters in Abuja—killing at least 23 people and injuring more than 80. A purported Boko Haram spokesman claimed responsibility for the attack and promised future targeting of US and Nigerian Government interests.

Boko Haram's capability has increased in 2014, with the group conducting near-daily attacks against a wide range of targets, including Christians, Nigerian security and police forces, the media, schools, politicians, and Muslims perceived as collaborators. Boko Haram continues to expand its activity into neighboring countries and has claimed responsibility for the kidnapping of 11 Westerners in Cameroon since early 2013, raising the group's international profile and emphasizing the growing threat it poses to Western and regional interests.

Boko Haram's unprecedented levels of violence—including the kidnapping of 276 schoolgirls in Borno State, Nigeria, in April 2014—have brought international condemnation as well as collaboration on security initiatives by the United States, United Kingdom, France, African partners, and others as Nigerian and other regional security forces continue to try to oust the group from northeastern Nigeria and its safe havens throughout the area.

# Central Asia Terrorism

*Imirat Kavkaz flag*

**Imirat Kavkaz, (IK, or Caucasus Emirate),** founded in late 2007 by now-deceased Chechen extremist Doku Umarov, is an Islamist militant organization based in Russia's North Caucasus. Its stated goal is the liberation of what it considers to be Muslim lands from Moscow. The group, now led by Ali Abu-Muhammad, also known as Aliaskhab Kebekov, regularly conducts attacks against Russian security forces in the North Caucasus. In the period 2010-2011, it carried out high-profile suicide bombings against civilian targets in Moscow that killed dozens. IK maintains ties with militants from the North Caucasus fighting alongside groups aiming to topple Bashar al-Asad in Syria. In the approach to the Sochi Olympic Games, Umarov on 2 July 2013 urged militants in Russia to target the Games, stating that Moscow "plan[s] to hold the Olympics on the bones of our ancestors, on the bones of many dead Muslims…and we mujahedin are obliged not to permit that." While there were attacks in Volgograd in the weeks before the event that killed more than 30 civilians, no attacks took place on site during the Games. The US State Department in May 2011 designated Imirat Kavkaz as a Specially Designated Terrorist group under Executive Order 13224.

**The Islamic Jihad Union (IJU)** is an extremist organization that splintered from the Islamic Movement of Uzbekistan in the early 2000s and is currently based in Pakistan's Federally Administered Tribal Areas. The IJU, which is committed to toppling the government in Uzbekistan, conducted two attacks there in 2004 and one in 2009. The IJU is also active in Afghanistan, where the group operates alongside the Taliban-affiliated Haqqani Network. The group has had particular success in recruiting German nationals and achieved international notoriety following the 2007 disruption of an IJU plot by the so-called Sauerland Cell to attack various targets in Germany.

**The Islamic Movement of Uzbekistan (IMU)** is an extremist organization that formed in the late 1990s and is currently based in Pakistan's Federally Administered Tribal Areas. The IMU seeks to overthrow the government in Uzbekistan and establish a radical Islamist caliphate in all of "Turkestan," which it considers to be the Central Asian region between the Caspian Sea and Xinjiang in western China. The IMU has become increasingly active in the Taliban-led insurgency in northern Afghanistan, providing the IMU with a springboard for future operations in Central Asia. A known IMU spokesperson in a video message delivered to Radio Liberty's Tajik service claimed responsibility for a September 2010 ambush against a military convoy in Tajikistan. The IMU in June 2014 joined Tehrik-e Taliban Pakistan fighters in a deadly siege of Karachi International Airport that killed 37.

# Communist Party of Philippines/ New People's Army (CPP/NPA)

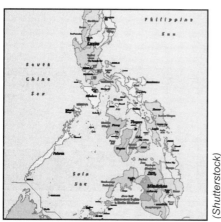

*(Shutterstock)*

**aka** CPP/NPA; Communist Party of the Philippines; the CPP; New People's Army; the NPA

**Description**: The Communist Party of the Philippines/New People's Army (CPP/NPA) was designated as a Foreign Terrorist Organization on August 9, 2002. The military wing of the Communist Party of the Philippines (CPP) – the New People's Army (NPA) – is a Maoist group formed in March 1969 with the aim of overthrowing the government through protracted guerrilla warfare. Jose Maria Sison, the Chairman of the CPP's Central Committee and the NPA's founder, reportedly directs CPP and NPA activity from the Netherlands, where he lives in self-imposed exile. Luis Jalandoni, a fellow Central Committee member and director of the CPP's overt political wing, the National Democratic Front (NDF), also lives in the Netherlands and has become a Dutch citizen. Although primarily a rural-based guerrilla group, the NPA had an active urban infrastructure to support its terrorist activities and, at times, used city-based assassination squads.

**Activities**: The CPP/NPA primarily targeted Philippine security forces, government officials, local infrastructure, and businesses that refused to pay extortion, or "revolutionary taxes." The CPP/NPA charged politicians running for office in CPP/NPA-influenced areas for "campaign permits." In addition to its focus on Philippine governmental targets, the CPP/NPA has a history of attacking U.S. interests in the Philippines. In 1987, the CPP/NPA conducted direct actions against U.S. personnel and facilities, killing three American soldiers in four separate attacks in Angeles City. In 1989, the CPP/NPA issued a press statement claiming responsibility for the ambush and murder of Colonel James Nicholas Rowe, chief of the Ground Forces Division of the Joint U.S.-Military Advisory Group.

Over the past few years, the CPP/NPA has continued to carry out killings, raids, kidnappings, acts of extortion, and other forms of violence which are directed mainly against domestic and security force targets. In May 2013, the Armed Forces of the Philippines reported that from 2011 through the first quarter of 2013, 383 people, including 158 civilians, were killed in encounters between the CPP/NPA and government forces. The NPA continued to use explosive and improvised explosive devices to target police and security forces throughout 2014.

**Strength**: The Philippine government estimates there are 4,000 CPP/NPA members.

**Location/Area of Operation**: Rural Luzon, Visayas, and parts of northern and eastern Mindanao. There are also cells in Manila and other metropolitan centers.

# Hamas

*Hamas flag*

HAMAS formed in late 1987 at the beginning of the first Palestinian intifada (uprising). Its roots are in the Palestinian branch of the Muslim Brotherhood, and it is supported by a robust sociopolitical structure inside the Palestinian territories. The group's charter calls for establishing an Islamic Palestinian state in place of Israel and rejects all agreements made between the PLO and Israel. HAMAS' strength is concentrated in the Gaza Strip and areas of the West Bank.

HAMAS has a military wing known as the Izz al-Din al-Qassam Brigades that has conducted many anti-Israel attacks in both Israel and the Palestinian territories since the 1990s. These attacks have included large-scale bombings against Israeli civilian targets, small-arms attacks, improvised roadside explosives, and rocket attacks.

The group in early 2006 won legislative elections in the Palestinian territories, ending the secular Fatah party's hold on the Palestinian Authority and challenging Fatah's leadership of the Palestinian nationalist movement. HAMAS continues to refuse to recognize or renounce violent resistance against Israel and in early 2008 conducted a suicide bombing, killing one civilian, as well as numerous rocket and mortar attacks that have injured civilians. The US Government has designated HAMAS a Foreign Terrorist Organization.

HAMAS in June 2008 entered into a six-month agreement with Israel that significantly reduced rocket attacks. Following the temporary calm, HAMAS resumed its rocket attacks, which precipitated a major Israeli military operation in late December 2008. After destroying much of HAMAS' infrastructure in the Gaza Strip, Israel declared a unilateral cease-fire on 18 January 2009.

HAMAS and Fatah in April 2011 agreed to form an interim government and hold elections, reaffirming this pledge in February 2012. HAMAS departed its long-time political headquarters in Damascus in February and dispersed throughout the region as Syrian President Bashar al-Asad's crackdown on opposition in the country made remaining in Syria untenable for the group. In May 2012, HAMAS claimed to have established a 300-strong force to prevent other Palestinian resistance groups from firing rockets into Israel. Conflict broke out again in November.

In July 2014, the uneasy calm between HAMAS and Israel broke down completely after three Israeli teenagers were kidnapped and killed in the West Bank in June—deaths ascribed by Israel to HAMAS—and a Palestinian was killed by Israeli settlers in revenge. Retaliatory rocket attacks by HAMAS's military wing and other Palestinian militants in the Gaza Strip escalated into the longest and most lethal conflict with Israel since 2009.

# Haqqani Network

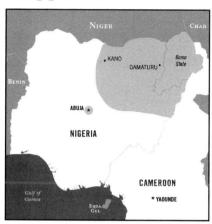

*Sirajuddin Haqqani*

The Haqqani Network is a Sunni Islamist militant organization founded by Jalaluddin Haqqani, who emerged as a top Afghan warlord and insurgent commander during the anti-Soviet war; he was a member of the Hezb-e-Islami faction led by renowned mujahedin commander Younis Khalis. Jalaluddin later allied with the Afghan Taliban as that group's Minister of Tribal and Border Affairs when the Taliban held power in Afghanistan during the mid-to-late 1990s. He was a known associate of Usama Bin Ladin and was recognized as one of Bin Ladin's closest mentors during the al-Qa'ida founder's formative years in the 1980s Afghan war. Sirajuddin Haqqani, Jalaluddin's son, currently leads the day-to-day activities of the group, along with several of his closest relatives.

The Haqqani Network is primarily based in North Waziristan, Pakistan, and conducts cross-border operations into eastern Afghanistan and Kabul. The group is primarily composed of members of the Zadran tribe. The Haqqanis are considered the most lethal and sophisticated insurgent group targeting US, Coalition and Afghan forces in Afghanistan, and typically conduct coordinated small-arms assaults coupled with rocket attacks, IEDs, suicide attacks, and attacks using bomb-laden vehicles.

The Haqqani Network is responsible for some of the highest-profile attacks of the Afghan war, including the June 2011 assault on the Kabul Intercontinental Hotel, conducted jointly with the Afghan Taliban, and two major suicide bombings—in 2008 and 2009—against the Indian Embassy in Kabul. In September 2011, the Haqqanis participated in a day-long assault against major targets in Kabul, including the US Embassy, International Security Assistance Force (ISAF) headquarters, the Afghan Presidential Palace, and the Afghan National Directorate of Security headquarters. More recently, in October 2013, Afghan security forces intercepted a truck bomb deployed by the Haqqanis against Forward Operating Base Goode in Paktiya Province. The device, which did not detonate, contained some 61,500 pounds of explosives and was the largest truck bomb ever built. The group is also involved in a number of criminal activities in Afghanistan and Pakistan, including extortion, kidnapping for ransom, and smuggling.

The US Government in 2012 designated the Haqqani Network as a Foreign Terrorist Organization because of its involvement in the Afghan insurgency, attacks on US military and civilian personnel and Western interests in Afghanistan, and because of its ties to the Taliban and al-Qa'ida. Key members have also been individually designated.

# Hezb-E-Islami Gulbuddin (HIG)

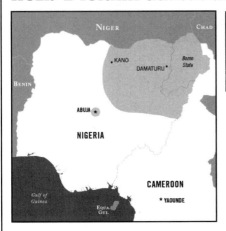

*Gulbuddin Hekmatyar*

Hezb-e-Islami, or "Party of Islam," is a political and paramilitary organization in Afghanistan founded in 1976 by former Afghan prime minister Gulbuddin Hekmatyar, who has been prominent in various Afghan conflicts since the late 1970s. Hezb-e Islami Gulbuddin (HIG) is an offshoot of that original Hezb-e-Islami, and is a virulently anti-Western insurgent group whose goal is to replace the Western-backed Afghan Government with an Islamic state rooted in sharia in line with Hekmatyar's vision of a Pashtun-dominated Afghanistan. His group conducts attacks against Coalition forces, Afghan Government targets, and Western interests in Afghanistan. HIG is distinct from Hezb-e-Islami Afghanistan (HIA), a legal Afghan political party composed of, among others, some reconciled HIG members. HIG shares most elements of Taliban ideology and HIG insurgents cooperate with the Taliban in some parts of Afghanistan despite some ideological differences.

Hekmatyar and his deputies, Ghairat Baheer and Qutbuddin Hilal, continue to participate sporadically in negotiations with the Afghan Government. Hilal even ran for Afghan president in the country's April 2014 election. HIG, however, strongly opposes the proposed Bilateral Security Agreement with the United States and, after Hilal's failed presidential bid, boycotted the subsequent election run-off.

The group has conducted some widely publicized attacks during the past few years even while negotiations were under way. Most recently, HIG spokesman Haroon Zarghoon claimed responsibility for a suicide VBIED attack in Kabul on 10 February 2014, which killed at least two US civilians and wounded two other Americans and seven Afghan nationals. HIG was also responsible for a 16 May 2013 suicide VBIED attack in Kabul, which destroyed a US armored SUV and killed two US soldiers, four US civilian contractors, eight Afghans—including two children—and wounded at least 37 others. The attack marked the deadliest incident against US personnel in Kabul in over a year.

# Hizballah

*Hizballah flag*

Formed in 1982 in response to the Israeli invasion of Lebanon, Hizballah (the "Party of God"), a Lebanon-based Shia terrorist group, advocates Shia empowerment globally. Hizballah has been involved in numerous anti-US terrorist attacks, including the suicide truck bombings of the US Embassy in Beirut in April 1983, the US Marine barracks in Beirut in October 1983, and the US Embassy annex in Beirut in September 1984, as well as the hijacking of TWA 847 in 1985 and the Khobar Towers attack in Saudi Arabia in 1996.

Hizballah has participated in the Lebanese Government since 1992. With the 2004 passage of UN Security Council Resolution 1559, which called for the disarmament of all armed militias in Lebanon, Hizballah has focused on justifying its retention of arms by casting itself as the defender of Lebanon against Israeli aggression. On 12 July 2006, Hizballah kidnapped two Israeli soldiers, sparking the 2006 war in which Hizballah claimed victory by virtue of its survival. It has since sought to use the conflict to justify its need to retain its arms as a Lebanese resistance force. In May 2008, Hizballah militants seized parts of Beirut. In negotiations to end the violence, Hizballah gained veto power in the government and retained its arms and secure communications.

In July 2011 the UN Special Tribunal for Lebanon (STL) indicted four Hizballah members—including a senior Hizballah official—for the assassination of former Lebanese Prime Minister Rafiq al-Hariri, who was killed by a car bomb in Beirut on 14 February 2005. Hizballah leader Hasan Nasrallah has publicly stated that Hizballah will not allow any members to be arrested, and continues to paint the STL as a proxy of Israel and the United States.

In February 2008, Hizballah's military chief 'Imad Mughniyah was killed by a vehicle bomb in Damascus. Nasrallah publicly blamed Israel and continues to promise retaliation. Additionally, Hasan al-Laqis, a senior Hizballah military leader, was shot and killed outside his home on 3 December 2013. Hizballah accused Israel of responsibility for the killing, although Tel Aviv denied involvement.

Although Hizballah's leadership is based in Lebanon, the group has established cells worldwide. Nasrallah publicly indicated in May 2013 that Hizballah was supporting Bashar al-Asad's regime by sending fighters to Syria. The European Union designated Hizballah's military wing as a terrorist organization on 22 July 2013, following the March conviction of a Hizballah member in Cyprus, the July 2012 bus bombing in Bulgaria, and the group's intervention in Syria.

# Islamic State of Iraq and the Levant (ISIL)

*Abu Bakr al-Baghdadi*

The Islamic State of Iraq and the Levant (ISIL)—formerly known as al-Qa'ida in Iraq and Islamic State of Iraq—was established in April 2004 by long-time Sunni extremist Abu Mus'ab al-Zarqawi, who the same year pledged his group's allegiance to Usama Bin Ladin. ISIL targeted Coalition forces and civilians using high-profile tactics such as vehicle-borne improvised explosive devices (VBIEDs), suicide bombers, and hostage executions, to pressure foreign countries and companies to leave Iraq, push Iraqis to stop supporting the United States and the Iraqi Government, and attract additional cadre to its ranks.

Following al-Zarqawi's death in June 2006, ISIL's new leader, Abu Ayyub al-Masri, announced in October 2006 the formation of the Islamic State of Iraq, led by Iraqi national Abu 'Umar al-Baghdadi, in an attempt to politicize the group's terrorist activities and place an "Iraqi face" on their efforts.

In 2007, ISIL's continued targeting and repression of Sunni civilians in Iraq caused a widespread backlash—known as the Sunni Awakening—against the group. The development of the Awakening Councils—composed primarily of Sunni tribal and local community leaders—coincided with a surge in Coalition and Iraqi Government operations, resulting in a decreased attack tempo beginning in mid-2007.

ISIL's current leader, Abu Bakr al-Baghdadi, assumed power following the death of both Abu Ayyub al-Masri and Abu 'Umar al-Baghdadi in April 2010. Under his authority, the group has continued conducting high-profile attacks across Iraq. ISIL has expanded its ranks through prison breaks and integration of fighters drawn to the Syrian conflict.

In April 2013, Abu Bakr al-Baghdadi publicly declared the group's presence in Syria under the name ISIL and that ISIL had founded the al-Nusrah Front in Syria. Al-Nusrah Front in June 2013 publicly pledged allegiance to al-Qa'ida leader Ayman al-Zawahiri. The disagreement and ISIL's hardline ideology caused a backlash in Syria. ISIL rejected al-Nusrah Front, Syrian opposition enemies, and al-Qa'ida's efforts to force the group to leave Syria.

In February 2014, al-Qa'ida publicly stated ISIL was no longer a branch of al-Qa'ida, a status the group had held since 2004. ISIL in April 2014 responded to the disavowal by publicly attacking al-Qa'ida as being unfit for Usama Bin Ladin's legacy and stating that ISIL was a better example for jihadists. Major ISIL-led efforts to overthrow the Iraqi Government erupted in June 2014, freeing prisoners and gaining access to more weapons and vehicles usable in Iraq or Syria. In late June 2014, ISIL declared the establishment of an Islamic caliphate under the name the "Islamic State" and called for all Muslims to pledge allegiance to the group.

# Jaish-E-Mohammed (JEM)

JEM flag

Jaish-e-Mohammed (JEM)—also known as the Army of Mohammed, Khudamul Islam, and Tehrik ul-Furqaan among other names—is an extremist group based in Pakistan. It was founded by Masood Azhar in early 2000 upon his release from prison in India. The group's aim is to unite Kashmir with Pakistan and to expel foreign troops from Afghanistan. JEM has openly declared war against the United States. Pakistan outlawed JEM in 2002, and by 2003 JEM had splintered into Khuddam ul-Islam (KUI), headed by Azhar, and Jamaat ul-Furqan (JUF), led by Abdul Jabbar. Pakistani authorities detained Abdul Jabbar for suspected involvement in the December 2003 assassination attempts against President Pervez Musharraf but released him in August 2004. Pakistan banned KUI and JUF in November 2003.

JEM continues to operate openly in parts of Pakistan despite the 2002 ban on its activities. Since JEM founder Masood Azhar's release in 2000, JEM has conducted many lethal terrorist attacks, including a suicide bombing of the Jammu and Kashmir legislative assembly building in the Indian-administered Kashmir capital of Srinagar in October 2001 that killed more than 30. In July 2004, Pakistani authorities arrested a JEM member wanted in connection with the 2002 abduction and murder of US journalist Daniel Pearl. In 2006 JEM claimed responsibility for a number of attacks, including the killing of several Indian police officials in Srinagar. JEM members also were involved in the 2007 Red Mosque uprising in Islamabad. Asmatullah Moavia, a militant currently associated with Tehrik-e Taliban Pakistan, split from the group after the Red Mosque incident because of disagreements over how to react to it. In 2009, Pakistani authorities detained several JEM members suspected of taking part in a 3 March attack on the Sri Lankan cricket team in Lahore.

In June 2008, JEM reportedly was working to resolve its differences with other Pakistani extremist groups and began shifting its focus from Kashmir to Afghanistan in order to step up attacks against US and Coalition forces. Rogue factions of JEM, in conjunction with other regional groups, may conduct attacks against Western interests in Pakistan as well as attack Pakistani Government entities.

JEM has at least several hundred armed supporters located in Pakistan, India's southern Kashmir and Doda regions, and in the Kashmir Valley. Supporters are mostly Pakistanis and Kashmiris, but also include Afghans and Arab veterans of the Afghan war against the Soviets. The group uses light and heavy machine guns, assault rifles, mortars, improvised explosive devices, and rocket-propelled grenades in its attacks. The US State Department designated JEM a Foreign Terrorist Organization in 2001.

# Jemaah Islamiyah (JI)

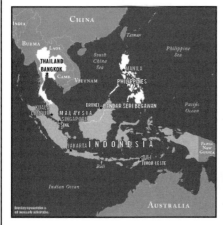

JI flag

Jemaah Islamiyah (JI) is an Indonesia-based clandestine terrorist network formed in the early 1990s to establish an Islamic state encompassing southern Thailand, Malaysia, Singapore, Indonesia, Brunei, and the southern Philippines. Its operatives, who trained in camps in Afghanistan and the southern Philippines, began conducting attacks in 1999. The network's existence was discovered in late 2001 after Singaporean authorities disrupted a cell that was planning to attack targets associated with the US Navy. JI is responsible for a series of lethal bombings targeting Western interests in Indonesia and the Philippines from 2000-2005, including attacks in 2002 against two nightclubs in Bali that killed 202 people; the 2003 car bombing of the JW Marriott hotel in Jakarta that killed 12; the 2004 truck bombing of the Australian Embassy that killed 11; and the 2005 suicide bombing of three establishments in Bali that killed 22. A JI splinter group led by Noordin Mat Top in July 2009 conducted suicide bombings at two hotels in Jakarta.

Southeast Asian governments since 2002 have arrested more than 300 suspected terrorists, significantly degrading JI's network. Thai authorities detained the network's operations chief in 2003. Indonesian police killed JI's most experienced bombmaker in 2005 and arrested its two senior leaders in mid-2007. Malaysian authorities arrested two senior JI operatives in Kuala Lumpur in early 2008 and in April 2009 recaptured fugitive Singapore JI leader Mas Selamat Kasteri, who escaped from his Singaporean prison cell in early 2008. Indonesian police in September 2009 killed Noordin Mat Top.

Since 2009, JI has been overshadowed by the activities of its splinter groups and other Indonesia-based terrorists, some of whom are experienced operatives previously affiliated with JI; others are convicted terrorists who completed prison sentences and have since resumed their activities. Indonesian terrorist Umar Patek—arrested by Pakistani authorities in Abbotabad in January 2011 and repatriated seven months later—was convicted in June 2012 for his role in the 2002 Bali bombings and sentenced to 20 years in prison. In November 2012, Philippine security forces killed senior Indonesian JI leader Sanusi.

# Lashkar-e-Jhangvi (LJ)

Lashkar-e-Jhangvi (LJ) was founded in 1996 as a militant offshoot of Sipah-i-Sahaba Pakistan, a Deobandi and anti-Shia group that emerged in the mid-1980s in reaction to class-based conflict and the domestic Pakistani Shia revival that followed the Iranian revolution. LJ seeks to transform Pakistan into a Deobandi-dominated Sunni state, and primarily targets Shia and other religious minorities.

Akram Lahori is the leader of LJ but in 2002 was arrested, later convicted of sectarian killings, and is currently incarcerated. Lahori officially remains LJ's amir and Malik Mohammad Ishaq, one of LJ's founding members, is believed to have taken command since his release from prison in 2011. According to Pakistani media reporting, LJ consists of at least eight loosely coordinated cells spread across Pakistan with independent chiefs for each cell. At least seven of these cells—Lashkar-e-Jhangvi Al Alami, Asif Chotoo group, Akram Lahori group, Naeem Bukhari group, Qari Zafar group, Qari Shakeel group, and Farooq Bengali group—are active in Pakistan's largest city, Karachi. Many are linked to al-Qa'ida and Tehrik-e Taliban Pakistan (TTP) but still recognize Ishaq as the head of LJ. In particular, LJ cells also often coordinate with TTP factions in Karachi when targeting law enforcement agencies and Shia.

LJ collaborates and has overlapping membership with other Pakistan-based radical Sunni groups including al-Qa'ida and TTP. Pakistani authorities suspected LJ collaborated with these groups in the 2009 attack on the Pakistan Army General Headquarters in Islamabad and in several attacks in 2010 targeting Pakistan's Criminal Investigation Department. LJ members reportedly also have been linked to a number of high-profile kidnappings and killings of Westerners in the region, such as the 1997 killing of four US oil workers in Karachi, the 2002 kidnapping and execution of US journalist Daniel Pearl, the August 2010 kidnapping of the son-in-law of the former Chairman of the Joint Chiefs of Staff Committee, and the August 2011 kidnapping of a US citizen that was later publicly claimed by al-Qa'ida.

In 2013, LJ claimed credit for some of the most deadly sectarian attacks in Pakistan's history. In January, a billiard hall in Quetta, Balochistan Province, was hit by two blasts, first by a suicide bomber and about 10 minutes later by a car bomb, killing 92 people and injuring more than 120, mostly Shia. In February, explosives hidden in a water tanker exploded in a crowded market in Hazara town, a Shia-dominated area on the edge of Quetta. The blast killed 81 people and wounded 178, stoking anger and frustration among Shia at the authorities' inability or unwillingness to crack down on LJ.

# Lashkar-e-Tayyiba (LT)

Lashkar-e-Tayyiba (LT), also known as Army of the Righteous, is one of the largest and most proficient of the Kashmir-focused militant groups. LT formed in the early 1990s as the military wing of Markaz-ud-Dawa-wal-Irshad, a Pakistan-based Islamic fundamentalist missionary organization founded in the 1980s to oppose the Soviets in Afghanistan. Since 1993, LT has conducted numerous attacks against Indian troops and civilian targets in the disputed Jammu and Kashmir state, as well as several high-profile attacks inside India itself. Concern over new LT attacks in India remains high. The United States and United Nations have designated LT as an international terrorist organization. The Pakistani Government banned LT and froze its assets in 2002. In June 2014, the US Treasury Department imposed sanctions on two additional LT leaders and the US State Department amended the Foreign Terrorist Organizations and Specially Designated Global Terrorist designations for LT to include four additional front organizations. In April 2012 two senior LT leaders were designated by the US State Department Rewards for Justice program.

The Indian Government has charged LT with committing the 26–29 November 2008 attacks in Mumbai, in which gunmen using automatic weapons and grenades attacked several sites, killing more than 160 people. Pakistani authorities have detained and are prosecuting several LT leaders for the Mumbai attacks. David Headley, an American citizen who acknowledged attending LT training camps, pleaded guilty in March 2010 to scouting targets for the Mumbai attacks. On 21 November 2012, India executed the lone surviving Mumbai attacker—Ajmal Kasab, a Pakistani—after the Indian Supreme Court upheld his death sentence.

LT's exact size is unknown, but the group probably has several thousand members. Elements of LT are active in Afghanistan and the group also recruits internationally, as evidenced by the arrest in the United States of Jubair Ahmed in 2011, Headley's arrest in 2009, and the indictment of 11 LT terrorists in Virginia in 2003. LT maintains facilities in Pakistan, including training camps, schools, and medical clinics. In March 2002, senior al-Qa'ida lieutenant Abu Zubaydah was captured at an LT safehouse in Faisalabad, suggesting that some LT members assist the group.

LT coordinates its charitable activities through its front organization, Jamaat-ud-Dawa (JuD), which spearheaded humanitarian relief to the victims of the October 2005 earthquake in Kashmir. JuD activities, however, have been limited since December 2008 by the UN's designation of the group as an alias for LT.

# Liberation Tigers of Tamil Eelam (LTTE)

*LTTE flag*

*(Shutterstock)*

**aka** Ellalan Force; Tamil Tigers

**Description**: Founded in 1976 and designated as a Foreign Terrorist Organization on October 8, 1997, the Liberation Tigers of Tamil Eelam (LTTE) became a powerful Tamil secessionist group in Sri Lanka. Despite its military defeat at the hands of the Sri Lankan government in 2009, the LTTE's international network of sympathizers and financial support persists.

**Activities**: Although the LTTE has been largely inactive since its military defeat in Sri Lanka in 2009, in the past the LTTE was responsible for an integrated battlefield insurgent strategy that targeted key installations and senior Sri Lankan political and military leaders. It conducted a sustained campaign targeting rival Tamil groups, and assassinated Prime Minister Rajiv Gandhi of India in 1991 and President Ranasinghe Premadasa of Sri Lanka in 1993. Although most notorious for its cadre of suicide bombers, the Black Tigers, LTTE also had an amphibious force, the Sea Tigers, and a nascent air wing, the Air Tigers. Fighting between the LTTE and the Sri Lanka government escalated in 2006 and continued through 2008.

In early 2009, Sri Lankan forces recaptured the LTTE's key strongholds, including their capital of Kilinochchi. In May 2009, government forces defeated the last LTTE fighting forces, killed LTTE leader Prabhakaran and other members of the LTTE leadership and military command, and declared military victory. There have been no known attacks in Sri Lanka that could verifiably be attributed to the LTTE since the end of the war, but a total of 13 LTTE supporters, several of which had allegedly planned attacks against U.S. and Israeli diplomatic facilities in India, were arrested in Malaysia in 2014.

LTTE's financial network of support continued to operate throughout 2014.

**Strength**: Exact strength is unknown.

**Location/Area of Operation**: Sri Lanka and India

**Funding and External Aid**: The LTTE used its international contacts and the large Tamil diaspora in North America, Europe, and Asia to procure weapons, communications, funding, and other needed supplies. The group employed charities as fronts to collect and divert funds for its activities.

# Lord's Resistance Army (LRA)

Joseph Kony

LRA flag

The Lord's Resistance Army (LRA) is a Ugandan rebel group currently operating in the border region of the Democratic Republic of the Congo (DRC), the Central African Republic (CAR), and South Sudan. Joseph Kony established the LRA in 1988 with the claim of restoring the honor of his ethnic Acholi people and to install a government based on his personal version of the Ten Commandments. Kony claims to channel various spirits who direct him to oust Ugandan President Yoweri Museveni; however, under Kony's leadership, LRA soldiers conduct violence for the sake of violence, primarily against civilians, rather than fighting to advance a political agenda. Since 2005, the LRA is believed to have committed hundreds of attacks resulting in well over 5,000 deaths and considerably more wounded and kidnapped.

The LRA has its roots in the conflict between the Acholi tribe of northern Uganda and other tribes in southern Uganda that began during Idi Amin Dada's regime (1971-1979). Power changed hands between two equally ruthless Acholi leaders after Idi Amin was overthrown, but the Acholi were forced to flee back to the north when Museveni seized power in 1986. Alienated Acholi troops subsequently formed a less extreme Holy Spirit movement to counter the Ugandan government. However, following their defeat in 1988, a more violent movement—the LRA— emerged under Kony. LRA soldiers quickly gained a reputation for murder, torture, rape, and mutilations aimed primarily at Acholi communities, as well as abducting tens of thousands of children over the years to use as sex slaves and child soldiers.

In 2002 Uganda launched "Operation Iron Fist" to defeat the insurgency in northern Uganda, but this only increased attacks and caused a dramatic increase in the number of internally displaced people. In 2005 and 2006, the LRA shifted forces to the DRC, during which time the rebellion took the form of a regional militia that terrorized populations in the DRC, CAR, Uganda, and what is now South Sudan.

In May 2010 the US Congress passed the "Lord's Resistance Army Disarmament and Northern Uganda Recovery Act," which follows the US State Department inclusion of the LRA on the Terrorist Exclusion List in 2001 and designation of Joseph Kony as a Specially Designated Global Terrorist under Executive Order 13324 in 2008. In October 2011 the United States sent a force of 100 soldiers—in an advisory role—to regional militaries aimed at removing Kony from the battlefield. In March 2014 the United States announced it was sending additional soldiers and military aircraft to increase its support to the hunt for Kony.

# National Liberation Army (ELN)

*ELN flag*

(Shutterstock)

**aka** ELN; Ejercito de Liberacion Nacional

**Description**: The National Liberation Army (ELN) was designated as a Foreign Terrorist Organization on October 8, 1997. The ELN is a Colombian Marxist-Leninist group formed in 1964. It is primarily rural-based, although it also has several urban units. The ELN remains focused on attacking economic infrastructure, in particular oil and gas pipelines and electricity pylons, and extorting foreign and local companies. The Colombian government began exploratory peace talks with the ELN in January 2014, although formal peace negotiations had not started by year's end.

**Activities**: The ELN engages in kidnappings, hijackings, bombings, drug trafficking, and extortion activities. The group also uses intimidation of judges, prosecutors, and witnesses; and has been involved in the murders of teachers and trade unionists. The group has targeted Colombia's infrastructure, particularly oil pipelines and equipment. In recent years, including 2014, the ELN launched joint attacks with the Revolutionary Armed Forces of Colombia (FARC), Colombia's largest terrorist organization.

During 2014, the ELN launched fewer attacks against oil pipelines, but according to Colombian authorities, the group caused more damage than in 2013. The ELN was responsible for eighty percent of the pipeline attacks in 2014. On June 20, the ELN bombed a police station in Bogota injuring three people. On June 29, the group attacked a pipeline in Arauca department which resulted in 13 people injured and suspended production at the Occidental Petroleum Corporation's oil field. In a demonstration of its ability to attack the capital city and in advance of the August presidential election, the ELN placed five leaflet bombs in Bogota on July 29, with several exploding prior to detection. On September 14, an ELN sniper shot dead two workers sent to repair a damaged section of an oil pipeline that had been bombed by the group near the town of Teorama, Norte de Santander.

**Strength**: Approximately 2,000 armed combatants and an unknown number of active supporters.

**Location/Area of Operation:** Mostly in the rural and mountainous areas of northern, northeastern, and southwestern Colombia, as well as the border regions with Venezuela.

**Funding and External Aid:** The ELN draws its funding from the illicit narcotics trade and from extortion of oil and gas companies. Additional funds are derived from kidnapping ransoms. There is no known external aid.

# Terrorism In North And West Africa

Mokhtar Belmokhtar

Al-Murabitun, which seeks to "unite all Muslims from the Nile to the Atlantic in jihad against Westerners" and "liberate Mali from France," according to the group's public announcement, was formed when veteran jihadist Mokhtar Belmokhtar in August 2013 merged his al-Mulathamun Battalion with Al-Tawhid Wal Jihad in West Africa (TWJWA). The merger formalized an already close relationship between two of the most active terrorist groups in North and West Africa. The two groups—both offshoots of al-Qa'ida in the Lands of the Islamic Maghreb (AQIM)—conducted numerous attacks against Westerners in North and West Africa prior to their merger, including the January 2013 attack on the I-n-Amenas gas facility in Algeria that killed nearly 40 Westerners, including three Americans, and a joint operation in May 2013 in Niger simultaneously targeting a French uranium mine and a Nigerian military barracks.

French CT operations have killed at least four senior leaders and dozens of rank-and-file members of al-Murabitun—including its titular leader, Abu Bakr al-Masri—in Mali since November 2013, possibly preventing the group from carrying out a high-profile attack in the region. However, al-Murabitun has conducted small-scale but lethal attacks against UN targets in Mali and remains the most potent threat in the Sahel because of Belmokhtar's anti-West agenda and vast network of extremists. In its initial announcement, the new group pledged allegiance to al-Qa'ida senior leadership and its commitment to the philosophy of jihad put forward by Usama Bin Ladin, suggesting a focus on anti-Western attacks, and in two separate statements in 2014 the group reaffirmed its allegiance to Ayman al-Zawahiri and restated its intent to continue to attack France and its allies.

Tawhid Wal Jihad in West Africa (TWJWA), also known as the Movement for Unity and Jihad in West Africa (MUJAO), was founded in late 2011 as an offshoot of AQIM and has coordinated terrorist attacks across North and West Africa. Since the French-led intervention in Mali began in mid-January 2013, TWJWA has conducted a majority of the attacks targeting French and African forces in the vicinity of Gao and Kidal, using suicide bombings, vehicle-borne improvised explosive devices, and landmines.

Al-Murabitun, an Arabic phrase meaning "The Sentinels," invokes a medieval dynasty of the same name—known in English as the Almoravids—that originated as a religious and military movement and whose nomadic founders emerged from present-day Western Sahara in the mid-11th century. The Almoravids ruled much of northwest Africa and southern Spain for nearly 100 years, professing a rigorous Islamic creed and imposing a strict form of sharia on the peoples they conquered.

# Palestinian Liberation Front (PLF)
## (Abu Abbas Faction)

Terrorist Threat

*(Shutterstock)*

**aka** PLF; PLF-Abu Abbas; Palestine Liberation Front

**Description**: The Palestinian Liberation Front – Abu Abbas Faction (PLF) was desig-nated as a Foreign Terrorist Organization on October 8, 1997. In the late 1970s, the Palestine Liberation Front (PLF) splintered from the Popular Front for the Liberation of Palestine-General Command (PFLP-GC), and then later split into pro-Palestinian Lib-eration Organization (PLO), pro-Syrian, and pro-Libyan factions. The pro-PLO faction was led by Muhammad Zaydan (a.k.a. Abu Abbas) and was based in Baghdad prior to Operation Iraqi Freedom.

Activities: Abbas's group was responsible for the 1985 attack on the Italian cruise ship Achille Lauro and the murder of U.S. citizen Leon Klinghoffer. The PLF was suspected of supporting terrorism against Israel by other Palestinian groups into the 1990s. In April 2004, Abu Abbas died of natural causes while in U.S. custody in Iraq. The PLF took part in the 2006 Palestinian parliamentarian elections but did not win a seat. In 2008, as part of a prisoner exchange between Israel and Hizballah, Samir Kantar, a PLF member – and purportedly the longest serving Arab prisoner in Israeli custody – was released from an Israeli prison.

After 16 years without claiming responsibility for an attack, the PLF claimed responsi-bility for two attacks against Israeli targets on March 14, 2008. One attack was against an Israeli military bus in Huwarah, Israel, and the other involved a PLF brigade firing at an Israeli settler south of the Hebron Mountain, seriously wounding him. On March 28, 2008, shortly after the attacks, a PLF Central Committee member reaffirmed PLF's commitment to using "all possible means to restore" its previous glory and to adhering to its role in the Palestinian "struggle" and "resistance" through its military. There were no known PLF attacks in 2014.

**Strength**: Estimates have placed membership between 50 and 500.

**Location/Area of Operation**: PLF leadership and membership are based in Lebanon and the West Bank and Gaza.

**Funding and External Aid:** Unknown

# Real IRA (RIRA)

(Shutterstock)

**aka** RIRA; Real Irish Republican Army; 32 County Sovereignty Committee; 32 County Sovereignty Movement; Irish Republican Prisoners Welfare Association; Real Oglaigh Na hEireann

**Description**: Designated as a Foreign Terrorist Organization on May 16, 2001, the Real IRA (RIRA) was formed in 1997 as the clandestine armed wing of the 32 County Sovereignty Movement, a "political pressure group" dedicated to removing British forces from Northern Ireland and unifying Ireland. The RIRA has historically sought to disrupt the Northern Ireland peace process and did not participate in the September 2005 weapons decommissioning. In September 1997, the 32 County Sovereignty Movement opposed Sinn Fein's adoption of the Mitchell principles of democracy and non-violence. Despite internal rifts and calls by some jailed members, including the group's founder Michael "Mickey" McKevitt, for a ceasefire and disbandment, the RIRA has pledged additional violence and continued to conduct attacks.

**Activities**: Many RIRA members are former Provisional Irish Republican Army members who left the organization after that group renewed its ceasefire in 1997. These members brought a wealth of experience in terrorist tactics and bomb making to the RIRA. Targets have included civilians (most notoriously in the Omagh bombing in August 1998), British security forces, and police in Northern Ireland. The Independent Monitoring Commission, which was established to oversee the peace process, assessed that RIRA members were likely responsible for the majority of the shootings and assaults that occurred in Northern Ireland.

The group remained active. In February 2013, two alleged RIRA members were arrested by Irish police while attempting to carry out the assassination of a local drug dealer. Police searched the van they were traveling in and found two loaded handguns and facemasks.

**Strength**: According to the Irish government, the RIRA has approximately 100 active members. The organization may receive limited support from IRA hardliners and Republican sympathizers who are dissatisfied with the IRA's continuing ceasefire and with Sinn Fein's involvement in the peace process.

**Location/Area of Operation:** Northern Ireland, Great Britain, and the Republic of Ireland.

# Revolutionary Armed Forces of Colombia (FARC)

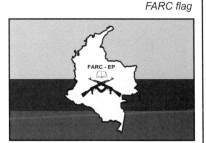

*FARC flag*

*(Shutterstock)*

**aka** FARC; Fuerzas Armadas Revolucionarias de Colombia

**Description**: Designated as a Foreign Terrorist Organization on October 8, 1997, the Revolutionary Armed Forces of Colombia (FARC) is Latin America's oldest, largest, most violent, and best-equipped terrorist organization. The FARC began in the early 1960s as an outgrowth of the Liberal Party-based peasant self-defense leagues, but took on Marxist ideology. Today, it only nominally fights in support of Marxist goals, and is heavily involved in illicit narcotics production and trafficking. The FARC has been responsible for large numbers of kidnappings for ransom in Colombia, and in past years has allegedly held as many as 700 hostages. The FARC's capacity has been degraded by a continuing Colombian military offensive targeting key FARC units and leaders that has, by most estimates, halved the FARC's numbers – estimated at approximately 8,000 in 2013 – and succeeded in capturing or killing a number of FARC senior and mid-level commanders. In August 2012, the Colombian President announced that exploratory peace talks between the Colombian government and the FARC were underway. Although the government and the FARC reached a tentative partial agreement on three of the five agreed upon points, no overall peace agreement was concluded by the end of 2014.

**Activities**: Over the years, the FARC has perpetrated a large number of high profile terrorist acts, including the 1999 murder of three U.S. missionaries working in Colombia, and multiple kidnappings and assassinations of Colombian government officials and civilians. In July 2008, the Colombian military made a dramatic rescue of 15 high-value FARC hostages. In 2014, the FARC focused on launching mortars at police stations or the military, placing explosive devices near roads or paths, and using snipers attacks, and ambushes. In 2014, FARC attacks on infrastructure, particularly on oil pipeline and energy towers, decreased. Security forces and government buildings were the most common terrorist targets, although civilian casualties occurred throughout the year. Although FARC attacks decreased in 2014, the group committed a number of significant attacks.

**Strength**: Approximately 8,000 to 9,000 members, with several thousand supporters.

**Location/Area of Operation:** Primarily in Colombia; however, FARC leaders and combatants have been known to use neighboring countries for weapons sourcing and logistical planning. The FARC often use Colombia's border areas with Venezuela, Panama, and Ecuador for incursions into Colombia; and used Venezuelan and Ecuadorian territory for safe haven.

# Tehrik-e Taliban Pakistan (TTP)

*Taliban flag*

The Taliban is a Sunni Islamist nationalist and pro-Pashtun movement founded in the early 1990s that ruled most of Afghanistan from 1996 until October 2001. The movement's founding nucleus—the word "Taliban" is Pashto for "students"—was composed of peasant farmers and men studying Islam in Afghan and Pakistani madrasas, or religious schools. The Taliban found a foothold and consolidated their strength in southern Afghanistan.

By 1994, the Taliban had moved their way through the south, capturing several provinces from various armed factions who had been fighting a civil war after the Soviet-backed Afghan government fell in 1992. The Taliban's first move was to institute a strict interpretation of Qur'anic instruction and jurisprudence. In practice, this meant often merciless policies on the treatment of women, political opponents of any type, and religious minorities.

Tehrik-e Taliban Pakistan (TTP) is an alliance of militant networks formed in 2007 to unify opposition against the Pakistani military. TTP's stated objectives are the expulsion of Islamabad's influence in the Federally Administered Tribal Areas and neighboring Khyber Pakhtunkhwa Province in Pakistan, the implementation of a strict interpretation of sharia throughout Pakistan, and the expulsion of Coalition troops from Afghanistan. TTP leaders also publicly say that the group seeks to establish an Islamic caliphate in Pakistan that would require the overthrow of the Pakistani Government. TTP historically maintained close ties to senior al-Qa'ida leaders, including al-Qa'ida's former head of operations for Pakistan.

Baitullah Mehsud, the first TTP leader, died on 5 August 2009, and his successor, Hakimullah Mehsud, died on 1 November 2013. TTP's central shura in November 2013 appointed Mullah Fazlullah as the group's overall leader. Fazlullah is staunchly anti-Western, anti-Islamabad, and advocates harsh tactics underscored by his ordering the November 2012 attempted assassination of education rights activist Malala Yousafzai. TTP since 2008 has repeatedly publicly threatened to attack the US homeland, and a TTP spokesman claimed responsibility for the failed vehicle-bomb attack in Times Square, New York City, on 1 May 2010. In June 2011, a spokesman vowed to attack the United States and Europe in revenge for the death of Usama Bin Ladin. A TTP leader in April 2012 endorsed external operations by the group and threatened attacks in the United Kingdom for its involvement in Afghanistan.

# Turkish Domestic Terrorism

Abdullah Ocalan

Kongra-Gel flag

The Revolutionary People's Liberation Party/Front (DHKP/C) was created in 1994 when its predecessor group, Devrimci Sol or Dev Sol, splintered after factional infighting. The Marxist-Leninist group espouses an anti-US, anti-NATO, and anti-Turkish establishment ideology and has targeted US interests intermittently for several decades, most recently in February 2013 when a suicide bomber targeted the US Embassy in Ankara. Its goals are the overthrow of the Turkish state, the removal of the US and NATO footprint from Turkey, and the abolition of one- to three-man prison cells, called F-type prisons, in Turkey.

In the 1990s Dev Sol began attacking foreign interests, including US military and diplomatic personnel and facilities. DHKP/C added suicide bombings to its tactics in 2001, in addition to improvised explosive devices and targeted assassinations. Increased attacks in 2003 probably were a reaction to Turkey's support of Operation Iraqi Freedom. DHKP/C entered an operational lull until mid-2012 when the group resumed attacks against Turkish police targets. Following the February 2013 US Embassy attack, DHKP/C has continued targeting Turkish Government and police interests, indicating that the group remained operationally viable despite crackdowns.

The Kurdistan People's Congress (Kongra-Gel or KGK, formerly the Kurdistan Workers' Party, PKK) is a Kurdish separatist group primarily active in part of northern Iraq and southeastern Turkey. Composed mostly of Turkish Kurds, the group in 1984 began a campaign of armed violence, including terrorism, which resulted in over 45,000 deaths. Historically, KGK directed operatives to target Turkish security forces, government offices, and villagers who opposed the group. The KGK's imprisoned leader, Abdullah Ocalan, in 2012 entered into peace negotiations with the Turkish Government, emphasizing the group's goals of obtaining constitutional guarantees for greater local autonomy and Kurdish cultural and political rights. The peace negotiations continued into 2014, though KGK leaders expressed frustration, charging the Turkish Government failed to establish legal and constitutional guarantees, and warned that lack of progress could make the talks collapse.

KGK and Turkish forces clashed repeatedly in 2011 and 2012, including an attack in October 2011 that killed 24 Turkish troops and was the deadliest incident since 1993. KGK also stepped up its kidnapping campaign against Turkish state employees and soldiers, which included the unprecedented abduction of a Turkish parliamentary deputy in August 2012.

# IX. The Terrorist Identities Datamart Environment (TIDE)

The Terrorist Identities Datamart Environment (TIDE) is the U.S. Government's (USG) central repository of information on international terrorist identities. The Intelligence Reform and Terrorism Prevention Act (IRTPA) of 2004 established NCTC in law, and mandated the Center serve as the "central and shared knowledge bank on known and suspected terrorists and international terror groups." TIDE is that knowledge bank and supports the USG's various terrorist screening systems or "watchlists" and the US Intelligence Community's overall counterterrorism mission.

The TIDE database includes, to the extent permitted by law, all information the USG possesses related to the identities of individuals known or appropriately suspected to be or to have been involved in activities constituting, in preparation for, in aid of, or related to terrorism (with the exception of purely domestic terrorism information). This information is available to counterterrorism professionals throughout the Intelligence Community, including the Department of Defense, via the web-based, read-only "TIDE Online."

*(FBI.GOV)*

Each day analysts create and enhance TIDE records based on their review of nominations received. NCTC exports a sensitive but unclassified subset of the data containing the terrorist identifiers to the Terrorist Screening Center (TSC) in near real time for use in the USG's consolidated watchlist. This consolidated watchlist, which is a critical tool for homeland security, supports screening processes to detect and interdict known and suspected terrorists at home and abroad – for example, the Transportation Security Administration's "No Fly" list and the Department of State's visa database, among others. For more information visit: www.fbi.gov/about-us/nsb/tsc/tsc_faqs.

As of December 2013, TIDE contained about 1.1 million persons, most containing multiple minor spelling variations of their names. U.S. Persons (including both citizens and legal permanent residents) account for about 25,000 of that total. In the last three years DTI has deleted over 50,000 records from TIDE, an average of over 16,500 per year, after they were determined to no longer meet the criteria for inclusion.

The Department of Homeland Security's (DHS) Traveler Redress Inquiry Program (DHS Trip) was launched in February 2007. Travelers can use this program to request resolution of possible watchlist misidentification issues with any of the department's component agencies at: http://www.dhs.gov/trip.

# IV(c). Domestic Terrorism

Contributor: Dr. Troy Mitchell.

Since September 11, 2001, the terrorist attacks and the U.S. response—now called the global war on terrorism—have changed the world, and the terrorist enterprise that we know as al-Qaeda has morphed into a globalized enterprise. As the most destructive day in the long, bloody history of terrorism, the casualties, economic damage, and outrage were unprecedented. The current status of al-Qaeda's network remains unclear, but it is certain that it and other terrorist groups continue to threaten the lives and well-being of civilians, at home and abroad, and the security of our friends and allies. This continuing danger leads to ongoing U.S. and international efforts to monitor, disrupt, and dismantle terrorist groups before they cause large-scale destruction to our people or our interests. The tremendous number and variation of terrorist organizations in the world preclude a single causal explanation for terrorism relative to every situation. Terrorist organizations appeal disproportionately to certain psychological types of people, namely, the socially alienated.

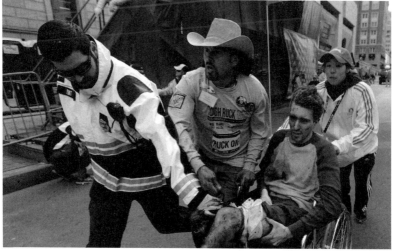

(AP Photo/Charles Krupa)

In this April 15, 2013 photo, an emergency responder and volunteers, including Carlos Arredondo in the cowboy hat, push Jeff Bauman in a wheel chair after he was injured in an explosion near the finish line of the Boston Marathon in Boston. The twin bombing at the Boston Marathon killed three people and wounded more than 260 others. Prosecutors say he and his brother, Tamerlan - ethnic Chechens who had lived in the United States for about a decade - carried out the attack in retaliation for U.S. wars in Muslim countries. Tamerlan died in a gunbattle with police.

Many Americans view terrorism as an unfortunate by-product of contemporary life. No one knows if the current campaign will be more successful than its predecessors, but we can more fully appreciate the difficulties ahead by examining features of the history of terror. That history shows how deeply implanted terrorism is in our culture, provides parallels worth pondering, and offers a perspective for understanding the uniqueness of September 11 and its aftermath.

# I. Terrorism in the United States
# [An FBI Retrospective: 1980-2005]

*Ref: TERRORISM 2002-2005, Federal Bureau of Investigation and Terrorism in the
United States 1999, Federal Bureau of Investigation.*

Many Americans view terrorism as an unfortunate by-product of contemporary life. Like
oil spills and aircraft disasters, acts of terrorism are considered one of the regrettable–
and often inexplicable–perils of modern society. However, terrorism is actually one of the
oldest forms of human conflict.

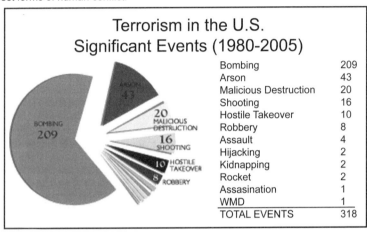

## Terrorism in the U.S.
## Significant Events (1980-2005)

| | |
|---|---|
| Bombing | 209 |
| Arson | 43 |
| Malicious Destruction | 20 |
| Shooting | 16 |
| Hostile Takeover | 10 |
| Robbery | 8 |
| Assault | 4 |
| Hijacking | 2 |
| Kidnapping | 2 |
| Rocket | 2 |
| Assasination | 1 |
| WMD | 1 |
| TOTAL EVENTS | 318 |

Terrorism is nothing new in the United States; the FBI has been investigating and helping
to prevent terrorist attacks since the 1920s. Since the mid-1980s, the FBI has published
Terrorism in the United States, an unclassified annual report summarizing terrorist activities in this country. While this publication provided an overview of the terrorist threat in
the United States and its territories, its limited scope proved inadequate for conveying
either the breadth or width of the terrorist threat facing U.S. interests or the scale of the
FBI's response to terrorism worldwide. To better reflect the nature of the threat and the
international scope of our response, the FBI expanded the focus of its annual terrorism
report in the 2000/2001 edition to include discussion of FBI investigations overseas.

TERRORIST INCIDENTS in the UNITED STATES 1980-2005

**318** TOTAL TERRORIST INCIDENTS

| TOTALS | '80 | '81 | '82 | '83 | '84 | '85 | '86 | '87 | '88 | '89 | '90 | '91 | '92 | '93 | '94 | '95 | '96 | '97 | '98 | '99 | '00 | '01 | '02 | '03 | '04 | '05 |
|---|---|---|---|---|---|---|---|---|---|---|---|---|---|---|---|---|---|---|---|---|---|---|---|---|---|---|
| | 29 | 42 | 51 | 31 | 14 | 7 | 25 | 9 | 9 | 4 | 7 | 5 | 4 | 12 | 1 | 1 | 3 | 3 | 6 | 11 | 8 | 14 | 8 | 6 | 5 | 5 |

The FBI divides terrorist-related activity into two categories:

- A **terrorist incident** is a violent act or an act dangerous to human life, in violation of the criminal laws of the United States, or of any state, to intimidate or coerce a government, the civilian population, or any segment thereof, in furtherance of political or social objectives.
- A **terrorism prevention** is a documented instance in which a violent act by a known or suspected terrorist group or individual with the means and a proven propensity for violence is successfully interdicted through investigative activity.

## Domestic Terrorism
Domestic terrorism is the unlawful use, or threatened use, of force or violence by a group or individual based and operating entirely within the United States or Puerto Rico without foreign direction committed against persons or property to intimidate or coerce a government, the civilian population, or any segment thereof in furtherance of political or social objectives.

## International Terrorism
International terrorism involves violent acts or acts dangerous to human life that are a violation of the criminal laws of the United States or any state, or that would be a criminal violation if committed within the jurisdiction of the United States or any state. These acts appear to be intended to intimidate or coerce a civilian population, influence the policy of a government by intimidation or coercion, or affect the conduct of a government by assassination or kidnapping. International terrorist acts occur outside the United States or transcend national boundaries in terms of the means by which they are accomplished, the persons they appear intended to coerce or intimidate, or the locale in which their perpetrators operate or seek asylum.

# Terror at Home
During the first 75 years of its history the FBI encountered a predominantly domestic terrorist threat that underlay larger criminal trends. Between the World Wars, this threat came primarily from right-wing extremists, then shifted to left-wing, socialist-oriented groups beginning in the 1950s and continuing into the 1980s. In the early 1980s, international terrorism–sponsored primarily by states or organizations–began to impact US interests overseas and led to legislation that extended the FBI's responsibilities to cover terrorist threats originating outside the United States and its territories. The 1990s saw a new era of domestic and international terrorism in which terrorists sought to inflict massive and indiscriminate casualties upon civilian populations. This threat grew as terrorists began to seek out unconventional weapons and weapons of mass destruction. The 1990s also saw the rise of terrorism pursued by loosely-affiliated extremists, with examples ranging from terrorists involved with domestic special interest causes to militants engaged in international jihad.

- Between 1980 and 1999, the FBI recorded 327 incidents or suspected incidents of terrorism in the United States. Of these, 239 were attributed to domestic terrorists, while 88 were determined to be international in nature. Combined, these acts resulted in the deaths of 205 persons and in the injury of over 2,037 more. During this same period, 130 planned acts of terrorism were prevented by U.S. law enforcement. Of these, 83 thwarted plots were being planned by domestic subjects; 47 plots were being planned by international extremists.
- (2002-2005) In keeping with a longstanding trend, domestic extremists carried out the majority of terrorist incidents during this period. Twenty three of the 24 recorded terrorist incidents were perpetrated by domestic terrorists
- The terrorism preventions for 2002 through 2005 present a more diverse threat picture. Eight of the 14 recorded terrorism preventions stemmed from right- wing extremism, and included disruptions to plotting by individuals involved with the militia, white supremacist, constitutionalist and tax protestor, and anti- abortion movements.

# II. Types of Domestic Terrorists
*Contributor: Dr. Troy Mitchell.*

Domestic terrorism involves groups or individuals who are based and operate entirely within the United States or its territories without foreign direction and whose acts are directed at elements of the U.S. Government or population. Domestic terrorist groups can represent right wing, left wing, or special interest orientations. Their causes generally spring from issues relating to American political and social concerns.

## Types of Domestic Threat

 **Right Wing**

 **Left Wing**

 **Special Interest Groups**

 **Lone Wolf**

## A. Right Wing
Right wing terrorist groups often adhere to the principles of racial supremacy and embrace antigovernment, antiregulatory beliefs. Generally, extremist right-wing groups engage in activity that is protected by constitutional guarantees of free speech and assembly. During the 1990s, right-wing extremists filed hundreds of groundless liens and other legal claims that clogged courts, disrupted the execution of legitimate civil proceedings, and, on many occasions, resulted in real financial loss to victimized individuals who had to defend against these illicit actions.

- Often adhere to conservative or reactionary principles.
- Such groups endorse racial supremacy, and / or embrace antigovernment and antiregulatory beliefs.
- Patriot movements, militias and "common-law" groups.
- Focused on racial supremacy and anti-government, as well as aspects of free speech and the right to an assembly
- Example terrorist groups: Ku Klux Klan, Neo-Nazis, Skinheads, Christian Identify, Black Separatist, Aryan Nation, World Church of the Creator (WCOTC), Posse Comitatus and other religious hate groups.

## B. Left Wing
Left wing groups generally profess a revolutionary socialist doctrine and view themselves as protectors of the people against the dehumanizing effects of capitalism and imperialism. They aim to bring about change in the United States and believe this change can be realized through revolution rather than through the established political process. From the 1960s to the 1980s, leftist-oriented extremist groups posed the most serious

domestic terrorist threat to the United States. In the 1980s, however, the fortunes of the leftist movement declined dramatically as law enforcement dismantled the infrastructure of many of these groups, and as the fall of Communism in Eastern Europe deprived the movement of its ideological foundation and patronage.

- Profess a revolutionary socialist doctrine and view themselves as protectors of the people against the "dehumanizing effects" of capitalism and imperialism.
- They are responsible for bombings, assassinations, robberies and planned attacks on infrastructure targets.
- Example terrorist groups: Weather Underground, Symbionese Liberation Army, and the Black Liberation Army
- The Cold War appeared to be a culminating point for the left-wing terrorist groups as the organization dissipated by losing their patronage and financial support.

## C. Special Interest Groups

Special interest terrorism differs from traditional right wing and left-wing terrorism in that extremist special interest groups seek to influence specific issues, rather than effect widespread political change. Special interest extremists conduct acts of politically motivated violence to force segments of society, including the general public, to change attitudes about issues considered important to their causes. The increasing level of violent and threatening activity perpetrated by extremists within the animal rights and environmental movements, in particular, appears to be increasing, not only in the United States, but also in Canada and especially throughout Europe.

- Extreme groups who seek to resolve specific issues, rather than affect more widespread political change.
- These groups occupy the extreme fringes of animal rights, pro-life, environmental, anti-nuclear and other political and social movements.
- Since 1990, more than 1200 criminal incidents were claimed by animal and environmental rights extremists
- Tactics range from spray-paint vandalizing to fire-bombings.
- Examples organizations: Animal Liberation Front (ALF) and Earth Liberation Front (ELF) are considered Eco-terrorists.

## D. Lone Wolf

Lone wolf terrorism is shown to be more prevalent in the United States than in the other countries under study. The cross-national analysis suggests that in the United States lone wolf terrorism has increased markedly during the past three decades; a similar increase does not appear to have occurred in the other countries under study. The numbers of casualties resulting from lone wolf terrorism have been relatively limited, and there is no evidence that the lethality of lone wolf terrorism is on the increase. The rates of psychological disturbance and social ineptitude are found to be relatively high among lone wolf terrorists. Lone wolf terrorists tend to create their own ideologies that combine personal frustrations and aversion with broader political, social, or religious aims. In this process, many lone wolf terrorists draw on the communities of belief and ideologies of validation generated and transmitted by extremist movements.

- Lone individuals have their own motivations and agenda.
- They are not supported by group activities, but may draw a few coconspirators in with them or ideological principles.
- McVeigh's retaliation motive (for the FBI assault on Ruby Ridge and ATF assault at Waco) led him to believe that bombing federal buildings prevented the government from continuing with its work.
- Eric Robert Rudolph seemingly targeted abortionists and homosexuals. He believed that by carrying out his attacks, he could influence the government to change laws and policy.

# III. What is Domestic Terrorism?

Domestic terrorists can be defined as people who commit crimes within the home-land and draw inspiration from U.S.-based extremist ideologies and movements. The FBI reported in 1999 that —"during the past 30 years, the vast majority—but not all—of the deadly terrorist attacks occurring in the United States have been perpetrated by domestic extremists." It is worth noting that in terms of casualties on U.S. soil, an act of domestic terrorism is second only to the events of 9/11. Timothy McVeigh's bombing of the Alfred P. Murrah Federal Building in Oklahoma City on April 19, 1995, claimed 168 lives and injured more than 500 others.

*(Oklahoma City Bombing/FBI.GOV)*

The FBI generally relies on two fundamental sources to define domestic terror-ism. First, the Code of Federal Regulations characterizes "terrorism" as including "the unlawful use of force and violence against persons or property to intimidate or coerce a government, the civilian population,  or any segment thereof, in furtherance of political or social objectives." Second, 18 U.S.C. Section 2331(5) more narrowly defines "domestic terrorism" and differentiates it from international terrorism and other criminal activity. This definition comes from Section 802 of the USA PATRIOT Act (P.L. 107-52). According to 18 U.S.C. Section 2331(5), domestic terrorism occurs primarily within U.S. territorial jurisdiction, and domestic terrorism involves

  (A) ... acts dangerous to human life that are a violation of the criminal laws of the United States or of any State;

  (B) appear to be intended—

  (i) to intimidate or coerce a civilian population;

  (ii) to influence the policy of a government by intimidation or coercion; or

  (iii) to affect the conduct of a government by mass destruction, assassination, or kidnapping....

According to the Federal Bureau of Investigation, domestic terrorists do not simply operate in the homeland, but they also lack foreign direction.  In fact, the Bureau's practical, shorthand definition of domestic terrorism is "Americans attacking Ameri-cans based on U.S.-based extremist ideologies."  The Department of Homeland Security (DHS) supports the same definition.

# IV. History of Domestic Terrorism

Terrorism is actually one of the oldest forms of human conflict. Before societies organized to wage war against each other, individuals and small bands engaged in terror tactics to achieve limited goals–to overthrow existing leaders, toward off potential rivals, or to frighten opposing groups from lands they wished to claim for themselves. A century ago America suffered a wave of violence carried out by anarchists. The anarchist movement started in Europe in the late 19th century. Anarchists longed for a stateless society, composed of self-governing workers' communes. Revolutionary anarchists believed the only way to accomplish their goal was to smash the existing order, and they carried out a string of high-profile political assassinations. As in Europe, they focused their anger on the ruling class, which in America meant the industrial nouveau riche. Grinding hours and bitter strikes provided the spark. The most sensational crime of all came in 1901: President William McKinley was shot and killed while shaking hands at the Pan-American Exposition in Buffalo, N.Y.

During the period from 1908 to 1982, the FBI dealt with two broad categories of domestic terrorism: right- and left-wing extremist groups. In the period between World War I and World War II, the domestic threat primarily came from right-wing groups, like the Ku Klux Klan, which often adhered to principles of racial supremacy or embraced antigovernment and antiregulatory beliefs in favor of individual freedoms.

Beginning in the 1950s, the most serious domestic terrorist threat shifted to leftist-oriented extremist groups that generally professed a revolutionary socialist doctrine and viewed themselves as protectors of the people against the adverse effects of capitalism and U.S. foreign policies. Some of the more sensational terrorist events during this latter period included the November 1, 1950, attempted assassination of President Truman at Blair House by two members of the National Party of Puerto Rico. On March 1, 1954, members of the same group opened fire on a session of the U.S. House of Representatives, injuring five congressmen. The 1958 commandeering of a Cuban airliner in flight from Miami inaugurated a decade of hijackings by Cuban revolutionaries.

During the 1970s and 1980s, Croatian nationalists and the anti-Castro Cuban group Omega 7 arose as prominent terrorist threats. Leftist groups, however, continued to remain active during these decades and committed numerous bombings, including the prominent March 1, 1971, bombing of the U.S. Senate building and the January 29, 1975, bombing of the U.S. State Department building, both attributed to the Weather Underground, and the January 24, 1975, bombing of Fraunces Tavern on Wall Street by the Armed Forces for Puerto Rican National Liberation (FALN) that resulted in four deaths and 53 people injured. The threat from leftist groups receded by the late 1980s as law enforcement dismantled their infrastructures. The dissolution of the communist Soviet Union in December 1991 into the democratic Russian Federation with a free market economy further deprived many of these groups of their ideological foundation and patronage.

Between 1980 and 1999, the FBI recorded 327 incidents or suspected incidents of terrorism in the United States. Of these, 239 were attributed to domestic terrorists, while 88 were determined to be international in nature. Combined, these acts resulted in the deaths of 205 persons and in the injury of over 2,037 more. During this same period, 130 planned acts of terrorism were prevented by U.S. law enforcement. Of these, 83 thwarted plots were being planned by domestic subjects; 47 plots were being planned by international extremists.

During the 1990s, however, the nature of domestic and international terrorism underwent recognizable changes in tactics and methodologies as terrorists aimed to inflict massive and indiscriminate casualties upon civilian populations. With respect to domestic terrorism, left-wing political groups and special interest terrorism—that is, terrorism committed by extremists who use violence to compel society to change its attitudes about specific causes—asserted themselves during the 1990s. Anarchists

# V. Lone Wolves: Are They Really Alone in the Radicalization Process?

*Ref: Dr. Tamara A. Mouras, American Military University's blog, In Public Safety, accessed Mar 2016 (http://inpublicsafety.com/2015/02/lone-wolves-are-they-really-alone-in-the-radicalization-process/)*

The term "lone wolf" is often used to describe individuals who act alone to commit terrorist acts. Lone wolf attacks are often motivated by political, religious, and/or ideological reasoning. But, are these individuals really acting alone?

# WANTED
## BY THE FBI

Suspect in Boston Marathon Bombings

### DZHOKHAR TSARNAEV

Captured | Captured

### DESCRIPTION

**Date(s) of Birth Used:** July 22, 1993
**Age:** 19 years old
**Height:** 5'9"

**Sex:** Male
**Race:** White

### CAUTION

The Federal Bureau of Investigation (FBI) is seeking the location of, and information about, Dzhokhar Tsarnaev, a suspect in the bombings at the Boston Marathon on April 15, 2013. These bombings resulted in the deaths of three victims and the injuries of more than 170 people.

**SHOULD BE CONSIDERED ARMED AND EXTREMELY DANGEROUS**

**If you have any information concerning this person, please call 1-800-CALL-FBI, 911, or submit information at https://bostonmarathontips.fbi.gov/. You may also contact your local FBI office or the nearest American Embassy or Consulate.**

*(FBI.GOV)*

## How Alone Are Lone Wolves?

Human beings, like many other animals, are instinctually pack animals. They typically learn with other humans in group settings. In the technology age, it is no longer necessary for individuals to be physically in a group setting. Rather, the Internet can provide potential terrorists with access to like-minded individuals who can provide the virtual encouragement needed for the radicalization process.

Close analysis of known lone wolf terrorists has shown that these individuals often have some level of contact with members of a terrorist organization. Often that contact is with a command and control structure via the Internet.

### Terrorism and the Internet

In my 2013 study, Law Enforcement Perspectives of Factors That May Lead to Radicalization, law enforcement respondents argued that the Internet is the primary tool for terrorist groups to recruit individuals. Through the Internet, extremist groups can use propaganda to expose individuals to brainwashing, provide a sanctuary for increased isolation from mainstream society, and provide a learning platform to share information on potential targets.

Lone wolves may radicalize within an Internet chatroom group that offers the emotional support and security that human beings often seek. Wanting to belong is considered a basic human need and is an important element of security and acceptance as evidenced in Maslow's Hierarchy of Needs. Individuals working and researching in the disciplines of criminal justice and homeland security must understand these needs and apply them to better understand lone wolf radicalization.

# How Maslow's Hierarchy of Needs Relates to Lone Wolf Behavior

Within Maslow's Hierarchy of Needs there are five levels of human needs:

- Psychological
- Safety
- Belongingness
- Esteem
- Self-actualization

The three needs most relevant to lone wolf analysis are belongingness, esteem, and self-actualization. Maslow stated that people are motivated to achieve certain needs and when one need is fulfilled a person seeks to fulfill the next one.

## Belongingness

According to Maslow, belongingness includes love and having roots that include family and friends. If there is a lack of love and affection from the immediate family and/or if there is significant family dysfunction, individuals will seek affection and love from other sources. Rex Hudson argued belonging to a group can provide moral support, family, and a purpose in life.

The most susceptible individuals are those who do not have such love and have a strong desire to become part of a family or group. As it relates to lone wolves, such desire for love and affection can be satisfied through an Internet chatroom with like-minded individuals and the possibility of becoming part of a group.

## Esteem

Esteem is when human beings search for acceptance, prestige, and achievement. Often times, individuals within the radicalization process are looking for a purpose in his or her life and are at a crossroads. By becoming part of an extremist chatroom they are given a new role, a new outlook on life, and a pathway to what they perceive as leading to success and prestige.

## Self-Actualization

Self-actualization is the need fulfilled when the lone wolf "becomes everything that one is capable of becoming." Self-actualization would fall into the phase of the radicalization process when an individual uses his or her capability to commit a terrorist activity.

# Reshaping our Approach to Lone Wolves

There is considerable evidence that lone wolf terrorists rarely act alone, particularly through the radicalization process. The human instinct to act as pack animals coupled with the desire to fulfill basic needs of belonging and acceptance strongly suggests that such terrorists need the support of others.

There must be further research and analysis done in order to understand how the lack of these basic needs may be contributing to the radicalization of lone wolves in the United States. With a greater understanding of this phenomenon we can provide more inclusive counter-radicalization strategies to prevent individuals from becoming radicalized to commit terrorism within the United States.

reemerged in the United States during this period and caused much of the criminal disruption during the 1999 World Trade Organization meeting in Seattle. The majority of domestic terrorism incidents from 1993 to 2001 were attributable to the left-wing special interest movements the Animal Liberation Front (ALF) and the Earth Liberation Front (ELF). Right-wing extremism, however, primarily in the form of domestic militias and conservative special interest causes, began to overtake left-wing extremism as the most dangerous, if not the most prolific, domestic terrorist threat to the country during the 1990s. In contrast to the ALF and the ELF, which have pursued a philosophy that avoids physical violence in favor of acts of property damage that cause their victims economic harm, right-wing extremists pursued a qualitatively different method of operation by targeting people.

The April 19, 1995, bombing of the Alfred P. Murrah Federal Building in Oklahoma City, Oklahoma, brought the threat of right-wing terrorism to the forefront of American law enforcement attention. The Oklahoma City bombing, which killed 168 people and injured 642 others, was an extreme manifestation of a grass-roots antigovernment movement that became prominent during the 1990s. Several factors fueled the growth of this movement, including the passage of gun control legislation, fears of increased United Nations involvement in domestic affairs, and several confrontations between members of right-wing groups and law enforcement officers at Waco, Texas, and Ruby Ridge, Idaho. These confrontations inspired Timothy McVeigh and Terry Nichols to carry out the Oklahoma City bombing, which coincided with the second anniversary of the destruction of the Branch Davidian compound near Waco.

The motivations behind another series of bombings in the mid-1990s illustrate the increasing prominence of terrorism in support of conservative special interest causes during this decade. On July 27, 1996, an explosion in Olympic Centennial Park killed two and injured 112 during the closing days of the Summer Olympics held in Atlanta, Georgia. Early the next year, two more bombings occurred: the first, on January 16, 1997, at a Birmingham, Alabama, health clinic; the second, on February 21, 1997, at the Otherside Lounge, a nightclub patronized by Atlanta's gay community. These latter bombings were distinctive in that the terrorist used secondary explosive devices with an apparent intent to target emergency responders.

The bombings in Oklahoma City, Atlanta, and Birmingham also brought an awareness of a new type of threat from those who may be sympathetic to extreme political or social ideologies, but who commit acts of violence outside of the auspices of structured terrorist organizations or without the prior approval or knowledge of these groups' leaders. The roles of McVeigh and Nichols in the Oklahoma City bombing, and the bombings by Rudolph, exemplify the FBI's "lone offender" category of terrorist for those who engage in terrorist activities free from organizational guidance.

On the morning of September 11, 2001, al-Qa'ida directed its ruthless ingenuity toward the further exploitation of civil aviation when 19 of its operatives hijacked four U.S. commercial airliners for use as suicide weapons against selected political, military, and economic targets on the U.S. East Coast. The hijackers used knives, boxcutters, and possibly pepper spray to commandeer the aircraft. Three of the aircraft struck their targets, destroying the Twin Towers of the World Trade Center in New York City and badly damaging the Pentagon in Arlington, Virginia. The fourth aircraft crashed into a remote field in Stonycreek Township, Pennsylvania, as passengers attempted to regain control of the airplane. All of the passengers on each of the aircraft were killed in the attack, as were more than 2,500 people in the Twin Towers and the Pentagon. In total, 2,972 people died in the September 11 attack, making it the most deadly act of terrorism ever committed. The September 11 attack also marked the first known suicide terrorist attack carried out in the United States since the FBI began keeping terrorist records.

Although the means and ends have evolved throughout history, the central elements of terrorism–fear, panic, violence, and disruption–have changed little through time.

# I. Hybrid & Future Threats

*Ref: TC 7-100, Hybrid Threat (Nov '10), chap. 1 and TRADOC Pamphlet 525-3-1, The U.S. Army Operating Concept: Win in a Complex World 2020-2040 (Oct '14), chap. 2.*

## I. Hybrid Threats

Hybrid threats are innovative, adaptive, globally connected, networked, and embedded in the clutter of local populations. They can possess a wide range of old, adapted and advanced technologies—including the possibility of weapons of mass destruction (WMD). They can operate conventionally and unconventionally, employing adaptive and asymmetric combinations of traditional, irregular, and criminal tactics and using traditional military capabilities in old and new ways. Understanding hybrid threats involves several key concepts, most of which are not actually new.

---

### Hybrid Threat

A hybrid threat is the diverse and dynamic combination of regular forces, irregular forces, and/or criminal elements all unified to achieve mutually benefitting effects.

The term "hybrid" has recently been used to capture the seemingly increased complexity of war, the multiplicity of actors involved, and the blurring between traditional categories of conflict. While the existence of innovative adversaries is not new, today's hybrid approaches demand that U.S. forces prepare for a range of conflicts. These may involve nation-state adversaries that employ protracted forms of warfare, possibly using proxy forces to coerce and intimidate, or non-state actors using operational concepts and high-end capabilities traditionally associated with states.

The emergence of hybrid threats heralds a dangerous development in the capabilities of what was labeled a "guerrilla" or "irregular" force in past conflicts. Hybrid threats can combine state-based, conventional military forces—sophisticated weapons, command and control, and combined arms tactics—with attributes usually associated with insurgent and criminal organizations.

Hybrid threats are characterized by the combination of regular and irregular forces. Regular forces are governed by international law, military tradition, and custom. Irregular forces are unregulated and as a result act with no restrictions on violence or targets for violence. The ability to combine and transition between regular and irregular forces and operations to capitalize on perceived vulnerabilities makes hybrid threats particularly effective. To be a hybrid, these forces cooperate in the context of pursuing their own internal objectives.

---

Threats can challenge U.S. access—directly and indirectly. They can attack U.S. national and political will with very sophisticated information campaigns as well as seek to conduct physical attacks on the U.S. homeland.

*See related discussion of "irregular warfare and insurgencies" on pp. 1-8 to 1-9.*

It is important to note that hybrid threats are not new. History is full of examples of how an adversary has prepared to use his relative perceived strengths against his opponent's perceived weaknesses:

- 1754 to 1763: regular British and French forces fought each other amidst irregular Colonialists fighting for the British and American Indians fighting for both sides.

- 1814: Peninsula War ended after the combination of regular and irregular allied forces from Britain, Portugal, and Spain prevented France from controlling the Iberian Peninsula.

- 1954 to 1976: Viet Cong and People's Army of Vietnam combined irregular and regular forces in fighting the French and U.S. forces. Viet Cong would organize into conventional and unconventional units.

- 2006: Hezbollah mixed conventional capabilities (such as anti-armor weapons, rockets, and command and control networks) with irregular tactics (including information warfare, non-uniformed combatants, and civilian shielding). The result was a tactical stalemate and strategic setback for Israel.

The U.S. Army will face hybrid threats that simultaneously employ some combination of regular forces, irregular forces, and/or criminal elements, to achieve their objectives. Hybrid threats will use an ever-changing variety of conventional and unconventional organizations, equipment, and tactics to create multiple dilemmas.

Hybrid threats seek to saturate the entire operational environment (OE) with effects that support their course of action and force their opponents to react along multiple lines of operation. A simple military attack may not present enough complexity to stretch resources, degrade intellectual capacity, and restrict freedom of maneuver. Instead, hybrid threats can simultaneously create economic instability, foster lack of trust in existing governance, attack information networks, provide a captivating message consistent with their goals, cause man-made humanitarian crises, and physically endanger opponents. Synchronized and synergistic hybrid threat actions can take place in the information, social, political, infrastructure, economic and military domains.

Opponents of hybrid threats will have difficulty isolating specific challenges. They will be forced to conduct economy of force measures on one or more of several lines of operation. Meanwhile, hybrid threats will continue to shift effort and emphasis to make all choices seem poor ones.

Hybrid threats are networks of people, capabilities, and devices that merge, split, and coalesce in action across all of the operational variables of the OE. Each separate actor and action of a hybrid threat can be defeated if isolated and the proper countermeasure is applied. By creating severe impacts across the total OE, a hybrid threat prevents its opponents from segregating the conflict into easily assailable parts. Often military action will be the least important of a hybrid threat's activities, only coming after exploitation of all the other aspects of the OE has paralyzed its opponent.

Hybrid threats can include criminals and criminal groups used in conjunction with both regular and irregular forces. A picture of this future was provided by the 2008 Russian-Georgian conflict, in which Russia employed the many criminal elements operating in South Ossetia to conduct the cleansing of ethnic Georgians from that region. Additionally, criminal organizations have the potential to provide much-needed funding to operations and facilitate the purchase of equipment. Adversaries will be enabled by WMD and technologies that allow them to be disruptive on a regional and area basis.

Swift tactical success is not essential to victory. The dimension of time favors those fighting the United States. An enemy need not win any engagement or battles; the enemy simply must not lose the war. Wearing down the popular support for U.S. operations by simply causing a political and military stalemate can be all that is required to claim victory or to change U.S. behavior or policy.

The most challenging attribute of our adversaries will be their ability to adapt and transition. Their speed, agility, versatility, and changeability are the keys to success in a fight against a larger, more powerful opponent.

## Hybrid Adaptation

Adaptation, broadly defined, is the ability to learn and adjust behaviors based on learning. Adaptation is closely linked to one's OE and its variables. Adversaries can approach adaptation from two perspectives: natural and directed.

Natural adaptation occurs as an actor (nation-state or non-state) acquires or refines its ability to apply its political, economic, military or informational power. Natural adaptation may be advanced through—

- Acquisition of technology, key capabilities, or resources (financial and material)
- Effective organization
- Effective use of the information environment or even key regional or global alliances

Directed adaptation refers to adaptation, based specifically on lessons learned, to counter U.S. power and influence. Counters to U.S. actions will be ever changing and likely conducted by a hybrid force. Hybrid threats will offer a mix of capabilities along the spectrum of conflict to counter U.S. military actions. Adversaries will learn from U.S. operations what works and what needs refinement. They will be whatever the U.S. force is not. Like natural adaptation, directed adaptation will inform issues of force design, military strategy, and operational designs.

Success goes to those who master the skills necessary to act, react, and adapt with speed and creativity. Enemies learn quickly and change, often unconstrained by rules or bureaucracy. While this may cause haphazard and incomplete change, it does allow a rapidity that is difficult to counter. Adversaries will continue to be adaptive in terms of using all available sources of power at their disposal.

## Hybrid Transitions

One of the most dangerous aspects of a hybrid threat is the ability of its components to transition in and out of various forms. Military forces, for example, can remove uniforms and insignia and other indicators of status and blend in with the local population. Insurgent forces might abandon weapons and protest innocence of wrongdoing. Criminals might don the accoutrements of a local police force in order to gain access to a key facility.

Hybrid threats will use the difficulties of positive identification of threat actors as threat actors to their advantage. OEs will be replete with many actors conducting activities counter to U.S. interests but without a clear visual signature as to their status as threats. Indeed, often these actors will be providing signatures similar to friendly or neutral actors.

Time-honored concepts of "conventional" and "unconventional" war and "traditional" methods versus "adaptive" methods are weapons to a hybrid threat. These concepts do not have meaning to a hybrid threat beyond their ability to be used against its opponents. Hybrid threats see war holistically and do not try to break it up into convenient pieces.

Hybrid threat forces will need to perform certain functions in order for them to succeed. Some functions at some points will best be performed by uniformed military forces. At other times or for other reasons, some functions will be best performed by irregular forces. At some points, both types of forces will be acting together. At others, they will shift between the status of regular and irregular. They may also use deception to shift between combatant and noncombatant status. Hybrid threats will present themselves in many ways but always maintain the ability to aggregate at the time and place of their choosing.

# II. Anticipated Threat and the Future Operating Environment

Diverse enemies will employ traditional, unconventional, and hybrid strategies to threaten U.S. security and vital interests. Threats may emanate from nation states or nonstate actors such as transnational terrorists, insurgents, and criminal organizations. Enemies will continue to apply advanced as well as simple and dual-use technologies (such as improvised explosive devices). Enemies avoid U.S. strengths (such as long-range surveillance and precision strike) through traditional countermeasures (such as dispersion, concealment, and intermingling with civilian populations). As new military technologies are more easily transferred, potential threats emulate U.S. military capabilities to counter U.S. power projection and limit U.S. freedom of action. These capabilities include precision-guided rockets, artillery, mortars, and missiles that target traditional U.S. strengths in the air and maritime domains. Hostile nation states may attempt to overwhelm defense systems and impose a high cost on the United States to intervene in a contingency or crisis. State and nonstate actors apply technology to disrupt U.S. advantages in communications, long-range precision fires, and surveillance. Enemy actions reduce U.S. ability to achieve dominance in the land, air, maritime, space, and cyberspace domains. Additionally, to accomplish political objectives, enemy organizations expand operations to the U.S. homeland. Enemies and adversaries will operate beyond physical battlegrounds and enemies will subvert efforts through infiltration of U.S. and partner forces (e.g., insider threat) while using propaganda and disinformation to effect public perception.

Paradoxically, the connectedness of networked devices within the U.S. presents adversaries with exploitable vulnerabilities.

While the United States must assess new and emerging threats, many current operational challenges will exist into the future. Harbingers of future conflict include competing powers (e.g., China and Russia), regional powers (e.g., Iran and the Democratic People's Republic of Korea (DPRK)), transnational terrorist networks (e.g., al Qaida, its affiliates, and transnational criminals), and cyber threats. The following are examples only and illustrate a limited number of threats for which future Army forces must prepare.

## A. Competing Powers

### People's Republic of China (PRC)

Though the People's Republic of China remains committed to stable relationships with neighbors and the U.S. in the near-term, it continues to pursue a long-term, comprehensive military modernization program designed to improve the capacity of its armed forces to fight and win short-duration, high-intensity regional contingencies. China's goal over time is to expand its influence to establish stability along its periphery. While China prefers to avoid direct confrontation with the U.S., it uses civilian assets to challenge actions such as U.S. surveillance flights. Moreover, China's behavior has created friction with regional neighbors including U.S. allies and partners. Territorial disputes with Japan over the Senkaku/Diaoyu islands; border disputes with India; and increased maritime pressure on the Philippines, Malaysia, Taiwan, and Vietnam are examples of China exerting power through force or threat of force. China works to negate U.S. advantages in space and cyberspace. China is developing significant anti-satellite capabilities, integrating cyber into all aspects of military operations, and developing sophisticated missiles and air defenses as part of an

# III. Characteristics of the Future Operational Environment

*Ref: TRADOC Pamphlet 525-3-1, The U.S. Army Operating Concept: Win in a Complex World 2020-2040 (Oct '14), pp. 10 to 12.*

The following five characteristics of the future operational environment are likely to have significant impact on land force operations.

## 1. Increased Velocity and Momentum of Human Interaction and Events

The speed at which information diffuses globally through multiple means increases the velocity, momentum, and degree of interaction among people. The diffusion of information via the Internet and social media amplifies and accelerates interaction between people, governments, militaries, and threats. Access to information allows organizations to mobilize people and resources locally, regionally, and globally. Disinformation and propaganda drive violence in support of political objectives.

## 2. Potential for Overmatch

Overmatch is the application of capabilities or use of tactics in a way that renders an adversary unable to respond effectively. Potential enemies invest in technologies to obtain a differential advantage and undermine U.S. ability to achieve overmatch. These technologies include long-range precision fires, air defense systems, electric fires, and unmanned aerial systems (UAS). Anti-access and area denial capabilities challenge the Joint Force's ability to achieve air dominance and sea control as well as its ability to project power onto land from the air and maritime domains. Potential enemies develop cyberspace capabilities such as disruptive and destructive malware and space capabilities such as anti-satellite weapons to disrupt U.S. communications and freedom of maneuver.

## 3. Proliferation of Weapons Of Mass Destruction (WMD)

WMD proliferation to diverse state and nonstate actors in the form of chemical, biological, radiological, nuclear, and high-yield explosive (CBRNE) weapons poses an increased threat to U.S. and international security. Adversaries share CBRNE knowledge, technology, and materiel. The risk of a nation losing control over nuclear assets increases as extremist organizations incite civil wars and establish control of territories, populations, and weapons. Moreover, directed energy and sophisticated CBRNE weapons could give adversaries unprecedented capabilities to threaten U.S. forces and civilian populations with mass casualties.

## 4. Spread of Cyberspace And Counter-Space Capabilities

The cyberspace and space domains grow in importance as global and regional competitors as well as nonstate actors invest in capabilities to protect their access and disrupt or deny access to others. A broad array of actors challenges the Joint Force's freedom of action in space and cyberspace. Enemies and adversaries collaborate as contests in space and cyberspace extend to and affect tactical operations.

## 5. Demographics and Operations among Populations, in Cities, and in Complex Terrain

The percentage of the world's population in urban areas will rise to sixty percent by 2030.22 Internal migration and higher birth rates contribute to increasing urbanization. Adversaries operate among the people in these urban areas and other complex terrain to avoid U.S. military advantages and they operate in cities because war, as a political phenomenon, is inherently about people. As cities grow, many governments fail to provide adequate security, employment, infrastructure, and services. Armed groups will exploit popular disaffection and weak governance. Urban areas become safe havens and support bases for terrorists, insurgents, or criminal organizations.

effort to challenge United States' ability to project power. Chinese doctrine calls for combining conventional and unconventional actions. The People's Liberation Army opened six combat training centers where it emphasizes combined arms operations and joint training. Chinese actions and force modernization efforts highlight the need for Army forces positioned forward or regionally engaged to prevent conflict, deter adversaries, and strengthen partners. Emerging Chinese capabilities also highlight the need for Army forces to project power from land into the air, maritime, space, and cyberspace domains.

## Russia

Russian annexation of the Crimean Peninsula and use of conventional and unconventional land forces in Ukraine suggest that Russia is determined to expand its territory and assert its power on the Eurasian landmass. Russia deployed and integrated a range of diplomatic, information, military, and economic means to conduct what some analysts have described as "non-linear" operations. Russia conducted operations to pursue its war aims below the threshold that would elicit a concerted North Atlantic Treaty Organization response. In addition, Russia used cyberspace capabilities and social media to influence perceptions at home and abroad and provide cover for large-scale military operations. While the long-term results of the incursion into Ukraine are not yet certain, Russia demonstrated the centrality of land forces in its effort to assert power and advance its interests in former Soviet states. Without a viable land force capable of opposing the Russian army and its irregular proxies, such adventurism is likely to continue undeterred. Russia's actions highlight the value of land forces to deter conflict as well as special operations and conventional force capability to project national power and exert influence in political contests.

# B. Regional Powers

## Iran

Iran's management of its nuclear aspirations will shape its role as a rising power in the Middle East. Iran, empowered by expanding sectarian conflicts in the greater Middle East, poses a hybrid threat to U.S. interests and allies in the region. As it continues to apply pressure on the region to erode and supplant U.S. power, Iran uses combinations of economic and diplomatic overtures with irregular forces to advance its interests. Iran develops partnerships with disenfranchised populations, religious factions, and criminal elements to create disorder focused on subverting the influence of the U.S. and partner nations. Iran also develops relationships with weak governments and uses those governments to advance its interests. For example, Iran's support for President Bashar al Assad in Syria is critical to its ability to sustain Lebanese Hezbollah, and Iran's support for militias in Iraq undermines government legitimacy and intensifies sectarian conflict. Iran avoids direct military confrontations while developing advanced capabilities and pursuing comprehensive military modernization. Iran's modernization efforts include the use of automated systems on land, sea, and air; ballistic missiles; and the development of nuclear capability. Iran is actively supporting militia in Iraq while confronting the Islamic State in Iraq and the Levant (ISIL). Iran has become a more capable cyber actor as well. Taken collectively, Iranian activity has the potential to undermine U.S. regional goals as it continues to confront the U.S. indirectly on a number of fronts.

## Democratic People's Republic of Korea (DPRK)

The DPRK, while in the same category as Iran, is at once a dangerous military threat and a failing state dependent upon the patronage of others, especially China. The DPRK is expanding its nuclear arsenal and improving its ballistic missile force to complement an aging but still large and capable conventional force. The DPRK's military possesses cyber and chemical-biological warfare capabilities. Key gov-

# C. Transnational Criminal Organizations

*Ref: TRADOC Pamphlet 525-3-1, The U.S. Army Operating Concept: Win in a Complex World 2020-2040 (Oct '14), chap. 2 and James R. Clapper, Director of National Intelligence, Statement for the Record, Worldwide Threat Assessment of the US Intelligence Community (Feb 9, 2016).*

**Transnational organized crime groups** will pose a persistent and at times sophisticated threat to the wealth, health, and security of people around the globe. Criminal groups' untaxed and unregulated enterprises drain state resources, crowd out legitimate commerce, increase official corruption, and impede economic competitiveness and fair trade. On occasion, transnational organized crime groups threaten countries' security, spur increases in social violence, or otherwise reduce governability.

- **Profit-minded criminals** generally do not seek the reins of political power but rather to suborn, co-opt, or bully government officials in order to create environments in which criminal enterprise can thrive.
- **Foreign-based transnational criminals** are increasingly using online information systems to breach sovereign borders virtually, without the need to send criminal operatives abroad to advance illicit businesses.
- **Organized crime and rebel groups in Africa** and elsewhere are likely to increase their involvement in wildlife trafficking to fund political activities, enhance political influence, and purchase weapons.

**Human trafficking** exploits and abused individuals and challenges international security. Human traffickers leverage corrupt officials, porous borders, and lax enforcement to orchestrate their illicit trade. This exploitation of human lives for profit continues to occur in every country in the world—undermining the rule of law and corroding legitimate institutions of government and commerce. Trafficking in persons has become a lucrative source of revenue for transnational organized crime groups and terrorist organizations and is estimated to produce tens of billions of dollars annually. For example, terrorist or armed groups—such as ISIL, the Lord's Resistance Army, and Boko Haram—engage in kidnapping for the purpose of sexual slavery, sexual exploitation, and forced labor. These activities might also contribute to the funding and sustainment of such groups.

We assess that the **ongoing global migration crises**—a post-WWII record 60 million refugees and internally displaced persons—will fuel an increase in the global volume of human trafficking victims as men, women, and children undertake risky migration ventures and fall prey to sex trafficking, forced labor, debt bondage and other trafficking crimes. This continuing rise in global displacement and dangerous migration, both forced and opportunistic movements within countries and across national borders, will probably allow criminal groups and terrorist organizations to exploit vulnerable populations.

Recent waves of migration from Central America to the U.S. – largely due to criminal violence – highlight second and third order threats to U.S. interests caused by transnational organized crime and weak governance. Ineffective governance provides an inviting environment for criminal organizations. Murders, kidnappings, and maimings in Central America equal or exceed violence associated with many political insurgencies in the Middle East and elsewhere. The region's militaries are engaged in support of law enforcement activities due to the severity of the problem and the inability of sometimes-corrupt police forces to cope with the problem. Criminal violence erodes state institutions and undermines governance. The threat from transnational organized crime highlights the need for Army special operations and regionally aligned forces to understand complex environments, operate with multiple partners, and conduct security force assistance.

ernment facilities, military installations, and weapons are located in underground shelters. Because economic, social, and political pressures on the DPRK leadership could lead to war or a collapse of the regime, the U.S. prepares for the deployment of substantial ground, air, and maritime forces to operate as part of a coalition alongside Republic of Korea (South Korea) forces and in defense of South Korea. The threat on the Korean peninsula highlights the need for Army forces to operate in a CBRNE environment.

## D. Transnational Terrorist Organizations

The emergence of ISIL is an example of how nonstate actors seize upon opportunities created by communal conflict and weak governance. ISIL is a nonstate actor that aims to create an Islamist militant state across large portions of Iraq, Syria, and surrounding areas. ISIL's military organization; ideological base; willingness to use murder and other forms of brutality against innocents; and ability to mobilize people, money, and weapons have enabled it to seize territory and establish control of populations and resources. ISIL exploits political opposition to governments to form alliances of convenience while acting to consolidate gains and marginalize competing insurgent groups through intimidation and coercion. ISIL moves into weakly governed spaces such as the Iraq-Syrian border where governments are unable to project power. These areas provide sanctuary and "strategic depth." ISIL uses social media and cyberspace to prosecute a propaganda campaign while using terrorist tactics (such as covert action, assassinations, destruction of historically significant property, extortion, and mass murder) to control populations and territory. The wider problem is ISIL's success combined with weaknesses of Middle Eastern governments has caused extremist Islam and terrorism to metastasize across much of the Middle East and North Africa. From Egypt to Yemen and from the Syrian Civil War to the disaster of Libya, the region is rife with weak governments and active terrorist groups.

## E. Technologies with Military Application

Emerging technologies hold promise for improving future force combat effectiveness. Because of the ease with which many technological advantages are copied or countered, the Army must emphasize how to combine multiple technological improvements and counter enemy efforts to adopt or disrupt new technologies. The U.S. Army's differential advantage over enemies derives, in part, from the integration of advanced technologies with skilled Soldiers and well-trained teams.

# IV. Conclusion

Future armed conflict will be complex, in part, because threats, enemies, and adversaries are becoming increasingly capable and elusive. State and nonstate actors employ traditional, unconventional, and hybrid strategies that threaten U.S. security and vital interests. The complexity of future armed conflict is due to increasing momentum of human interaction, threats emanating from dense and weakly governed urban areas, the availability of lethal weapon systems, and the proliferation of CBRNE threats. Enemies and adversaries will challenge U.S. competitive advantages in the land, air, maritime, space, and cyberspace domains. Advanced technologies will transfer readily to state and nonstate actors. Enemies possess the capability to threaten the U.S. homeland and project power from land into all other domains. Because these threats may originate in dense urban areas or remote safe havens, long-range strikes will prove insufficient to defeat them.

The complexity of future armed conflict, therefore, will require Army forces capable of conducting missions in the homeland or in foreign lands including defense support of civil authorities, international disaster relief and humanitarian assistance, security cooperation activities, crisis response, or large-scale operations.

# II. Hybrid Threat Components

*Ref: TC 7-100, Hybrid Threat (Nov '10), chap. 2.*

Through formal structure and informal agreement, military and state paramilitary forces can work in concert to varying degrees with insurgent, guerrilla, and criminal groups towards common ends. Typically, the common goal is the removal of U.S. and coalition forces from their area of operations. The goals of hybrid threat forces may or may not coincide with those of other actors in the same geographic area.

## Hybrid Threat Components

### I  Threats and Other Actors

A. Nation-State Actors
B. Non-State Actors
C. Regular Military Forces
D. Irregular Forces

### II  Enemy Combatants

A. Combatants
  • Enemy Combatant
  • Lawful Enemy Combatant
  • Unlawful Enemy Combatant
B. Paramilitary Forces
  • Paramilitary
  • Insurgent
  • Guerrilla
  • Terrorist
  • Mercenary
  • Criminal Organizations

### III  Weapons of Mass Destruction (WMD)

*Ref: TC 7-100, Hybrid Threat (Nov '10), chap. 2.*

# I. Threats and Other Actors

*Ref: TC 7-100, Hybrid Threat (Nov '10), pp. 2-1 to 2-3.*

There are many types of actors or participants in today's complex world environment. Some of the actors are countries (also called nation-states) and some are not. Nation-states are still dominant actors. However, some power is shifting to nontraditional actors and transnational concerns. There are many potential challenges to traditional concepts like balance of power, sovereignty, national interest, and roles of nation-state and non-state actors.

Of course, not all actors are threats. To be a threat, a nation or organization must have both the capabilities and the intention to challenge the United States. The capabilities in question are not necessarily purely military, but encompass all the elements of power available to the nation or organization.

Defining the actors in hybrid threat operations requires a dynamic situational awareness of change in a particular operational environment (OE). An order of battle or an appreciation of adversaries may transition abruptly or retain characteristics over an extended period. Similarly, the full band of PMESII-PT variables requires constant estimation and analysis to project or confirm the motivations, intentions, capabilities, and limitations of a hybrid threat. This section addresses significant categories of threats that can combine, associate, or affiliate in order to threaten or apply hybrid capabilities.

The key components of a hybrid threat, therefore, are two or more of the following:

- Military force
- Nation-state paramilitary force (such as internal security forces, police, or border guards)
- Insurgent groups (movements that primarily rely on subversion and violence to change the status quo).
- Guerrilla units (irregular indigenous forces operating in occupied territory)
- Criminal organizations (such as gangs, drug cartels, or hackers).

## A. Nation-State Actors

Nation-states fall into four basic categories according to their roles in the international community. The categories are core states, transition states, rogue states, and failed or failing states. Countries can move from one category to another, as conditions change.

The category of core states includes more than half of the nearly 200 countries in the world today. These are basically democratic (although to varying degrees) and share common values and interests. Within this larger group, there is an "inner core" of major powers. These are the advanced countries, including the United States, that generally dominate world politics. Most conflict with global consequences will involve the core states in some fashion or another.

Transition states are other larger, industrial-based countries, mostly emerging regional powers, that have the potential to become accepted among the core states, perhaps as major powers. High-end transition states are moving from an industrial-based society to an information-based society. Low-end transition states are seeking to move from an agricultural-based society to an industrial base. As states try to make this transition, there are cycles of political stability and instability, and the outcome of the transition is uncertain. Some transition states may successfully join the ranks of core states and even become major powers within that context. Others may become competitors.

Rogue states are those that are hostile to their neighbors or to core states' interests. These countries attack or threaten to attack their neighbors. They may sell or give armaments to other countries or non-state actors within or outside their region, thus threatening regional or international stability. They can sponsor international terrorism or even confront U.S. military forces operating in the region.

Failed or failing states are fragmented in such a way that a rule of law is absent. Their instability is a threat to their neighbors and the core states. The government has ceased to meet the needs of all its people, and at least parts of the country may have become virtually ungovernable. Entities other than the legitimate government institutions—such as large criminal organizations—may have filled the power vacuum and taken control. The real threat to U.S. forces may come from elements other than the military. In some cases, the government might be able to control the population and meet the people's needs, but only with outside support—perhaps from countries or groups opposed to U.S. interests. Failed or failing states often harbor groups antagonistic to the United States and its interests.

## B. Non-State Actors

Non-state actors are those that do not represent the forces of a particular nation-state. Such non-state elements include rogue actors as well as third-party actors.

Like rogue states, rogue actors are hostile to other actors. However, they may be present in one country or extend across several countries. Examples include insurgents, guerrillas, mercenaries, and transnational or subnational political movements. Particular sources of danger are terrorists and drug-trafficking or criminal organizations, since they may have the best technology, equipment, and weapons available, simply because they have the money to buy them. These non-state rogue actors may use terror tactics and militarily unconventional methods to achieve their goals.

Third-party actors may not be hostile to other actors. However, their presence, activities, and interests can affect the ability of military forces to accomplish their mission. These third-party actors can include refugees and internally displaced persons, international humanitarian relief agencies, transnational corporations, and news media.

These individuals and groups bring multiple sources of motivation, ideology, interests, beliefs, or political affiliations into consideration. They may be sources of civil unrest. Their presence may require military forces to consider the potential impacts of traffic congestion, demonstrations, sabotage, and information manipulation.

## C. Regular Military Forces

Regular military forces are the regulated armed forces of a state or alliance of states with the specified function of military offensive and defensive capabilities in legitimate service to the state or alliance. Traditional capabilities of regular military forces normally are intended to accomplish one or more of the following objectives:

- Defeat an adversary's armed forces
- Destroy an adversary's war-making capacity
- Seize or retain territory

Other legitimate functions of regular military forces can include a wide range of stability and support missions in concert with state policies and programs. These can include national disaster response, or assistance to province or district government to counter lawlessness, riot, or insurrection.

## D. Irregular Forces

Irregular forces are armed individuals or groups who are not members of the regular armed forces, police, or other internal security forces (JP 3-24). Irregular warfare is a violent struggle among state and non-state actors for legitimacy and influence over the relevant population(s) (JP 1).

# II. Enemy Combatants & Paramilitary Forces

Ref: TC 7-100, Hybrid Threat (Nov '10), pp. 2-3 to 2-7.

## A. Combatants

The DOD defines an enemy combatant as "in general, a person engaged in hostilities against the United States or its coalition partners during an armed conflict" (JP 1-02 from DODD 2311.01E). Other essential terms are lawful enemy combatant and unlawful enemy combatant.

### Enemy Combatant

In general, a person engaged in hostilities against the United States or its coalition partners during an armed conflict. The term enemy combatant includes both "lawful enemy combatants" and "unlawful enemy combatants." (DODD 2310.01E)

### Lawful Enemy Combatant

Lawful enemy combatants, who are entitled to protections under the Geneva Conventions, include members of the regular armed forces of a State party to the conflict; militia, volunteer corps, and organized resistance movements belonging to a State party to the conflict, which are under responsible command, wear a fixed distinctive sign recognizable at a distance, carry their arms openly, and abide by the laws of war; and members of regular armed forces who profess allegiance to a government or an authority not recognized by the detaining power. (DODD 2310.01E)

### Unlawful Enemy Combatant

Unlawful enemy combatants are persons not entitled to combat immunity, who engage in acts against the United States or its coalition partners in violation of the laws and customs of war during an armed conflict. ... [The] term unlawful enemy combatant is defined to include, but is not limited to, an individual who is or was part of or supporting ... forces that are engaged in hostilities against the United States or its coalition partners. (DODD 2310.01E)

## B. Paramilitary

*Combatants can be casually and incorrectly categorized without appropriate attention to what a particular term defines as the purpose, intent, or character of an enemy combatant. Several terms that can easily be misused include paramilitary forces, insurgents, guerrillas, terrorists, militia, and mercenaries. The discussion below provides DOD definitions of the first four terms.*

### Paramilitary

Paramilitary forces are "forces or groups distinct from the regular armed forces of any country, but resembling them in organization, equipment, training, or mission" (JP 3-24). Thus, there are various types of non-state paramilitary forces, such as insurgents, guerrillas, terrorist groups, and mercenaries. However, there are also nation-state paramilitary forces such as internal security forces, border guards, and police, which are specifically not a part of the regular armed forces of the country.

*Note. The term militia has acquired many definitions based on the situational context. This context may be the culture; historical traditions such as which group of people have familial, social, theological, or political power; and the external or self-descriptions such forces use in media affairs or propaganda. A generic definition of a militia can parallel the definition of a paramilitary force. However, a nation-state can also have militia that are considered an extension of its armed forces.*

## Insurgent

An insurgency is "the organized use of subversion and violence by a group or movement that seeks to overthrow or force change of a governing authority" (JP 3-24). Insurgent organizations have no regular table of organization and equipment structure. The mission, environment, geographic factors, and many other variables determine the configuration and composition of each insurgent organization and its subordinate cells. A higher insurgent organization can include organizations at regional, provincial, district, national, or transnational levels. Higher insurgent organizations can contain a mix of local insurgent and guerrilla organizations. Each of these organizations provides differing capabilities.

## Guerrilla

A guerrilla is "a combat participant in guerrilla warfare" (JP 1-02). Guerrilla warfare is "military and paramilitary operations conducted in enemy-held or hostile territory by irregular, predominantly indigenous forces" (JP 3-05.1). A prime characteristic of guerrilla operations is to attack points of enemy weakness and in conditions developed or selected by the guerrilla force. Deception and mobility are critical to achieving surprise and avoiding engagements unless the tactical opportunity weighs heavily in the favor of the guerrilla. At the tactical level, attacks are planned and conducted as sudden, violent, decentralized actions. Principles of rapid dispersion and rapid concentration facilitate these types of operation.

## Terrorist

A terrorist is "an individual who commits an act or acts of violence or threatens violence in pursuit of political, religious, or ideological objectives" (JP 3-07.2). A terrorist group is "any number of terrorists who assemble together, have a unifying relationship, or are organized for the purpose of committing an act or acts of violence or threatens violence in pursuit of their political, religious, or ideological objectives" (JP 3-07.2). Categorizing terrorist groups by their affiliation with governments or supporting organizations can provide insight in terrorist intent and capability. Terrorist groups can align as state-directed, state-sponsored, or non-state supported organizations. In some cases, the state itself can be a terrorist regime.

## Mercenary

Mercenaries are armed individuals who use conflict as a professional trade and service for private gain. Those who fall within that definition are not considered combatants. However, those who take direct part in hostilities can be considered unlawful enemy combatants. The term mercenary applies to those acting individually and in formed units. Soldiers serving officially in foreign armed forces are not mercenaries. Loan service personnel sent to help train the soldiers of other countries as part of an official training agreement between sovereign governments are not mercenaries even if they take a direct part in hostilities.

## Criminal Organizations

There is no part of the world that is criminal-free. Therefore, there will always be criminal elements present in any OE. The only question is whether those criminal organizations will find it in their interests to become part of a hybrid threat and to perform some of the functions required to achieve common goals and objectives.

Criminal organizations are normally independent of nation-state control. However, large-scale criminal organizations often extend beyond national boundaries to operate regionally or worldwide and include a political influence component. Individual criminals or small gangs do not normally have the capability to adversely affect legitimate political, military, and judicial organizations. However, large-scale criminal organizations can challenge governmental authority with capabilities and characteristics similar to a paramilitary force.

# III. Weapons of Mass Destruction (WMD)

The intent of hybrid threats to obtain and use weapons of mass destruction (WMD) is one of the most serious contemporary threats to regional neighbors or even the U.S. homeland. The means of attack can range from a highly sophisticated weapon system such as a nuclear bomb to a rudimentary improvised radiological device. The specter of chemical contamination or biological infection adds to the array of weapons. Although high-yield explosives have not been traditionally recognized as WMD, high-yield and some low-yield explosives have caused significant devastating effects on people and places. With any type of WMD, the hybrid threat's desired outcome could involve any or all of the following:

- Producing mass casualties
- Massive damage of physical infrastructure and/or the economy
- Extensive disruption of activities and lifestyles

The threat of WMD use is present across the entire spectrum of conflict. Potential exists for WMD use with individual acts of wanton damage or destruction of property or person, as well as operations conducted by organized violent groups or rogue states. Hybrid threats may include organizations with demonstrated global reach capabilities and the intention to acquire and use WMD. For example, an international terrorist network with WMD capability could target extragegional military forces either in their homeland or as they are deploying into the region. It would patiently await the opportunity to achieve maximum operational or strategic impact of its use of WMD.

Ultimately, a significant impact on a large population would be an intimidating psychological effect from physical and emotional stress. Simply stated, the potential for mass injury or death, as well as mass damage or destruction, presents a compelling requirement for protective measures and increased assurance to counter public harm, anxiety, and fear.

Three general trends with impact on hybrid threat use of WMD are micro-actors, sophistication, and overlap with transnational crime. Each of these trends can pose a critical danger by linking intent with WMD capability. Growing numbers of small independent actors can manipulate advanced technologies to gain knowledge and means while masking their operational or tactical plans. Sophistication involves a combination of global information systems, financial resources, and practical exchange of ideas. Transnational criminals demonstrate themselves to be a valuable network to assist other hybrid threat components with enhanced mobility, improved support, and concealed actions.

*See chapter 7, "Countering Weapons of Mass Destruction", and chapter 8, "Consequence Management" for further discussion.*

# III. Hybrid Threat Organizations

*Ref: TC 7-100, Hybrid Threat (Nov '10), chap. 6.*

The Hybrid Threat (HT) tailors its organizations to the required missions and functions. It determines the functions that must be performed in order to successfully accomplish its goals. Then it builds teams and organizations to execute those functions without regard to traditional military hierarchy, the law of war, or rules of engagement.

## Hybrid Threat Organizations

**I** Military Organizations

**II** Insurgent Organizations

**III** Guerrilla Organizations

**IV** Criminal Organizations

**\*** Hybrid Relationships

*Ref: TC 7-100, Hybrid Threat (Nov '10), chap. 6.*

## Task-Organizing

The HT will task-organize forces in a fashion that matches its available resources to its goals. Task organizations will often include more than purely military formations. The HT's regular military and irregular components are tailored forces depending on training requirements. FM 7-100.4 provides a baseline of organizational size, equipment, and weapons. Its organizational directories provide a very detailed listing of personnel and equipment. For some training requirements, the opposing force (OPFOR) order of battle (OB) might not need to include personnel numbers. Trainers and exercise planners can extract the appropriate pages from the organizational directories and tailor them by eliminating the detail they do not need and adding the necessary units from other pages to develop the required task organization.

*For more detail on organizations, refer to FM 7-100.4, which introduces baseline organizational structures of a flexible, thinking, and adaptive OPFOR.*

The baseline organizations presented in the organizational directories of FM 7-100.4 are intended to be tailored and task-organized in a manner that is appropriate for the training objectives. Depending on the training requirement, the OPFOR may be a large, medium, or small force. Its technology may be state-of-the-art, relatively modern, obsolescent, obsolete, or an uneven combination of these categories. Its ability to sustain operations may be limited or robust.

# I. Military Organizations

Regular military organizations of the HT will present conventional and unconventional capabilities. This TC is part of the TC 7-100 series, which includes OPFOR doctrine, organization, and equipment for trainers and educators to tailor specified threats for U.S. Army training requirements.

In the regular military forces of a nation-state that is part of the HT, six services generally comprise the armed forces. These include the Army, Navy, Air Force (which includes the national-level Air Defense Forces), Strategic Forces (with long-range rockets and missiles), Special-Purpose Forces (SPF) Command, and Internal Security Forces. The Internal Security Forces may be subordinate to the Ministry of the Interior rather than to the Ministry of Defense. The armed forces field some reserve component forces in all services, but most reserve forces are Army forces. In time of war, command and control relationships among state ministries may be consolidated for regular, reserve, militia, and other paramilitary-type armed forces, all under the Supreme High Command (SHC).

Baseline OPFOR organizations described in FM 7-100.4 do not constitute an OPFOR OB. Rather, they provide a framework from which trainers can develop a specific OPFOR OB appropriate for their particular training requirements. Within this framework, training scenario writers and exercise designers have considerable flexibility in determining what the OPFOR actually has in capabilities or limitations at a given point in time or a given location. In some cases, an organization taken straight from the OPFOR administrative force structure (AFS) in FM 7-100.4 may meet the requirements for a particular U.S. Army training environment. In most cases, however, task-organizing an OPFOR organization is appropriate in order to portray the correct array of OPFOR units and equipment for stressing the mission essential task list (METL) of U.S. units in a particular training environment.

## A. Special-Purpose Forces (SPF) Command

As part of an OPFOR, the SPF Command includes both SPF units and elite commando units. Four of the five other service components of the armed forces also have their own SPF. There are Army, Navy, and Air Force SPF. The Internal Security Forces also have their own SPF units. These service SPF normally remain under the control of their respective services or a joint operational or theater command. However, SPF from any of these service components could become part of joint SPF operations in support of national-level requirements. The SPF Command has the means to control joint SPF operations as required.

Any SPF units from the SPF Command or from other service components' SPF that have reconnaissance or direct action missions supporting strategic-level objectives or intelligence requirements would normally be under the direct control of the SHC or under the control of the SPF Command, which reports directly to the SHC. Also, any service SPF units assigned to joint SPF operations would temporarily come under the control of the SPF Command or perhaps the SHC. Most of the service SPF units are intended for use at the operational level. Thus, they can be subordinate to operational-level commands even in the AFS. In peacetime and in garrisons, SPF of both the SPF Command and other services are organized administratively into SPF companies, battalions and brigades.

In time of war, some SPF units from the SPF Command or from the Army, Navy, Air Force, or Internal Security Forces SPF may remain under the command and control of their respective service headquarters. However, some SPF units also might be allocated to operational or even tactical level commands during the task-organizing process.

*Refer to FM 7-100.4 for additional discussion on the strategic to tactical levels of SPF.*

# B. Internal Security Forces

Ref: TC 7-100, Hybrid Threat (Nov '10), pp. 6-2 to 6-3.

Hybrid & Future Threat

Internal security forces are part of an OPFOR structure for operations against internal threats to the state. In peacetime, the Chief of Internal Security heads the forces within the Ministry of the Interior that fall under the general label of "internal security forces." Most of the internal security forces are uniformed and use military ranks and insignia similar to those of the other services of the nation-state armed forces. Among the internal security forces, border guard, security, and SPF units most closely resemble regular military units of other services of the armed forces. However, units from the General Police directorate and Civil Defense Directorate can also perform military-like roles.

During wartime, some or all of the internal security forces from the Ministry of the Interior may become a sixth service component of the Armed Forces, with the formal name "Internal Security Forces." Internal Security Forces can be allocated to a theater command or to a task-organized operational or tactical level military command that is capable of controlling joint or interagency operations. In such command relationships or when missions share a common area of responsibility (AOR) with a military organization, units of the Internal Security Forces send liaison teams to represent them in the military organization's staff.

Various types on non-state actors might be part of the HT, affiliated with it, or support it in some manner. Even those internal security forces that do not belong to the HT, or support it directly or willingly, could be exploited or manipulated by the HT to support its objectives.

## General Police Directorate

The General Police Directorate has responsibility for national, district, and local police. In some circumstances, police forces at all three levels operate as paramilitary forces. They can use military-type tactics, weapons, and equipment. National Police forces include paramilitary tactical units that are equipped for combat, if necessary. These uniformed forces may represent the equivalent of an infantry organization in the regular armed forces.

Within the various national- and district-level police organizations, the special police are the forces that most resemble regular armed forces in their organization, equipment, training, and missions. Because some special police units are equipped with heavy weapons and armored vehicles, they can provide combat potential to conduct defensive operations if required. Special police units could be expected to supplement the armed forces.

## Civil Defense Directorate

The Civil Defense Directorate comprises a variety of paramilitary and nonmilitary units. While the majority of Civil Defense personnel are civilians, members of paramilitary units and some staff elements at the national and district levels hold military ranks. Civil Defense paramilitary units are responsible for the protection and defense of the area or installation where they are located. Even the nonmilitary, civil engineering units can supplement the combat engineers of the armed forces by conducting engineer reconnaissance, conducting explosive ordnance disposal, and providing force-protection construction support and logistics enhancements required to sustain military operations.

# II. Insurgent Organizations

Ref: TC 7-100, Hybrid Threat (Nov '10), pp. 6-3 to 6-5.

Insurgent organizations have no regular, fixed table of organization and equipment structure. The mission, environment, geographic factors, and many other variables determine the configuration and composition of each insurgent organization and its subordinate cells. Their composition varies from organization to organization, mission to mission, environment to environment. The structure, personnel, equipment, and weapons mix all depend on specific mission requirements, as does the size, specialty, number, and type of subordinates.

There are several factors that differentiate the structure and capability of an insurgent organization from the structure and capability of a guerrilla organization. Since the insurgent organization is primarily a covert organization, it typically has a cellular, networked structure. By comparison, guerrilla organizations often reflect a military structure such as battalion, company, platoon, or squad.

Insurgent organizations generally do not have some of the heavier and more sophisticated equipment that guerrilla organizations can possess. Weapons of the insurgents are generally limited to small arms, antitank grenade launchers, and improvised explosive devices (IEDs). There may be some crew-served weapons such the 82-mm mortar or 107-mm single-tube rocket launcher. In the event the insurgents require heavier weapons or capabilities, they might obtain them from guerrillas, or the guerrilla organization might provide its services depending on the relationship between the two organizations at the time.

Insurgent organizations are irregular forces. The baseline insurgent organizations in the FM 7-100.4 organizational directories represent the default setting for a typical insurgent organization. If an OPFOR OB has more than one local insurgent organization, no two insurgent organizations should look exactly alike. Trainers and training planners should vary the types and numbers of cells to reflect the irregular nature of such organizations. The FM 7-100.4 baseline array of possible cells for various functions is arranged in a line-and-block chart for convenience. However, they would typically be task-organized in a network-type structure.

In FM 7-100.4, the baseline organization charts and equipment lists for individual cells include many notes on possible variations in organization or in numbers of people or equipment within a given organization. When developing an OB for a specific insurgent organization for use in training, users may exercise some latitude in the construction of cells. Some cells might need to be larger or smaller than the "default" setting found in the organizational directories. Some entire cells might not be required, and some functional cells might be combined into a single cell performing multiple functions. However, trainers and training planners would need to take several things into consideration in modifying the "default" cell structures:

• What functions the insurgents need to be able to perform

• What equipment is needed to perform those functions

• How many people are required to employ the required equipment

• The number of vehicles in relation to the people needed to drive them or the people and equipment that must be transported

• Equipment associated with other equipment (for example, an aiming circle/goniometer used with a mortar or a day/night observation scope used with a sniper rifle)

# Local Insurgent Organization (Example)

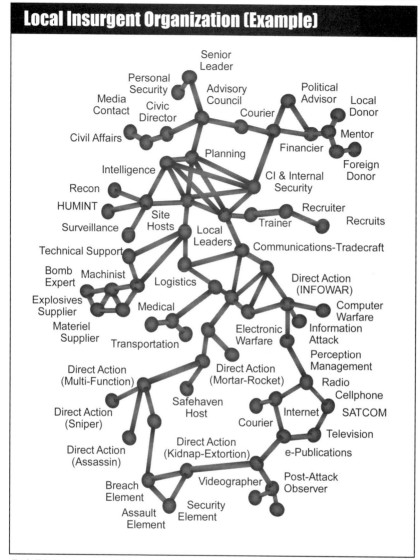

*Ref: TC 7-100, Hybrid Threat, fig. 6-1, p. 6-4.*

Any relationship of independent local insurgent organizations to regional or national insurgent structures may be one of affiliation or dependent upon a single shared or similar goal. These relationships are generally fluctuating and may be fleeting, mission-dependant, or event- or agenda-oriented. Such relationships can arise and cease due to a variety of reasons or motivations.

When task-organizing insurgent organizations, guerrilla units might be subordinate to a larger insurgent organization. However, they might be only loosely affiliated with an insurgent organization of which they are not a part. A guerrilla unit or other insurgent organization might be affiliated with a regular military organization. A guerrilla unit might also become a subordinate part of an OPFOR task organization based on a regular military unit.

## C. Reserves and Militia

Although all six services can field some reserve forces, most of the reserve forces are Army forces. All militia forces belong to the Army component. Overall planning for mobilization of reserves and militia is the responsibility of the state and its Organization and Mobilization Directorate of the General Staff. Each service component headquarters would have a similar directorate responsible for mobilization of forces within that service. Major geographical commands (and other administrative commands at the operational level and higher) serve as a framework for mobilization of reserve and militia forces.

During mobilization, some reserve personnel serve as individual replacements for combat losses in active units. Others fill positions, including professional and technical specialists, that were left vacant in peacetime in deference to requirements of the civilian sector. However, reservists also man reserve units that are mobilized as units to replace other units that have become combat-ineffective or to provide additional units necessary for large, sustained operations.

Like active force units, most mobilized reserve and militia units do not necessarily go to war under the same administrative headquarters that controlled them in peacetime. Rather, they typically become part of a task-organized operational- or tactical-level fighting command tailored for a particular mission. In most cases, the mobilized reserve units would be integrated with regular military units in such a fighting command. In rare cases, however, a reserve command at division level or higher might become a fighting command or serve as the basis for forming a fighting command based partially or entirely on reserve forces.

# III. Guerrilla Organizations

Guerrilla organizations may be as large as several brigades or as small as a platoon or independent hunter-killer (HK) teams. Even in the AFS organizational directories, some guerrilla units were already re-configured as HK units. In the fighting force structure represented in an OPFOR OB, some additional guerrilla units may become task-organized in that manner.

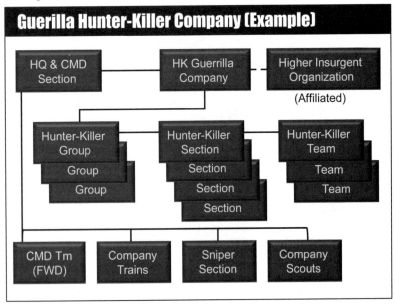

*Ref: TC 7-100, Hybrid Threat, fig. 6-2, p. 6-6.*

The structure of a guerrilla organization depends on several factors. These might include the physical environment, sociological demographics and relationships, economics, and/or support available from external organizations and countries. A guerrilla organization might be affiliated with forces from countries other than the state with which it is in conflict or other organizations external to the state sovereignty in contest. Some guerrilla organizations may constitute a paramilitary arm of an insurgent movement, while others may pursue guerrilla warfare independently from or loosely affiliated with an insurgent organization.

Compared to insurgent organizations as a whole, guerrilla organizations have a more military-like structure. Within this structure, guerrilla organizations have some of the same types of weapons as a regular military force. The guerrilla organization contains weapons up to and including 120-mm mortars, antitank guided missiles (ATGMs), and man-portable air defense systems (MANPADS), and can conduct limited mine warfare and sapper attacks.

# IV. Criminal Organizations

Criminal organizations are normally independent of nation-state control, and large-scale organizations often extend beyond national boundaries to operate regionally or worldwide. Individual criminals or small-scale criminal organizations do not have the capability to adversely affect legitimate political, military, and judicial organizations. However, large-scale criminal organizations do. The weapons and equipment mix varies based on type and scale of criminal activity. Criminal organizations can appear similar to the characteristics of a paramilitary organization.

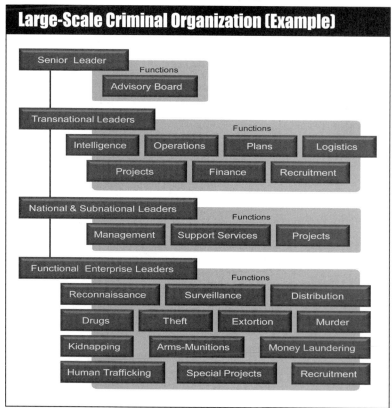

Ref: TC 7-100, Hybrid Threat, fig. 6-3, p. 6-7.

By mutual agreement, or when their interests coincide, criminal organizations may become affiliated with other actors, such as insurgent or guerrilla forces. Insurgents or guerrillas controlling or operating in the same area can provide security and protection to the criminal organization's activities in exchange for financial assistance, arms and materiel, or general logistical support. On behalf of the criminal organization, guerrilla or insurgent organizations can conduct—

- Diversionary actions
- Reconnaissance and early warning
- Money laundering, smuggling, or transportation
- Civic actions

Their mutual interests can include preventing U.S. or local government forces from interfering in their respective activities.

At times, criminal organizations might also be affiliated with nation-state military and/or paramilitary actors. In time of war, for instance, the state can encourage and materially support criminal organizations to commit actions that contribute to the breakdown of civil control in a neighboring country.

Criminal organizations may employ criminal actions, terror tactics, and militarily unconventional methods to achieve their goals. They may have the best technology, equipment, and weapons available, simply because they have the money to buy them. Criminal organizations may not change their structure in wartime, unless wartime conditions favor or dictate different types of criminal action or support activities.

Criminal organizations may conduct civic actions to gain and maintain support of the populace. A grateful public can provide valuable security and support functions. The local citizenry may willingly provide ample intelligence collection, counterintelligence, and security support. Intelligence and security can also be the result of bribery, extortion, or coercion.

# * Hybrid Relationships

The HT is a composite of many different groups. These groups will often have no standard, readily identifiable organizational relationship. What brings together the capabilities and intent of the components of the HT is a common purpose, typically opposition to U.S. goals. This unity of purpose can even bring together groups that normally would be fighting among themselves.

Affiliated organizations are cooperating toward a common goal despite having no formal command or organizational relationship. Affiliated organizations are typically nonmilitary or paramilitary groups such as criminal cartels, insurgencies, terrorist cells, or mercenaries.

Those irregular forces operating in a military unit's AOR that the unit may be able to sufficiently influence to act in concert with it for a limited time are affiliated forces. No "command relationship" exists between an affiliated organization and the unit in whose AOR it operates. In some cases, affiliated forces may receive support from the military unit as part of the agreement under which they cooperate.

# IV. Hybrid Threat Operations

*Ref: TC 7-100, Hybrid Threat (Nov '10), chap. 4.*

## I. Operational Designs

The HT employs three basic operational designs:

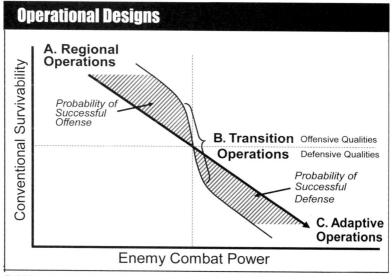

### Operational Designs

*Ref: TC 7-100, Hybrid Threat, fig. 4-1, p. 4-1.*

### A. Regional Operations *(see p. 2-26)*
Actions against regional adversaries and internal threats.

### B. Transition Operations *(see p. 2-27)*
Actions that bridge the gap between regional and adaptive operations and contain some elements of both. The HT continues to pursue its regional goals while dealing with the development of outside intervention with the potential for overmatching the HT's capabilities.

### C. Adaptive Operations *(see p. 2-28)*
Actions to preserve the HT's power and apply it in adaptive ways against overmatching opponents.

Each of these operational designs is the aggregation of the effects of tactical, operational, and strategic actions, in conjunction with the other three instruments of power, that contribute to the accomplishment of strategic goals. The type(s) of operations the HT employs at a given time will depend on the types of threats and opportunities present and other conditions in the operational environment (OE). Figure 4-1 above illustrates the HT's basic conceptual framework for the three operational designs.

# II. Principles of Operation (versus an Extraregional Power)

Ref: TC 7-100, Hybrid Threat (Nov '10), pp. 4-4 to 4-8.

The HT assumes the distinct possibility of intervention by a major extraregional power in any regional conflict. It views the United States as the most advanced extraregional force it might have to face. Like many other countries and non-state actors, the HT has studied U.S. military forces and their operations and is pursuing lessons learned based on its assessments and perceptions. The HT is therefore using the United States as its baseline for planning adaptive approaches for dealing with the strengths and weaknesses of an extraregional force. It believes that preparing to deal with intervention by U.S. forces will enable it to deal effectively with those of any other extraregional power. Consequently, it has devised the following principles for applying its various instruments of diplomatic-political, informational, economic, and military power against this type of threat.

## Access Limitation

Extraregional enemies capable of achieving overmatch against the HT must first enter the region using power-projection capabilities. Therefore, the HT's force design and investment strategy is focused on access limitation in order to—

- Selectively deny, delay, and disrupt entry of extraregional forces into the region
- Force them to keep their operating bases beyond continuous operational reach

This is the easiest manner of preventing the accumulation of enemy combat power in the region and thus defeating a technologically superior enemy.

## Control Tempo

The HT initially employs rapid tempo in an attempt to conclude regional operations before an extra-regional force can be introduced. It will also use rapid tempo to set conditions for access-limitation operations before the extraregional force can establish a foothold in the region. Once it has done that, it needs to be able to control the tempo—to ratchet it up or down—as is advantageous to its own operational or tactical plans.

## Cause Politically Unacceptable Casualties

The HT will try to inflict highly visible and embarrassing losses on enemy forces to weaken the enemy's domestic resolve and national will to sustain the deployment or conflict. Modern wealthy nations have shown an apparent lack of commitment over time. They have also demonstrated sensitivity to domestic and world opinion in relation to conflict and seemingly needless casualties. The HT believes it can have a comparative advantage against superior forces because of the collective psyche and will of the HT forces and their leadership to endure hardship or casualties, while the enemy may not be willing to do the same.

## Neutralize Technological Overmatch

Against an extraregional force, the HT's forces will forego massed formations, patterned echelonment, and linear operations that would present easy targets for such an enemy. The HT will hide and disperse its forces in areas of sanctuary that limit the enemy's ability to apply his full range of technological capabilities. However, the HT can rapidly mass forces and fires from those dispersed locations for decisive combat at the time and place of its own choosing.

The HT will attempt to use the physical environment and natural conditions to neutralize or offset the technological advantages of a modern extraregional force. It trains its forces to operate in adverse weather, limited visibility, rugged terrain, and urban environments that shield them from the effects of the enemy's high-technology weapons and deny the enemy the full benefits of his advanced C2 and reconnaissance, intelligence, surveillance, and target acquisition (RISTA) systems.

## Change the Nature of Conflict

The HT will try to change the nature of conflict to exploit the differences between friendly and enemy capabilities. To do this, it can take advantage of the opportunity afforded by phased deployment by an extraregional enemy. Following an initial period of regionally-focused conventional operations, the HT will change its operations to focus on preserving combat power and exploiting enemy ROE. This change of operations will present the fewest targets possible to the rapidly growing combat power of the enemy. It is possible that enemy power-projection forces, optimized for a certain type of maneuver warfare, would be ill suited to continue operations. (An example would be a heavy-based projection force confronted with combat in complex terrain.)

## Allow No Sanctuary

The HT seeks to deny enemy forces safe haven during every phase of a deployment and as long as they are in the region. The resultant drain on manpower and resources to provide adequate force-protection measures can reduce the enemy's strategic, operational, and tactical means to conduct war and erode his national will to sustain conflict.

Along with dispersion, decoys, and deception, the HT uses urban areas and other complex terrain as sanctuary from the effects of enemy forces. Meanwhile, its intent is to deny enemy forces the use of such terrain. This forces the enemy to operate in areas where the HT's fires and strikes can be more effective.

Terror tactics are one of the effective means to deny sanctuary to enemy forces. Terrorism has a purpose that goes well beyond the act itself. The goal is to generate fear. For the HT, these acts are part of the concept of total war. HT-sponsored or -affiliated terrorists or independent terrorists can attack the enemy anywhere and everywhere. The HT's special-purpose forces (SPF) can also use terror tactics and are well equipped, armed, and motivated for such missions.

The HT is prepared to attack enemy forces anywhere on the battlefield, at overseas bases, at home stations, and even in military communities. It will attack his airfields, seaports, transportation infrastructures, and lines of communications (LOCs). These attacks feature coordinated operations by all available forces, using not just terror tactics, but possibly long-range missiles and weapons of mass destruction (WMD).

## Employ Operational Exclusion

The HT will apply operational exclusion to selectively deny an extraregional force the use of or access to operating bases within the region or near it. In doing so, it seeks to delay or preclude military operations by the extraregional force. For example, through diplomacy, economic, or political connections, information campaigns, and/or hostile actions, the HT might seek to deny the enemy the use of bases in other foreign nations. It might also attack population and economic centers for the intimidation effect, using long-range missiles, WMD, or SPF.

## Employ Operational Shielding

The HT will use any means necessary to protect key elements of its combat power from destruction by an extraregional force, particularly by air and missile forces. This protection may come from use of any or all of the following:

- Complex terrain
- Noncombatants
- Risk of unacceptable collateral damage
- Countermeasure systems
- Dispersion
- Fortifications
- INFOWAR

# A. Regional Operations

Against opponents from within its region, the HT may conduct "regional operations" with a relatively high probability of success in primarily offensive actions. HT offensive operations are characterized by using all available HT components to saturate the OE with actions designed to disaggregate an opponent's capability, capacity, and will to resist. These actions will not be limited to attacks on military and security forces, but will affect the entire OE. The opponent will be in a fight for survival across many of the variables of the OE: political, military, economic, social, information, and infrastructure.

HT offensive operations seek to—

- Destabilize control
- Channel actions of populations
- Degrade key infrastructure
- Restrict freedom of maneuver
- Collapse economic relationships
- Retain initiative

These operations paralyze those elements of power the opponent possesses that might interfere with the HT's goals.

The HT may constantly shift which components and sets of components act to affect each variable. For example, regular forces may attack economic targets while criminal elements simultaneously act against an enemy military base or unit in one action, and then in the next action their roles may be reversed. In another example, information warfare (INFOWAR) assets may attack a national news broadcast one day, a military command and control (C2) network the next day, and a religious gathering a day later. In addition to military, economic, and information aspects of the OE, HT operations may include covert and overt political movements to discredit incumbent governments and serve as a catalyst to influence popular opinion for change. The synergy of these actions creates challenges for opponents of the HT in that it is difficult to pinpoint and isolate specific challenges.

The HT may possess an overmatch in some or all elements of power against regional opponents. It is able to employ that power in an operational design focused on offensive action. A weaker regional neighbor may not actually represent a threat, but rather an opportunity that the HT can exploit. To seize territory or otherwise expand its influence in the region, the HT must destroy a regional enemy's will and capability to continue the fight. It will attempt to achieve strategic decision or achieve specific regional goals as rapidly as possible, in order to preclude regional alliances or outside intervention.

During regional operations, the HT relies on its continuing strategic operations to preclude or control outside intervention. It tries to keep foreign perceptions of its actions during a regional conflict below the threshold that will invite in extraregional forces. The HT wants to achieve its objectives in the regional conflict, but has to be careful how it does so. It works to prevent development of international consensus for intervention and to create doubt among possible participants. Still, at the very outset of regional operations, it lays plans and positions forces to conduct access-limitation operations in the event of outside intervention.

# B. Transition Operations

Transition operations serve as a pivotal point between regional and adaptive operations. The transition may go in either direction. The fact that the HT begins transition operations does not necessarily mean that it must complete the transition from regional to adaptive operations (or vice versa). As conditions allow or dictate, the "transition" could end with the HT conducting the same type of operations as before the shift to transition operations.

The HT conducts transition operations when other regional and/or extraregional forces threaten its ability to continue regional operations in a conventional design against the original regional enemy. At the point of shifting to transition operations, the HT may still have the ability to exert all instruments of power against an overmatched regional enemy. Indeed, it may have already defeated its original adversary.

However, its successful actions in regional operations have prompted either other regional actors or an extraregional actor to contemplate intervention. The HT will use all means necessary to preclude or defeat intervention.

Although the HT would prefer to achieve its strategic goals through regional operations, it has the flexibility to change and adapt if required. Since the HT assumes the possibility of extraregional intervention, its plans will already contain thorough plans for transition operations, as well as adaptive operations, if necessary.

When an extraregional force starts to deploy into the region, the balance of power begins to shift away from the HT. Although the HT may not yet be overmatched, it faces a developing threat it will not be able to handle with normal, "conventional" patterns of operation designed for regional conflict. Therefore, the HT must begin to adapt its operations to the changing threat.

While the HT is in the condition of transition operations, an operational- or tactical-level commander will still receive a mission statement in plans and orders from his higher authority stating the purpose of his actions. To accomplish that purpose and mission, he will use as much as he can of the conventional patterns of operation that were available to him during regional operations and as much as he has to of the more adaptive-type approaches dictated by the presence of an extraregional force.

Even extraregional forces may be vulnerable to "conventional" operations during the time they require to build combat power and create support at home for their intervention. Against an extraregional force that either could not fully deploy or has been successfully separated into isolated elements, the HT may still be able to use some of the more conventional patterns of operation. The HT will not shy away from the use of military means against an advanced extraregional opponent so long as the risk is commensurate with potential gains.

Transition operations serve as a means for the HT to retain the initiative and pursue its overall strategic goals. From the outset, one of the HT's strategic goals would have been to defeat any outside intervention or prevent it from fully materializing. As the HT begins transition operations, its immediate goal is preservation of its instruments of power while seeking to set conditions that will allow it to transition back to regional operations. Transition operations feature a mixture of offensive and defensive actions that help the HT control the tempo while changing the nature of conflict to something for which the intervening force is unprepared. Transition operations can also buy time for the HT's strategic operations to succeed.

There are two possible outcomes to transition operations. If the extraregional force suffers sufficient losses or for other reasons must withdraw from the region, the HT's operations may begin to transition back to regional operations, again becoming primarily offensive. If the extraregional force is not compelled to withdraw and continues to build up power in the region, the HT's transition operations may begin to gravitate in the other direction, toward adaptive operations.

# C. Adaptive Operations

Generally, the HT conducts adaptive operations as a consequence of intervention from outside the region. Once an extraregional force intervenes with sufficient power to overmatch the HT, the full conventional design used in regionally-focused operations is no longer sufficient to deal with this threat. The HT has developed its techniques, organization, capabilities, and strategy with an eye toward dealing with both regional and extraregional opponents. It has already planned how it will adapt to this new and changing threat and has included this adaptability in its methods.

The HT's immediate goal is survival. However, its long-term goal is still the expansion of influence. In the HT's view, this goal is only temporarily thwarted by the extraregional intervention. Accordingly, planning for adaptive operations focuses on effects over time. The HT believes that patience is its ally and an enemy of the extraregional force and its intervention in regional affairs.

The HT believes that adaptive operations can lead to several possible outcomes. If the results do not completely resolve the conflict in its favor, they may at least allow it to return to regional operations. Even a stalemate may be a victory, as long as it preserves enough of its instruments of power and lives to fight another day.

When an extraregional power intervenes, the HT has to adapt its patterns of operation. It still has the same forces and technology that were available to it for regional operations, but must use them in creative and adaptive ways. It has already thought through how it will adapt to this new or changing threat in general terms. It has already developed appropriate branches and sequels to its core plans and does not have to rely on improvisation. During the course of combat, it will make further adaptations, based on experience and opportunity.

Even with the intervention of an advanced extraregional power, the HT will not cede the initiative. It may employ military means so long as this does not either place its survival at risk or risk depriving it of sufficient force to remain a significant influence in its region after the extraregional intervention is over. The primary objectives are to—

- Preserve power
- Degrade the enemy's will and capability to fight
- Gain time for aggressive strategic operations to succeed

The HT will seek to conduct adaptive operations in circumstances and terrain that provide opportunities to optimize its own capabilities and degrade those of the enemy. It will employ a force that is optimized for the terrain or for a specific mission. For example, it will use its antitank capability, tied to obstacles and complex terrain, inside a defensive structure designed to absorb the enemy's momentum and fracture his organizational framework.

The types of adaptive actions that characterize adaptive operations can also serve the HT well in regional or transition operations, at least at the tactical and operational levels. However, once an extraregional force becomes fully involved in the conflict, the HT will conduct adaptive actions more frequently and on a larger scale.

# V. Hybrid Threat Tactics

*Ref: TC 7-100, Hybrid Threat (Nov '10), chap. 5.*

## I. Tactical Concepts

Initiative and mobility characterize tactics the HT would use while establishing and preserving bases in which to train, self-sustain, prepare for future missions, and evolve organizational capability. Concurrently, collective tactical actions can have strategic consequences of denying an enemy a secure area or making it politically untenable to remain. Actions are aimed at keeping an enemy physically and psychologically stressed from constant harassment and disruption when a distinct defeat or destruction of an enemy is not practical.

### Tactical Concepts

**A** Synergy of Regular and Irregular Forces

**B** Info Warfare as a Key Weapon System

**C** Complex Battle Positions

**D** Systems Warfare

**E** Adapting by Function

*Ref: TC 7-100, Hybrid Threat, chap. 5.*

Tactical actions can encompass a range of activities that can include the following:
- Collection of intelligence
- Coercion for fiscal or logistic support
- Assassination of designated enemy leaders or officials
- Sabotage by small loosely affiliated groups of irregular forces
- More traditional major offensive and defensive actions between regular military forces

*See following pages for an overview and further discussion of HT tactical concepts.*

# Tactical Concepts

*Ref: TC 7-100, Hybrid Threat (Nov '10), pp. 5-1 to 5-3.*

Initiative and mobility characterize tactics the HT would use while establishing and preserving bases in which to train, self-sustain, prepare for future missions, and evolve organizational capability. Concurrently, collective tactical actions can have strategic consequences of denying an enemy a secure area or making it politically untenable to remain. Actions are aimed at keeping an enemy physically and psychologically stressed from constant harassment and disruption when a distinct defeat or destruction of an enemy is not practical.

## A. Synergy of Regular and Irregular Forces

The HT understands that the environment that would produce the most challenges to U.S. forces is one in which conventional military operations occur in concert with irregular warfare. The HT's concept is not just one of making do with what is available, but is primarily one of deliberately created complexity.

Each component of the HT brings a capability to bear. The synergy of these capabilities is not to be understated. Operational environments (OEs) by their very nature provide a myriad of complexities across all the operational variables. The HT seeks to introduce additional complexity through the use of an ever-shifting array of forces, technologies, and techniques.

## B. Information Warfare as a Key Weapon System

HT tactical actions will be often be designed to achieve information warfare (INFOWAR) objectives rather than purely military ones. Information and its management, dissemination, and control have always been critical to the successful conduct of tactical missions. Given today's tremendous advancements in information and information systems technology, this importance is growing in scope, impact, and sophistication. The HT recognizes the unique opportunities that INFOWAR gives tactical commanders. Therefore, it continuously strives to incorporate INFOWAR activities in all tactical missions and battles.

INFOWAR may help degrade or deny effective enemy communications and blur or manipulate the battlefield picture. In addition, INFOWAR helps the HT achieve the goal of dictating the tempo of combat. Using a combination of perception management activities, deception techniques, and electronic warfare (EW), the HT can effectively slow or control the pace of battle. For example, the HT may selectively destroy lucrative enemy targets. It could also orchestrate and execute a perception management activity that weakens the enemy's international and domestic support, causing hesitation or actual failure of the operation. It executes deception plans to confuse the enemy and conceal intentions.

INFOWAR also supports the critical mission of counterreconnaissance at the tactical level. The HT constantly seeks ways to attack, degrade, or manipulate the enemy's reconnaissance, intelligence, surveillance, and target acquisition (RISTA) capabilities. All enemy target acquisition systems and sensors are potential targets.

## C. Complex Battle Positions (CBP)

The HT reduces exposure to enemy standoff fires and RISTA by utilizing complex battle positions (CBPs) and cultural standoff. CBPs are designed to protect the units within them from detection and attack while denying their seizure and occupation by the enemy. Commanders occupying CBPs intend to preserve their combat power until conditions permit offensive action. In the case of an attack, CBP defenders will engage only as long as they perceive an ability to defeat aggressors. Should the defending commander feel that his forces are decisively overmatched, he will attempt a withdrawal in order to preserve combat power.

CBPs have the following characteristics that distinguish them from simple battle positions :
- Limited avenues of approach. (CBPs are not necessarily tied to an avenue of approach.)
- Avenues of approach are easily observable by the defender.
- 360-degree fire coverage and protection from attack. (This may be due to the nature of surrounding terrain or engineer activity such as tunneling.)
- Engineer effort prioritizing camouflage, concealment, cover, and deception (C3D) measures; limited countermobility effort which might reveal the CBP location.
- Large logistics caches.
- Sanctuary from which to launch local attacks.

C3D measures are critical to the success of a CBP, since the defender generally wants to avoid enemy contact. Additionally, forces within a CBP will remain dispersed to negate the effects of precision ordinance strikes. Generally, once the defense is established, non-combat vehicles will be moved away from troop concentrations to reduce their signature on the battlefield.

Cultural standoff is the fact that protection from enemy weapon systems can be gained through actions that make use of cultural differences to prevent or degrade engagement. Examples of cultural standoff are—
- Using a religious or medical facility as a base of fire
- Firing from within a crowd of noncombatants
- Tying prisoners in front of battle positions and onto combat vehicles

## D. Systems Warfare

The HT will disaggregate enemy combat power by destroying or neutralizing vulnerable single points of failure in enemy warfighting functions. A system is a set of different elements so connected or related as to perform a unique function not performable by the elements or components alone. The essential ingredients of a system include the components, the synergy among components and other systems, and some type of functional boundary separating it from other systems. Therefore, a "system of systems" is a set of different systems so connected or related as to produce results unachievable by the individual systems alone. The HT views the OE, the battlefield, its own instruments of power, and an opponent's instruments of power as a collection of complex, dynamic, and integrated systems composed of subsystems and components.

Systems warfare serves as a conceptual and analytical tool to assist in the planning, preparation, and execution of warfare. With the systems approach, the intent is to identify critical system components and attack them in a way that will degrade or destroy the use or importance of the overall system.

The primary principle of systems warfare is the identification and isolation of the critical subsystems or components that give the opponent the capability and cohesion to achieve his aims. The focus is on the disaggregation of the system by rendering its subsystems and components ineffective. While the aggregation of these subsystems or components is what makes the overall system work, the interdependence of these subsystems is also a potential vulnerability.

## E. Adapting by Function

The HT will choose the most effective option for executing each combat function, without regard to original purpose, laws of war, or military hierarchy. For example, a child on a street corner with a cell phone may be the most effective means of providing early warning to the leaders involved in a tactical action. If so, the HT will employ that option, even if more sophisticated or expensive RISTA devices or techniques are available.

The HT will typically acquire a capability to permit it to act with freedom with respect to its natural, regional enemies. These capabilities will be adapted to exploit their pertinent characteristics to best advantage against enemy forces.

# II. Functional Tactics

The HT employs functional tactics. It determines the functions that need to be performed as part of an action to bring about its success. Then it allocates appropriate actors to each function and synchronizes the effort.

A number of different functions must be executed each time an HT force attempts to accomplish a mission. An HT commander identifies the specific functions he intends his various subordinate forces or elements to perform. The functions do not change, regardless of where the force or element might happen to be located on the battlefield. However, the function of a particular force or element may change during the course of the battle. While the various functions required to accomplish any given mission can be quite diverse, they can be broken down into two very broad categories: action and enabling.

*Note. In larger groupings of forces, HT commanders refer to the subordinates performing various functions as forces. In smaller groupings, commanders call them elements.*

## A. Action Functions

The action function is performed by the set of capabilities that actually accomplish a given mission. One part of the unit or grouping of units conducting a particular action is normally responsible for performing the primary function or task that accomplishes the goal or objective of that action. In most general terms, therefore, that part can be called the action force or action element. In most cases, however, the higher commander will give the action force or element a more specific designation that identifies the specific function it is intended to perform, which equates to achieving the objective of the higher command's mission.

## B. Enabling Functions

The enabling function is performed by a set of capabilities that acts to assist those capabilities performing the action function. In relation to the force(s) or element(s) conducting the action function, all other parts of the organization or grouping of organizations conducting an action provide enabling functions of various kinds. In most general terms, therefore, each of these parts can be called an enabling force or enabling element. However, each subordinate force or element with an enabling function can be more clearly identified by the specific function it performs.

# I. Forms of Terrorism (Tactics & Techniques)

*Ref: U.S. Army TRADOC G2 Handbook No. 1 (Version 5.0), A Military Guide to Terrorism in the Twenty-First Century (Aug '07), chap. 4; Terrorism in the United States 1999, Federal Bureau of Investigation; and TERRORISM 2002-2005, Federal Bureau of Investigation.*

Terrorism is one of the oldest forms of human conflict. Before societies organized to wage war against each other, individuals and small bands engaged in terror tactics to achieve limited goals–to overthrow existing leaders, toward off potential rivals, or to frighten opposing groups from lands they wished to claim for themselves.

*(Combating Terrorism Center)*

Although the means and ends have evolved throughout history, the central elements of terrorism–fear, panic, violence, and disruption–have changed little through time. As the world enters the 21st Century, terrorism remains a vexing problem–an anachronistic fixture of human relations as paradoxically human and inhuman in the third Millennium as it was before the dawn of recorded history.

If terrorism was not unique to the 20th Century, the remarkable technological and social advances of the second Millennium's closing century created unprecedented opportunities for terrorists, both in terms of the destruction they could create and the level of public anxiety their acts could generate.

The modern era of terrorism–beginning approximately in the late 1960s and continuing through to today–has been the most destructive in history. Over 14,000 international terrorist attacks have taken place worldwide since 1968. These attacks have resulted in more than 10,000 deaths.

While U.S. interests–primarily commercial and diplomatic facilities, U.S.-flagged aircraft, and U.S. nationals–have been a common target for terrorist attacks overseas, U.S. soil remained largely untouched by serious acts of international terrorism until the 1990s, when the World Trade Center bombing and several thwarted plots to

# I. Terrorism Trends (Sept. 11, 2001-Present)

Ref: TERRORISM 2002-2005, Federal Bureau of Investigation, pp. 47 to 48.

Beginning in the late 1950s the most serious terrorist threat to U.S. civil aviation came in the form of hijackings of commercial aircraft. In these incidents, the aircraft provided hijackers both transportation to diverted destinations and a ready supply of hostages for leverage in their negotiations with government authorities. By the late 1980s—as seen in the 1988 bombing of Pan Am flight 103 over Lockerbie, Scotland, and in the prevented "Manila Air" plot of 1994—the threat to civil aviation began to include the targeting of commercial aircraft and their passengers and crews for destruction.

On the morning of September 11, 2001, al-Qa'ida directed its ruthless ingenuity toward the further exploitation of civil aviation when 19 of its operatives hijacked four U.S. commercial airliners for use as suicide weapons against selected political, military, and economic targets on the U.S. East Coast. The hijackers used knives, boxcutters, and possibly pepper spray to commandeer the aircraft. Three of the aircraft struck their targets, destroying the Twin Towers of the World Trade Center in New York City and badly damaging the Pentagon in Arlington, Virginia. The fourth aircraft crashed into a remote field in Stonycreek Township, Pennsylvania, as passengers attempted to regain control of the airplane. All of the passengers on each of the aircraft were killed in the attack, as were more than 2,500 people in the Twin Towers and the Pentagon. In total, 2,972 people died in the September 11 attack, making it the most deadly act of terrorism ever committed. The September 11 attack also marked the first known suicide terrorist attack carried out in the United States since the FBI began keeping terrorist records.

The threat of terrorism is expected to continue from both international and domestic sources. Internationally, at least two operational trends are evident in the militant Islamic jihad movement. First is a preference for high-casualty, high-profile attacks directed against lower-risk, unofficial, so-called "soft" targets, as traditional military and diplomatic targets become increasingly hardened. Second, the dissolution of much of al-Qa'ida's structure by international military and law enforcement efforts has resulted in the dispersal of its multinational trainees to pursue their own regional agendas. The following terrorist incidents from September 11, 2001, through 2005 may involve both trends:

- On October 12, 2002, a nightclub bombing on the Indonesian island of Bali killed approximately 200 people, including seven Americans, and on August 5, 2003, a bombing of the JW Marriott Hotel in Jakarta, Indonesia, resulted in 15 deaths. Both of these bombings have been attributed to members of the Jemaah Islamiyya terrorist organization, a Southeast Asian-based terrorist network with links to al-Qa'ida.

- On May 12 and November 9, 2003, al-Qa'ida operatives conducted bombings of residential compounds that housed Western workers in Riyadh, Saudi Arabia. The first incident claimed dozens of lives and injured nearly 200 others. The second resulted in 18 deaths and over 120 injuries.

- On May 16, 2003, five nearly simultaneous explosions in Casablanca, Morocco, killed 41 people and injured approximately 100 others. Although no definitive evidence links al-Qa'ida to the bombings in Casablanca, the Sunni extremist group responsible for this attack may have al-Qa'ida ties.

- On March 11, 2004, a series of 10 bombs detonated on four commuter trains in Madrid, Spain. The near simultaneous explosions killed 191 people and injured more than 1,400 others. Spanish police have traced responsibility for the attack to Moroccan Islamic militants with ties to al-Qa'ida.

- On July 7, 2005, four coordinated bomb blasts struck London's public transit system during the morning rush hour. Fifty-two people were killed and approximately 700 injured in the attack, including the death of one American and the wounding of four others. The London bombing was distinctive in having involved "homegrown" jihadist terrorists operating in a Western, predominantly non-Muslim country.

The use of WMD against civilian targets represents the most serious potential international and domestic terrorism threat facing the United States today and provides a glimpse into emerging terrorist scenarios of the 21st century. A variety of intelligence reporting indicates that al-Qa'ida has energetically sought to acquire and experiment with biological, chemical, and radiological weapons of mass destruction. The January 2003 arrests in the United Kingdom of Algerian extremists suspected of producing the biological toxin ricin exemplifies the interest some Islamic militants have in the operational use of such agents. In April 2004, Jordanian authorities disrupted a plot by Islamic extremists to generate a cloud of cyanide gas in Amman.

Ricin and the bacterial agent anthrax are emerging as the most prevalent agents involved in WMD investigations. Prior to the fall of 2001, there had been no criminal cases involving the actual use of anthrax in the United States. In September and October of that year, however, several anthrax-tainted letters were received in Florida, New York, New Jersey, Connecticut, and the District of Columbia. The contaminations resulted in five fatalities and 22 infections. On February 2, 2004, in an incident for which no threat was made or threat letter identified, ricin was discovered on the automated mail opening system used in the Washington, D.C., office of U.S. Senate Majority Leader William Frist. Both the anthrax mailings of 2001 and the 2004 ricin incident remain under investigation by the FBI, and their connection to domestic or international terrorism has not been determined.

## Legislative Action

In his September 20, 2001, address to a Joint Session of Congress and the American people, President Bush declared a war to disrupt global terrorism, beginning with al-Qa'ida. The war on terrorism has included military action to overthrow Afghanistan's Taliban government and Sadaam Hussein's Baathist regime in Iraq, as well as a multifaceted campaign involving diplomacy, economic sanctions, covert intelligence operations, and law enforcement action. In the weeks immediately following the September 11, 2001, attack, Congress and the President enacted legislation and policies intended to minimize the possibility of another catastrophic act of terrorism from occurring on U.S. soil.

On October 26, 2001, Congress passed the Uniting and Strengthening America by Providing Appropriate Tools Required to Interrupt and Obstruct Terrorism Act of 2001 (USA PATRIOT Act), which includes changes to national security authorities, criminal and immigration laws, and money-laundering and victim assistance statutes. The USA PATRIOT Act improved the processes by which federal law enforcement officials obtain legal authority for conducting surveillance and allowed for greater information sharing between criminal investigators and intelligence collectors. The act modified the definition of terrorism as a federal crime to include several offenses likely to be committed by terrorists, including certain computer crimes and a number of violent crimes involving aircraft. New federal offenses include attacks on mass transportation systems, vehicles, facilities, or passengers; harboring or concealing persons who have committed or are about to commit an act of terrorism; expansion of the prohibition against providing material support or resources to terrorists; and possessing a biological agent or toxin of a type or in a quantity that is not reasonably justified for specifically defined purposes. Additionally, the inclusion of the International Money Laundering Abatement and Financial Anti-Terrorism Act of 2001 into the USA PATRIOT Act significantly increased the United States' ability to combat the financing of terrorism. On October 29, 2001, President Bush issued Homeland Security Presidential Directive No. 2 (HSPD-2). Among its provisions, HSPD-2 offers federal guidance for keeping foreign terrorists and their supporters out of the United States through entry denial, removal, and prosecution.

# II. Tomorrow's Terrorist Trends
*Ref: Terrorism in the United States 1999, Federal Bureau of Investigation, pp. 38-41.*

Statistics indicate that the vast majority of terrorist attacks worldwide continue to be perpetrated with conventional weapons such as bombs, firearms, and limited-range rockets. However, the terror-causing potential of a variety of unconventional weapons may draw growing attention from terrorists in the new Millennium.

Chemical, biological, and radiological weapons–often collectively referred to as weapons of mass destruction (WMD)–have the potential to kill large numbers of people and cause mass fear. A subcategory of this threat, known as agroterrorism, involves the intentional contamination of human food sources. Modern society's growing use of computerized information systems as key tools in the maintenance of basic infrastructure offers other avenues of stealthy destruction. Cyberterrorism, involving the use of computers to steal, alter, or destroy information, will continue to plague the 21st Century as the global populace becomes increasingly adept in and reliant on the use of computers. Even more exotic dangers, such as high-energy radio frequency and electromagnetic pulse weapons, will add to the counterterrorism and infrastructure protection issues of the new Millennium.

## Chemical, Biological, and Radiological Terrorism
WMD CASES–those cases primarily dealing with the threatened use or procurement of chemical, biological, or radiological materials with intent to harm–have shown a steady increase since 1995. Most of these cases have involved hoaxes rather than actual use of a weapon of mass destruction, and most of these threats have been directed against locations such as office buildings, schools, federal government facilities, court houses, and women's reproductive health centers.

Although the state of WMD use appears relatively unsophisticated in the United States today, the destructive possibilities inherent in even their unsophisticated use, and the possibility that an individual or group may decide to explore more advanced methods, require law enforcement to be vigilant regarding this threat. Incidents in other countries–such as the 1995 Aum Shinrikyo sarin gas attack on the Tokyo subway system that killed 12 and injured approximately 5,000 individuals–demonstrate the need to guard against and prepare for WMD terrorism in the United States. The FBI's National Domestic Preparedness Office (NDPO), created in 1998, is one element of this ongoing effort. The NDPO serves as an information clearinghouse for federal programs supporting state and local emergency responder communities in the area of WMD-related domestic preparedness planning, training, exercises, equipment research and development, information sharing, and health/medical issues.

## Agroterrorism
WHILE all WMD incidents are troubling, cases related to contamination of food supplies suggest a disturbing twist on this threat. An attack against agriculture, livestock, or other food supplies with a biological, chemical, or radiological weapon is known as agroterrorism. As in any type of terrorism, there can be a wide variety of motives behind agroterrorism, and the results of a successful attack can be serious.

The FBI has investigated consumer product and food-tampering violations since the early 1980s. The most significant attack against a food supply in the United States occurred in Dalles, Oregon, in 1984. Followers of the Bagwan Shree Rajneessh cult sprayed salmonella on salad bars in several area restaurants, causing 751 people to become ill. This was an unannounced biological attack; it was not determined to be a biological attack until a year later. WMD threats against U.S. food supplies still occur significantly less often than WMD threats to other targets, and agriculture and livestock in the United States have never been attacked. But the potential for widespread injury, and even death, as a result of agroterrorism has required law enforcement and public health agencies to continuously improve their coordination and vigilance.

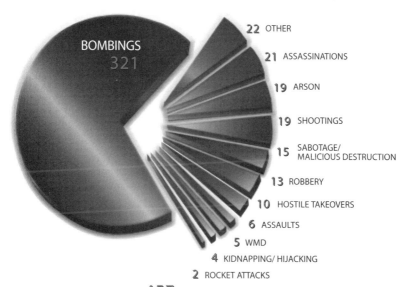

# TERRORISM
## by Event
# 1980-1999

BOMBINGS
321

22 OTHER

21 ASSASSINATIONS

19 ARSON

19 SHOOTINGS

15 SABOTAGE/ MALICIOUS DESTRUCTION

13 ROBBERY

10 HOSTILE TAKEOVERS

6 ASSAULTS

5 WMD

4 KIDNAPPING/ HIJACKING

2 ROCKET ATTACKS

457 TOTAL INCIDENTS OR PLANNED ACTS

ª Figures include terrorist incidents, suspected terrorist incidents, and preventions.

## Cyberterrorism

The threat of physical attacks on critical U.S. infrastructure—such as electric power, telecommunications, banking and finance, gas and oil, and transportation– has always been a source of concern. Electronic, information-based attacks, however, constitute a relatively new and growing threat. One subset of this threat is terrorists' use of computers and the Internet. Terrorists are known to use information technology and the Internet to formulate plans, raise funds, spread propaganda, recruit new members, and communicate securely. However, there have also been cases of terrorist groups using cyber-based attacks to inflict damage on their enemies' information systems.

## Conclusion

The counterterrorism challenges in the next Millennium are evolving today. In practice, the vast majority of terrorist attacks have been committed with conventional means such as bombs and bullets, rather than unconventional methods such as chemical, biological, radiological, cyber, radio frequency, and electromagnetic pulse weapons. Conventional explosives and firearms are relatively easy to procure, handle, transport, and use. In comparison, more high-tech weapons often require sophisticated scientific knowledge or difficult-to-acquire hardware. Yet this very complexity may contribute to the fear evoked by these unseen and often indiscriminate weapons. This terror effect, in addition to the threat of mass murder and destruction, may make such weapons attractive to certain types of terrorists. Certainly, many of these weapons have already been used: from sarin gas in Tokyo to malicious computer viruses aimed at U.S. Government networks, terrorists have proved that at least some of these weapons are feasible. But in other cases the arrests of those who attempt to commit acts of violence with these weapons have prevented their use, while those who do manage to launch an attack are often caught and incarcerated.

attack targets in the United States ushered in a new understanding of the international terrorist threat confronting the United States. During the past 30 years, the vast majority–but not all–of the deadly terrorist attacks occurring in the United States have been perpetrated by domestic extremists.

# III. Terrorist Tactics and Techniques

The terrorist uses a wide array of tactics and techniques in conducting terror. This section is not an exhaustive presentation of methods or approaches. One norm regarding terror operations is the use of surprise, secrecy, innovation, and indirect methods of attack. Tactics are as broad and diverse as the resources of the terrorist cell and the imagination of the group leader. Use of the Internet and training exchanges information among terrorists on tactics that yield success. Terrorists continue to improve techniques as field tests demonstrate degrees of effectiveness in real-world situations such as Chechnya, Kashmir, Afghanistan, the Balkans, and Iraq.

The terrorist will utilize tactics, forces, and weapons specifically tailored to a particular mission. Terrorist operations are individualistic in that each is planned for a specific target and effect.

A terrorist relies upon prior planning and reconnaissance to counter and overmatch the target. If changes to the target or unexpected conditions render success unlikely, the terrorist may cancel the operation and return later or choose a different target and continue his planning and attack process.

In many regions of the world, terrorism challenges political stability, economic progress, and democratic initiatives. To discuss the likelihood of particular terrorist threats to U.S. military forces, defining operational area and contemporary operational environment provides a setting of where and how particular threats may emerge.

*See pp. 3-11 to 3-18 for further discussion.*

# IV. Circumstances and Influences

A principal consideration in terrorist targeting is the psychological impact of an attack on a selected audience. Attacking U.S. forces can provide a psychological impact that serves the goals of the terrorist. Assessing risk to potential targets will often focus less on specific military value, and consider the value to a terrorist intention to cause fear and anxiety.

Terrorists might consider one civilian casualty more effective than several military casualties, considering the psychological impact and resulting media coverage. Soft targets could achieve the most significant attention while employing minimal risk to their own assets. A saying attributed to several terrorists is, "Why hunt wolves when here are so many sheep about?" Furthermore, a recurring number of civilian deaths and mayhem can be an effective tool in a campaign of terror to break the resolve of a population and discourage a popularly elected representative government.

# II. Terrorist Planning & Execution

*Ref: JP 3-26, Counterterrorism (Nov '09), pp. II-17 to II-21, and U.S. Army TRADOC G2 Handbook No. 1 (Version 5.0), A Military Guide to Terrorism in the Twenty-First Century (Aug '07), app. A.*

Terrorist operations typically are planned in great detail with the objectives of minimizing risk, achieving the highest probability of success, and attaining the widest publicity of their actions. Terrorists seek to avoid adversary strengths and concentrate on their weaknesses. Terrorist tactics are aligned with their overall plans which attempt to use the successful achievement of their operational objectives to realize the accomplishment of their strategic goals. Their approaches to planning and execution follow.

## Terrorist Planning Cycle

| | |
|---|---|
| **I** | **Broad Target Selection** |
| **II** | **Intelligence Gathering and Surveillance** |
| **III** | **Specific Target Selection** |
| **IV** | **Pre-attack Surveillance and Planning** |
| **V** | **Rehearsals** |
| **VI** | **Actions on the Objective** |
| **VII** | **Escape and Exploitation** |

*Ref: JP 3-26, Counterterrorism (Nov '09), fig. II-3, p. II-18.*

Terrorist operational planning can be analyzed according to requirements common to all operations. The planning and operation cycle is valid for traditional hierarchically organized groups, as well as decentralized "network" type organizations. The differences between the two organizations are the location of the decision maker at the various steps of the cycle, and the method of task organizing and providing support for the operations.

# I. Broad Target Selection

This phase of planning is the collection of information on a large number of potential targets, some of which may never be attacked, or seriously considered for attack. Personnel who are not members of a terrorist organization's cadre, but lower-level active or even passive supporters may be used for data collection and target surveillance. This phase also includes open source and general information collection. Potential targets are identified through the media, Internet research, and elicitation of unwitting sources.

Potential targets are screened based on symbolic value and their potential to generate high profile media attention. Objectives of the terrorist group influence the selection of a person or facility as a worthy target. This includes the risk and likely casualty figures achieved by the attack. The number of preliminary targets that can be screened is limited only by the capabilities of the group to collect information from sympathizers and open sources. Targets that are considered vulnerable and which would further the terrorist organization's goals are selected for the next phase of intelligence collection.

# II. Intelligence Gathering and Surveillance

Targets showing potential vulnerabilities are given a higher priority of effort. The type of surveillance employed depends on the priority and type of target. Elements of information typically gathered include:

## Practices, Procedures, and Routines

For facilities, this includes scheduled deliveries, work shift changes, identification procedures and other observable routines. For individuals, it can include regularly scheduled errands, appointments, and activities.

## Residence and Workplace

This category applies primarily to the physical layout and individual activities at the two places the target typically spends the most time.

## Transportation and Routes of Travel

For individuals, this is the mode of transport and common routes to any regular destination. For facilities and conveyances, it addresses ingress and egress points, types of vehicles allowed on the grounds, or availability of transportation into the target site.

## Security Measures

Intelligence gathering and surveillance of security measures include a myriad of potential collection areas, depending on the complexity of the security around the target. Presence of a guard force; the reaction time of response units; any hardening of structures, barriers, or sensors; personnel, package, and vehicle screening procedures; and the type and frequency of emergency reaction drills are examples of key collection objectives. This is one of the most important areas of information for attack site selection, since the intent is to bypass and avoid security measures, and be able to strike the target during any period.

# III. Specific Target Selection

Target selection for actual planning considers several factors prior to a decision to proceed or not proceed. A decision to proceed requires continued intelligence collection against the chosen target. Targets not receiving immediate consideration will still be collected against for future opportunities. Selection factors include:

- Does success affect a larger audience than the immediate victim(s)?
- Will the target attract high profile media attention?
- Does success make the desired statement to the correct target audience(s)?
- Is the effect consistent with objectives of the group?
- Does the target provide an advantage to the group by providing the group an opportunity to demonstrate its capabilities?
- What are costs versus benefits of conducting the operation?

# IV. Pre-attack Surveillance and Planning

Members of the actual operational cells begin to appear during this phase. Either trained intelligence and surveillance personnel, or members of the cell organized to conduct the operation conduct this phase of planning. Consequently, the level of intelligence expertise and operational competency increases correspondingly. During this phase, information is gathered on the target's patterns over time, usually days to weeks, sometimes longer depending on the complexity of the target. It allows the attack team to confirm the information gathered from previous surveillance and reconnaissance activities, but with greater focus based upon the planning conducted thus far. The type of surveillance employed depends on the target's activities. The information gained is then used to:

- Conduct security studies
- Conduct detailed preparatory operations
- Recruit specialized operatives as needed
- Establish a base of operations in the target area (e.g., safe houses, caches)
- Design and test escape routes
- Decide on type of weapon or attack

# V. Rehearsals

As with conventional military operations, rehearsals are conducted to improve the odds of success, confirm planning assumptions, and develop contingencies. Terrorists also rehearse to test security reactions to particular attack profiles. Terrorists use both their own operatives and unwitting people to test target reactions. Typical rehearsals include:

- Deployment into target area
- Actions on the objective
- Escape routes
- Equipment and weapon performance

Tests in the target area are conducted to confirm:

- Target information gathered to date
- Target pattern of activities
- Physical layout of target or operation area
- Security force reactions (state of alert, timing, size of response, equipment, routes)

# VI. Actions on the Objective

Once terrorists reach the execution phase of the operation, the odds of success favor the terrorist and are clearly against the target. Terrorists attempt to minimize time spent conducting the actual operation to reduce their vulnerability to discovery or countermeasures. With the exception of barricade-style hostage taking operations, terrorists normally plan to complete their actions before immediate security forces can react. Terrorists conducting planned operations possess important tactical advantages. As the attacker, they possess the initiative, giving them the advantage of surprise; choice of time, place, and conditions of attack; employment of diversions and secondary or follow-on attacks; and employment of security and support positions to neutralize target reaction forces and security measures.

# VII. Escape and Exploitation

Terrorist TTPs

Escape plans are usually well rehearsed and executed. Successful escape further enhances the effect of fear and terror from a successful operation. The exception is a suicide operation, where the impact is enhanced by the willingness to die in achieving the attack. Even in suicide attacks, however, there are usually support personnel and "handlers" who must deliver the suicide asset to the target, and subsequently make their escape.

Exploitation is the primary objective of all terrorist operations. Terrorist operations must be exploited properly and publicized to create their intended effect. Media control measures, prepared statements, and a host of other preparations are made to effectively exploit a successful operation. These are timed to take advantage of media cycles for the selected target audiences (TAs). By quickly capturing and exploiting images themselves, the adversary can rapidly leverage events to influence the public via self produced media (Internet, radio, television, text messaging, podcast, Weblogs (blogs), etc.) and gain an advantage within the information environment.

Unsuccessful operations are disavowed when possible. The perception that a group has failed severely damages the organization's prestige and makes it appear vulnerable, or worse, ineffective. Once a terrorist organization is perceived as ineffective, it becomes more difficult to impact target audiences or recruit members.

In addition to the impact on the target, successful attacks bring perceived favorable attention, notoriety and support (such as money and recruits) to the terrorist group conducting the operation. If the group conducting the operation subscribes to a revolutionary ideology, they will see each success as gradually inspiring more revolutionary fervor in the population they are attempting to influence. Any success encourages the terrorists to conduct further operations, and improves their ability to do so through increased support and experience.

# III. Terrorist Operations & Tactics

Ref: JP 3-26, Counterterrorism (Nov '09), pp. II-22 to II-25, and U.S. Army TRADOC G2 Handbook No. 1 (Version 5.0), A Military Guide to Terrorism in the Twenty-First Century (Aug '07), chap. 4.

The ensuing discussion presents the most common types of terrorist operations and tactics. It is not intended to be an exhaustive discussion of the subject since the combination of methods and approaches is virtually unlimited. However, common themes in terrorist operations are surprise, secrecy, innovation, and indirect methods of attack. Terrorist tactics are broad and diverse. Additionally, with the use of the Internet and common training bases, terrorist groups exchange information on tactics that can yield success.

## Forms of Terrorist Tactics

| | |
|---|---|
| • Threat or Hoax | • Raid or Ambush |
| • Arson | • Seizure |
| • Sabotage | • Assassination |
| • Bombing | • WMD |
| • Kidnapping | • Aircraft Threats |
| • Hostage Taking | • Maritime Threats |
| • Hijacking | • Suicide Tactics |

Ref: Adapted from JP 3-26, Counterterrorism (Nov '09), fig. II-4, p. II-23.

# I. Terrorist Operational Considerations

The terrorist utilizes tactics, forces, and weapons specifically tailored to the particular mission. Terrorist operations are unique, in that each is planned for a specific target and effect. Terrorists normally expose only as much of their resources and personnel as are absolutely necessary to accomplish a mission in order to avoid capture or destruction. A conventional military force would approach an operation with plans to concentrate forces and keep excess combat power on hand to meet contingencies, ensure mission success, and prepare for follow-on missions. A terrorist takes a minimal force and relies upon prior planning and reconnaissance to match the force, weapons, and methods to the target. If changes to the target, or unexpected conditions render success unlikely, the terrorist group will most often cancel or postpone the operation, regroup, update its plan, and adapt to whatever conditions are required to ensure a successful operation. For major terrorist operations, mission accomplishment is often followed by a disbanding of the force, a return of terrorists to their cells and covers, and formation of new task groups for future operations.

In addition to adaptive and flexible organizations, terrorists also employ specific equipment built or procured for a particular operation. Because of the lag time between development of a new technology and military acquisition and fielding, terrorists can sometimes procure equipment superior to standardized military models. As an example, instead of purchasing hundreds of identical radios constructed to meet all likely uses, a terrorist group may only procure the quantity it needs of the

# II. Forms of Terrorist Tactics

Ref: JP 3-26, Counterterrorism (Nov '09), chap. 2, pp. 2-22 to 2-25 and U.S. Army TRADOC G2 Handbook No. 1 (Version 5.0), A Military Guide to Terrorism in the Twenty-First Century (Aug '07), chap. 4.

Terrorist tactics take many forms. Some are accomplished as independent actions. Others may be undertaken as part of other coordinated activities. The more common types of terrorist tactics are described below.

## Threat or Hoax

Terrorist groups use threats and hoaxes to coerce or preclude actions by a targeted individual or population. Threats and hoaxes can dull the effectiveness of counter or preventive measures when a targeted individual or population loses situational awareness, or disperses finite assets against many possible threats. This tactic also can be used to gain information concerning the target's response to a potential attack. It also can be combined with an actual attack to circumvent fixed security measures as a diversion tactic. While there is limited evidence that terrorists use hoaxes to achieve their aims, the potential exists for them to use them, so JFCs should consider this possibility when conducting CT operations.

## Arson

Arson is a destructive technique usually used in sabotage operations against property. It is most often used for symbolic attacks and to create economic effects.

## Sabotage

Sabotage is the planned destruction of the target's equipment or infrastructure. Its purpose is to inflict both psychological and physical damage. Sabotage demonstrates how vulnerable the target is to the terrorist group's actions. Sabotage can have significant economic impacts, as well as the additional effects of creating mass casualties.

## Bombing

Bombs, to include IEDs, vehicle-borne IEDs, and suicide bombers (wearing explosives or in vehicles with IEDs), are the favored weapon of terrorists. They are highly destructive, are flexible enough to be tailored to the mission, do not require the operator to be present, and have a significant psychological impact. They may be used as a technique to conduct other operations, such as sabotage or assassination, or can simply be a tactic to create terror through destruction and casualties.

## Kidnapping

Kidnapping is usually conducted against a prominent individual(s) for a specific reason. The most common reasons are ransom, some demanded action such as release of a fellow terrorist; or the desire to publicize a demand or an issue. The risk to terrorist groups is generally lower in kidnapping as compared to hostage taking because the kidnapped victim is typically moved to a location controlled by the group. A kidnap victim may be killed once a terrorist group achieves its objective or perceives its demands will not be met. The success of kidnapping relies upon balancing the value of the victim to the government, organization, or social group with the costs of meeting the kidnappers' demands. Kidnapping (and hostage taking) can also be used as a means of financing the terrorist organization.

## Hostage Taking

Hostage taking is typically an overt seizure of people to gain publicity for a cause, political concessions, political asylum, release of prisoners, or ransom. Killing of hostages may occur once the terrorist group believes that it has fully exploited the media coverage from the situation. Unlike kidnapping victims, hostages usually are not prominent figures. Because of high risk from retaliation or CT operations, terrorists usually attempt to hold hostages in a neutral or friendly area.

## Hijacking

Hijacking involves the forceful commandeering of a conveyance. Normally associated with aircraft, it may also include ships, trains, vehicles or other forms of conveyance. The type of hijacking depends on the purpose of the terrorists. Purposes range from hostage taking activities, procuring a means of escape, or as a means of destruction.

## Raid or Ambush

A terrorist raid is similar in concept to a conventional military operation, but usually is conducted with smaller forces against targets marked for destruction, hijacking, or hostage/barricade operations. In some cases, the raid is designed to allow control of the target for the execution of another operation. An ambush is a surprise attack characterized by violent execution and speed of action. Its objective may be to cause mass casualties, assassinate an individual, or disrupt security operations.

## Seizure

Seizure of a critical element of infrastructure typically is a physical site of notoriety or importance to a target population, or a media or communications node that could gain widespread attention in one way or another (e.g., pirated broadcasts or disruption of service).

## Assassination

An assassination is a deliberate action to kill specific, usually prominent, individuals such as political leaders, notable citizens, collaborators, or particularly effective government officials, among others. A terrorist group will assassinate people it cannot intimidate, those who have left the group, people who support the "enemy," or people who have some symbolic significance to the enemy or world community. Terrorist groups may refer to these killings as "punishment" or "justice" as a way of legitimizing them. Assassinations are an effective psychological tool of terrorist tactics.

## WMD

This category acknowledges a broad range of chemical, biological, radiological, and nuclear (CBRN) weapons. A WMD capability would allow for catastrophic results and could be delivered through numerous means.

## Aircraft Threats

A man portable air defense system (MANPADS) is a significant threat in the hands of terrorists. There are a number of surface-to-air weapons that terrorists can use to attack aircraft. Weapons can be as simple as a rocket propelled grenade (RPG) normally used in surface-to-surface combat or as sophisticated as a Stinger or similar Igla air defense missile.

## Maritime Threats

Likely operations conducted by maritime terrorism include suicide attacks on commercial and military vessels, and hijacking for the following purposes: (1) carrying out a subsequent suicide attack on a ship or port (2) seeking ransom (3) smuggling weapons and explosives (4) simple piracy. (Graham Gerard Ong, "Next Stop, Maritime Terrorism," Viewpoints (12 September 2003): 1; available from http://www.iseas.edu.sg/viewpoint/ggosep03.pdf; Internet; accessed 2 April 2004.)

## Suicide Tactics

Suicide tactics are particular methods of delivering a bomb or conducting an assassination. The prevalent suicide tactic in use today involves an individual wearing or carrying an explosive device to a target and then detonating the bomb, or driving an explosive laden vehicle to a target and then detonating the bomb.

# III. Terrorist Methods, Target Types, and Their Psychological Impact

*Ref: Dr. Michael A. Bozarth, http://psychologyofterrorism.com (accessed Mar '16).*

### Difference Between Terror & Terrorism

Terror involves inflicting fear and anxiety on the victim(s) Terror can be goal oriented or gratuitous:

- produce "positive" political, social, economic, or religious change
- extortion for financial gain
- pathological desire to inflict suffering

Terrorism is directed towards "positive" change for a larger group, is seldom 'self-serving' and often 'sacrificing'. Criminal terror benefits the individual, extortion for financial or social gain, and often involves frank or borderline psychopathology.

Terrorists seek change through the use of fear and intimidation, but this seldom involves mentally disturbed individuals. Some people use terror gratuitously, and this usually involves mentally disturbed individuals.

## Terrorist's Method to Accomplish Goals

A terrorist's method is to instill "terror" in target audience to force capitulation by using the most terrifying means available, including kidnapping, assassination, IEDs, CBRNs by affecting many more people than directly affected by physical actions. Additionally, media and government-response play a critical role in the impact of terrorism.

Terrorist tactics probably work best against democracies, where targeting civilian populations has the greatest effect (i.e., civilians elect the government which sets the policy the terrorists wish to change). In contrast, "soft targets" have little influence on totalitarian government leadership, whereas "hard targets" can erode totalitarian control (through attrition) or even instigate a coup de tat.

### Relative Terror Value for Audience Population

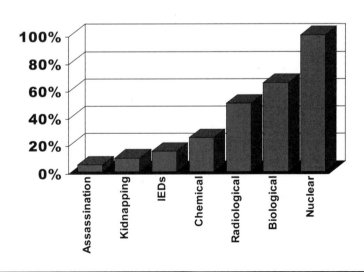

# Widening the "Target" to 'Hit the Mark'

Terrorists increase their range of targets to achieve their goal. Most terrorist organizations include civilian targets, often preferred over hard targets.

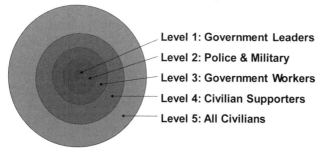

Level 1: Government Leaders
Level 2: Police & Military
Level 3: Government Workers
Level 4: Civilian Supporters
Level 5: All Civilians

## Terror Value of Soft Targets

Most people probably believe that hard targets have a higher impact value than soft targets. This is generally true for conventional military campaigns but this is not true for terrorist campaigns against democracies. Hard targets are generally protected and high value, but difficult to hit. Examples include:

- high-ranking government officials
- military bases and installations
- fortified police stations (e.g., Northern Ireland)

Targets are usually selected for maximum 'terror' impact. In addition to being easier to attack, soft targets actually have a higher terror value for the average citizen than do most hard targets (e.g., killing people "like me" makes the threat more personal and increases the individual terror value). Soft targets are unprotected, and are easier to hit. Examples:

- **Individuals**: local civic officials, celebrities, clergy, rich & famous, average citizens
- **Places with people**: shopping malls, schools, hospitals, theaters, sports venues, parks
- **Symbols**: historic monuments, national landmarks & parks

Terrorists seek to instill "terror" in target audience to force capitulation by using the most terrifying means available by affecting many more people than directly effected by physical actions. Terrorists strive to instill terror in a much larger audience. Media plays an important role.

### Tokyo Subway Attack
Sarin gas attack by Aum Shinrikyo cult, 20 March 1995

12 Killed

5,700 physically injured

9,000+ psychologically 'injured'

10,000's terrorized

### Beltway Snipers
Washington DC region, 02 - 24 October 2002

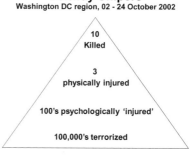

10 Killed

3 physically injured

100's psychologically 'injured'

100,000's terrorized

### 9-11 Attack on America
World Trade Center & Pentagon, 11 September 2001

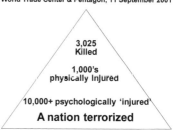

3,025 Killed

1,000's physically injured

10,000+ psychologically 'injured'

A nation terrorized

# IV. Terrorist Target Venues:
# Public Places, Businesses, Workplaces

*Ref: Miller, Erin. "Mass-Fatality, Coordinated Attacks Worldwide, and Terrorism in France."*
*Background Report, START (2015). Access at: http://www.start.umd.edu/publications*

Workplace violence is recognized as a specific category of violent crime that calls for distinct responses from employers, law enforcement, and the community. Contrary to popular opinion, sensational multiple homicides represent a very small number of workplace violence incidents.

The reality -- as evidenced by the tragic events of 9/11, Charlie Hedbo, San Bernandino, and the Paris attacks, just to name a few -- is that a large number of terrorist attacks occur in public venues that are actually workplaces. This brings to light a different perspective of workplace violence than just the traditional law enforcement definition.

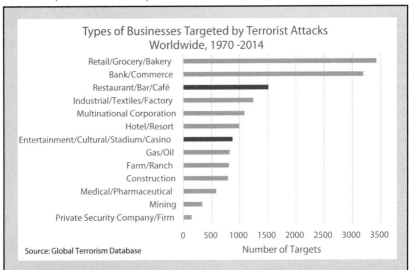

Types of Businesses Targeted by Terrorist Attacks Worldwide, 1970 -2014

Source: Global Terrorism Database · Number of Targets

*The terrorist attacks that occurred in New York, Washington, D.C., and Pennsylvania on September 11, 2001, were a tragic reminder to the Nation of the threat posed by international terrorism. With the exception of the attack on the Pentagon, the targets chosen by the terrorists were not military in nature, but were workplaces where thousands of people work every day to support their families and their country.*

*Workplace violence was put in a new context that day. Prior to 9/11, this type of violence was viewed as perpetrated by disgruntled employees, customers, or a domestic violence/stalking relationship that surfaces at a workplace. Since that time, America's workplaces have to be prepared not only to face the more traditional internal workplace threats, but now have to consider the external threat of terrorism.*

*Robert S. Mueller, III from "Workplace Violence: Issues in Response", 2003 Director of the FBI (2001-2013)*

The attacks in Paris reportedly targeted several "soft" targets where large numbers of civilians gather without extraordinary security measures in place. The targets included several restaurants, a theater where a concert was being held, and a sports arena where a soccer match was being held.

The Global Terrorism Database classifies these particular types of targets as businesses, subcategorized as "restaurants/bars/cafés" and entertainment/cultural/stadiums/casinos." Between 1970 and 2014, more than 2,300 of these types of targets were attacked by terrorists. Among the most deadly attacks on these restaurant/entertainment targets were two coordinated attacks targeting tourists at Paddy's Bar and the Sari Club in Kuta, Indonesia in October 2002. These attacks, which were claimed by al-Qa'ida and also attributed to members of Jemaah Islamiyah, killed more than 200 people and wounded more than 300 others. Later that same month, Chechen rebels attacked Dubrovka Theater in Moscow, holding more than 900 people hostage. After a three-day standoff, Russian special forces filled the building with an unidentified gas intended to subdue the perpetrators.

Over this entire 45-years, the most terrorist attacks against restaurant/entertainment targets took place in Iraq (342), the United Kingdom (167), Spain (131), Colombia (122), and France (118). However, nearly all of the attacks in Iraq took place in the 21st century and were carried out by ISIL and its predecessors. In contrast, attacks in Western Europe and Latin America were somewhat more concentrated in the 1970s, 1980s, and 1990s, and were most commonly attributed to perpetrator organizations like ETA, FARC, PKK, IRA, and the FLNC.

# Attacks Against Transportation Targets

*Miller, Erin. Terrorism in Belgium and Western Europe; Attacks against Transportation Targets; Coordinated Terrorist Attacks." Background Report, START (2016).*

In the aftermath of the March 22, 2016 attacks in Brussels, Belgium, START compiled the following statistics from the Global Terrorism Database. Early reports on the Brussels attacks indicate that the perpetrators executed a series of coordinated attacks targeting an airport and a subway station with explosives. Two of the attacks were reportedly carried out by suicide bombers. More than 30 people were killed, and more than 200 people were injured across both locations. The Islamic State of Iraq and the Levant (ISIL) claimed responsibility for the attack.

More than 7,400 terrorist attacks worldwide between 1970 and 2014 targeted some form of transportation, including airports and aircraft. These types of targets made up 5.3 percent of all terrorist attacks, and 9.1 percent of all terrorist attacks on civilian targets (excluding attacks against government, military, or police).

- Recently, attacks on transportation targets have been somewhat less prevalent, comprising 3.0 percent of all attacks and 5.5 percent of attacks against civilian targets between 2010 and 2014.
- The tactic of targeting of transportation infrastructure was not used uniformly around the world. Among countries that experienced at least 50 terrorist attacks against civilian targets between 1970 and 2014, the highest proportion of attacks against transportation targets took place in China (52.1%) and the lowest was in Central African Republic (1.1%).
- Terrorist attacks against transportation targets were slightly less likely to be carried out by suicide attackers (2.0% of attacks), compared to attacks against other types of targets (2.7%).
- Terrorist attacks against transportation targets worldwide were slightly more likely to be part of coordinated, multi-part attacks (13.5 percent of attacks), compared to attacks against other types of targets (12.5%).

The types of transportation most frequently targeted in terrorist attacks worldwide were buses and trains, which comprised 61.6 percent of all transportation targets worldwide between 1970 and 2014. In contrast, airports represented 6.4 percent of all transportation targets, and subway systems made up in 1.9 percent of all transportation targets.

The average lethality of terrorist attacks against transportation targets between 1970 and 2014 was 2.8 deaths per attack. This is 22 percent higher than the average lethality of attacks against other types of targets (2.3 deaths per attack).

# V. Mass-Fatality Terrorist Attacks

Ref: Miller, Erin. "Mass-Fatality, Coordinated Attacks Worldwide, and Terrorism in France." Background Report, START (2015). Access the full report at: http://www.start. umd.edu/publications

On November 13, 2015 assailants carried out a series of coordinated attacks at locations in Paris, France, including a theater where a concert was being held, several restaurants, and a sporting event. These attacks reportedly killed more than 120 people and wounded more than 350 others. The Islamic State of Iraq and the Levant (ISIL) claimed responsibility for the attack.[1] To provide contextual information on coordinated, mass-fatality attacks, as well as terrorism in France and the attack patterns of ISIL, START has compiled the following information from the Global Terrorism Database.

Between 1970 and 2014, there have been 176 occasions on which terrorist attacks killed more than 100 people (excluding perpetrators), in a particular country on a particular day. This includes both isolated attacks, multiple attacks, and multi-part, coordinated attacks. The first such event took place in 1978, when an arson attack targeting the Cinema Rex Theater in Abadan, Iran killed more than 400 people.

Since the Cinema Rex attack, and until 2013, 4.2 such mass-fatality terrorist events happened per year, on average. In 2014, the number increased dramatically when 26 mass-fatality terrorist events took place in eight different countries: Afghanistan (1), Central African Republic (1), Iraq (9), Nigeria (9), Pakistan (1), South Sudan (1), Syria (3), and Ukraine (1).

The occurrence of a series of attacks on a particular day that result in large numbers of casualties may or may not be indicative of explicit coordination among perpetrators. Nearly half (11) of the 26 days in 2014 in which more than 100 victims were killed by terrorists in a single country involved the Islamic State of Iraq and the Levant (ISIL) as perpetrators. In Nigeria, all nine of the highly lethal days involved the perpetrator group Boko Haram. Other perpetrator groups responsible for attacks on these high-lethality days include the Taliban in Afghanistan, militia groups in the Central African Republic, Tehrik-i-Taliban Pakistan (TTP), Sudan People's Liberation Movement in Opposition (SPLM-IO), al-Nusrah Front, and the Luhansk People's Republic and the Donetsk People's Republic, both in Ukraine.

Between 2000 and 2014, there were 83 days on which more than 100 people were killed by terrorist attacks in a single country. These attacks took place in 25 countries in North and South America, Europe, the Middle East, Africa, and Asia; however, they were especially concentrated in Iraq and Nigeria.

Although Western Europe has historically experienced thousands of terrorist attacks, highly lethal attacks like the recent events in Paris are extremely unusual. The deadliest terrorist attacks in Western Europe between 2000 and 2014 took place in Madrid, Spain, on March 11, 2004 when assailants attacked six different transportation targets with explosives. Four of the devices detonated, killing 191 people and wounding more than 1,800.

On July 22, 2011, Anders Breivik killed 77 people and wounded 75 in terrorist attacks involving explosives and firearms in Oslo and Utøya, Norway.

| Number of Times more than 100 People were Killed by Terrorist Attacks on a Single Day in a Single Country, 2000-2014 | |
|---|---|
| Iraq | 29 |
| Nigeria | 13 |
| Pakistan | 6 |
| India | 4 |
| Syria | 4 |
| Nepal | 3 |
| Afghanistan | 2 |
| Angola | 2 |
| Russia | 2 |
| Sudan | 2 |
| Yemen | 2 |
| Central African Republic | 1 |
| Chad | 1 |
| China | 1 |
| Colombia | 1 |
| Democratic Republic of the Congo | 1 |
| Indonesia | 1 |
| Philippines | 1 |
| Somalia | 1 |
| South Sudan | 1 |
| Spain | 1 |
| Sri Lanka | 1 |
| Uganda | 1 |
| Ukraine | 1 |
| United States | 1 |

Source: Global Terrorism Database

Preliminary data from 2015 suggest that the unusual frequency of mass casualty terrorist attacks in 2014 has continued. Between January and June 2015 there were 11 occasions in which terrorist attacks killed more than 100 people in a single country on a single day. Of these events, which took place in Iraq (2), Kenya (1), Nigeria (3), Syria (4), and Yemen (1), seven involved ISIL or Islamic State provinces

[1] Reuters. (2015, November 14). Timeline of Paris attacks according to public prosecutor. Retrieved on November 14, 2015 from http://www.reuters.com/article/2015/11/14/us-france-shooting-timeline-idUSKCN0T31BS20151114

# VI. Coordinated Attacks

*Ref: Miller, Erin. "Mass-Fatality, Coordinated Attacks Worldwide, and Terrorism in France." Background Report, START (2015). Access the full report at: http://www.start. umd.edu/publications*

Like the recent attacks in Paris, some of the highly lethal terrorist attacks described above were carried out as part of coordinated events in which perpetrators execute multiple attacks simultaneously, or nearly simultaneously, typically in a single country or city. Between 2000 and 2014, 14 percent of all terrorist attacks that occurred worldwide were conducted in coordination with other attacks.

On average, individual attacks that were carried out as part of a coordinated event were slightly more deadly, causing 2.84 total fatalities on average, compared to isolated attacks, which caused 2.35 total fatalities on average. The average number of perpetrator fatalities among attacks that were part of a coordinated event were slightly higher as well—0.39 perpetrator deaths per attack, compared to 0.33 for isolated attacks.

## Locations

More than 10,000 coordinated terrorist attacks took place in 104 countries between 2000 and 2014. Much like terrorism in general, these attacks were concentrated among a small number of countries. More than half of all coordinated attacks (54%) took place in Iraq, Pakistan, India, Nigeria, and Afghanistan.

Among countries that experienced more than 50 attacks between 2000 and 2014, France had the highest proportion of attacks that were carried out as part of multi-part, coordinated events, with 40 percent. The majority of these (87%) were carried out in Corsica by separatists including the Corsican National Liberation Front (FLNC), causing property damage but no deaths and few injuries.

| Lethality of Coordinated Terrorist Attacks among Countries with the Highest Percentage of Coordinated Terrorist Attacks, 2000-2014 | | | | | |
|---|---|---|---|---|---|
| Country | Total Attacks | % Coordinated Attacks | Total Fatalities | Perpetrator Fatalities | Victim Fatalities |
| France | 331 | 40% | 0 | 0 | 0 |
| South Sudan | 57 | 35% | 763 | 293 | 470 |
| Bangladesh | 480 | 35% | 27 | 5 | 22 |
| Nigeria | 2170 | 33% | 4592 | 776 | 3816 |
| Myanmar | 123 | 32% | 26 | 0 | 26 |
| Spain | 412 | 29% | 198 | 5 | 193 |
| Indonesia | 472 | 29% | 318 | 17 | 301 |
| Chile | 63 | 29% | 0 | 0 | 0 |
| China | 111 | 28% | 196 | 118 | 78 |
| Greece | 442 | 27% | 0 | 0 | 0 |
| Macedonia | 101 | 27% | 1 | 0 | 1 |
| Cameroon | 79 | 27% | 56 | 43 | 13 |
| South Africa | 69 | 26% | 2 | 0 | 2 |
| United States | 289 | 25% | 3009 | 20 | 2989 |
| Burundi | 159 | 24% | 108 | 34 | 74 |
| Ukraine | 918 | 24% | 104 | 33 | 71 |
| Syria | 834 | 22% | 1240 | 233 | 1007 |
| Egypt | 743 | 22% | 105 | 8 | 97 |
| Italy | 97 | 22% | 0 | 0 | 0 |
| Ethiopia | 53 | 21% | 16 | 0 | 16 |

Source: Global Terrorism Database

## Perpetrators

The perpetrator of the attack was unidentified for 40 percent of all coordinated terrorist attacks that took place worldwide between 2000 and 2014. The remaining 60 percent were disproportionately carried out by a relatively small number of perpetrator groups. While the recent attack in Paris shares similarities with the November 2008 attack in Mumbai, India, the perpetrator group in that attack, Lashkar-e-Taiba (LeT), is not among the most frequent perpetrators of coordinated attacks.

In contrast, ISIL, under its current incarnation, carried out more than 750 coordinated attacks during this time period—specifically in 2013 and 2014. However, this is a conservative assessment because the Global Terrorism Database records the names of perpetrator organizations at the time of the attack. Thus, it is important to note that al-Qa'ida in Iraq (AQI), ISIL's predecessor, carried out at least 400 coordinated attacks as well. Also, 25 coordinated attacks were attributed to the Islamic State of Iraq (ISI), another identity previously assumed by ISIL, and several other coordinated attacks were carried out by provinces of the Islamic State, including the Sinai Province and the Tripoli Province.

Other organizations that have carried out more than a hundred coordinated attacks include Boko Haram in Nigeria, the Taliban in Afghanistan, the Communist Party of India-Maoist and unaffiliated Maoists in India, al-Shabaab primarily in Somalia and Kenya, Tehriki-i-Taliban Pakistan, the Revolutionary Armed Forces of Columbia (FARC), the New People's Army (NPA) in the Philippines, Fulani militants in Nigeria and the Central African Republic, and al-Qa'ida in the Arabian Peninsula (AQAP).

In addition, at least 50 coordinated attacks between 2000 and 2014 were carried out by individuals who reportedly were not affiliated with a particular terrorist organization or group. These attacks took place in 10 countries; however, 30 of them (60%) occurred in the United States and were carried out in pursuit of a wide variety of ideological goals. Eighteen of the attacks were part of a series in which a single perpetrator motivated by anti-government sentiment planted pipe bombs in mailboxes in five U.S. states.

## Weapons: Explosives and Firearms

The recent attacks in Paris reportedly involved both explosives and firearms. These two types of weapons are those most commonly used in terrorist attacks worldwide. Between 2000 and 2014, explosives were used in 58 percent of all terrorist attacks, and firearms were used in 34 percent of all terrorist attacks. However both firearms and explosives were used much more rarely—in less than 4 percent of all attacks.

Attacks that involved firearms were somewhat more deadly than those involving explosives, causing 3.1 fatalities on average (including perpetrator deaths), compared to 2.4. Despite the potential for explosives to cause mass casualties in certain cases, they were also more frequently used in attacks that are non-lethal (57%), either because they targeted only property or were unsuccessful at causing human casualties. In comparison, 24 percent of all attacks involving only firearms worldwide between 2000 and 2014 were non-lethal.

Attacks that involved both explosives and firearms caused, on average, 6.8 deaths per attack. This rate of lethality is 2.8 times that of all attacks overall, and attacks involving explosives. It is 2.2 times the average lethality of attacks involving firearms.

# Mass Casualty Explosives Attacks in Iraq and Afghanistan

*Ref: Miller, Erin. "Mass Casualty Explosives Attacks in Iraq and Afghanistan." Background Report, START (Jun 2017). Access the full report at: http://www.start.umd.edu/publications*

In the aftermath of a series of deadly terrorist attacks in Baghdad and Kabul involving vehicle bombs, START has compiled information from the Global Terrorism Database (GTD) on terrorism in Iraq and Afghanistan and the use of explosives—particularly vehicle-borne explosives and suicide tactics—in terrorist attacks.

## Global Context

As illustrated in the figure below, terrorist violence in Iraq and Afghanistan has accounted for a substantial proportion of terrorism worldwide in the 21st century. The total number of deaths caused by terrorist attacks in these two countries comprised nearly half (46%) of all fatalities worldwide between 2004 and 2016.1 During this period, 13 percent of the fatalities from terrorist attacks in Iraq and 15 percent of the fatalities from terrorist attacks in Afghanistan resulted from attacks against combatant targets.

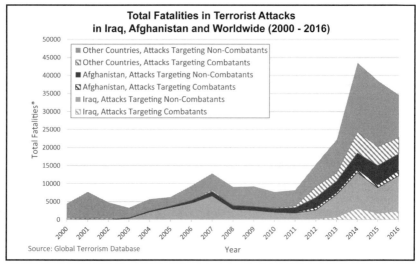

**Total Fatalities in Terrorist Attacks in Iraq, Afghanistan and Worldwide (2000 - 2016)**

Legend:
- Other Countries, Attacks Targeting Non-Combatants
- Other Countries, Attacks Targeting Combatants
- Afghanistan, Attacks Targeting Non-Combatants
- Afghanistan, Attacks Targeting Combatants
- Iraq, Attacks Targeting Non-Combatants
- Iraq, Attacks Targeting Combatants

Total Fatalities*

Source: Global Terrorism Database     Year

The peak in 2014 coincides with the sharp increase in terrorist violence carried out by the Islamic State of Iraq and the Levant (ISIL), particularly in Iraq, and by the Taliban in Afghanistan. Terrorist attacks and total fatalities from attacks attributed to the Taliban in Afghanistan continued to increase in 2015 before declining slightly in 2016. In contrast, the terrorist activity of ISIL in Iraq declined slightly in 2015 before increasing again in 2016. The global pattern during this time period indicates that the number of terrorist attacks and the number of resulting fatalities declined in 2015 and 2016, largely as a result of patterns of activity outside Iraq and Afghanistan, including substantial decreases in terrorist violence in Nigeria and Pakistan.

## Types of Targets

Although terrorism in Iraq and Afghanistan between 2004 and 2016 took place in the context of war and insurgency, civilian (non-military) targets represent the majority of targets of terrorist attacks in both countries. The figure below shows the types of targets of terrorist attacks in Iraq and Afghanistan during this time period. The GTD records up to three targets per attack; however, only 8 percent of attacks in Iraq and 12 percent of attacks in Afghanistan involved more than one distinct target.

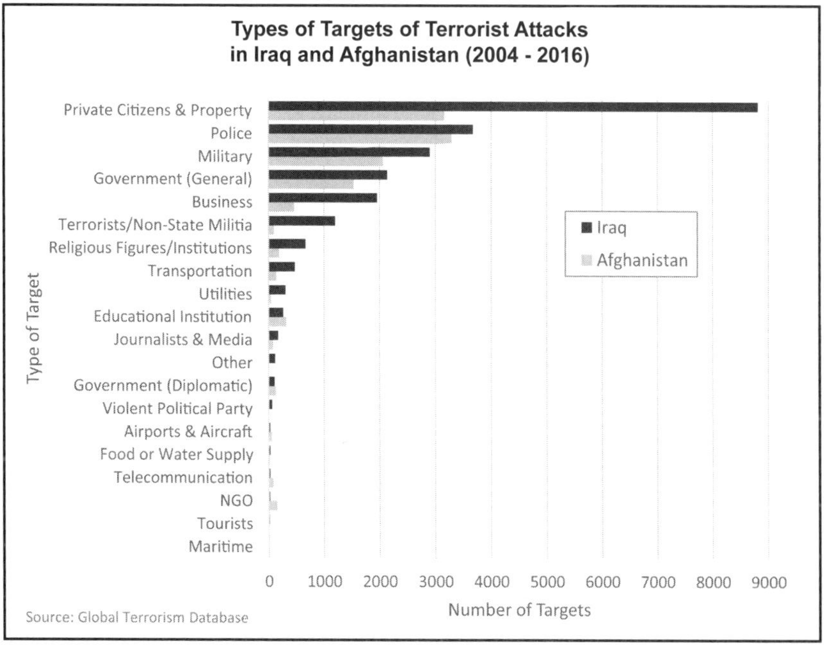
Types of Targets of Terrorist Attacks
in Iraq and Afghanistan (2004 - 2016)
Private Citizens & Property
Police
Military
Government (General)
Business
Terrorists/Non-State Militia
Religious Figures/Institutions
Transportation
Utilities
Educational Institution
Journalists & Media
Other
Government (Diplomatic)
Violent Political Party
Airports & Aircraft
Food or Water Supply
Telecommunication
NGO
Tourists
Maritime
Type of Target
Iraq
Afghanistan
0
1000
2000
3000
4000
5000
6000
7000
8000
9000
Number of Targets
Source: Global Terrorism Database

In Iraq, more than one-third (38%) of all targets of terrorism were classified as private citizens and property. These targets were most frequently unspecified civilians; open marketplaces or plazas; personal vehicles; or private citizens targeted according to their religious identity. In Afghanistan, targets classified as private citizens also included people who were targeted according to their occupation, such as construction workers and engineers, or doctors and other medical personnel, particularly those involved in vaccination programs. In certain cases, the Taliban claimed responsibility for attacks targeting private citizens and suggested that the victims were spies or criminals.

Terrorist attacks against police in Iraq and Afghanistan most frequently involved security forces, police patrols, and police checkpoints; however, attacks targeting police buildings (headquarters or stations) were disproportionately deadly. In Iraq in particular, attacks targeting police buildings resulted in twice as many deaths per attack (6.1) than attacks against police targets in general (3.0). Dozens of attacks in Iraq targeted police recruits and training facilities, resulting in more than 700 deaths and more than 1,300 injuries.

Government targets of terrorism in both Iraq and Afghanistan were typically either government personnel (other than police or military personnel) or government buildings/facilities. In Afghanistan, terrorist attacks targeting election-related entities such as polling stations and election officials were also relatively common. In Iraq, however, terrorist attacks frequently targeted politicians and political party gatherings. Diplomatic facilities and personnel (listed separately in Figure 2) comprised 5 percent of all government targets of terrorist attacks in Iraq, and 8 percent of all government targets of terrorist attacks in Afghanistan.

Terrorist attacks against business targets in Afghanistan were considerably less common than attacks on business targets in Iraq. In Afghanistan, these targets most frequently included construction firms and personnel, private security firms and personnel, and hospitals/clinics. Retail stores, hotels, banks, restaurants, and entertainment venues combined comprised one-fifth (20%) of all business targets in Afghanistan. In Iraq, however, these same types of businesses where civilian crowds often gather represented more than half (53%) of all businesses targeted in terrorist attacks.

Continued on next page

Continued on next page

# Mass Casualty Explosives Attacks in Iraq and Afghanistan (Cont.)

*Ref: Miller, Erin. "Mass Casualty Explosives Attacks in Iraq and Afghanistan." Background Report, START (Jun 2017). Access the full report at: http://www.start.umd.edu/publications*

## Attacks Involving Explosives

Between 1970 and 2016, more than 170,000 terrorist attacks took place around the world and more than half of these attacks (52%) involved the use of an explosive device. Explosives used in these attacks included suicide and vehicle bombs as well as roadside bombs, grenades, and rockets.

| | | Total Explosives Attacks | Total Attacks | Percent Explosives Attacks | Rank Total Attacks |
|---|---|---|---|---|---|
| Country | Region | | | | |
| Iraq | Middle East | 17,079 | 22,131 | 77.2 % | 1 |
| Pakistan | South Asia | 7,709 | 13,631 | 56.6 % | 2 |
| Afghanistan | South Asia | 6,195 | 11,304 | 54.8 % | 3 |
| India | South Asia | 4,795 | 10,958 | 43.8 % | 4 |
| Colombia | South America | 3,250 | 8,162 | 39.8 % | 5 |
| Peru | South America | 3,175 | 6,087 | 52.2 % | 7 |
| Philippines | Southeast Asia | 2,207 | 6,209 | 35.6 % | 6 |
| United Kingdom | Western Europe | 2,204 | 5,094 | 43.3 % | 9 |
| El Salvador | Central America | 2,103 | 5,320 | 39.5 % | 8 |
| France | Western Europe | 2,029 | 2,643 | 76.8 % | 19 |

**Ten Countries that Experienced the Most Terrorist Attacks Involving Explosives (1970 - 2016)**

Although 189 countries experienced a terrorist attack involving the use of an explosive device between 1970 and 2016, these attacks were concentrated geographically. More than half (57%) of all explosives attacks occurred in just 10 countries. These countries are listed in the tabel above in order of the overall prevalence of attacks involving explosives. The table also includes the total number of terrorist attacks in each country, the percent of attacks in each country that involved an explosive device, and each country's worldwide rank in terms of total attacks.

The five highest-ranked countries (Iraq, Pakistan, Afghanistan, India, and Colombia) were ranked identically in terms of the number of terrorist attacks they experienced overall. More than 19 percent of all attacks involving explosive devices occurred in Iraq alone. In comparison, 13 percent of all terrorist attacks worldwide took place in Iraq.

The 10 highest-ranked countries differ in terms of the percentage of attacks that involved explosive devices. Whereas more than 75 percent of all attacks in Iraq and France involved the use of an explosive device, the method was far less prevalent in Colombia, Philippines, and El Salvador, where it represented less than 40 percent of all attacks. This suggests that attacks involving the use of firearms, arson, or other weapons were more prevalent in these countries.

The countries in this list represent different regions around the world. Three countries (Pakistan, Afghanistan, and India) are located in South Asia, two countries (Colombia and Peru) are in South America, two countries (United Kingdom and France) are in Western Europe, and one country is in each of the Middle East (Iraq), Southeast Asia (Philippines), and Central America (El Salvador).

## Casualties/Lethality

Attacks involving explosive devices were collectively less lethal, on average, compared with other types of attacks. While attacks involving explosives killed 1.7 people on average, other methods claimed 2.5 lives on average. There are several potential explanations for this disparity. For example, it may be that although attacks involving explosives have the potential to be extremely deadly, they were often used to target property rather than people. Alternatively, perhaps attacks involving explosives are more complex to execute and as a result they were more likely to be unsuccessful, even if the perpetrators intended for the attack to be deadly.

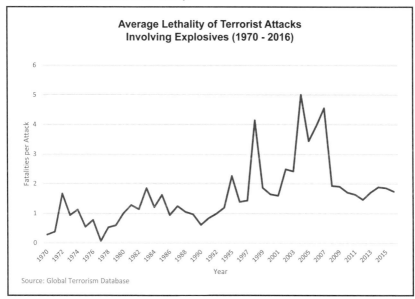

**Average Lethality of Terrorist Attacks Involving Explosives (1970 - 2016)**

Source: Global Terrorism Database

One-third (34%) of all attacks involving explosive devices between 1970 and 2016 resulted in at least one fatality, compared to more than half (58%) of attacks that did not include explosives. However, among attacks that were lethal, those that involved explosives were deadlier than those that did not. For attacks in which at least one person was killed, those involving explosive devices resulted in 5.0 deaths on average, compared to 4.3 deaths, on average, in attacks in which the perpetrators relied on other types of weapons.

The average lethality of all attacks involving explosive devices increased over time, as shown in Figure 3. From 1970 to 1994, the average lethality for these attacks never exceeded two people killed per attack. However, the average lethality increased steadily from 1990 through 1998 and then again from 2001 through 2007. The average lethality of attacks involving explosive devices peaked with more than five people killed per attack in 2004. Since 2008, the average lethality of terrorist attacks involving explosives stabilized at fewer than two people killed per attack.

## Tactics

Attacks involving explosive devices represented a diverse set of tactics used by perpetrators of terrorism, including the use of roadside bombs, grenades, or rockets, as well as suicide bombings and vehicle bombings. These different types of delivery mechanisms for explosive devices resulted in somewhat different outcomes in terms of lethality. In general, suicide bombings killed 7.9 people on average, and injured 19.9 others. In vehicle bombings, 4.3 people were killed and 12.6 people were injured on average. For vehicle bombings, those figures were influenced by the high lethality of explosives-laden vehicles driven by suicide bombers, which killed an average of 8.0 people and injured an additional 21.6 people. In contrast, other explosives-laden vehicle attacks killed 2.8 people and injured 9.4, on average. This suggests that the combination of suicide bombers and vehicles was the most lethal strategy.

Terrorist TTPs

# VII. Terrorist Attack Threats to U.S. Forces

*Ref: U.S. Army TRADOC G2 Handbook No. 1 (Version 5.0), A Military Guide to Terrorism in the Twenty-First Century (Aug '07), pp. 4-4 to 4-12.*

Why attack U.S. military forces? During the twenty year period from 1980 to 1999, thirteen specifically domestic military targets were attacked by terrorist activities. Large numbers of U.S. military forces located in varied areas of the world make military forces a lucrative target. Accessibility is one key factor. For example, during the 1970s to 1990s U.S. military installations and personnel were frequently targeted in by anti-NATO European terrorists and by state sponsored terrorists acting on behalf of a variety of regimes. These attacks generally struck at military targets that were not engaged in hostilities but were accessible to terrorists of the geographic region. Today, the expansive presence of U.S. military forces is clearly evident in the Middle East and Persian Gulf region, and many other regions of the world due to political and economic factors as a global superpower.

Several terrorist rationales exist for targeting U.S. military forces. Whether terrorism comes from an individual with a single issue concern or a terrorist organization with global reach, many factors are considered in target selection, vulnerability analysis, and risk management before attacking a target. With the variety of terrorist motivations and goals, the reasons to target U.S. military forces or individuals are equally varied. The most common rationales are:

## Identify Target Accessibility
Presence of military members, units, and activities in large numbers makes an inviting target. Presence of U.S. forces in some regions of the world may offend particular political or religious sensibilities and can be presented as a justification for terrorist attack.

## Symbolic Value
Commitment of military forces is a significant indicator of national interest and carries major political consequences. Targeting military forces can often achieve a greater notoriety for terrorists than targeting civilian targets such as diplomats, commercial businessmen, or government officials and facilities.

## Demonstrate Organizational Capability
Terrorist action that demonstrates the capability to negate U.S. military operations security and force protection can promote individual terrorist or organizational terrorist agenda when they attack U.S. military forces.

## Delay or Prevent Movements
Disruption of transportation may take place by sabotage or direct attack upon the unit being transported and its mode of transportation. Methods of attack would be selected depending upon their effectiveness versus the mode of unit transport. Air, rail and sea are normal modes of transport for long voyages or distances, but may also be motor transportation means such as buses or organic unit vehicles to move to a destination. Weapons likely to be employed include bombs, antitank rockets, rocket propelled grenades, and small arms gunfire. In some cases, sophisticated shoulder fired missiles could be used. Sabotage may be designed to produce maximum casualties in the ensuing crash, derailment, or fire. In January 2003, intelligence sources detected the targeting of chartered aircraft participating in the build up of forces against Iraq. In the past, U.S. domestic terrorists have derailed U.S. passenger and cargo trains. Attacks on ships in port and at sea are within the capabilities of selected transnational and international terror groups.

Destroying facilities such as docks, airfields, refueling facilities, and cargo terminals at intermediate stops or at the final destination is another way for terrorists to prevent or delay deployment. Attacking critical private infrastructure through physical and cyber means could cause similar effects. Adding depth to a conflict does not necessarily require the projection of physical terrorist assets and weapons into more distant countries. If timed to coincide with the arrival or departure of military units, such destructive attacks could cause significant casualties.

## Degrade Social Environment

Terrorists prefer an environment that is chaotic. A fluid, poorly policed or uncontrolled situation often permits normally suspicious activities to go unnoticed. However, hostile environments put military forces on their guard, reduce the opportunities to get close to targets without being challenged or detained, and increase the difficulty of achieving any degree of operational surprise.

## Disrupt Economic Environment

Other terrorist incidents indicate the potential for disrupting deployments or materiel in transit. The tensions of political, environmental, and economic impacts add to the specific damage or destruction of an incident.

## Influence U.S. Policy

Terrorists can attack U.S. military forces with the intent to force a change in U.S. policy. The desire to discredit U.S. Federal, state, and local governments can result in military members, units, or infrastructure being targeted by domestic terror groups.

**Table 4-1.**

| Terrorist Targeting U.S. Military Forces | | |
|---|---|---|
| **Target Environment** | **Attack Means** | **Attack Rationale** |
| **Deployed** Forces | ◆ Threat-Hoax<br>◆ Arson<br>◆ Sabotage<br>◆ Kidnapping | **Select Accessible Target**<br>within means of terrorist cell<br><br>**Diminish Symbolic Prestige**<br>of nation-coalition-alliance<br><br>**Gain Notoriety**<br>for terrorist cell or ideology |
| **In-Transit** Forces | ◆ Hostage Taking<br>◆ Assassination<br>◆ Bombing<br>◆ Gunfire-RPG | **Delay-Prevent Movements**<br>of US military forces<br><br>**Reduce Operational Capability**<br>of US military forces |
| **Institutional** Forces | ◆ Raid-Ambush<br>◆ Seizure<br>◆ Aerial-MANPADS<br>◆ WMD | **Degrade Social Stability-Trust**<br>of nation and region<br><br>**Disrupt Economic Confidence**<br>of nation-supporting nations<br><br>**Influence Political Policy**<br>of nation-supporting nations |

newest, most capable radio appropriate for the operation. The only real limitation is funding and availability of the equipment when it is needed. As with equipment, terrorist organizations choose weapons that are tailored to the particular operation. If a particular weapon Is not available, the terrorist is adept at creating a weapon from available sources to suit the mission.

Although several types of operations may satisfy a particular objective, terrorist groups often develop expertise in one or more types of operations, and less specialization in others.

# VIII. Terrorist IO & Public Relations Activities

The Internet provides terrorists and extremists the means to spread their radical ideology, an ad hoc means of operational connectivity, and a link to the full-media spectrum for public relations. The Internet facilitates their recruiting, training, logistic support, planning, fund-raising, etc. The internet is also a powerful tool to conduct the equivalent of media facilitated IO against the United States and PNs. Although not yet typical, terrorists may employ electronic attacks to disrupt communications, or banking, or to project disinformation and propaganda in support of their cause. From the terrorist perspective, media coverage is an important measure of the success of a terrorist act and a means of countering US and PN IO and SC activities. News reports, streaming videos on websites, blogs, and editorials can amplify (some unwittingly) the psychological effects of a terrorist incident and aid terrorists in publicizing the event globally to a much wider audience, and potentially gain further recognition of their radical ideology.

*See pp. 3-25 to 3-28 for further discussion.*

*(Shutterstock.com)*

# IV. Active Shooters & Ideological Homicides

Editor's Note: Although not always classified or perceived as terrorist incidents, the following related topics and special report by the FBI's Critical Incident Response Group (CIRG) and START are presented as related to discussion/examination of terrorism.

## I. Active Shooters

*Ref: Blair, J. Pete, and Schweit, Katherine W. (2014). A Study of Active Shooter Incidents, 2000 - 2013. Texas State University and Federal Bureau of Investigation, U.S. Department of Justice, Washington D.C. 2014.*

Active shooter is a term used by law enforcement to describe a situation in which a shooting is in progress and an aspect of the crime may affect the protocols used in responding to and reacting at the scene of the incident. Unlike a defined crime, such as a murder or mass killing, the active aspect inherently implies that both law enforcement personnel and citizens have the potential to affect the outcome of the event based upon their responses.

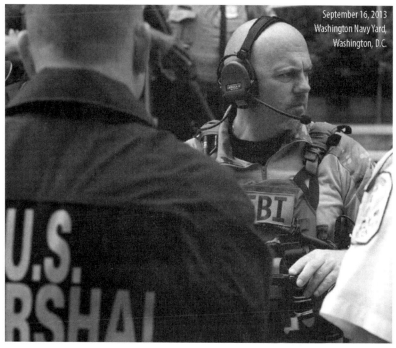

September 16, 2013
Washington Navy Yard,
Washington, D.C.

*(Sept 2013 Washington Navy Yard Shooting/Shane T. McCoy/U.S. Marshals)*

The agreed-upon definition of an active shooter by U.S. government agencies— including the White House, U.S. Department of Justice/FBI, U.S. Department of Education, and U.S. Department of Homeland Security/Federal Emergency Management Agency—is "an individual actively engaged in killing or attempting to kill people in a confined and populated area."

# Active Shooter Incidents (2000-2013)

*Ref: Blair, J. Pete, and Schweit, Katherine W. (2014). A Study of Active Shooter Incidents, 2000 - 2013. Texas State University and Federal Bureau of Investigation, U.S. Department of Justice, Washington D.C. 2014, pp. 6-8.*

In 2013, the president signed into law the Investigative Assistance for Violent Crimes Act of 2012, which granted the attorney general the authority to assist in the investigation of "violent acts and shootings occurring in a place of public use" and in the investigation of "mass killings and attempted mass killings at the request of an appropriate law enforcement official of a state or political subdivision."

## Findings

In this study, the FBI identified 160 active shooter incidents, noting they occurred in small and large towns, in urban and rural areas, and in 40 of 50 states and the District of Columbia.

Though incidents occurred primarily in commerce and educational environments (70.0%), they also occurred on city streets, on military and other government properties, and in private residences, health care facilities, and houses of worship. The shooters victimized young and old, male and female, family members, and people of all races, cultures, and religions.

The findings establish an increasing frequency of incidents annually. During the first 7 years included in the study, an average of 6.4 incidents occurred annually. In the last 7 years of the study, that average increased to 16.4 incidents annually. This trend reinforces the need to remain vigilant regarding prevention efforts and for law enforcement to aggressively train to better respond to—and help communities recover from—active shooter incidents.

The findings also reflect the damage that can occur in a matter of minutes. In 63 incidents where the duration of the incident could be ascertained, 44 (70%) of 63 incidents ended in 5 minutes or less, with 23 ending in 2 minutes or less. Even when law enforcement was present or able to respond within minutes, civilians often had to make life and death decisions, and, therefore, should be engaged in training and discussions on decisions they may face.

### Incidents Annually

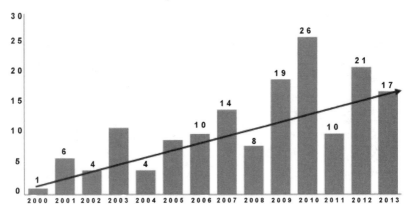

As expected, therefore, many incidents ended before police arrived. Of the 160 incidents, at least 107 (66.9%) ended before police arrived and could engage the shooter, either because a citizen intervened, the shooter fled, or the shooter committed suicide or was killed by someone at the scene.

# Snapshot of Active Shooter Incidents

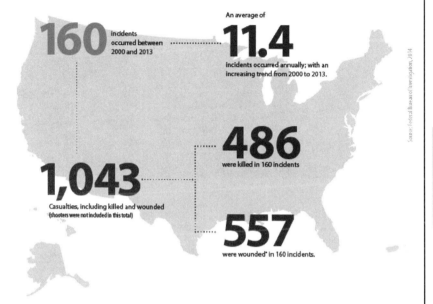

**160** incidents occurred between 2000 and 2013

An average of

**11.4** incidents occurred annually; with an increasing trend from 2000 to 2013.

*Source: Federal Bureau of Investigation, 2014*

**486** were killed in 160 incidents

**1,043** Casualties, including killed and wounded (shooters were not included in this total)

**557** were wounded* in 160 incidents.

## Incidents

- An average of 11.4 incidents occurred annually.
- An average of 6.4 incidents occurred in the first 7 years studied, and an average of 16.4 occurred in the last 7 years.
- 70.0% of the incidents occurred in either a commerce/business or educational environment.
- Shootings occurred in 40 of 50 states and the District of Columbia.
- 60.0% of the incidents ended before police arrived.

## Casualties

- Casualties (victims killed and wounded) totaled 1,043. The individual shooters are not included in this total.
- A total of 486 individuals were killed.
- A total of 557 individuals were wounded.
- In 64 incidents (40.0%), the crime would have fallen within the federal definition of "mass killing"—defined as "three or more" killed—under the new federal statute.

## Shooters

- All but 2 incidents involved a single shooter.
- In at least 9 incidents, the shooter first shot and killed a family member(s) in a residence before moving to a more public location to continue shooting.
- In at least 6 incidents, the shooters were female.
- In 64 incidents (40.0%), the shooters committed suicide; 54 shooters did so at the scene of the crime.
- At least 5 shooters from 4 incidents remain at large.

*(FBI.GOV)*

## Resolutions

The majority of the 160 incidents (90 [56.3%]) ended on the shooter's initiative—sometimes when the shooter committed suicide or stopped shooting, and other times when the shooter fled the scene.

There were at least 25 incidents where the shooter fled the scene before police arrived. In 4 additional incidents, at least 5 shooters fled the scene and were still at large at the time the study results were released.

In other incidents, it was a combination of actions by citizens and/or law enforcement that ended the shootings. In at least 65 (40.6%) of the 160 incidents, citizen engagement or the shooter committing suicide ended the shooting at the scene before law enforcement arrived.

Of those:

- In 37 incidents (23.1%), the shooter committed suicide at the scene before police arrived.

- In 21 incidents (13.1%), the situation ended after unarmed citizens safely and successfully restrained the shooter. In 2 of those incidents, 3 off-duty law enforcement officers were present and assisted.

- Of note, 11 of the incidents involved unarmed principals, teachers, other school staff and students who confronted shooters to end the threat (9 of those shooters were students).

- In 5 incidents (3.1%), the shooting ended after armed individuals who were not law enforcement personnel exchanged gunfire with the shooters. In these incidents, 3 shooters were killed, 1 was wounded, and 1 committed suicide.

- The individuals involved in these shootings included a citizen with a valid firearms permit and armed security guards at a church, an airline counter, a federally managed museum, and a school board meeting.

- In 2 incidents (1.3%), 2 armed, off-duty police officers engaged the shooters, resulting in the death of the shooters. In 1 of those incidents, the off-duty officer assisted a responding officer to end the threat.

Even when law enforcement arrived quickly, many times the shooter still chose to end his life. In 17 (10.6%) of the 160 incidents, the shooter committed suicide at the scene after law enforcement arrived but before officers could act.

In 45 (28.1%) of the 160 incidents, law enforcement and the shooter exchanged gunfire. Of those 45 incidents, the shooter was killed at the scene in 21, killed at another location in 4, wounded in 9, committed suicide in 9, and surrendered in 2.

# Active Shooter Casualties

*Ref: Blair, J. Pete, and Schweit, Katherine W. (2014). A Study of Active Shooter Incidents, 2000 - 2013. Texas State University and Federal Bureau of Investigation, U.S. Department of Justice, Washington D.C. 2014, pp. 9-10.*

A total of 1,043 casualties occurred during the incidents included in this study (486 killed, 557 wounded). If a shooter died as a result of the incident, that individual was not included in the casualty totals. In addition, a small number of those identified as wounded were not injured by gunfire but rather suffered injuries incidental to the event, such as being hit by flying objects/shattered glass or falling while running. For the purposes of this study, the FBI did not seek to isolate the exact number of individuals that fell into this category, when research did not allow for that type of injury to be easily discerned.

The median number of individuals killed in each incident was 2, and the median number of individuals wounded in each incident was 2. The FBI found that 64 incidents (40.0%) would have been categorized as falling within the new federal definition of "mass killing," which is defined as "three or more killings in a single incident."

At least 25 (15.6%) of the 160 incidents involved shootings at more than one location. Several casualties involved family members or individuals who had a close personal relationship with the shooter. In at least 15 (9.4%) of the 160 incidents, the shooters targeted family members, resulting in the deaths of 20 and the wounding of 1. In 9 of these incidents, or about half, the shooters then moved on to another location and continued shooting.

Of note, male shooters also acted violently against women with whom they had or once had a romantic relationship. In 16 (10.0%) of the 160 incidents, the shooters targeted current, estranged, or former wives as well as current or former girlfriends. In 12 incidents, the women were killed; in 3 incidents, the women sustained significant injuries but survived; and in 1 incident, the shooter could not find the woman. While perpetrating this violence, an additional 42 people were killed and another 28 were wounded.

**A Study of 160 Active Shooter Incidents in the United States Between 2000-2013: Broken Down by Casualty Type; Killed or Wounded**

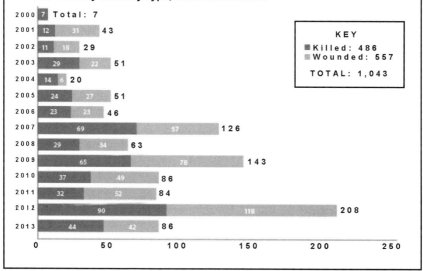

# II. Ideological Homicides

*Ref: Parkin, William S., Steven M. Chermak, Joshua D. Freilich, and Jeff Gruenewald.
"Twenty-Five Years of Ideological Homicide Victimization in the United States of
America," Report to the Office of University Programs, Science and Technology
Directorate, U.S. Department of Homeland Security. START (2016).*

Over the last 25 years in the United States, attacks inspired by al-Qa'ida and its associated movement (AQAM) have killed nearly seven-and-a-half times more people than
far-right extremists (FRE) have killed in one-fifth as many incidents.

However, if you remove two outlier events – the September 11th terrorist attacks and
the Oklahoma City Bombing – far-right extremists have killed nearly four times as
many people as AQAM extremists. Excluding the September 11th and Oklahoma City
bombing victims (2,977 and 168, respectively):

- 62 individuals were killed by AQAM offenders in 38 incidents (1.6 victims per
  homicide incident) and
- 245 individuals were killed by FRE offenders in 177 incidents (1.4 victims per
  homicide incident).

## Targeting/Victims

For victim type, the majority of AQAM victims were civilian targets, while the second
largest category was government victims. For the government victims, this is partially
connected to another variable, which shows more than 20 percent of AQAM victims
were in the military and killed in the line of duty.

Compared to this, FRE victims were most often targeted for racial or ethnic reasons, specifically as their status as minorities. This was followed by civilian targets (28.1%) and then
government targets, primarily law enforcement officers killed in the line of duty (12.7%).

For the most part, these two types of ideological victimization appear to be more
unique than similar. It is thus important to, as this study did, disaggregate the study of
terrorism by ideology. Victims of AQAM were killed at different times and in different locations when compared to FRE victims. AQAM victims were killed in events that more
often had multiple victims, where others were injured, and the use of a firearm was
the primary weapon of the offender. FRE victims were more often the sole victim (both
fatal and not), and although a firearm was still the primary weapon used, they were
more likely than AQAM victims to be stabbed or beaten to death. Although both sets of
victims had disproportionate numbers of individuals killed in the line of duty, especially
when one considers the percentage of the general population engage in active military
or law enforcement service at any given point in time, AQAM victims were more likely
to be military, while FRE victims were more likely to be law enforcement.

In some ways, AQAM victims appear to have characteristics that are slightly closer
to that of "typical" homicide victims and even the general population. This could be a
mechanism of the fact that AQAM victims are much more likely to be random or representative victims than are FRE victims. In these circumstances, it could be argued
that a victim's routine activities and lifestyle play a larger role in their risk of ideological victimization. If an individual is fatally victimized by an AQAM offender depends
on whether they are in the proverbial wrong place at the wrong time. FRE victims,
however, are more likely to be targeted purposefully for assassination based on the
offender's previous knowledge of the individual. In these circumstances, their lifestyle
and routine activities only dictate when and where, not if, they are victimized. These
victimization patterns over the last 25 years demonstrate that ideological victimization from terrorist and extremist violence varies across ideologies and underlines the
importance of future research in the fields of criminology and victimology in attempting
to understand these differences and reduce victimization risk.

# V. Media, Disinformation & Radical Propaganda

*Ref: JP 3-26, Counterterrorism (Nov '09), pp. II-6, II-25, and V-15 to V-16; and U.S. Army TRADOC G2 Handbook No. 1 (Version 5.0), A Military Guide to Terrorism in the Twenty-First Century (Aug '07), pp. I-2, 5-16 and 5-17.*

## I. Terrorist IO and Public Relations Activities

Terrorism, like a theatrical play, can be viewed as a deliberate presentation to a large audience in order to gain attention, spotlight a particular message, and seek a response favorable to the actor. The purpose of such actions can have sinister impact on national, regional, and global populations. Global communications provide a stage for near instantaneous media exploitation. Anxiety can increase as random or deliberate acts of terror often target civilians as victims. Similar to a play, the objective of the experience is to affect the feelings and attitudes of the audience.

*(Shutterstock.com)*

At the fundamental level, terrorism is a psychological act that communicates through the medium of violence or the threat of violence. Terrorist strategies are aimed at publicly causing damage to symbols or inspiring fear. Timing, location, and method of attacks accommodate media dissemination and ensure wide-spread reporting to maximize impact. In its purest form, a terrorist operation often will have the goal of manipulating popular perceptions, and strives to achieve this by controlling or dictating media coverage. This control need not be overt, as terrorists analyze and exploit the dynamics of major media outlets and the pressure of the "news cycle." In considering possible terrorist targets, a massive destructive attack launched against a target that does not attract media coverage may not be a suitable target for the intended effect and targeted population. When the attack is meant to influence a population outside of the area of interest to the terrorists (i.e., the US) in order to influence decision making, a small attack against a "media accessible" target may be a more lucrative target than a larger one of less publicity.

# II. Media, Disinformation & Radical Propaganda

*Contributor: Dr. Tamara Mouras, Criminal Justice & Homeland Security Professor.*

The aspect of examining the dynamics of media and terrorism are often dictated by the perspective and/or lens one is viewing this phenomenon. It is most important to have a clear and concise knowledge and understanding of the term domestic terrorism in which to base how media outlets can provide for disinformation of false rhetoric and radical propaganda that may lead to an individual down the path of terrorism. The inaccurate transfer of information along with a constant stream of propaganda that is filled with radical and extreme ideology can influence the rise of domestic terrorist activity in the United States.

It is also important to note terrorists are not made overnight and terrorist activity does follow a pattern known as the radicalization process to terrorism. We can notice and witness factors associated with the radicalization process of an individual when there is a heightened media (Mass Media and/or Internet Social Media) consumption do to some form of feeling of disenfranchisement, alienation and/ or life stressors in a vulnerable individual's life course. The radicalization process is a funnel perspective that weighs heavily on the theory that individuals go through a process of redefining their world view, their life's mission, their ideas and perspectives to a belief system bent on the incorporation of extreme beliefs. These extreme beliefs can transcend into violent terrorist activity. Mass media outlets both Mass Media and Internet Social Media play a crucial role in this personal and radical psychological transformation of an individual and/or group.

When examining media outlets there are various types of media avenues to consider when exploring the link between terrorism, disinformation of false or misleading material, and radical propaganda as it relates to the rise of domestic terrorism. Mass Media outlets which include both left and right views and Internet Social Media cites are all viewed and utilized by terrorists and terrorist's organizations. However, each media outlet is utilized quite differently. It is vital to distinguish between these two media arenas of news filters (Mass Media and Internet Social Media). Internet Social Media outlets can be widely assembled and produced quite easily. The spread of radical Internet sites providing religious, political, and even economic justification for violent attacks is increasingly aggressive (Mouras, 2013).

Before a terrorist organization can plan and carry out any terrorist activity they have to build a base of believers. Internet Social media is platform often used by terrorists groups and/or organizations in which to build their support/base, recruit and inspire willing subjects. To inspire mass amounts of individuals often includes disinformation of materials and radical rhetoric. Propaganda is not without its intentional and/or inaccurate information to help move an individual's belief system into a belief system filled with hatred and disdain for the enemy which is often initiated towards The United States. Violent anti-Western rhetoric and actions by local groups, and the growing number of radical, self-generating cells is of concern to law enforcement (Mouras, 2013).

Internet Social Media websites are used to recruit like-minded individuals to a cause. Often times this cause is false and misleads many individuals down a path of radicalization to terrorism for an ideology that is bent on the goal of selling information to help recruit individuals. Terrorists organizations also promote and sell propaganda that generates large amounts of sympathy of individuals searching for meaning in their life. When examining the human makeup and human dynamics most humans want to belong to some like-minded group and radical Internet websites may fulfill this need of wanting to belong. The success of a terrorist organization and fulfillment of a terrorist attack is only as strong or deep as the number of individuals who consider themselves part of the terrorist organization. The reasoning for this is because many of the radicalized individuals will filter out of the radicalization process leaving only a few individuals who will make the complete transformation into an active violent terrorist. There are various reasoning's for disengagement in the radicalization process to terrorism. Some individuals, while they believe in the cause, will realize the act of violence is something they do not want to be involved with. Others will have a shift in their life such as a new relationship or a new job and will start to feel as though the world is not against them anymore. Others will have an intervention from a family member which deters them from further activity.

Because there are high numbers of individuals who will disengage from the process of radicalization to terrorism the extreme rhetoric of disinformation must be constant (24 hours/365 days) and filled with propaganda tools that are aimed at the recruitment and motivation of sympathizers to their cause and also the cause of the alienated individual themselves. How do terrorist organization motivate? When we examine this through the lens of domestic terrorism the reasoning includes disinformation of false materials and radical propaganda aimed at the perceived social injustices of disenfranchised segments of the population, economic backlash on lower-socioeconomic groups, and/or political repression of religious groups. Terrorist organizations are aiming their message to perceived victims of American mainstream society and/or government. Terrorist organizations are constantly and steadily sending messages, pictures, events and announcements encouraging violent action for the perceived wrongs.

An internet Social media outlet (such as FaceBook, Twitter, Renren, YouTube, Instagram, vk.com, Meetup, and Secret) is the number one tool in which terrorists organizations can reach their potential terrorist pool. Without Internet Social Media terrorist groups would not have the capability or numbers to carry out the violent terrorist activity witnessed today in the 21st century. Internet Social media websites can easily be built, run, updated and have little to no censorship in the type of information that can be displayed to vulnerable individuals looking to right the wrong society has placed upon them in The United States leaving the pool of potential terrorists at numbers which cannot be counted.

The second type of media which is examined is the influence of Mass Media channels and/or outlets. Mass Media outlets allow for terrorists organizations and groups to view the so called "fruit of their labor." Mass Media provides a 24 hour continuous coverage of events, predominantly negative and violent in nature to be readily available for viewer consumption at any time across the world. Mass Media channels provide terrorist organizations a complete analysis of their violent terrorist event hour-by-hour, lay claim to the responsibly of the terrorist event, provide a center stage character for the world to view, provide a rationale for their cause, therefore, helping to recruit more individuals into the terrorist organization, and gives the American public a large consumption of terrorist activity on a daily basis.

There is some debate of whether this large amount of violent consumption available through Mass Media outlets desensitizes the general American public to the violent nature of terrorist organizations and terrorist attacks. The question remains how the United States Criminal Justice Agencies can provide for disengagement measures without impinging upon the Freedom of Speech and Freedom of Press rights in which the U.S. Constitution provides safe guards for.

Mass Media and Internet Social Media outlets operate on the legality of protection by U.S. Constitutional Rights. Freedom of Speech is a double edge sword as this U.S. Constitutional Right is one of the compelling aspects of the United States freedoms in which this country's civil liberties are built upon. Censorship may produce feelings of a perceived wrong initiated by the government possibly creating even more radical groups to spring up across the United States. At the other end of the sword is the issue of whether Freedom of Speech and Freedom of Press is allowing for extreme rhetoric and speech to influence human psychological behavior. Words have meaning, words inspire and words influence. This concept can be used at both edges of the sword. Words can inform, educate, inspire creativity and provide for constructive debate generating new and innovative ideas. However, words can inspire extreme views and influence violent behavior in humans that may lead to domestic terrorist activity.

*Mouras, T. A. (2013). Law enforcement perspectives of factors that may lead to radicalization. Capella University). ProQuest Dissertations and Theses, 168. Retrieved from http://search.proquest.com.library.capella.edu/docview/1319282147?accountid=27965.*

Media control measures, prepared statements, and a host of other preparations are made to effectively exploit a successful operation. These are timed to take advantage of media cycles for the selected target audiences (TAs). By quickly capturing and exploiting images themselves, the adversary can rapidly leverage events to influence the public via self produced media (Internet, radio, television, text messaging, podcast, Weblogs (blogs), etc.) and gain an advantage within the information environment.

The Internet provides terrorists and extremists the means to spread their radical ideology, an ad hoc means of operational connectivity, and a link to the full-media spectrum for public relations. The Internet facilitates their recruiting, training, logistic support, planning, fund-raising, etc. The internet is also a powerful tool to conduct the equivalent of media facilitated IO against the United States and PNs. Although not yet typical, terrorists may employ electronic attacks to disrupt communications, or banking, or to project disinformation and propaganda in support of their cause. From the terrorist perspective, media coverage is an important measure of the success of a terrorist act and a means of countering US and PN IO and SC activities. News reports, streaming videos on websites, blogs, and editorials can amplify (some unwittingly) the psychological effects of a terrorist incident and aid terrorists in publicizing the event globally to a much wider audience, and potentially gain further recognition of their radical ideology.

Violent Extremist Organizations (VEOs) use the Internet and some mass media for organizational support, intelligence gathering, and offensive actions. Uses of the Internet include command and control, training, dissemination of information and ideology, perception management, and propaganda, as well as open source intelligence gathering. Mass media and other influence networks are used to deliver disinformation and propaganda to further extremist objectives. Extremists are resourceful and adaptive in using IO in support of their own strategic communications strategy to gain and maintain ideological support, fundraise and recruit, and influence key audiences. Because VEOs are not constrained by truth or accuracy, they can exploit the information environment with considerable effect.

Terrorists will attempt to exploit US vulnerabilities to information dominance. Casualty avoidance and the media effect are interrelated perceptions held by many potential adversaries of the US social and political situation. Terrorists may believe the US. is extremely casualty averse and that images and news of casualties will be easy to deliver to the American public in their living rooms. While this effect may be overemphasized, promotion of goals, acts, and demands are significant part of terrorist operations.

Since the terrorists prepare their operations around a desired media effect, they will be prepared and vocal or visual for reporting coverage. They can orchestrate supporting events and interviews to reinforce the desired message. Terrorists have well-established methods of presenting disinformation and false perspectives. Frequently, military reluctance to comment on ongoing operations in the media for operational security (OPSEC) reasons can assist the terrorist. If no balanced information comes from official sources in a timely manner, the media will use the information readily available from the terrorist as a primary source for reporting the story.

# Counterterrorism Overview/Introduction

*Ref: JP 3-26, Counterterrorism (Oct '14), chap. 1.*

Terrorists use many forms of unlawful violence or threats of violence to instill fear and coerce governments or societies to further a variety of political, social, criminal, economic, and religious ideologies. Terrorists threaten the national power, sovereignty, and interests of the United States and our allies. Terrorists organize and operate in a number of ways. Some operate within transnational networks, others operate as small independent groups, and others operate alone. The terrorist threat is amplified by the proliferation of weapons of mass destruction (WMD) and their potential use by terrorists. The United States strives to enlist the support of the international community, adapts alliances, and creates new partnerships to facilitate regional solutions that contain and defeat terrorists, their organizations, and networks.

# I. The Nature of Warfare and Terrorism

Warfare is the mechanism, method, or modality of armed conflict against an enemy. It is the "how" of waging war. The US military recognizes two basic forms of warfare: traditional and irregular. Terrorism is principally a tool of irregular warfare, but it is seen in unlawful actions of state and non-state actors during traditional warfare.

## Terrorism

Terrorism is the unlawful use of violence or threat of violence, often motivated by religious, political, or other ideological beliefs, to instill fear and coerce governments or societies in pursuit of goals that are usually political. Non-state actors use unlawful violence to influence states or populations to achieve their goals, and state actors may use unlawful acts of violence to create effects when lawful conflict between nations does not exist. Terrorism is not in and of itself an ideology or a form of war. Terrorism is a tactic used by organizations trying to achieve specific goals. Terrorist tactics are used by a wide variety of actors, including insurgents such as al-Qa'ida in Iraq's effort to replace what they identified as a Shia-led government; nationalists such as Pakistan-based Lashkar-e-Tayyiba's efforts to eliminate the influence of a foreign power; armed separatists such as the Euskadi Ta Askatasuna in Spain; or a state attempting to influence another by the murder, kidnapping, or hostage taking of another state's diplomats or citizenry. The defeat of terrorism is therefore better understood through the prism of terrorists' goals rather than their acts of terrorism.

## Counterterrorism (CT)

CT activities and operations are taken to neutralize terrorists, their organizations, and networks in order to render them incapable of using violence to instill fear and coerce governments or societies to achieve their goals.

The purpose of CT is to disrupt, isolate, and dismantle terrorist organizations and networks to render them incapable of striking the homeland, US facilities and personnel, or US interests abroad. CT also includes crisis response operations to respond to imminent terrorist threats or incidents when preemption and preclusion are not successful.

Successful CT campaigns require geographic combatant commanders (GCCs) and other JFCs to apply the tenets of other joint doctrine: counterinsurgency (COIN), stability operations, security cooperation, and foreign internal defense (FID). These other activities are specifically designed to change political, social, economic, and other factors that comprise the environment from which terrorists emanate and sustain themselves. Depending on the operational environment, a GCC may support CT through stability operations, COIN, counterdrug, counter WMD, information operations, military information support operations (MISO), FID, security force assistance (SFA), and other joint activities and operations.

# II. Counterterrorism Goals

With core tenets as the foundation of all CT efforts, the United States aims to achieve eight overarching near-term CT goals. Taken together, these goals articulate a framework for the success of the US global CT mission. These goals are:

- Protect the American people, homeland, and American interests, along with those of our allies and partners
- Identify, locate, disrupt, degrade, dismantle, and defeat extremist organizations and networks along with their affiliates and adherents
- Prevent terrorist development, acquisition, and use of WMD
- Eliminate terrorist safe havens
- Build enduring CT partnerships and capabilities
- Degrade links between terrorist organizations, networks, and their affiliates and adherents (attack the network)
- Counter violent extremist ideology and its resonance; diminish the specific drivers of violence that it exploits
- Deprive terrorists of their enabling resources and functions: money, personnel, and weapons

While there will never be a complete eradication of terrorism, the *National Strategy for Counterterrorism* reflects the reality that success will only come through the sustained, steadfast, and systematic application of all elements of national power simultaneously across the globe. The United States must use all means to defend against terrorist attacks on the United States, its citizens, and its interests around the world. It is imperative not only to forge a diverse and powerful coalition to combat terrorism today, but also to work with our international partners to build lasting mechanisms for combating terrorism while fostering trust, coordination, and cooperation.

# III. Pursuing a Whole-of-Government Effort

In order to succeed at the tactical through the strategic levels, commanders and civilian leadership should develop a rapid, coordinated, and effective CT effort that reflects and leverages the full capabilities and resources of the entire United States Government (USG). This approach integrates the capabilities and authorities of each department and agency, ensuring the right tools are applied at the right time for the right situation in a manner that is consistent with US law and supports USG objectives.

JP 3-26 is designed to guide joint force commanders' (JFCs') application of Department of Defense (DOD) counterterrorism (CT) capabilities in planning, executing, and assessing CT operations. CT is part of the broader construct of combating terrorism, which includes actions such as antiterrorism and CT, taken to fight terrorism throughout the entire threat spectrum.

# I. National Approach for Counterterrorism

*Ref: JP 3-26, Counterterrorism (Oct '14), chap. 3.*

The Secretary of Homeland Security is the principal federal official for domestic incident management. The Secretary of Homeland Security coordinates federal operations within the United States to anticipate, prepare for, respond to, and recover from terrorist attacks. The Attorney General of the United States, generally acting through the Director of the Federal Bureau of Investigation (FBI), leads law enforcement response to, and criminal investigations of, terrorist acts or threats within the United States and its territories. The Secretary of Defense (SecDef) may, at the request of the Attorney General, support domestic CT activities and operations. If a terrorist incident exceeds the FBI's capacity, the President may direct DOD to provide domestic CT assistance within Constitutional and statutory limits.

> *"US CT [counterterrorism] efforts require a multidepartmental and multinational effort that goes beyond traditional intelligence, military, and law enforcement functions. We are engaged in a broad, sustained, and integrated campaign that harnesses every tool of American power—military, civilian, and the power of our values—together with the concerted efforts of allies, partners, and multilateral institutions."*
>
> *President Barack Obama, National Strategy for Counterterrorism, June 28, 2011*

## I. National Strategy for Counterterrorism

The National Strategy for Counterterrorism formalizes the approach that President Obama and his Administration have been pursuing and adapting to prevent terrorist attacks and to deliver devastating blows against al-Qa'ida, including the successful mission to kill Usama bin Laden.

The latest National Strategy for Counterterrorism was published in June 2011.

For the past decade, the preponderance of the United States' CT effort has been aimed at preventing the recurrence of an attack on the Homeland directed by al-Qa'ida. That includes disrupting plots as well as working to constrain al-Qa'ida's ability to plan and train for attacks by shrinking the size and security of its safehavens.

*See the following pages for an overview and fact sheet.*

## II. National Security Council (NSC)

The National Security Council manages the interagency process with respect to CT and all national security-related issues and certain selected actions. The interagency process is designed to advance the President's policy priorities and to serve the national interest by ensuring that all agencies and perspectives that can contribute to achieving these priorities participate in making and implementing policy. Thus, the National Security Council is the key integrator of the President's whole-of-government CT policy and strategies, which requires interagency coordination at the Principals Committee, Deputies Committee, and supporting interagency policy committees, and the efforts of the National Security Council Staff. The key interagency policy committee of CT is the Counterterrorist Security Group, which is led by the Assistant to the President for Homeland Security and Counterterrorism.

# National Strategy for Counterterrorism (Published June 2011)

*Ref: Fact Sheet: National Strategy for Counterterrorism, https://www.whitehouse.gov/ the-press-office/2011/06/29/fact-sheet-national-strategy-counterterrorism (Accessed Mar 2016).*

> *"As a country, we will never tolerate our security being threatened, nor stand idly by when our people have been killed. We will be relentless in defense of our citizens and our friends and allies. We will be true to the values that make us who we are. And on nights like this one, we can say to those families who have lost loved ones to al Qaeda's terror: Justice has been done."*
>
> *--President Barack Obama, May 1, 2011*

The National Strategy for Counterterrorism, found at http://www.whitehouse.gov/sites/ default/files/counterterrorism_strategy.pdf formalizes the approach that President Obama and his Administration have been pursuing and adapting for the past two and half years to prevent terrorist attacks and to deliver devastating blows against al-Qa'ida, including the successful mission to kill Usama bin Laden.

Rather than defining our entire national security policy, this counterterrorism strategy is one part of President Obama's larger National Security Strategy, which seeks to advance our enduring national security interests, including our security, prosperity, respect for universal values and global cooperation to meet global challenges.

This Strategy builds upon the progress we have made in the decade since 9/11, in partnership with Congress, to build our counterterrorism and homeland security capacity as a nation. It neither represents a wholesale overhaul—nor a wholesale retention—of previous policies and strategies.

## Threat

This Strategy recognizes there are numerous nations and groups that support terrorism to oppose U.S. interests, including Iran, Syria, Hezbollah and HAMAS, and we will use the full range of our foreign policy tools to protect the United States against these threats.

However, the principal focus of this counterterrorism strategy is the network that poses the most direct and significant threat to the United States—al-Qa'ida, its affiliates and its adherents.

- **Al-Qa'ida** has murdered thousands of our citizens, including on 9/11.
- Al-Qa'ida **affiliates**—groups that have aligned with al-Qa'ida—have attempted to attack us, such as Yemen-based al-Qa'ida in the Arabian Peninsula's (AQAP) failed attempt to bomb a Detroit-bound airliner on December 25, 2009.
- Al-Qa'ida **adherents**—individuals, sometimes American citizens, who cooperate with or are inspired by al-Qa'ida—have engaged in terrorism, including the tragic slaughter of our service members at Fort Hood in 2009.

## Our Ultimate Objective

This Strategy is clear and precise in our ultimate objective: we will disrupt, dismantle, and ultimately defeat al-Qa'ida—its leadership core in the Afghanistan-Pakistan region, its affiliates and adherents to ensure the security of our citizens and interests.

## Our Posture

We are at war. We are waging a broad, sustained, integrated and relentless campaign that harnesses every element of American power to defeat al-Qa'ida.

## Our Goals

To defeat al-Qa'ida, we are pursuing specific counterterrorism goals, including:

- Protecting our homeland by constantly reducing our vulnerabilities and adapting and updating our defenses.
- Disrupting, degrading, dismantling and defeating al-Qa'ida wherever it takes root.
- Preventing terrorists from acquiring or developing weapons of mass destruction.
- Eliminating the safehavens al-Qa'ida needs to train, plot and launch attacks against us.
- Degrading links between al-Qa'ida, its affiliates and adherents.
   Countering al-Qa'ida ideology and its attempts to justify violence.
- Depriving al-Qa'ida and its affiliates of their enabling means, including illicit financing, logistical support, and online communications.

## Our Principles

Our pursuit of these goals is guided by several key principles, including:

- Upholding core American values, including rule of law and the privacy, civil rights, and civil liberties of all Americans;
- Harnessing every tool at our disposal, including intelligence, military, homeland security and law enforcement, and maximizing cooperation between communities;
- Building partnerships to with international institutions and partners so that nations can take the fight to al-Qa'ida, its affiliates and adherents in their own countries;
- Applying tools appropriately, recognizing that different threats in different regions demand different tools;
- Building a culture of preparedness and resilience at home to prevent terrorist attacks and ensure we can quickly recover should an attack occur.

## Devastating Blows Against Al-Qa'ida

Guided by this Strategy, we have achieved significant progress against al-Qa'ida over the past two and a half years.

We have put al-Qa'ida under more pressure than at any time since 9/11, affecting its ability to attract new recruits and making it harder for al-Qa'ida to train and plot attacks.

Al-Qa'ida's leadership ranks have been decimated, with more key leaders eliminated in rapid succession than at any time since 9/11.

Virtually every major al-Qa'ida affiliate has lost its key leader or operational commander.

More than half of al-Qa'ida's leadership has been eliminated, including Usama bin Laden

## "On a Path to Defeat"

As President Obama stated in his June 22 remarks on our way forward in Afghanistan, "we have put al Qaeda on a path to defeat, and we will not relent until the job is done."

- Information seized from his compound reveals bin Laden's concerns about al-Qa'ida's long-term viability.
- Bin Laden clearly saw that al-Qa'ida is losing the larger battle for hearts and minds.
- Bin Laden knew that he had failed to portray America as being at war with Islam.
- He knew that al-Qa'ida's murder of so many innocent civilians, most of them Muslims, had deeply and perhaps permanently tarnished al-Qa'ida's image in the world.

# Relationship of Homeland Security, Homeland Defense, & DSCA

Ref: JP 3-28, Defense Support of Civil Authorities (Jul '14), pp. I-2 to I-3 and app. A.

Perhaps one of the greatest challenges for a military staff is operating in or near the homeland and being subject to the inherent legal and jurisdictional responsibilities that accompany such operations. This challenge is set against the evolving range of threats to the homeland–to countering transnational organizations and individual actors of concern internal and external to the US.

## Homeland Security (HS)

Homeland security is a concerted national effort to prevent terrorist attacks within the US; reduce America's vulnerability to terrorism, major disasters, and other emergencies; and minimize the damage and recover from attacks, major disasters, and other emergencies that occur. HS is an integral element of a broader US national security and domestic policy. Protecting the US from terrorism is the cornerstone of HS.

HS describes the intersection of evolving threats and hazards with traditional governmental and civic responsibilities for civil defense, emergency response, law enforcement, customs, border control, and immigration. In combining these responsibilities under one overarching construct, HS breaks down longstanding stovepipes of activity that have been exploited by those seeking to harm the US.

The President of the United States is uniquely responsible for the safety, security, and resilience of the nation. The President leads the overall HS policy direction and coordination. Individual United States Government (USG) departments and agencies, in turn, are empowered by law and policy to fulfill various aspects of the HS mission. DHS has the following missions:

- Preventing terrorism and enhancing security
- Securing and managing US borders
- Enforcing and administering immigration laws
- Safeguarding and securing cyberspace
- Ensuring resilience to disasters
- However, as a distributed system, no single entity has the mission to directly manage all aspects of HS

## Homeland Defense (HD)

Homeland defense is the protection of US sovereign territory, the domestic population, and critical infrastructures against external threats and aggression or other threats, as directed by the President.

DOD is the federal agency with lead responsibility for HD, which may be executed by DOD alone or include support from other USG departments and agencies.

## Defense Support to Civil Authority (DSCA)

Defense Support of Civil Authorities (DSCA) is support provided in response to requests for assistance from civil authorities for domestic emergencies, law enforcement support, and other domestic activities, or from qualifying entities for special events.

The Armed Forces of the United States and Department of Defense (DOD) agencies may be called upon for defense support of civil authorities (DSCA) to support a **whole-of-government** response in support of civil authorities, although not specifically organized, trained, or equipped for the support of civil authorities. The US Armed Forces have a historic precedent and enduring role in supporting civil authorities during times of emergency, and this role is codified in **national defense strategy** as a primary mission of DOD.

# Homeland Defense Relationships

Relationships Between Homeland Defense, Defense Support of Civil Authorities, and Homeland Security Missions

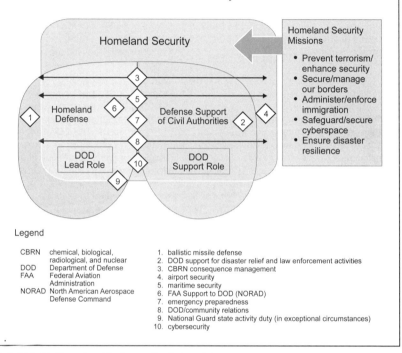

Ref: JP 3-27, Homeland Defense, fig. A-1, p. A-2.

*Refer to our series of related Homeland Defense, DSCA, Disaster and National Response SMARTbooks for further discussion. The US Armed Forces have a historic precedent and enduring role in supporting civil authorities during times of emergency, and this role is codified in national defense strategy as a primary mission of DOD. In the past decade alone, natural disasters of considerable severity resulted in 699 Presidential Disaster Declarations, an average of nearly six per month. Disaster management (or emergency management) is the term used to designate the efforts of communities or businesses to plan for and coordinate all the personnel and materials required to either mitigate the effects of, or recover from, natural or man-made disasters, or acts of terrorism.*

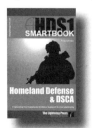

# III. US Government Counterterrorism Roles

## A. Department of Homeland Security (DHS)

DHS leads the unified national effort to secure the United States. Key among its strategic goals is to prevent, protect, respond, and recover from acts of terrorism.

## B. Department of State (DOS)

As the lead US foreign affairs agency, DOS formulates, represents, and implements the President's foreign policy. The Secretary of State is the President's principal advisor on foreign policy and the person chiefly responsible for US representation abroad, except for CT within regions where the responsibility lies with the military commander as designated by the President.

DOS has six regional bureaus that address foreign policy considerations on a regional basis. The assistant secretaries of the regional bureaus are key actors in CT activities and operations policy in their assigned regions. Furthermore, the DOS Bureau of Counterterrorism publishes an annual country report on terrorism and manages US policy for a whole-of-government approach to CT. The DOS Bureau of Counterterrorism maintains the Foreign Terrorist Organizations List that provides justification for the President to block or freeze tangible property and freeze financial accounts of individuals or terrorist organizations pursuant to Executive Order 13224, *Blocking Property and Prohibiting Transactions With Persons Who Commit, Threaten to Commit, or Support Terrorism.* This tool is designed to sever terrorists' organizations logistics and resources. These efforts are worked through PNs where the United States maintains country teams under the leadership of COMs.

## C. Chief of Mission (COM)

The COM is the personal representative of the President and the official USG representative in the host country. The COM is responsible for the conduct of relations with the host government and is the primary channel for communications with that government. The COM directs, coordinates, and supervises all USG executive branch employees in that effort, except those under the command of a US military commander. CT activities and operations conducted by DOD and other USG departments and agencies require COM concurrence prior to execution, unless otherwise directed by the President.

## D. Department of Justice (DOJ)

The Attorney General investigates acts or incidents that may constitute a violation of federal laws related to acts of terrorism or the use or threatened use of WMD. This authority is exercised through the FBI. The Attorney General, generally acting through the FBI, in coordination with the Secretary of State and the COM, will assume lead responsibility for the law enforcement investigation of terrorist or WMD incidents abroad. The FBI's tasks may include taking custody of suspected terrorists, lawful transfer of custody of suspected terrorists, forensic examination of material collected of possible intelligence or criminal prosecution value, and hostage negotiation support.

## E. The Department of the Treasury (TREAS)

TREAS's role in CT is to lead the USG efforts to locate, track, and seize suspected terrorist financial assets. TREAS may use a variety of Presidential, statutory, and regulatory authorities, including economic and financial sanctions. For threats not responsive to diplomatic outreach and not suitable for military action, TREAS economic and financial capabilities often provide unique tools to contribute to achievement of the President's CT policy and strategies.

# F. National Counterterrorism Center (NCTC)

The mission of NCTC is to analyze terrorist threats, share information with PNs, and integrate all instruments of national power to ensure unity of effort. NCTC also provides assistance to the operational elements of the USG that disrupt, isolate, and dismantle terrorist organizations and prevent future attacks.

NCTC is staffed by personnel from multiple USG departments and agencies. NCTC serves as the primary organization in the USG to integrate and analyze all intelligence pertaining to CT, except for information pertaining exclusively to domestic terrorism. It serves as the USG's central and shared database on known and suspected terrorists and international terrorist groups. NCTC also provides USG departments and agencies with terrorism intelligence analysis and other information.

NCTC conducts strategic operational planning for CT activities across the USG, integrating all instruments of national power to ensure unity of effort. NCTC ensures effective integration of CT plans and synchronization of operations across more than 20 USG departments and agencies engaged in CT efforts.

As part of NCTC's mission, it maintains the authoritative database of all known or suspected terrorist identifiers maintained by the USG. The Defense Combating Terrorism Center gathers, evaluates, and nominates all known or suspected terrorist identifiers collected by DOD to NCTC for inclusion on the National Known or Suspected Terrorist Watch List maintained by the Terrorist Screening Center, and dissemination to front-line screening organizations, like Customs and Border Patrol, Consular Affairs, and state and local law enforcement.

*See p. 1-34 for further discussion.*

# G. National Joint Terrorism Task Force (NJTTF)

The NJTTF is an interagency coordination organization that provides liaison from FBI Headquarters to local joint terrorism task forces and participating agencies and serves as a conduit for information on threats and leads. It is located in the NCTC, where it also works with NCTC personnel to analyze data and plan antiterrorism strategies. The NJTTF shares information among its 80 members—officers, agents, and analysts—who then pass the information onto the 48 different agencies they represent. Those agencies—from the law enforcement, intelligence, homeland security, defense, diplomatic, and public safety sectors—include the DHS, the US military, and federal, state, and local partners. Men and women from the US Secret Service, Federal Air Marshals, New York City Police Department, DOD counterintelligence organizations (Naval Criminal Investigative Service, Air Force Office of Special Investigations, and Army Counterintelligence), Federal Bureau of Prisons, Amtrak Police, and dozens of other organizations work together every day to counter terrorist planning and operations.

# IV. The Role of the FBI in Counterterrorism

As an intelligence-driven and a threat-focused national security organization with both intelligence and law enforcement responsibilities, the mission of the FBI is to protect and defend the United States against terrorist and foreign intelligence threats, to uphold and enforce the criminal laws of the United States, and to provide leadership and criminal justice services to federal, state, municipal, and international agencies and partners.

## FBI Priorities

The FBI focuses on threats that challenge the foundations of American society or involve dangers too large or complex for any local or state authority to handle alone. In executing the following priorities, the FBI—as both a national security and law enforcement organization—will produce and use intelligence to protect the nation from threats and to bring to justice those who violate the law.

**The FBI's top priority is protecting the U.S. from terrorist attacks.**

# The FBI's National Security Mission

Ref: https://www.fbi.gov/about-us/nsb

The FBI's national security mission is to lead and coordinate intelligence efforts that drive actions to protect the United States.

The FBI's goal is to develop a comprehensive understanding of the threats and penetrate national and transnational networks that have a desire and capability to harm us. Such networks include: terrorist organizations, foreign intelligence services, those that seek to proliferate weapons of mass destruction, and criminal enterprises.

In order to be successful, we must understand the threat, continue to integrate our intelligence and law enforcement capabilities in every FBI operational program, and continue to expand our contribution to the Intelligence Community knowledge base.

Because national security and criminal threats are often intertwined, our ability to integrate intelligence and investigations makes us uniquely situated to address our nation's threats and vulnerabilities.

## FBI's National Security Branch (NSB)

The National Security Branch (NSB) was established on September 12, 2005, in response to a presidential directive and Weapons of Mass Destruction (WMD) Commission recommendation to create a "National Security Service" combining the missions, capabilities, and resources of the FBI's counterterrorism, counterintelligence, and intelligence elements under the leadership of a senior FBI official.

In July 2006, the NSB created the WMD Directorate to integrate components previously distributed throughout the FBI. The NSB also includes the Terrorist Screening Center, which provides crucial, actionable intelligence to state and local law enforcement, and the High-Value Detainee Interrogation Group, an interagency body whose members collect intelligence from key terror suspects to prevent attacks against the United States and its allies.

Combining the FBI's national security workforce and mission under one leadership umbrella enhances our contribution to the national intelligence effort and allows us to leverage resources from our intelligence community, federal, state, local, tribal, private, and foreign partners.

### Mission

The NSB carries out the FBI's responsibilities as the lead intelligence and law enforcement agency in the nation to detect, deter, and disrupt national security threats to the United States and its interests. While maintaining the Bureau's goal to preserve civil liberties, the branch collects and analyzes intelligence pertaining to national security threats and shares this information with our public, private, federal, state, local, and tribal partners.

### NSB Components

- **The Counterterrorism Division** works with intelligence and law enforcement partners to provide a centralized, comprehensive, and intelligence-driven approach to address international and domestic terrorism-related matters. It also oversees the more than 100 JTTFs nationwide.

- **The Counterintelligence Division** is charged with preventing and investigating foreign intelligence activities within the United States. The Counterintelligence Division targets both traditional and emerging nontraditional threats and investigates espionage activities using both intelligence and law enforcement techniques. The Counterintelligence Division is home to the FBI's Counterproliferation Center.

- **The Directorate of Intelligence** is the FBI's dedicated national intelligence workforce, with clear authority and responsibility for all FBI intelligence functions. The DI's mission is to provide strategic support, direction, and oversight to the FBI's intelligence program, and it carries out its functions through embedded intelligence elements at FBI Headquarters and through Field Intelligence Groups in each field division.

- **The Weapons of Mass Destruction Directorate** leads efforts to deny state and non-state sponsored adversaries access to WMD materials and technologies, to detect and disrupt the use of WMD, and to respond to WMD threats and incidents.

- **The Terrorist Screening Center** consolidates the government's approach to terrorist screening by creating and maintaining a single comprehensive watchlist of known or suspected terrorists, and making this consolidated list available to all federal, state, and local screeners through its 24/7 call center.

- **The High-Value Detainee Interrogation Group** is an interagency body, housed within the NSB, and staffed with members from various IC agencies. Its mission is to gather and apply the nation's best resources to collect intelligence from key terror suspects in order to prevent terrorist attacks against the United States and its allies.

# FBI's Joint Terrorism Task Forces (JTTFs)

The FBI's JTTFs are our nation's front line on terrorism: small cells of highly trained, locally based, passionately committed investigators, analysts, linguists, SWAT experts, and other specialists from dozens of U.S. law enforcement and intelligence agencies.

When it comes to investigating terrorism, they do it all: chase down leads, gather evidence, make arrests, provide security for special events, conduct training, collect and share intelligence, and respond to threats and incidents at a moment's notice.

The task forces are based in 104 cities nationwide, including at least one in each of our 56 field offices. A total of 71 of these JTTFs have been created since 9/11; the first was established in New York City in 1980.

Today, the JTTFs include approximately 4,000 members nationwide—more than four times the pre-9/11 total—hailing from over 500 state and local agencies and 55 federal agencies (the Department of Homeland Security, the U.S. military, Immigration and Customs Enforcement, and the Transportation Security Administration, to name a few).

**The benefits of JTTFs?** They provide one-stop shopping for information regarding terrorist activities. They enable a shared intelligence base across many agencies. They create familiarity among investigators and managers before a crisis. And perhaps most importantly, they pool talents, skills, and knowledge from across the law enforcement and intelligence communities into a single team that responds together.

**Their contributions?** More than we could possibly capture here, but JTTFs have been instrumental in breaking up cells like the "Portland Seven," the "Lackawanna Six," and the Northern Virginia jihad. They've foiled attacks on the Fort Dix Army base in New Jersey, on the JFK International Airport in New York, and on various military and civilian targets in Los Angeles. They've traced sources of terrorist funding, responded to anthrax threats, halted the use of fake IDs, and quickly arrested suspicious characters with all kinds of deadly weapons and explosives.

The task forces coordinate their efforts largely through the interagency National Joint Terrorism Task Force, working out of FBI Headquarters. JTTFs are working 24/7/365 to protect you, your families, and your communities from terrorist attack.

Counter-terrorism

The FBI is the lead domestic terrorism agency in the U.S., working to identify and prevent domestic terrorism acts before they occur and investigate them when they do take place. We're also the lead federal agency in responding to a domestic terrorism crisis situation, functioning as the on-scene manager for the U.S. government.

# V. Department of Defense

Within DOD, CT activities and operations are normally executed by GCCs, subordinate theater special operations command (TSOC) commanders, and other JFCs. and SOF each bring certain competencies to CT efforts. Conventional forces and SOF skills and capabilities complement each other. The scope, intensity, and duration of each specific operation will dictate the missions to be accomplished, and the JFCs must determine the right joint force mix to employ. Conventional forces and SOF each possess unique capabilities that can produce even greater warfighting potential for the JFCs when integrated into a holistic global CT campaign with numerous theater CT operations. Flexible C2, specific mission-generation processes, clear mission approval levels, and integration of all appropriate partners at the strategic, operational, and tactical levels improves the CT effectiveness of both Conventional forces and SOF. CT is a core task of SOF, but global demand for CT activities and the varied conditions under which the broad range of CT activities occur dictate that SOF cannot be the sole force engaged in CT operations.

## A. Geographic Combatant Commanders (GCCs)

The principal JFC responsible for CT activities and operations is the GCC. The GCC detects, deters, and prevents attacks against the United States, its territories, and bases, and employs appropriate force to defend the nation should deterrence fail. The GCC is also the single point of contact for military matters within the assigned area of responsibility (AOR), excluding areas within the United States.

## B. Theater Special Operations Command (TSOC)

A TSOC is a subordinate unified command of United States Special Operations Command (USSOCOM). It is the primary theater special operations organization capable of performing synchronized, continuous CT activities and operations. It is the organization through which a GCC exercises C2 of attached SOF as designated. SecDef has delegated operational control (OPCON) of TSOCs and attached SOF tactical units to their respective GCCs via the Global Force Management Implementation Guidance. A GCC normally exercises OPCON of attached SOF through the commander, theater special operations command (CDRTSOC). The GCC may exercise OPCON of subordinate forces directly from the TSOC or through a special operations command-forward (SOC-FWD), which is a small, scalable, operational-level headquarters that provides a forward-deployed, persistent presence, C2 capability. If conditions warrant greater SOF engagement, a SOC-FWD can transition to a joint task force. The SOC-FWD develops a close working relationship with members of the country team and PN armed forces and those of the HN, and helps the TSOC commander execute the role as a JFC and theater special operations advisor.

## C. USSOCOM

USSOCOM is a functional combatant commander (FCC) with transregional responsibilities. The Commander, United States Special Operations Command (CDRUS-SOCOM) synchronizes plans for global operations against terrorist networks, in coordination with other combatant commands (CCMDs), the Services, and, as directed, appropriate USG departments and agencies. During the conduct of CT activities and operations, CDRUSSOCOM is normally a supporting commander to the GCC in whose AOR the CT effort occurs.

# The FBI Counterterrorism Fly Team

*Ref: https://www.fbi.gov/about-us/investigate/terrorism/counterterrorism-fly-team*

The FBI's Counterterrorism Division Fly Team can respond quickly to dangerous threats and major terrorist attacks around the country and across the globe.

**Genesis:** On June 21, 2002, the FBI Director announced to Congress the establishment of the Fly Team as a significant counterterrorism initiative under the reorganization plan to refocus the Bureau's mission and priorities following the 9/11 terrorism attacks.

**What is it exactly?** A small, highly trained cadre of counterterrorism investigators—including special agents and intelligence analysts—based at FBI Headquarters who stand ready to deploy anywhere in the world on a moment's notice.

**Fly Team mission:** To bring the FBI's strategic and tactical counterterrorism capabilities to bear in partnership with other U.S. government agencies and foreign partner-nation entities in critical overseas locations to detect, penetrate, and disrupt terrorist networks. Specific training and skills include:

- Counterterrorism subject matter expertise
- Advanced interview and interrogation
- Human intelligence operations
- Evidence collection and sensitive site exploitation
- Digital media exploitation and forensics
- Explosive post blast investigations
- Biometrics
- Advanced tactical and force protection skills
- Advanced medical training
- Tactical evasive driving
- Hostage survival and resistance training
- Foreign language skills (Arabic, French, Somali, Spanish)
- Foreign weapons knowledge and proficiency
- Advanced surveillance techniques

**How often has the Fly Team been called?** Since its creation, the Fly Team has conducted hundreds of strategic deployments throughout the Middle East and North Africa, South Asia, the Horn of Africa, and the war zones of Iraq & Afghanistan. The Fly Team has also responded to numerous counterterrorism critical incidents over the years, with recent examples include the Boston Marathon bombing; Benghazi, Libya – U.S. Consulate Attack; Nairobi, Kenya - Westgate Mall attack; Kampala, Uganda – World Cup bombing; **and** Abuja, Nigeria – Boko Haram kidnapping of school girls.

# VI. Global Nature of Counterterrorism Operations

Ref: JP 3-26, Counterterrorism (Oct '14), p. III-5 to III-7.

*(Searching Documents/ U.S. Army photo by Spc. Philip Diab)*

## Global SOF Network

All SOF CT forces, whether based in the continental United States (CONUS) or forward-stationed, are part of the global SOF network where all SOF coordinate, exchange information and intelligence, and otherwise synchronize their efforts in support of the GCCs. They are able to connect with cross-functional, multiorganizational entities in CONUS and around the world allowing global collaboration to counter transregional and regional terrorist threats. The key CT organization in each AOR is the TSOC and its subordinate assigned and attached organizations and supporting forces.

Terrorist networks operate in a transnational environment that is not confined by boundaries, borders, or regions. To defeat this type of organization, USSOCOM provides continuous threat monitoring, 24/7 planning and reaction, as directed, and global capabilities that are not confined by department or agency geographic regions.

## Partner Nations

DOS engages US partners through the regional levels with regional teams or the sub-regional level with country teams. DOD works together with DOS and other interagency elements through the GCCs to implement US CT strategy. US strategy against terrorist organizations and individuals associated with terrorist organizations are a mixture of diplomatic, informational, military, and economic options as stated above. The GCC's CT operations are coordinated with allies and integrated into developing foreign partner SOF and conventional forces, and focus on mutual threats to United States and partner sovereignty. PNs' strategies focus on regional threats or adversaries and improving security. Military engagement planning occurs at the country team levels and the CCMD level to support US regional security interests and mitigate PN security concerns.

## Partner Nation Contributions

| Combat Forces | Troops<br>Ships<br>Aircraft<br>Staff/Noncommissioned Officers<br>Trainers | |
|---|---|---|
| **Non-Combat Forces** | Diplomatic Support | • Diplomatic recognition<br>• Opening embassy or mission<br>• Supporting United Nations Security Council resolutions |
| | Financial Support | • Debt forgiveness<br>• Unfreezing assets<br>• Direct financial assistance |
| | Logistics, Lift, and Sustainment | • Logistic infrastructure<br>• Strategic air and sea lift<br>• Intertheater air lift |
| | Basing, Access, and Overflight Support | • Basing rights<br>• Access to facilities<br>• Overflight rights |
| | Stabilization and Reconstruction Support | • Humanitarian assistance<br>• Public infrastructure |
| | Governance and Ministerial Support | • Constitutional support<br>• Ministerial mentoring<br>• Civil service training support |

Ref: JP 3-26 Counterterrorism, fig. III-1, p. III-6.

# US CT Strategy with Foreign Partners

US strategy against terrorist organizations and individuals associated with terrorist organizations are a mixture of diplomatic and security options. The US DOD CT enterprise, coordinated with allies and integrated into developing PN SOF, focuses on mutual threats to United States and partner sovereignty.

Military engagement with partners and advising and assisting them to develop CT capabilities are key tools in US CT strategy and leverages SOF regional orientation and expertise that creates an enduring CT partner in the region and often elsewhere.

Indigenous and surrogate forces may be employed to support or conduct CT operations. These indigenous forces may resemble those used during unconventional warfare operations or campaigns. Generally, SOF work with and through irregular forces in unconventional warfare, which are armed individuals or groups who are not members of the regular armed forces, police, or other internal security forces.

Generally, when SOF conduct CT with or through indigenous or surrogate elements, they team with members of the regular armed forces, police forces, or other internal security forces of a PN. A PN may have the national will to apprehend or expel terrorists from inside their borders, but lack the CT resources and expertise to act. Using USG assets to remove terrorists unilaterally from the civilian populace on behalf of a foreign government may present collateral diplomatic, political, and legal risks. In these circumstances, pursuing terrorists with or through regular indigenous forces or surrogates offers several advantages. They generally speak the local language, are sensitive to local culture, and have personal knowledge of the civilian populace. More importantly, they may be legally empowered by their national or local governments to conduct military or law enforcement operations within national borders to impose national will.

The Joint Special Operations Command, a subordinate unified command of US-SOCOM, has assigned and attached subordinate units and may deploy to support GCC's training, exercises, activities, and operations.

*Refer to JP 3-05, Special Operations, for a detailed description of SOF core activities.*

In addition to the responsibilities assigned in Title 10, USC, Section 167, the President has assigned CDRUSSOCOM responsibility for preparing forces to conduct CT activities and operations in support of SecDef-directed and GCC activities and operations, as well as the following tasks:

- Integrate DOD strategy, plans, and intelligence priorities for operations against terrorist networks designated by SecDef
- Plan campaigns against designated terrorist networks
- Provide military representation to US national agencies and international agencies for matters related to global operations against terrorist networks
- Integrate theater security cooperation activities, deployments, and capabilities that support campaigns against designated terrorist networks in coordination with GCCs and make priority recommendations to SecDef
- Plan operational preparation of the environment (OPE) and, as directed, execute OPE or synchronizing execution of OPE in coordination with GCCs
- Execute global operations against terrorist networks as directed

# II. Fundamentals of Counterterrorism

Ref: JP 3-26, Counterterrorism (Oct '14), chap. 2.

## I. Counterterrorism across the Range of Military Operations (ROMO)

JFCs use CT capabilities in a wide variety of combat and noncombat situations to build a cohesive CT operation or support the theater campaign plan. Activities and operations are normally performed by forces with regional expertise, long-term relations, and specific CT equipment and training. GCC CT operations and campaigns may take place across the range of military operations from the activities of engaging local CT forces and governments, developing indigenous CT security capabilities, deterring terrorist threats; to crisis response operations to counter terrorist incidents or limited CT contingencies; and when required, CT operations in support of major operations and campaigns to counter local, regional, or global terrorist threats.

(Dept of Army Photo)

## A. Military Engagement, Security Cooperation, and Deterrence Activities

The primary purpose of military engagement and security cooperation activities, which may include CT activities, is to enable the GCC to build indigenous capabilities that deter terrorist acts and shape the operational environment to a desired set of conditions that facilitate stability and future operations. Shaping activities include development of PN and friendly military capabilities, information exchange and intelligence sharing, intelligence operations, identification and development of infrastructure and logistics capabilities, interagency coordination, and other efforts to ensure access to critical regions across the globe.

CT as a part of military engagement is a noncombat activity conducted by CT forces. GCCs conduct routine military engagements to build trust and confidence, share information, coordinate mutual activities, maintain influence, build defense relationships, and develop allied and friendly military capabilities for self-defense and multinational operations. CT forces engage with nations' military or civilian security forces and authorities.

Security cooperation that involves interaction with PN or host nation (HN) CT defense forces builds relationships that promote US CT interests and develops indigenous and PN CT capabilities and capacities. These activities provide US CT forces with peacetime and contingency access to critical regions around the world. Security cooperation includes activities such as FID, SFA, combined training and exercises, and similar noncombat activities.

Deterrence prevents terrorist acts by presenting a credible threat of specific counteraction that would deny the success of an organization's use of terrorism and/or degrade its legitimacy or capabilities and influence over a population. Deterrence of an adversary who uses terrorism to achieve objectives is a difficult task. Military engagement and security cooperation activities can help deter future terrorist acts by presenting a credible threat that US and regional partner CT action would render the organization ineffective. Deterrence in one region may force terrorists to move to another, which may deter or disrupt the organization temporarily.

*Refer to JP 3-07.2, Antiterrorism, for more information.*

# B. Crisis Response and Limited Contingency Operations

## Crisis Response

The President and SecDef can respond to imminent terrorist threats or actual acts of terrorism by executing Chairman of the Joint Chiefs of Staff or GCC's CT crisis response plans. CT crisis response operations are rapid, relatively small-scale, of limited duration, and may involve multiple threat locations.

The Secretary of State has responsibility for matters involving protection of US citizens and interests and protection of all USG personnel on official duty abroad, other than personnel under command of a GCC. During a military crisis response, the President may direct the application of CT capabilities to resolve threats and incidents. This requires significant coordination and support from the National Security Council, Department of State (DOS), COM, and the country team, other USG departments and agencies, PNs for basing and/or forces, and the HN government and security forces. DOS employs its emergency action plans or post plans to highlight roles and responsibilities during potential hostage situations which could impact CT planning and CT activities.

In US domestic territory, crisis response is led by the Director of the FBI for the Attorney General. The Attorney General may request support from SecDef if a crisis exceeds the FBI's capacities. DOD support to the FBI/Department of Justice (DOJ) will require a Presidential proclamation or executive order if the joint force is likely to use deadly force.

## Limited Contingency Operations

A crisis response or limited contingency operation can be a single small-scale, limited-duration operation or a significant part of a major operation of extended duration involving combat. The associated general strategic and operational objectives are to protect US interests and prevent surprise attack or further conflict. Included are operations to ensure the safety of American citizens and US interests while

# II. Principles of Counterterrorism

*Ref: JP 3-26, Counterterrorism (Oct '14), p. II-1 to II-2.*

The principles of joint operations are formed around the traditional nine principles of war—objective, offensive, mass, economy of force, maneuver, unity of command, security, surprise, and simplicity. To these, joint doctrine adds three principles based on operations over the last few decades—restraint, perseverance, and legitimacy. The principles of joint operations apply to CT activities and operations, but of particular importance are legitimacy and objective.

## A. Legitimacy

Legitimacy is a condition based upon the perception by specific audiences of the legality, morality, or rightness of a set of actions, and of the propriety of the authority of the individuals or organizations in taking them. Legitimate CT operations strengthen support for the goals and activities of CT and help isolate terrorists from the public. Legitimacy can be decisive in addressing enduring terrorist threats.

## B. Objective

Objectives direct operations toward a clearly defined, decisive, and achievable goal. Clearly defined goals enable effective collaboration and unity of effort, which focuses CT operations to use scarce resources efficiently. Finally, by identifying and pursuing appropriate goals, CT may enhance legitimacy and earn enduring support.

In addition to the traditional tenets, CT requires collaboration, balance, and precision.

## C. Collaboration

Collaboration between USG departments and agencies, partner nations (PNs), and allies is necessary to ensure unity of effort through ongoing coordination, cooperation, and information sharing. CT operations include interagency and multinational partners during both planning and execution. Collaboration creates a common and increased understanding of the operational environment, and must be managed in order to preserve the precision and capabilities of forces conducting CT operations.

## D. Balance

The purpose of balanced action is to provide the appropriate type and scale of operations and activities to create desired effects. Balance is critical to CT operations as overly offensive or aggressive action risks eroding the legitimacy and support. Conversely, overly defensive action cedes the initiative to the terrorists and provides them the time and space to potentially grow into strategic threats.

## E. Precision

The purpose of precision is to limit unnecessary collateral damage. CT operations must be scalable in application and effect to address everything from individual actions by small groups of terrorists to enduring operations as part of a campaign to dismantle large terrorist networks. Precision helps preserve legitimacy by limiting unnecessary collateral damage.

maintaining and improving US ability to operate with multinational partners to deter the hostile ambitions of potential aggressors. CT activities during limited contingencies may include intelligence operations to identify terrorists and gain insights into terrorist organizations identified as an imminent threat to a US mission abroad. After terrorists and their organizations are located, CT forces may conduct strikes or raids to neutralize or reduce the threats, and other operations as directed by SecDef or GCC to protect US interests.

## C. Major Operations and Campaigns

When required to achieve national strategic objectives or protect national interests, the US national leadership may decide to conduct a major operation or campaign involving large-scale combat. The JFC may employ CT forces in support of all phases of operations to attack adversary state and non-state actors' use of unlawful violence. CT operations in support of major operations and campaigns are sustained and may occur simultaneously in multiple operational areas.

# III. Counterterrorism and Types of Activities and Operations

Joint doctrine characterizes the employment of US military by types of activities and operations in order to describe the nature of the effort, tasks, tactics, and other aspects to inform future operations, training, and professional education—CT is a type of operation. There are three broad types of CT activities: advise and assist activities; overseas CT activities; and support to civil authorities activities.

## A. Advise and Assist Activities

Advise and assist activities are all US military efforts to improve other nations' ability to provide security for its citizens, govern, provide services, prevent terrorists from using the nation's territory as a safe haven, and promote long-term regional stability.
*See facing page for further discussion.*

## B. Overseas CT Activities

### 1. Offense, Defense, and Stability Operations

Combat operations vary widely depending on the context of the operation and the objective. Major operations and campaigns, whether or not they involve large-scale combat, will normally include some level of offense, defense, and stability operations. Although defense may be the stronger force posture, it is the offense that is normally decisive in combat. In striving to achieve military strategic objectives quickly and at the least cost, JFCs will normally seek the earliest opportunity to conduct decisive offensive operations. Nevertheless, during sustained offensive operations, selected elements of the joint force may need to pause, defend, resupply, or reconstitute, while other forces continue the attack. Transitioning between offense and defense requires agility. Simultaneously, in many combat operations, the JFC will conduct stability operations to maintain or reestablish a safe and secure environment and provide essential governmental services, emergency infrastructure reconstruction, or humanitarian relief. The JFC may need to conduct a broad spectrum of CT operations to help secure the population during offensive, defensive, and stability operations.

Stability operations are military missions, tasks, and activities conducted outside the United States, in coordination with other government agencies to maintain or reestablish a safe and secure environment and to provide essential governmental services, emergency infrastructure reconstruction, and humanitarian relief. The JFC integrates and synchronizes stability operations with other operations within each major operation or campaign phase. Stability operations support USG stabilization

# Advise and Assist Activities

Ref: JP 3-26, Counterterrorism (Oct '14), p. II-4 to II-5.

Advise and assist activities include:

## 1. Nation Assistance

Nation assistance is a broad term for civil or military assistance, other than foreign humanitarian assistance (FHA), rendered to a nation by foreign forces within that nation's territory based on agreements mutually concluded between nations. Nation assistance includes security assistance, FID, and other programs.

Security assistance refers to a group of programs by which the United States provides defense articles, military training, and other defense-related services to foreign nations by grant, loan, credit, or cash sales. Security assistance equips, trains, and develops capabilities and capacities in foreign CT forces. A GCC theater campaign plan may include activities to provide security assistance to a nation's military and, when authorized, civilian CT forces, and may be combined with similar security assistance to neighboring countries to develop a regional CT capability to address cross-border terrorist threats and act in a coordinated effort.

## 2. Foreign Internal Defense (FID)

FID programs encompass the diplomatic, economic, informational, and military support provided to another nation to assist its fight against subversion, lawlessness, insurgency, terrorism, and other threats to their security. US military support to FID focuses on the operational assistance to HN personnel and collaborative planning with interorganizational and HN authorities to anticipate, preclude, and counter threats. FID supports HN internal defense and development programs. US military involvement in FID has historically been focused on helping a nation defeat an organized movement attempting to overthrow its lawful government.

## 3. Foreign Humanitarian Assistance (FHA)

FHA consists of DOD activities, normally in support of the US Agency for International Development or DOS, conducted outside of the United States and its territories to directly relieve or reduce human suffering, disease, hunger, or privation. The assistance provided supplements or complements the efforts of the HN civil authorities or agencies that may have the primary responsibility for providing humanitarian assistance.

## 4. Security Force Assistance (SFA )

SFA consists of DOD activities that contribute to unified action by the USG to support the development of the capacity and capability of foreign security forces and their supporting institutions. Foreign security forces are duly constituted military, paramilitary, police, and constabulary forces of a state. Foreign security forces consist of civilian and military organizations, to include law enforcement, border security, intelligence, SOF, and conventional forces. SFA and foreign security forces are integral to successful FID, COIN, and stability operations. SFA may provide US CT force information, intelligence, and access to the HN.

*Refer to TAA2: Military Engagement, Security Cooperation & Stability SMARTbook (Foreign Train, Advise, & Assist) for further discussion. Topics include Security Cooperation & Security Assistance (Train, Advise, & Assist), Stability Operations (ADRP 3-07), Peace Operations (JP 3-07.3), Counterinsurgency Operations (JP & FM 3-24), Civil-Military Operations (JP 3-57), Multinational Operations (JP 3-16), Interorganizational Coordination (JP 3-08), and more.*

efforts and contribute to USG initiatives to build partnerships. These initiatives set the conditions for interaction with multinational partners, competitors, adversary leaders, military forces, and relevant populations by developing and presenting information and conducting activities that affect their perceptions, will, behavior, and capabilities. The JFC will likely conduct them in coordination with interorganizational partners and the private sector in support of HN authorities. The JFC may need to conduct a broad spectrum of CT activities and operations from improving the capabilities of HN CT forces to conducting strikes and raids on terrorist organizations.

## 2. Counterinsurgency (COIN)

An insurgency may devolve into organizations merely focused on terrorism because of many factors, such as lack of popular support, loss of leadership, or desperation. An insurgent applies military power against military forces, a terrorist unlawfully uses violence against civilians. Thus, a JFC may be simultaneously conducting COIN operations and CT.

## 3. Peace Operations (PO)

The diplomatic, information, economic, and military efforts to return a nation to stability and legitimate governance may be spoiled by terrorist actions. The JFC should assess the requirement for CT activities and operations during PO. The POs' fundamental requirement for impartiality requires the JFC to act on behalf of the peace process and not show preference for any faction or group over another and also applies to belligerents. Impartiality does not apply to possible spoilers such as terrorists. The JFC, within the command and operational framework of the specific PO, should determine if actors hostile to the peace process use terrorist tactics and design CT activities and operations with USG, HN, and PO partners.

## 4. Counterdrug Operations

Counterdrug operations are civil or military actions taken to reduce or eliminate illicit drug trafficking. Counterdrug activities are provided by DOD to support foreign military forces and law enforcement agencies to detect, monitor, and counter the production and distribution of illegal drugs. DOD policy recognizes that illicit drug traffickers and terrorists often use the same methods, and that in many cases, traffickers and terrorists are one and the same. Narcoterrorism is terrorism that is linked to illicit drug trafficking. It may take the form of drug traffickers using terrorist tactics to protect and further illicit drug production or trade. Insurgents can also use illicit drug production or trade to fund their operations. Both narco-driven and narco-funded terrorists may be countered by CT operations.

## 5. Noncombatant Evacuation Operation (NEO)

NEOs are conducted to assist DOS in evacuating US citizens, DOD civilian personnel, and designated HN and third country nationals whose lives are in danger from locations in a foreign nation to an appropriate safe haven due to events that may have been caused by terrorists. Within the country, the ambassador is designated as the responsible authority for the NEO.

*Refer to TAA2: Military Engagement, Security Cooperation & Stability SMARTbook (Foreign Train, Advise, & Assist) for further discussion. Topics include Security Cooperation & Security Assistance (Train, Advise, & Assist), Stability Operations (ADRP 3-07), Peace Operations (JP 3-07.3), Counterinsurgency Operations (JP & FM 3-24), Civil-Military Operations (JP 3-57), Multinational Operations (JP 3-16), Interorganizational Coordination (JP 3-08), and more.*

## 6. Countering WMD

The intersection of states, state-sponsored terrorism, nonstate terrorists, and WMD proliferation represents one of the greatest security challenges facing the United States. Terrorists have the ability to use chemical, biological, radiological, and nuclear (CBRN) weapons and even toxic industrial materials to conduct attacks that can cause catastrophic mass casualties and panic in support of any terrorist aim.

*See chapters seven and eight for more information.*

## 7. MISO

MISO attempt to change the behavior of foreign governments, organizations, groups, and individuals in a manner favorable to the JFC. MISO are integral to CT approaches to counter the terrorists' ideology, support moderate alternatives, establish an information capability with HNs, build HN CT capacities, and attack VEOs and their infrastructure and networks.

# C. Defense Support of Civil Authorities (DSCA)

DSCA is support provided by US Armed Forces, DOD civilians, DOD contract personnel, DOD component assets, and National Guard forces (when SecDef, in coordination with the governors of the affected states, elects and requests to use those forces in Title 32, United States Code [USC] status), or when federalized in response to requests for assistance from civil authorities for domestic emergencies, law enforcement support, and other domestic activities, or from qualifying entities for special events. DSCA includes support to prepare, prevent, protect, respond, and recover from domestic incidents including terrorist attacks, major disasters both natural and man-made, and domestic special events. DSCA is provided in response to requests from civil authorities and upon approval from appropriate authorities.

*Refer to The Homeland Defense & DSCA SMARTbook (Protecting the Homeland / Defense Support to Civil Authority) for complete discussion. Topics and references include homeland defense (JP 3-28), defense support of civil authorities (JP 3-28), Army support of civil authorities (ADRP 3-28), multi-service DSCA TTPs (ATP 3-28.1/MCWP 3-36.2), DSCA liaison officer toolkit (GTA 90-01-020), key legal and policy documents, and specific hazard and planning guidance.*

# IV. Joint Intelligence Preparation of the Operational Environment (JIPOE)

The joint intelligence preparation of the operational environment (JIPOE) process is used to characterize the operational environment and provide a disciplined methodology for applying a holistic view to the analysis of adversary capabilities and intentions. During CT operations JIPOE places far greater emphasis on understanding the civil population and critical infrastructure. Additionally, JIPOE helps combat terrorism by supporting force protection measures, counterintelligence, and other security-related activities. The JIPOE process consists of four basic steps that ensure the systematic analysis of all relevant aspects of the operational environment. The process is both continuous and cyclical in that JIPOE is conducted both prior to and during CT operations as well as during planning for follow-on missions. All joint staff headquarters sections, not just the intelligence section, are involved in the JIPOE process.

## Critical Factors Analysis

Critical factors analysis for CT starts by analyzing the centers of gravity (COGs) of terrorist organizations and their networks and then determining their critical capabilities, requirements, and vulnerabilities. This allows the JIPOE team to recognize decisive points and what shaping operations are necessary to successfully execute CT operations.

# V. Counterterrorism Analytical Framework

Ref: JP 3-26, Counterterrorism (Oct '14), fig. II-1, p. II-9.

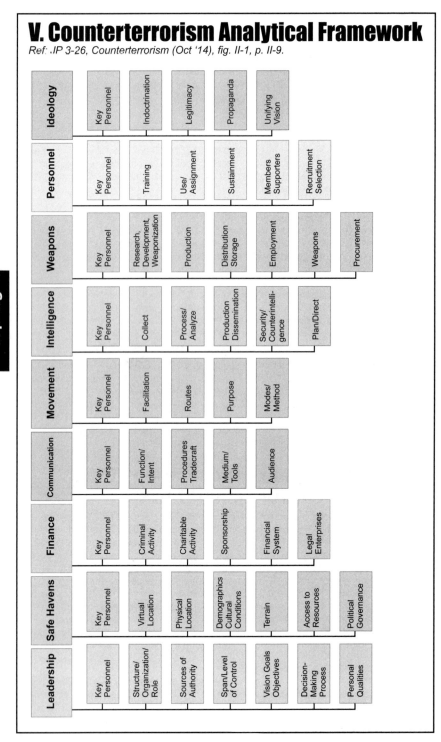

Chap 4

# III. Command, Planning & Assessment

Ref: JP 3-26, Counterterrorism (Oct '14), chap. 4.

> "Now, make no mistake, our nation is still threatened by terrorists… But we have to recognize that the threat has shifted and evolved from the one that came to our shores on 9/11. With a decade of experience now to draw from, this is the moment to ask ourselves hard questions—about the nature of today's threats and how we should confront them."
>
> President Barack Obama, National Defense University, May 23, 2013

# I. Command of Counterterrorist Operations

## A. General Tenets

### 1. Command

Command is the exercise of authorities, as specified by SecDef or delegated by a superior JFC, by a properly designated commander over forces assigned or attached to the command. The JP-1, Doctrine for the Armed Forces of the United States, command framework applies to command of CT forces, but because of the unbounded nature of terrorist organizations that operate within and astride GCCs' boundaries, creating a CT command structure that maintains unity of command and achieves unity of action and effort is challenging.

### 2. Unity of Command

Unity of command means all forces operate under a single commander with the requisite authority to direct all forces employed in pursuit of a common purpose, and no two commanders may exercise the same command relationship over the same force at any one time. The diverse nature of SOF component capabilities and missions, the small size of numerous operational elements that often cross geographically large operations areas, and working with HN forces and/or among indigenous populations make SOF unity of command difficult. The guiding principle is to place all SOF forces under a single JFC with the requisite command authorities and relationships to coordinate special operations among all supporting and supported units. Unless otherwise directed by the President or SecDef, a special operations activity or mission is conducted under the command of the GCC in whose AOR the activity or mission is to be conducted. A GCC normally achieves unity of command of SOF through the CDRTSOC. A commander, joint special operations task force normally provides SOF unity of command for a JFC subordinate to a GCC. CDRTSOC or commander, joint special operations task force, may also be designated the joint force special operations component commander under a JFC.

Also, CDRUSSOCOM must maintain the capability to exercise command of a selected special operations mission if directed by the President or SecDef with the approval of the President.

SecDef may create unity of command across multiple GCC AORs by establishing simultaneous command relationships, such as OPCON, between a CT JFC and multiple GCCs. Each GCC exercises OPCON of the JFC and those CT forces operating in the GCC's AOR; the OPCON does not apply to the JFC's CT forces operating in

Counter-terrorism

other GCCs' AORs. This maintains unity of command because no GCC exercises OPCON of the same forces, only those forces within the GCC's AOR. Furthermore, SecDef, CDRUSSOCOM, or the GCC may enhance unity of command by creating a support command relationship between a supporting CT JFC, not assigned or apportioned to the GCC, and the supported TSOC commander.

### 3. Unity of Effort and Unified Action

Unity of effort is the coordination and cooperation toward common objectives, as a result of unified action even if the participants are not necessarily part of the same command or organization. Unified action is the synchronized, coordinated, and integrated activities of government and nongovernment entities with those of the military to achieve common objectives. Through unified action CT forces are often employed as part of a whole-of-government effort, operating with other joint forces, various interagency partners, and multinational partners, intergovernmental organizations, NGOs, and HN forces and organizations. This requires the SOF commanders to coordinate and synchronize special operations with other efforts. Unity of effort is an essential complement to unity of command.

# B. Command Relationships and Authorities for Counterterrorist Activities and Operations

Title 10, USC, Section 164, is the statutory authority for combatant command (command authority). SecDef, FCCs, GCCs, JFCs, and tactical commanders delegate requisite authorities to subordinate commanders at all levels by establishing command relationships. JP 1, Doctrine for the Armed Forces of the United States, delineates and describes the types of command authority.

*Refer to JP 1, Doctrine for the Armed Forces of the United States, for a complete discussion of command authorities, relationships, transfer of forces, and C2.*

### Counterterrorist Support Command Relationships Establishing Directives

Unless limited by the establishing directive, the supported commander will have the authority to exercise general direction of the supporting effort, including designation and prioritization of targets or objectives, timing and duration of the supporting action, and other instructions necessary for coordination and efficiency.

Unless limited by the establishing directive, the supporting commander has the responsibility to ascertain the needs of the supported commander and take action to fulfill them within existing capabilities, consistent with priorities and requirements of other assigned tasks. The supporting commander determines the forces, tactics, methods, procedures, and communications to be employed in providing this support. The supporting commander will advise and coordinate with the supported commander on matters concerning the employment and limitations (e.g., logistics) of such support, assist in planning for the integration of such support into the supported commander's effort as a whole, and ensure that support requirements are appropriately communicated within the supporting commander's organization.

# C. Command Relationships and Assignment and Transfer of Counterterrorist Forces

When a force is assigned, reassigned, or attached, SecDef will specify the command relationship the gaining CCDR will exercise and the losing commander will relinquish. Forces, not command relationships, are transferred between commands. Forces assigned or attached to a CCMD may be further assigned or attached within the CCMD by the CCDR, who will also delegate the appropriate command relationship.

# Command Relationships

Ref: JP 3-26, Counterterrorism (Oct '14), p. IV-3 to IV-4.

The nature of terrorist threats requires SecDef, CDRUSSOCOM, GCCs, and JFCs to establish flexible and often complex command relationships to ensure CT forces have the required agility to coordinate with all DOD, interagency, and foreign partners, and to pursue terrorists across military and governmental boundaries. Following is an overview of these authorities and their use in CT activities and operations.

## Combatant Command (Command Authority)

Title 10, USC, Section 167, lists CT as a special operations activity of USSOCOM, which has forces specifically trained and equipped to conduct CT activities and operations. Special operations activities and missions are normally conducted under the OPCON of a specific GCC.

## Operational Control (OPCON)

Unless otherwise directed by SecDef, when USSOCOM CT forces are transferred to a GCC, the gaining GCC exercises OPCON over those CT forces. In addition to US-SOCOM provided CT forces, the gaining GCC has OPCON over permanently forward-stationed CT forces. In both cases—forces provided by CDRUSSOCOM and those permanently under a GCC's OPCON—the GCC normally exercises OPCON through the TSOC commander, unless otherwise directed by SecDef.

## Tactical Control (TACON)

A GCC or TSOC commander may delegate tactical control to subordinate commanders to direct CT activities and operations, and control assigned or attached forces or designated forces made available for tasking.

## Support

Support is a command relationship especially useful for JFCs employing CT forces that must operate across multiple commands and operational areas because it creates flexibility for the JFC. A support relationship is established when a CT force must operate in another organization's operational area or across multiple GCCs' AORs to effectively coordinate and pursue terrorists. Thus, a supporting CT force commander may be in support of two or more GCCs/JFCs simultaneously to effectively address cross-boundary threats. The support relationship enables CT forces to address terrorist threats thereby complementing forces conducting other operations, such as stability, COIN, FID, offense, defense, etc.

SecDef or common superior commander assigns roles and responsibilities and grants authorities to the supporting and supported commanders in an establishing directive or order that creates the command relationship. An establishing directive is essential to ensure unity of effort. The support command relationship is used by SecDef to establish and prioritize CT support between and among CCDRs, and to create command relationships for national CT forces with CCMDs and TSOCs to address terrorist threats within and that transcend GCCs' AORs.

Effective employment of CT forces may require a JFC to be a supporting commander to two or more supported commanders simultaneously. When there is a conflict over prioritization between component commanders, SecDef or common superior commander will have final adjudication. When the supporting commander cannot fulfill the needs of the supported commander, either the supported or supporting commander will notify the establishing authority. The establishing authority will provide a solution.

In support of Title 10, USC, Section 167, and delineated through the Global Force Management Implementation Guidance, SecDef assigns all CONUS-based CT forces to USSOCOM and attaches permanently forward-stationed CT forces to the respective GCC, who exercises OPCON over them. SecDef may direct CDRUS-SOCOM to temporarily transfer CONUS-based CT forces, attach them to a GCC and delegate OPCON or tactical control, and establish support command relationships with each TSOC in order to facilitate employment of CT forces within and astride GCC AORs and coordinate and pursue transregional terrorist threats. SecDef may authorize CDRUSSOCOM to establish support command relationships where CT forces simultaneously support one or more TSOCs. The support command relationships are set up through the affected GCCs.

## D. Command and Control of Counterterrorist Forces

The C2 fundamentals and processes described in JP 1, Doctrine for the Armed Forces of the United States, apply to CT activities and operations. Of special concern to the JFC conducting CT activities and operations is the need to create a flexible and responsive C2 structure, one that enables coordination at all appropriate levels, rapid decision making and approval, and timely action, and maintains unity of effort. In complex operational environments, the JFC may use the support command relationship to provide the organizational agility necessary for CT operations. In all cases, commanders exercising command authority over SOF should:

- Provide for a clear and unambiguous CT chain of command to create unity of command with the requisite authority to accomplish assigned tasks.
- Establish clear command relationships to achieve unity of effort. Clearly define authorities, roles, and relationships and ensure subordinate commanders, staff principals, and leaders of C2 nodes and liaisons understand their authorities and role in decision making and controlling, and their relationships with others.
- Provide for sufficient CT staff experience and expertise to plan, conduct, support, and assess operations.
- Ensure that requisite CT liaisons are in place and know their roles, responsibilities, and authorities.

# II. Elements of Operational Design for Counterterrorism Planning

Joint operation planning integrates military action and capabilities with those of other instruments of national power in time, space, and purpose in unified action to achieve the JFC's objectives.

## A. Operational Approach

The purpose of joint operation planning is to integrate military activities and operations with those of other instruments of national power in time, space, and purpose in unified action to create effects that achieve the JFC's objectives and attain the end state.

A JFC uses the operational approach to understand the operational environment and the problem while describing the visualization of a broad approach for attaining the desired end state. The operational approach uses elements of operational design—termination criteria, military end state, objectives, effects, COG, approaches, lines of operation (LOOs) and lines of effort (LOEs), CT defeat mechanism, etc.—to provide details and facilitate detailed planning.

*See facing page for an overview and further discussion.*

# Operational Approach

Ref: JP 3-26, Counterterrorism (Oct '14), p. IV-6 to IV-7 and JP 5-0, Joint Operation Planning (Aug '11), pp. III-5 to III-6.

The JFC and staff develop plans and orders through the application of operational art and operational design and by using the joint operation planning process (JOPP). They combine art and science to develop products that describe how **(ways)** the joint force will employ its capabilities **(means)** to achieve the military end state **(ends)**. **Operational art** is the application of creative imagination by commanders and staffs— supported by their skill, knowledge, and experience. **Operational design** is a process of iterative understanding and problem framing that supports commanders and staffs in their application of operational art with tools and a methodology to conceive of and construct viable approaches to operations and campaigns. Operational design results in the **commander's operational approach**, which broadly describes the actions the joint force needs to take to reach the end state.

Figure IV-1 below illustrates the operational approach concept to CT operational planning. The figure shows five LOEs, each of which applies specific CT defeat mechanisms—disrupt, isolate, dismantle, and enable—to achieve the objectives supported by the LOE and create desired conditions by changing the physical or behavioral political, military, economic, social, informational, and infrastructure environment.

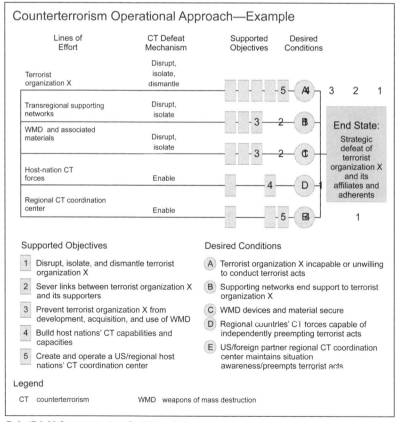

Counterterrorism Operational Approach—Example

Ref: JP 3-26 Counterterrorism, fig. IV-1, p. IV-7.

# B. Termination Criteria

The JFC derives CT termination criteria from national policy and strategy to establish the end state and conditions required to end military operations. The JFC must know the national strategic end state and conditions, understand the US policy nuances among different terrorist organizations, and maintain contact with the national leadership for potential changes during the planning and execution of CT operations.

Terrorist organizations often operate in and receive support from many countries. This means CT planning termination criteria are normally organization-based rather than country-based, except perhaps where a country is a sponsor of terrorism. The JFC's understanding of national strategic end state and conditions develops termination criteria for joint CT operations against terrorist organizations as the starting point for operational design because they enable development of the military end state, conditions, and objectives. The following examples of CT termination criteria conditions support the national end state of defeating terrorist organization X.

# C. Military End State

Military end state is the set of required conditions that defines achievement of all military objectives. It normally represents a point in time and/or circumstances beyond which the President does not require the military instrument of national power as the means to achieve remaining national objectives. CT activities and operations are seldom the primary military effort in a whole-of government CT effort, but they are often a major complementing effort. In any situation, military CT activities and operations may be only one of many USG instruments of national power employed.

## Examples of CT Termination Criteria (Conditions)

Terrorist organization X lacks the capability to plan, conduct, or support operations that threaten countries within the region where it operates, other countries, and the US homeland and its interests abroad.

Countries where terrorist organization X operates are willing and able to disrupt attack planning, facilitation, and operations against countries in the region and the US homeland and interests abroad and safe havens are eliminated.

Countries where terrorist organization X operates have secured their weapons of mass destruction.

US and foreign partners are positioned to maintain situational awareness and able to identify potential use of terrorism in order to preempt reemergence of terrorists.

# D. Objectives

An objective is a clearly defined, decisive, and attainable goal toward which every military operation should be directed. The purpose of CT operations is to achieve military objectives that change conditions and attain the end state. Because national CT strategy and guidance may provide national strategic end state and objectives individually for each terrorist operation and organization of importance to the defense of the homeland, they may be useful without significant additional guidance at the theater and operational levels. Military objectives are the basis for identifying the military tasks that have to be accomplished in order to achieve an objective and change conditions.

# E. Effects

An effect is a physical and/or behavioral change in the state of a system resulting from an action, a set of actions, or another effect. The use of desired effects in planning can help a commander and staff determine the operational tasks required to achieve objectives and clarify the relationship among COGs, decisive points, LOOs, LOEs, objectives, military end state, and termination criteria. During execution of CT operations in complex situations the proximate cause of effects can be difficult to predict. While effects may be created by the conduct of missions at the tactical level, their contribution to achieving an objective is measured at the operational and higher levels. Sufficient intelligence is required to predict direct effects reliably, and indirect effects are difficult to foresee. JFCs must appreciate that unpredictable third-party action, unintended consequences of friendly operations, and the fog and friction of conflict will contribute to the uncertainty of effect assessments.

## Examples of CT Effects

Terrorist organization X is incapable of conducting attacks within countries from which it operates, in other countries, or US against persons or facilities.

Links between terrorist organization X and violent extremist organizations are severed and the development of new links is prevented.

Countries in which terrorist organization X operates have trained and equipped civilian or military forces able to independently conduct effective CT operations.

Countries in which terrorist organization X operates participate in a US and foreign partner regional CT coordination center to maintain situational awareness of terrorist organization X, and coordinate and take action to preempt terrorist acts.

# F. Centers of Gravity (COG)

Analysis of friendly and adversary COGs is a key step in operational design. Joint force intelligence analysts identify adversary COGs, determining from which elements the adversary derives freedom of action, physical strength (means), and the will to fight. The J-2, in conjunction with other operational planners, then attempts to determine if the tentative or candidate COGs truly are critical to the adversary's strategy. This analysis is a linchpin in the planning effort. Others on the joint force staff conduct similar analysis to identify friendly COGs. Once COGs have been identified, JFCs and their staffs determine how to attack enemy COGs while protecting friendly COGs. The protection of friendly strategic COGs such as public opinion and US national capabilities typically requires efforts and capabilities beyond those of just the supported CCDR. An analysis of the identified COGs in terms of critical capabilities, requirements, and vulnerabilities is vital to this process.

An objective is always linked to a COG. The JFC needs to identify and analyze friendly and enemy COGs during planning. In CT planning, there may be different COGs at the strategic, operational, and tactical levels, especially when addressing terrorist movements that have transregional or global participants. Terrorist organizations may coalesce around a strategic COG in a global or transregional effort to change political, military, economic, or social conditions. The JFC's analysis of COGs at all levels is important because it guides the application of military capabilities and is exceedingly dependent upon detailed and continuous joint and interagency intelligence and analysts with long-term focus.

The JFC must determine the COG(s) at each level and apply CT capabilities appropriately in order to efficiently and effectively use CT resources and achieve the CT objectives, as the JFC continuously analyzes and refines COGs to adjust to friendly and terrorist actions. Furthermore, the JFC must recognize that CT operations are normally complementing efforts to other military and USG actions to protect a foreign country and the homeland from terrorist acts. As such, COGs associated with terrorist organizations may also be addressed by stability operations, COIN, FID, and other military and civilian efforts to change the environment within the country or region so that terrorists do not have the support of the population and lack the legitimacy required for continued support within and outside of the country and region.

The JFC further analyzes each COG to determine its critical capabilities, requirements, and vulnerabilities. The JFC must have sufficient CT capabilities, authorities, and approvals, to include interagency and often HN approvals, to take advantage of a terrorist's critical vulnerabilities.

A JFC should focus efforts against critical vulnerabilities that will do the most decisive or significant damage to a terrorist's COG. In selecting the vulnerabilities for attack, the JFC must analyze the vulnerability for its accessibility, redundancy, ability to recuperate, and impact on the civilian populace, and balance those factors against friendly capabilities to affect those vulnerabilities. In CT operations, the freedom of action for CT forces is essential and may be reduced substantially when vulnerability factors are not balanced properly, especially the effect CT forces' actions may have on the civilian population. Additionally, critical capabilities, requirements, and vulnerabilities may change as the JFC applies CT capabilities and the terrorists react and modify their strategy.

*See facing page for further discussion.*

# G. Direct and Indirect Approaches & Decisive Points

A direct approach attacks the enemy's COG by applying combat power directly against it. An indirect approach attacks the enemy's COG by applying combat power against a series of decisive points that lead to the defeat of the COG. Understanding the relationship among a COG's critical capabilities, requirements, and vulnerabilities can illuminate direct and indirect approaches to the COG. Most critical factors will be decisive points. When dealing with terrorists, the JFC must consider how actions against decisive points will affect not only the enemy but also the relevant population and their behavior and relationships with the terrorist and friendly forces. A CT campaign or operation is normally a sustained indirect approach to defeat a terrorist organization and its support networks. A JFC employing CT forces must selectively focus a series of actions against terrorists' critical vulnerabilities until the cumulative effects lead to achieving the objectives and attaining the end state determined by the President and SecDef. National policy does not always require defeat of terrorist organizations; it may direct the containment of the threat, monitoring it, and be prepared to take action if required.

# H. Lines of Operation (LOOs) and Lines of Effort (LOEs)

## Lines of Operation (LOOs)

A LOO defines the interior or exterior orientation of a friendly force in relationship to an enemy force that connects actions on nodes and/or decisive points related in time and space to an objective(s). Interior lines refer to a force operating from a central position allowing it to mass combat power against a specific portion of an enemy force. Exterior lines mean a force converges on an enemy force, offering opportunities for encirclement. Major operations are typically designed using LOOs to tie offensive, defensive, and stability tasks to the geographic and opposing force-oriented objectives.

## Lines of Effort (LOEs)

A LOE links multiple tasks and missions using the logic of purpose—cause and effect—to focus efforts toward establishing operational and strategic conditions. LOEs are used when COGs and decisive points do not involve friendly force orientation toward an enemy force as seen in LOOs. CT planning uses LOEs to link tasks, effects, and decisive points to objectives to achieve the desired conditions and attain the end state, and are particularly useful when CT force orientation at the operational and strategic levels has little relevance. CT force orientation at the tactical level may involve LOOs, or a combination of LOOs and LOEs. Furthermore, the JFC planning

# Centers of Gravity (COG)

*Ref: JP 3-26, Counterterrorism (Oct '14), p. IV-9 to IV-10 and JP 5-0, Joint Operation Planning (Aug '11), pp. III-5 to III-6.*

The JFC must determine the COG(s) at each level and apply CT capabilities appropriately in order to efficiently and effectively use CT resources and achieve the CT objectives, as the JFC continuously analyzes and refines COGs to adjust to friendly and terrorist actions. Furthermore, the JFC must recognize that CT operations are normally complementing efforts to other military and USG actions to protect a foreign country and the homeland from terrorist acts. As such, COGs associated with terrorist organizations may also be addressed by stability operations, COIN, FID, and other military and civilian efforts to change the environment within the country or region so that terrorists do not have the support of the population and lack the legitimacy required for continued support within and outside of the country and region.

## Counterterrorist Operational Level Center of Gravity Analysis—Example

| Terrorist Organization X | | CT Forces |
|---|---|---|
| • Key leaders<br>• Permissive operating environment | **Center of Gravity** | • Interagency/foreign partner collaboration<br>• US political will to act |
| • Leadership capacity to communicate, plan, and C2<br>• Maintain contact with other terrorists and local tribal leaders<br>• Freedom of movement to operate, resupply, recruit, and train<br>• Transregional media production capabilities<br>• Financial and logistics access | **Critical Capabilities** | • US interagency/foreign partner CT enterprise focused on threat<br>• Communications network with all relevant interagency/foreign partners<br>• Freedom of movement<br>• Financial and other resources<br>• Force structure tuned to CT activities and operations<br>• Strategic, operational, and tactical mobility |
| • Transregional communications networks<br>• Safe havens<br>• Experienced cadre<br>• Access to smuggling routes, black markets, local criminals, and tribes | **Critical Requirements** | • Trust among interagency/foreign partners<br>• Transregional C2 structure<br>• Regional basing and support<br>• Access to regions where terrorists base, receive support, operate |
| • Unsecure communications networks<br>• Leadership lack of OPSEC within safe havens–training camps, etc.<br>• Leadership internal rifts<br>• Delegitimizing criminal activities<br>• Hostage for ransom activities | **Critical Vulnerabilities** | • Acquiring sufficient intelligence<br>• Timeliness of authorities to act<br>• Interaction with foreign forces<br>• OPSEC when operating independent of Department of Defense facilities |

Legend

| | |
|---|---|
| C2 command and control | OPSEC operations security |
| CT counterterrorism | |

*Ref: JP 3-26 Counterterrorism, fig. IV-2, p. IV-10.*

**(Counterterrorism) III. Command, Planning & Assessment  4-33**

CT operations may combine CT LOEs with those of corresponding DOS, FBI, and other interagency CT partners, which brings to bear capabilities, expertise, and authorities of multiple elements of the USG and facilitates unity of effort when addressing complex CT problems.

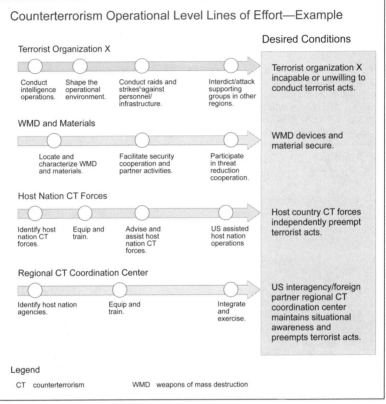

## Counterterrorism Operational Level Lines of Effort—Example

**Desired Conditions**

**Terrorist Organization X**

Conduct intelligence operations. → Shape the operational environment. → Conduct raids and strikes against personnel/ infrastructure. → Interdict/attack supporting groups in other regions.

Terrorist organization X incapable or unwilling to conduct terrorist acts.

**WMD and Materials**

Locate and characterize WMD and materials. → Facilitate security cooperation and partner activities. → Participate in threat reduction cooperation.

WMD devices and material secure.

**Host Nation CT Forces**

Identify host nation CT forces. → Equip and train. → Advise and assist host nation CT forces. → US assisted host nation operations

Host country CT forces independently preempt terrorist acts.

**Regional CT Coordination Center**

Identify host nation agencies. → Equip and train. → Integrate and exercise.

US interagency/foreign partner regional CT coordination center maintains situational awareness and preempts terrorist acts.

Legend

CT   counterterrorism          WMD   weapons of mass destruction

Ref: JP 3-26 Counterterrorism, fig. IV-3, p. IV-12.

Commanders synchronize activities along complementary LOOs to achieve the end state.

- **Interior Lines.** A force operates on interior lines when its operations diverge from a central point. Interior lines usually represent central position, where a friendly force can reinforce or concentrate its elements faster than the enemy force can reposition.

- **Exterior Lines.** A force operates on exterior lines when its operations converge on the enemy. Operations on exterior lines offer opportunities to encircle and annihilate an enemy force.

*Refer to JFODS4: The Joint Forces Operations & Doctrine SMARTbook (Guide to Joint, Multinational & Interorganizational Operations) for further discussion of the remaining elements of operational design. Topics and chapters include joint doctrine fundamentals, joint operations, joint operation planning, joint logistics, joint task forces, information operations, multinational operations, and interorganizational coordination.*

# I. Counterterrorist Defeat Mechanism
Ref: JP 3-26, Counterterrorism (Oct '14), p. IV-11 to IV-13.

The defeat mechanism complements the understanding achieved by a COG analysis of a problem by suggesting means to solve it. It is a useful tool to describe the main effects a commander wants to create along a LOO or LOE. The defeat mechanism is to identify, disrupt, isolate, and dismantle terrorist organizations, plus enable HN and PN CT forces that lead to the organization's defeat. Terrorists often reside in remote or inaccessible areas, avoid presenting their organizations to direct attack, blend with populations, and hide their activities until ready to take action. Defeating terrorist organizations requires the application of persistent pressure, eroding their ability to operate, and denying them the ability to instill fear or coerce populations and governments through violence. This requires enduring activities targeting both a terrorist organization's operational capability and its capacity to gain and employ resources. Attacking terrorist organizations requires specifically trained and equipped CT forces, working with interagency partners and independently or with HNs and PNs.

## Disrupt
CT disruption is the direct attack of terrorist nodes that are identified during the JIPOE process. All source analysis conducted by specialized intelligence organizations, integrating intelligence provided by USG and PNs, facilitates the identification and targeting of key network nodes. Disruption contributes to degrading terrorist capabilities by eliminating or temporarily neutralizing organizational nodes. Terrorists do not normally mass their forces for engagement, thus CT disruption attacks terrorist nodes to capture or kill terrorists, destroy communications, capture resources, and neutralize materiel required for terrorist acts. The effect of disruption is degradation of the organization's ability to commit acts of terrorism.

## Isolate
Isolation limits a terrorist organization's ability to organize, train, plan, or conduct operations effectively by denying communications, resources, recruits, and access to supporting population(s) and/or governments. The effect of isolation is a diminished organization, unable to grow or maintain its size, cutting off logistic support, and eliminating its ability to publicize its cause.

## Dismantle
Dismantling exploits the effects of disruption and isolation that further expose the organization to attack. Dismantling may include capturing or killing of remaining key personnel and neutralizing materiel essential to the organization's terrorist capabilities. The effect of dismantling may include dislocation, a shift of terrorist acts to another region or multiple dispersed locations, terrorists unable to acquire recruits or funding to maintain its organization, or members leave the organization for other pursuits.

## Enable
Enabling is the advise and assist activities made by US CT forces to ensure HN and PN military and civilian CT forces have sufficient capabilities and capacities to contain or defeat organizations that commit acts of terrorism to further their goals. In addition to providing equipment, training, and operational support, enabling may include sustained military engagement with HN and PN in regional CT coordination centers to maintain situational awareness and to preempt terrorists before they can strike.

# III. Assessment

*Ref: JP 3-26, Counterterrorism (Oct '14), p. IV-13 to IV-14 and JP 5-0, Joint Operation Planning (Dec '06), pp. D-2 to D-6.*

Assessment is the process to measure progress toward achieving objectives, attaining the desired end state and associated conditions, or performing tasks. The JFC assesses operations continuously to determine when to adjust operations—such as shifting priority of effort or transitioning to another phase—in order to ensure the joint force achieves its objectives and attains the military end state.

The assessment criteria of measures of effectiveness (MOEs) and measures of performance (MOPs) play key roles in determining a commander's critical information requirements (CCIRs). The CCIRs consist of priority intelligence requirements that focus on the adversary and operational environment, and friendly force information requirements, which address the status of friendly forces and supporting capabilities. Both may include MOEs and MOPs and assessment indicators associated with them in the form of information requirements.

The assessment process is a continuous cycle that begins during mission analysis when the JFC and staff consider what to measure and how to measure it to determine progress toward accomplishing a task, creating an effect, or achieving an objective to attain the desired end state. The JFC and staff determine relevant assessment actions and measures during planning to help guide operational design because these considerations can affect the sequence and type of actions along LOOs and LOEs. During execution the JFC and staff continually monitor progress toward accomplishing tasks, creating an effect, achieving an objective, attaining conditions relevant to the end state, or attaining the end state.

Criteria in the forms of **MOEs and MOPs** aid in determining progress toward performing tasks, achieving objectives, and attaining end state conditions.

## Measures of Effectiveness (MOEs)

MOEs are criteria used to assess changes in system behavior, capability, or operational environment that is tied to measuring the attainment of an end state, achievement of an objective, or creation of an effect. MOEs help measure changes in conditions, both positive and negative. MOEs help to answer the question, Are we doing the right things? MOEs are used at the strategic, operational, and tactical levels to assess the impact of military operations and measure changes in the operational environment, changes in system behavior, or changes to adversary capabilities. MOEs are based on observable or collectable indicators.

## Measures of Performance (MOPs)

MOPs are criteria used to assess friendly actions that are tied to measuring task accomplishment. MOPs help to answer questions such as Was the action taken? or Were the tasks completed to standard? A MOP confirms or denies that a task has been properly performed. MOPs are commonly found and tracked at all levels in execution matrixes. MOPs are also heavily used to evaluate training. MOPs help to answer the question, Are we doing things right?

*Refer to JFODS4: The Joint Forces Operations & Doctrine SMARTbook (Guide to Joint, Multinational & Interoganizational Operations) for complete discussion of assessment criteria -- to include measures of effectiveness and measures of performance. Related topics include commander's critical information requirements (CCIRs), priority intelligence requirements, (PIRs) and friendly force information requirements (FFIRs).*

# IV. Counterterrorism Operations

*Ref: JP 3-26, Counterterrorism (Oct '14), chap. 5.*

## I. Nature of Counterterrorism Operations

Effective CT requires the sustained global CT effort of all relevant USG departments and agencies and PNs, each with unique capabilities, perspectives, and authorities. Over time, by locating and defeating terrorist organizations and networks, they will be rendered incapable or unwilling to use terrorism to achieve their goals. CT activities and operations may support COIN operations, stability operations, or other major operations and campaigns. CT activities and operations are especially useful in irregular warfare to bring military and civilian capabilities to bear in a focused manner against state and non-state actors who use terrorism.

*(Dept of Defense Photo)*

The DOD core of a global CT enterprise is forces specifically trained and equipped to conduct CT operations against transregional terrorists. An effective CT enterprise is founded upon trust between its members and the ability to work as a team to counter terrorist recruitment, logistics, actions, and planning. The CT enterprise can be decisive when it maintains a sustained look at a terrorist organization globally, uninhibited by USG regional boundaries, rapidly obtains decisions at the national level, and takes action at the tactical level with a speed greater than that of the terrorists. The CT enterprise may take action using a variety of capabilities and authorities, ranging from customs inspection and confiscation, unmanned aerial vehicle strikes, indictment, arrests, and diplomatic consultation to HN action or other USG and foreign efforts.

The ends of CT operations are the elimination of a terrorist's ability or willingness to conduct terrorist acts against the homeland/US facilities and interests abroad or facilitate other terrorist organizations to act against the United States. The ways of CT operations are to capture, kill, or otherwise neutralize terrorist leadership and key subordinates, isolate terrorists from their supporting administrative and logistic infrastructure, and dismantle their capabilities and bases. The means of CT operations are the application of whole-of-government and multinational CT capabilities operating seamlessly through the levels of warfare to disrupt, isolate, and dismantle the nation's most dangerous and difficult terrorist organizations. Additionally, means include influencing relevant populations and impacting the operational environment.

> *"It takes a network to defeat a network...an effective network involves much more than relaying data. A true network starts with robust communications connectivity, but also leverages physical and cultural proximity, shared purpose, established decision-making processes, personal relationships, and trust. Ultimately, a network is defined by how well it allows its members to see, decide, and effectively act."*
>
> Stanley McChrystal, General, United States Army (Retired), "It Takes a Network," Foreign Policy, February 22, 2011

## Information Operations (IO)

Information operations can create and/or sustain desired and measurable effects on terrorist organizations and networks while protecting and defending the JFC's own forces' actions, information, and information systems. Information-related capabilities such as electronic warfare, cyberspace operations, MISO, and military deception should be applied to CT operations as a means to influence extremists, their supporters, and the mainstream populace. Within an operational area there will be a number of target audiences and there will likely be multiple synchronized themes, messages, and means of delivery required for each. The timing, method, and speed of message delivery will affect which side will gain the upper hand in public opinion. In order to be most effective, narratives and messages should be coordinated among the interagency partners, PNs, and intergovernmental organizations, and should consider NGOs and private sector entities in the operational area.

## Counter Threat Finance (CTF) Planning

Counter threat finance (CTF) is an interagency effort to detect, counter, contain, disrupt, deter, or dismantle the transnational financing of state and non-state adversaries threatening US national security. This includes persons and entities that provide financial and material support to terrorists and their networks, including WMD.

In accordance with Title 10, USC, Section 113, Department of Defense Directive 5205.14, DOD Counter Threat Finance (CTF) Policy, establishes DOD policy and assigns DOD responsibilities for the conduct of CTF. CTF is a consideration in all steps of the integrated financial operations process and is a primary concern in evaluation of projects, selection of conduits or implementers, and assessment.

Threat finance intelligence collection, exploitation, analysis, and dissemination of financial information is an essential intelligence support element of CTF activities. Effective CTF requires a global effort. CTF activities include, but are not limited to, countering narcotics trafficking, proliferation activities, WMD networks, trafficking in persons, weapons trafficking, precursor chemical smuggling, terrorist revenue and logistics, anticorruption, and other such activities that generate revenue through illicit networks. It is critical for those conducting CTF to maintain a strong link with financial execution elements. CTF operators must coordinate and share information with those executing integrated financial operations before contracts are approved and funded.

# II. Levels of Warfare and Counterterrorism
Ref: JP 3-26, Counterterrorism (Oct '14), p. V-2 to V-3.

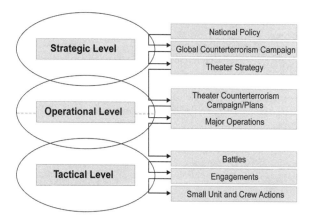

## Strategic Level

At the strategic level, a nation articulates the national (or multinational in the case of an alliance or coalition) guidance that addresses strategic objectives in support of strategic end states and develops and uses national resources to achieve them. The President, aided by the National Security Council Staff, establishes CT policy and national strategic objectives in the National Strategy for Counterterrorism that includes national goals and end states as well as establishing the interagency framework for achieving them. At the strategic level, SecDef translates national CT strategic objectives into military strategic objectives that facilitate theater planning. Theater planning links national strategic policy, strategy, objectives, and end states that address global and transregional adversaries to DOD global objectives and end states, as established in the Guidance for Employment of the Force. DOD then develops global campaign plans to address inherently global and transregional threats that exceed the authority of a single GCC. The CCDRs along with the combat support agencies participate in development of global campaign plans that inform their regional efforts.

## Operational Level

The operational level links the national and military CT strategic objectives and end states to the tactical level by design and execution of theater campaign plans with day-to-day activities and developing plans for contingency operations that may occur within the AORs. The CT enterprise is where interagency capabilities and authorities coalesce into unified whole-of-government action. It operates across all levels of warfare but is centered between the strategic and operational levels to national decision makers and with the intelligence and operations elements at the regional operational and tactical levels in order to make timely decisions. At this level, the GCCs develop and execute theater campaigns in support of the global campaigns and execute operations at the tactical level to achieve theater military objectives and the global CT objectives and activities.

## Tactical Level

The tactical level of warfare is where battles and engagements are planned and executed to achieve military objectives assigned to tactical units or task forces. SOF contain units dedicated to CT operations and should be a JFC's first choice. When SOF CT forces are not available, the most appropriate and available force may be used. GCCs normally rely on TSOCs to execute OPCON over CT operations within their AOR.

# III. Find, Fix, Finish, Exploit, and Analyze (F3EAD) Process for CT

Ref: JP 3-26, Counterterrorism (Oct '14), pp. V-3 to V-5.

CT forces use the find, fix, finish, exploit, analyze, and disseminate (F3EAD) process to plan for and execute all CT operations against terrorists and terrorist organizations and networks. The F3EAD is a continuous analytical and operational process where the analytical effort underpins all portions of the process and is conducted concurrently and continuously. This process analyzes a terrorist organization's structure, capabilities, and intentions to help develop courses of action to eliminate its capability to commit terrorist acts. CT planners identify COGs and decisive points where application of CT capabilities will produce desired effects. This process involves all members of the CT enterprise. For those not in the CT enterprise, dissemination is required to inform those who may require the information. At the tactical and operational level, this process serves as a continuous cycle to prosecute known CT targets and discover and identify future targets. The cycle also serves to focus resources on strategic CT priorities.

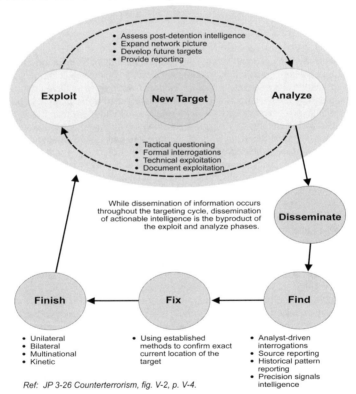

Ref: JP 3-26 Counterterrorism, fig. V-2, p. V-4.

## A. Find

The purpose of "find" is to locate a specific node, preferably a COG or decisive point, in a terrorist organization that, if found and neutralized, would reduce its ability to commit terrorist acts. A node may be an individual, communications and Internet, weapons, destructive devices, and other material used for or that supports acts of terrorism. Finding is a complex analytical effort that requires tenacity among a broad set of intelligence at all decisive CT levels of warfare and use of authorities unique to individual departments, agencies, or organizations. Find requires multiskilled intelligence professionals, seamlessly wedded with operation planners and executors with interagency cooperation and coordination.

## B. Fix

The purpose of "fix" is to predict the location of a target with sufficient specificity that tactical operational elements can engage the target. When the find phase culminates in sufficient intelligence, the analysts continue their efforts and are joined by more tactical focused analytical and operations personnel for the fix phase to produce actionable intelligence and operation plans. Fixing a target is a complex process that requires rapid integration of information, intelligence, and assets in close and continuous partnerships with the CT enterprise partners. The information derived from the exploitation of a fix facilitates the selection of appropriate follow-on actions in the subsequent finish phase.

## C. Finish

The purpose of "finish" is to neutralize a node in a terrorist organization by capturing, killing, or otherwise rendering the node ineffective and incapable of continuing its role in the terrorist organization. The finished concept of operations is dependent on the mission, enemy, terrain and weather, troops and support available, time available, and civilian presence and may entail use of a variety of platforms or any combination of infiltration and exfiltration methods. Finish may also employ standoff strikes, or low-visibility capabilities. US finish operations require approval by a JFC, as authorized by the President and SecDef. HN military or civilian forces, partners, and USG law enforcement or other agencies may often be the preferred finish capabilities. During finishing operations, intelligence and other capabilities maintain focus on the node for situational awareness for tactical operators and involve commanders and staffs before, during, and after the operations.

## D. Exploit

The purpose of "exploit" is to optimize the value of the finish operation through questioning and screening individuals found at the finish site, collecting all material that may contain useful intelligence and information, analyzing it on site, and movement to another location for thorough examination. Exploitation is obtaining detailed information from technical and forensic examination of documents, cell phones, computers, biometric information, weapons, bomb making and other materials. The on-site screening and questioning of persons and analysis may lead to immediate follow-on finish operations, or at least contribute to the total intelligence and information picture obtained from the operation. Exploited information may assist in subsequent legal proceedings. Site exploitation teams normally conduct the on-site collection and immediate analysis, including the questioning of persons found on site and determine their value for detaining them for future interrogations. Exploitation is a continuous process; a steady build of information on the selected target(s) activities further refining the analysts' understanding of the network's operations, key nodes, and COGs. Successful exploitation requires a supporting dissemination architecture that provides the developed intelligence to the operations participants to facilitate planning and execution.

## E. Analyze

The purpose of "analyze" is to place the intelligence and information obtained from finish operations into the greater body of knowledge about the terrorist organization in order to further disrupt it. DOD's multiple intelligence agencies cannot by themselves provide a complete intelligence context. Rather it requires all USG departments and agencies. The analyze phase occurs across the levels of warfare and involves processing digital media, documents, clothing, weapons, and equipment on site and forwarding material beyond the analysts' capabilities to other members of the CT enterprises for timely analysis. The analyze phase is the foundation of the F3EAD process. It continuously expands the understanding of terrorist organizations and informs all other phases of F3EAD. It is in the analyze process that the unique capabilities of the different USG departments and agencies come together.

# IV. Legal Considerations

## A. Application of the Law of War

It is DOD policy that members of the DOD components comply with the law of war during all armed conflicts, however such conflicts are characterized, and in all other military operations. Law of war is that part of international law that regulates the conduct of armed hostilities. It encompasses all international law for the conduct of hostilities binding on the United States or its individual citizens, including treaties and international agreements to which the United States is a party, and applicable customary international law. The law of war rests on fundamental principles of military necessity, unnecessary suffering, proportionality, and distinction (discrimination). JFCs must ensure CT operations in numerous locations across the globe comply with these legal requirements where an armed conflict exists.

## B. Legal Basis for Use of Force

Nearly every military decision and action has potential legal considerations and implications. A legal basis must exist for every decision to use military force. In a general sense, under customary international law as reflected in the United Nations Charter and elsewhere, the United States has the inherent right of self defense against hostile acts or demonstrations of hostile intent toward the United States or its citizens, including the use of force in anticipatory self-defense. Additionally, US forces may be acting under a United Nations Security Council resolution to take action to restore international peace and security in a particular area. Actions within the sovereign territory of another state should be based on either the consent of that state, a United Nations Security Council resolution, or a Presidential determination that such action is necessary either in response to an armed attack or in anticipation of an imminent threat to the security of the United States. Normally, for a given operation, the JFC has approved rules of engagement (ROE) for overseas operations or rules for the use of force (RUF) for operations within the homeland or while conducting official DOD security functions outside US territory. These ROE/RUF govern the use of military force and were developed based on the legal and operational considerations for the situation.

## C. ROE and RUF

For operations, the responsibility and authority for using military force is generally delegated from the President through SecDef to the supported CCDR/JFC in the form of approved plans/orders with either ROE for operations overseas or RUF for DSCA within the homeland or while conducting official DOD security functions outside US territory. When compared to major combat operations, ROE for some smaller-scale operations (i.e., some CT operations) may be more restrictive and detailed, especially in an urban environment, due to national policy concerns for the impact on civilians, their culture, values, and infrastructure. A JFC may begin operations with different ROE/RUF for each type of mission, and especially for CT operations. The JFC responsible for CT should determine early in the planning stage what the required ROE/RUF should be, including anticipating the need for serial changes based on the need for escalation of force, changing phases of an operation, branches/sequels to a plan, etc. Dependent upon the required level of approval for any changes, that JFC must take anticipatory action if the serial changes are to be timely enough for effective operations. When conducting multinational CT operations, the use of military force may be influenced by the differences between United States and HN or PN ROE/RUF. Commanders at all levels must take proactive steps to ensure an understanding of ROE by the individual Service member because a single errant act could cause significant adverse political consequences.

*For more detailed discussion on restraint (a joint operations principle) and ROE/RUF, refer to JP 3-0, Joint Operations.*

# D. Detainee Operations

CT operations may result in detainees. Proper handling of detainees is essential not only for possible exploitation purposes, but also for prevention of violations of the law (civil or military). Improper handling of detainees may undermine the legitimacy of US CT operations. However, regardless of the detainees' legal status, US forces must treat all detainees humanely and be prepared to properly control, maintain, protect, and account for detainees in accordance with applicable US law, the law of war, and applicable US policy. Inhumane treatment of detainees is prohibited by the Uniform Code of Military Justice, domestic and international law, and DOD policy. Accordingly, the stress of combat operations, the need for intelligence, or provocations by captured or detained personnel does not justify deviation from this obligation.

# E. Domestic Military CT Operations

Domestic CT operations are considered part of homeland security under the lead of DHS. DHS is considered primary for coordinating Executive Branch efforts to detect, prepare for, prevent, protect against, respond to, and recover from terrorist attacks within the United States. DOJ supports DHS for CT, but could also be the primary federal agency for some situations. If tasked to support the primary agency for domestic CT operations, DOD would be in a supporting role, which would include any support for law enforcement purposes.

If a CT situation should formally transcend into a matter of homeland defense (HD), then DOD is the lead for action and interagency coordination for HD. Domestic CT operations raise additional legal concerns due to the likely intersection with civil authorities and US persons. When participating in domestic CT operations JFCs must be particularly aware of the status of their forces, the legal basis for their use of force, the authority for conducting the operation and any specific limitations, and the characterization, treatment, and authorized activities regarding all persons and property encountered in their operations.

SecDef retains the authority to approve use of DOD resources for DSCA where it is unlikely that use of military force will be required. The Joint Staff Joint Director of Military Support validates requests for assistance, determines what DOD capabilities are available to fulfill the requests, coordinates for SecDef approval to use DOD assets, and allocates forces to the CCDR with responsibility for that area of the United States.

In domestic situations, the Constitution, federal law, and DOD policy limit the scope and nature of military actions. The President has the authority to direct the use of the military against terrorist groups and individuals in the United States for other than law enforcement actions (i.e., national defense, emergency protection of life and property, and to restore order). The National Guard has a unique role in domestic military operations. Under control of the respective states, National Guard units in Title 32, USC, and state active duty status can support a variety of tasks for HD and DSCA. National Guard forces in state active duty or Title 32, USC, status can perform direct law enforcement tasks that Title 10, USC, forces cannot perform due to constraints in the Posse Comitatus Act. In its maritime law enforcement role under DHS, the United States Coast Guard (USCG), as a Service under DHS, has jurisdiction in both US territorial waters and on the high seas as prescribed in law.

*Refer to The Homeland Defense & DSCA SMARTbook (Protecting the Homeland / Defense Support to Civil Authority) for complete discussion. Topics and references include homeland defense (JP 3-27), defense support of civil authorities (JP 3-28), Army support of civil authorities (ADRP 3-28), multi-service DSCA TTPs (ATP 3-28.1/MCWP 3-36.2), DSCA liaison officer toolkit (GTA 90-01-020), key legal and policy documents, and specific hazard and planning guidance.*

# V. Identity & Weapons Technical Intel
Ref: JP 3-26, Counterterrorism (Oct '14), fig. II-1, p. II-9.

## Identity Intelligence (I2)

I2, which supports the find, fix, exploit, and analyze phases of the F3EAD process, results from the fusion of identity attributes (biologic, biographic, behavioral, and reputational information related to individuals) and other information and intelligence collected across all intelligence disciplines. I2 utilizes enabling intelligence activities, like biometrics-enabled intelligence, forensics-enabled intelligence, and document and media exploitation, to discover the existence of unknown potential threat actors by connecting individuals to other persons, places, events, or materials; analyzing patterns of life; and characterizing their level of potential threats to US interests. I2 supports the identification of key adversary personnel, persons of interest, and their support and facilitation networks. I2 operations combine the synchronized application of biometrics, forensics, and document and media exploitation capabilities with intelligence and identity management processes to establish identity, affiliations, and authorizations in order to deny anonymity to the adversary and protect US/PN assets, facilities, and forces. The I2 operations process results in discovery of true identities; links identities to events, locations, and networks; and reveals hostile intent. These outputs enable tasks, missions, and actions that span the range of military operations. Additionally, biometrics-enabled intelligence and corresponding I2 products support the persistent identification and targeting of adversaries, which enables a range of military and civilian functions.

*For more information on I2, refer to JP 2-0, Joint Intelligence.*

## Weapons Technical Intelligence (WTI)

WTI is particularly suited for CT and provides a fuller understanding of the operational environment through the technical and forensic exploitation of improvised weapons. WTI uses information derived from the exploitation of weapons to link and identify associations between people, places, and things leading to identification of suspected terrorists and threat networks that employ or source those weapons. Synchronizing this information and products with I2 and the intelligence disciplines ensures that the threat is more fully understood in order to take appropriate actions. Commanders may concentrate these exploitation functions in an element of the intelligence directorate of a joint staff to synchronize the unique planning considerations and requirements, such as force protection and specialized skills, posed by the improvised weapons threat. The effects of WTI are amplified through information sharing throughout DOD, interagency partners, and PNs.

*For more information on WTI, refer to JP 3-15.1, Counter-Improvised Explosive Device Operations; JP 2-01.3, Joint Intelligence Preparation of the Operational Environment; and the Weapons Technical Intelligence Handbook.*

# Critical Infrastructure

Ref: NIPP 2013, National Infrastructure Protection Plan: Partnering for Critical Infrastructure Security and Resilience, Dept of Homeland Security (2013) and DCSINT Handbook No. 1.02, Critical Infrastructure (Aug '06).

Critical infrastructure is a term used by governments to describe assets that are essential for the functioning of a society and economy - the infrastructure.

The U.S. has had a wide-reaching Critical Infrastructure Protection Program in place since 1996. The Patriot Act of 2001 defined critical infrastructure as those "systems and assets, whether physical or virtual, so vital to the United States that the incapacity or destruction of such systems and assets would have a debilitating impact on security, national economic security, national public health or safety, or any combination of those matters."

Since 2009, numerous national policies have continued to shape the way the Nation addresses critical infrastructure security and resilience and national preparedness.

On February 12, 2013, the President issued PPD-21, Critical Infrastructure Security and Resilience, which explicitly calls for the development of an updated national plan. The directive builds on the extensive work done to date to protect critical infrastructure, and describes a national effort to share threat information, reduce vulnerabilities, minimize consequences, and hasten response and recovery efforts related to critical infrastructure. It also identifies 16 critical infrastructure sectors, listed below:

## Critical Infrastructure Sectors (16)

- **Chemical**
- **Commercial Facilities**
- **Communications**
- **Critical Manufacturing**
- **Dams**
- **Defense Industrial Base**
- **Emrgency Services**
- **Energy**
- **Financial Services**
- **Government Facilities**
- **Healthcare & Public Health**
- **Information Technology**
- **Nuclear Reactors, Materials, Waste**
- **Transportation Systems**
- **Waste & Wastewater Systems**

Ref: NIPP 2013, National Infrastructure Protection Plan (2013), p. 9.

The President also issued Executive Order 13636: Improving Critical Infrastructure Cybersecurity in February of 2013, which calls for the Federal Government to closely coordinate with critical infrastructure owners and operators to improve cybersecurity information sharing and collaboratively develop and implement risk-based approaches to cybersecurity. The executive order directs the Federal Government to develop a technology-neutral cybersecurity framework to reduce cyber risk to critical infrastructure; promote and incentivize the adoption of strong cybersecurity practices; increase the volume, timeliness, and quality of information sharing related to cyber threats; and incorporate protection for privacy and civil liberties into critical infrastructure security and resilience initiatives.

The National Plan is aligned with the goal of PPD-8, National Preparedness, of "a secure and resilient Nation with the capabilities required across the whole community to prevent, protect against, mitigate, respond to, and recover from the threats and hazards that pose the greatest risk." These five PPD-8 mission areas are central to a comprehensive approach for enhancing national preparedness and critical infrastructure risk management activities across all five mission areas contribute to achieving the National Preparedness Goal. In addition, the National Plan is consistent with the National Planning Frameworks and Interagency Operational Plans developed pursuant to PPD-8. The scope of the National Plan is not meant to and does not alter the implementation and execution of prevention activities, as described in the Prevention Federal Interagency Operational Plan. The National Plan scope comprises activities that often support and abut prevention activities designed to avoid, prevent, or stop an imminent threat or actual attacks.

Two additional policy documents that align with this National Plan include the President's Climate Action Plan, issued in June 2013, and the National Strategy for Information Sharing and Safeguarding (NSISS), issued in December 2013. The Climate Action Plan establishes a number of strategic objectives and directs Federal agencies to take further action to better prepare America for the impacts of climate change, including enhancing the resilience of infrastructure. The NSISS identifies as one of 16 national priorities the need to establish "information-sharing processes and sector-specific protocols with private sector partners, to improve information quality and timeliness and secure the Nation's infrastructure."

The National Plan acknowledges that the Nation's critical infrastructure is largely owned and operated by the private sector; however, Federal and SLTT governments also own and operate critical infrastructure, as do foreign entities and companies.

## Defense Critical Infrastructure Program (DCIP)

19 August 2005, The Department of Defense issued a Directive Number 3020.40, the subject being the Defense Critical Infrastructure Program (DCIP). This directive superseded earlier plans and programs written in the late 90's. Directive 3020.40 provided new definitions, policies, and updates on responsibilities concerning the identification, assessment, and security enhancements required for defense of critical infrastructures.

Most recently the Department of Defense issued the Defense Critical Infrastructure Program (DCIP) Interim Implementation Guidance, dated 13 July 2006. This document references DoD Directive 3020.40 and Homeland Security Presidential Directive 7 among others. This document provides additional definitions as well as DCIP Acronyms, Procedures and Assessment Standards.

On 17 April 2002 the Department of Defense announced the establishment of the U.S. Northern Command (USNORTHCOM). All existing homeland defense and civil support missions previously executed by other organizations would be consolidated under USNORTHCOM. USNORTHCOM, located at Peterson Air Force Base, Colorado Springs, Colorado, began the arduous task of planning, organizing and coordinating military support to all of the nation's homeland defense and civil support missions.

*See pp. 5-12 and 5-18 to 5-21 for further discussion.*

# I. The Protection Challenge

Ref: National Strategy for Physical Protection of Critical Infrastructure and Key Assets (Feb '03), p. viii and p. 9.

## The Importance of Critical Infrastructures

America's critical infrastructure sectors provide the foundation for our national security, governance, economic vitality, and way of life. Furthermore, their continued reliability, robustness, and resiliency create a sense of confidence and form an important part of our national identity and purpose. Critical infrastructures frame our daily lives and enable us to enjoy one of the highest overall standards of living in the world.

The facilities, systems, and functions that comprise our critical infrastructures are highly sophisticated and complex. They include human assets and physical and cyber systems that work together in processes that are highly interdependent. They also consist of key nodes that, in turn, are essential to the operation of the critical infrastructures in which they function.

## The Importance of Key Assets

Key assets and high profile events are individual targets whose attack—in the worst-case scenarios—could result in not only large-scale human casualties and property destruction, but also profound damage to our national prestige, morale, and confidence

Individually, key assets like nuclear power plants and dams may not be vital to the continuity of critical services at the national level. However, a successful strike against such targets may result in a significant loss of life and property in addition to long-term, adverse public health and safety consequences. Other key assets are symbolically equated with traditional American values and institutions or U.S. political and economic power. Our national icons, monuments, and historical attractions preserve history, honor achievements, and represent the natural grandeur of our country. They celebrate our American ideals and way of life and present attractive targets for terrorists, particularly when coupled with high profile events and celebratory activities that bring together significant numbers of people.

## The Protection Challenge

| | |
|---|---|
| Agriculture and Food | 1,912,000 farms; 87,000 food-processing plants |
| Water | 1,800 federal reservoirs; 1,600 municipal waste water facilities |
| Public Health | 5,800 registered hospitals |
| Emergency Services | 87,000 U.S. localities |
| Defense Industrial Base | 250,000 firms in 215 distinct industries |
| Telecommunications | 2 billion miles of cable |
| Energy Electricity | 2,800 power plants |
| Oil and Natural Gas | 300,000 producing sites |
| Tran sportation Aviation | 5,000 public airports |
| Passenger Rail and Railroads | 120,000 miles of major railroads |
| Highways, Trucking, and Busing | 590,000 highway bridges |
| Pipelines | 2 million miles of pipelines |
| Maritime | 300 inland/costal ports |
| Mass Transit | 500 major urban public transit operators |
| Banking and Finance | 26,600 FDIC insured institutions |
| Chemical Industry and Hazardous Materials | 66,000 chemical plants |
| Postal and Shipping | 137 million delivery sites |
| Key Assets National Monuments and Icons | 5,800 historic buildings |
| Nuclear Power Plants | 104 commercial nuclear power plants |
| Dams | 80,000 dams |
| Government Facilities | 3,000 government owned/operated facilities |
| Commercial Assets | 460 skyscrapers |

*These are approximate figures.

Critical Infrastructure

# II. Defining Critical Infrastructures, their Components, and their Threats

There are certain systems in place within the United States today that are taken for granted. Americans expect to pick up the phone and have a dial tone, turn a switch and have power, adjust their thermostat and make their home warmer or cooler, be able to move from one part of the U.S. to another, turn a faucet for drinking water and call 911 and receive aid. These infrastructures which support our everyday life are much more fragile than we think. A simple act of Mother Nature or the deliberate act of a terrorist can disrupt or destroy these systems and delay their return to normalcy.

Some infrastructures at the national level are so vital that their incapacity would have a devastating affect on the defense and economic security of our entire country. We have seen over the past decade how a single attack can adversely impact multiple areas of our lives. The term "Critical Infrastructure" came into vogue in the last decade to describe those systems that keep the nation secure.

Today the term "Critical Infrastructure" is defined as "systems and assets, whether physical or virtual, so vital to the United States that the incapacity or destruction of such systems and assets would have a debilitating impact on the security, national economic security, national health or safety, or any combination of those matters."[6]

The assets mentioned above are further sub-divided into three categories:

- **Physical** – Physical assets may include both tangible property (e.g., facilities', components, real estate, animals, and products) and the intangible (e.g., information). Physical protection becomes an even more difficult task when one considers that 85% of the nation's critical infrastructures are not federally owned. Proper protection of physical assets requires cooperation between all levels of the government and within the private sector.

- **Human** – Human assets include both the employees to be protected and the personnel who may present an insider threat (e.g., due to privileged access to control systems, operations, and sensitive area and information). Those individuals who are identified as critical require protection as well as duplication of knowledge and authority.

- **Cyber** – Cyber assets include the information hardware, software, data, and the networks that serve the functioning and operation of the asset. Damage to our electronic and computer networks would cause widespread disruption and damage, including casualties. Cyber networks link the United State's energy, financial and physical securities infrastructures.

Terrorists throughout the world are already exploiting information technologies and the Internet to plan attacks, raise funds, spread propaganda, collect information, communicate securely and recruit. As terrorists gain experience and technology, cyber attacks on all infrastructures becomes an increasing threat.

Since the late 1990's commissions and organizations were formed to review the vulnerabilities of U.S. critical infrastructures and determine the best courses of action to protect them. The current definition of Critical Infrastructure Protection (CIP) used by the Department of Defense is, "The actions taken to prevent, remediate, or mitigate the risks resulting from vulnerabilities of critical infrastructure assets. Depending on the risk, these actions could include changes in tactics, techniques, or procedures; adding redundancy; selection of another asset; isolation or hardening; guarding, etc.

A later section will discuss how to determine which infrastructures are critical to an organization. But once determined critical, how do we protect these infrastructures? After identifying those infrastructures that are critical to our organization, we need to look at them from the threats' point of view. The threat could be a man-made or natural attack or occurrence on any of the three above mentioned areas. The Army has developed methods to view "ourselves" from the threat's perspective.

The Contemporary Operational Environment (COE) is a dynamic and adaptive process for being more aware, better prepared, and ready to counter any adversity that could negatively impact an operation or task. These variables allow U.S. planners to understand impacts and changes within a "state", country or situation. These same variables can be used to view ourselves in a form of "Red Teaming". Red teaming is "a technique that involves viewing a potential target from the perspective of an attacker to identify its hidden vulnerabilities, and to anticipate possible modes of attack. Red teaming deepens understanding of options available to adaptive adversaries and provides groups an insight into their vulnerabilities. The result of a good red teaming session will provide a basis for plans to mitigate risks to your critical infrastructures.

To understand the complex interactions of the COE, a framework of "systems" assists in assessing and gaining situational awareness. Joint doctrine uses systems of Political, Military, Economic, Social, Infrastructure, and Information (PMESII) to shape and conduct missions. PMESII, with other variables such as physical environment and time, affect circumstances and influence operations throughout the domains of air, land, sea, and space. This broader perspective, combined with mission, enemy and belligerents, friendly forces and partners, cultural sensitivities and resolve, are critical to mission success. Defining physical environmental conditions include terrain or urban settings (super-surface, surface and subsurface features), weather, topography, and hydrology. The variable of time influences action such as planning, multi-echelon decision cycles, tempo of operations, and projected pacing of popular support for operations. Whether a real world threat or an opposing force created to simulate relevant conditions for training readiness, PMESII and other variables such as physical environment and time describe the OE.

# III. The Threat's Viewpoint

Systems Warfare is a technique or method that identifies critical systems components and attacks them to degrade or destroy the use or importance of the overall system. The enemy targets "single points of failure" to cripple larger systems. Examples of systems that might be targeted by systems warfare are; logistics, command and control, Medical evacuation, commerce, and transportation. A tactical level example is an enemy attacking a fuel convoy so that combat vehicles such as tanks or personnel carriers cannot pursue him. The enemy cannot defeat the tanks or personnel carrier's superior armor or weapons capabilities, but he can target that which supports the tank and personnel carrier. The fuel convoy is the "weak link" in the combat system that the enemy can attack and achieve a greater success. The enemy came to this realization, and identified the weak link through analysis of our systems.

> "To build and implement a robust strategy to protect our critical infrastructures and key assets from further terrorist exploitation, we must understand the motivations of our enemies as well as their preferred tactics and targets."
>
> The National Strategy for the Physical Protection of Critical Infrastructures and Key Assets, February 2003

# IV. Department of Homeland Security (DHS)

The Department of Homeland Security (DHS) was established on 25 November 2002, by the Homeland Security Act of 2002. DHS is designed to work in the civilian arena to protect the United States within, at, and outside its borders. Its goal is to prepare for, prevent, and respond to domestic emergencies, particularly terrorism. DHS defines Critical Infrastructure as "systems and assets, whether physical or virtual, so vital to the United States that the incapacity or destruction of such systems and assets would have a debilitating impact on security, national economic security, national public health or safety, or any combination of those matters."

# V. Critical Infrastructures (National Level)

*Ref: NIPP 2013, National Infrastructure Protection Plan: Partnering for Critical Infrastructure Security and Resilience, Dept of Homeland Security (2013), pp. 15-20.*

The National Plan organizes critical infrastructure into 16 sectors and designates a Federal department or agency as the lead coordinator—Sector-Specific Agency (SSA)—for each sector (refer to Appendix B for the roles and responsibilities of SSAs). The sector and cross-sector partnership council structures described in previous NIPPs remain the foundation for this National Plan and are depicted in Table 1 below:

| Critical Infrastructure Sector | Sector Specific Agency | Critical Infrastructure Partnership Advisory Council | | |
| | | Sector Coordinating Councils (SCCs) | Government Coordinating Councils (GCCs) | Regional Consortia |
| --- | --- | --- | --- | --- |
| Chemical | Department of Homeland Security | 3 | 3 | |
| Commercial Facilities ⓘ | | 3 | 3 | |
| Communications ⓘ | | 3 | 3 | |
| Critical Manufacturing | | 3 | 3 | |
| Dams | | 3 | 3 | |
| Emergency Services ⓘ | | 3 | 3 | |
| Information Technology ⓘ | | 3 | 3 | |
| Nuclear Reactors, Materials & Waste | | 3 | 3 | |
| Food & Agriculture | Department of Agriculture, Department of Health and Human Services | 3 | 3 | |
| Defense Industrial Base ⓘ | Department of Defense | 3 | 3 | |
| Energy ⓘ | Department of Energy | 3 | 3 | |
| Healthcare & Public Health ⓘ | Department of Health and Human Services | 3 | 3 | |
| Financial Services ⓘ | Department of the Treasury | Uses separate coordinating entity | 3 | |
| Water & Wastewater Systems ⓘ | Environmental Protection Agency | 3 | 3 | |
| Government Facilities | Department of Homeland Security, General Services Administration | Sector does not have an SCC | 3 | |
| Transportation Systems ⓘ | Department of Homeland Security, Department of Transportation | Various SCCs are broken down by transportation mode or subsector. | 3 | |

*(Columns spanned by vertical labels: Critical Infrastructure Cross-Sector Council; Federal Senior Leadership Council; State, Local, Tribal and Territorial Government Coordinating Council; Regional Consortium Coordinating Council.)*

ⓘ Indicates that a sector (or a subsector within the sector) has a designated information-sharing organization.

*National Monuments and Icons along with the Postal and Shipping sector were removed in the 2013 update to the NIPP.*

Sector and cross-sector council structures include:

## Sector Coordinating Councils (SCCs)
Self-organized, self-run, and self-governed private sector councils consisting of owners and operators and their representatives, which interact on a wide range of sector-specific strategies, policies, activities, and issues. SCCs serve as principal collaboration points between the government and private sector owners and operators for critical infrastructure security and resilience policy coordination and planning and a range of related sector-specific activities.

## Critical Infrastructure Cross-Sector Council
Consisting of the chairs and vice chairs of the SCCs, this private sector council coordinates cross-sector issues, initiatives, and interdependencies to support critical infrastructure security and resilience.

## Government Coordinating Councils (GCCs)
Consisting of representatives from across various levels of government (including Federal and SLTT), as appropriate to the operating landscape of each individual sector, these councils enable inter-agency, intergovernmental, and cross-jurisdictional coordination within and across sectors and partner with SCCs on public-private efforts.

## Federal Senior Leadership Council (FSLC)
Consisting of senior officials from the SSAs and other Federal departments and agencies with a role in critical infrastructure security and resilience, the FSLC facilitates communication and coordination on critical infrastructure security and resilience across the Federal Government.

## State, Local, Tribal, and Territorial Government Coordinating Council (SLTTGCC)
Consisting of representatives from across SLTT government entities, the SLTTGCC promotes the engagement of SLTT partners in national critical infrastructure security and resilience efforts and provides an organizational structure to coordinate across jurisdictions on State and local government guidance, strategies, and programs.

## Regional Consortium Coordinating Council (RC3)
Comprises regional groups and coalitions around the country engaged in various initiatives to advance critical infrastructure security and resilience in the public and private sectors.

## Information Sharing Organizations
Organizations including Information Sharing and Analysis Centers (ISACs) serve operational and dissemination functions for many sectors, subsectors, and other groups, and facilitate sharing of information between government and the private sector. ISACs also collaborate on a cross-sector basis through a national council.

The sector and cross-sector partnership approach described above is designed to be scalable and allow individual owners and operators of critical infrastructure and other stakeholders across the country to participate. It is intended to promote consistency of process to enable efficient collaboration between disparate parts of the critical infrastructure community, while allowing for the use of other viable partnership structures and planning processes. This concept has proved successful and can be leveraged at the State, local, tribal, and territorial levels as well as within and across regions to build, form, or expand existing networks; identify proven practices; adapt to or adopt lessons learned; and leverage practices, processes, or plans as appropriate.

# VI. National Infrastructure Protection: Key Concepts

Ref: NIPP 2013, National Infrastructure Protection Plan: Partnering for Critical Infrastructure Security and Resilience, Dept of Homeland Security (2013), p. 7.

The National Plan relies on several key concepts, which remain consistent with the 2009 NIPP. At the same time, the Plan is informed by and updated to reflect the evolving critical infrastructure risk, policy, and operating environments.

The key concepts described below provide context for this critical infrastructure environment. An understanding of these key concepts influences the state of critical infrastructure and shapes the community's approach to ensuring security and resilience.

- **Critical infrastructure** represents "systems and assets, whether physical or virtual, so vital to the United States that the incapacity or destruction of such systems and assets would have a debilitating impact on security, national economic security, national public health or safety, or any combination of those matters." The National Plan acknowledges that the Nation's critical infrastructure is largely owned and operated by the private sector; however, Federal and SLTT governments also own and operate critical infrastructure, as do foreign entities and companies.

- **PPD-21 defines security** as "reducing the risk to critical infrastructure by physical means or defens[ive] cyber measures to intrusions, attacks, or the effects of natural or manmade disasters." There are several elements of securing critical infrastructure systems, including addressing threats and vulnerabilities and sharing accurate information and analysis on current and future risks. Prevention and protection activities contribute to strengthening critical infrastructure security.

- **Resilience**, as defined in PPD-21, is "the ability to prepare for and adapt to changing conditions and withstand and recover rapidly from disruptions...[it] includes the ability to withstand and recover from deliberate attacks, accidents, or naturally occurring threats or incidents." Having accurate information and analysis about risk is essential to achieving resilience. Resilient infrastructure assets, systems, and networks must also be robust, agile, and adaptable. Mitigation, response, and recovery activities contribute to strengthening critical infrastructure resilience.

- Security and resilience are strengthened through **risk management**. Risk refers to the "potential for an unwanted outcome resulting from an incident, event, or occurrence, as determined by its likelihood [a function of threats and vulnerabilities] and the associated consequences;" risk management is the "process of identifying, analyzing, and communicating risk and accepting, avoiding, transferring, or controlling it to an acceptable level at an acceptable cost." 3

- **Partnerships** enable more effective and efficient risk management. Within the context of this National Plan, a partnership is defined as close cooperation between parties having common interests in achieving a shared vision. For the critical infrastructure community, leadership involvement, open communication, and trusted relationships are essential elements to partnership.

# I. Identifying Vulnerabilities in Critical Infrastructure

Ref: DCSINT Handbook No. 1.02, Critical Infrastructure (Aug '06), section III.

> "The War against America and its allies will not be confined to Iraq...As for similar operations taking place in America; it's only a matter of time. They are in the planning stages, and you will see them in the heart of your land as soon as the planning is complete"
>
> Osama Bin Laden, al-Jazeera, 19 January 2006

The definition of critical infrastructure has been given and examples of the critical infrastructures of the United States are provided, but what are our critical infrastructures within our own areas of responsibility, influence and interest? Some of these are provided to us by our higher organizations and their commands. Those higher infrastructures and parts of infrastructures located in our areas of responsibility are listed to us and we ensure their protection. These areas can be labeled Mission Essential Vulnerable Areas (MEVAs). Unfortunately a list of critical infrastructures and sites is not always provided; oftentimes staffs have to decide what are their critical infrastructures and the key assets supporting them. The staff or command will need to understand the infrastructures, how they function and which parts they need to protect.

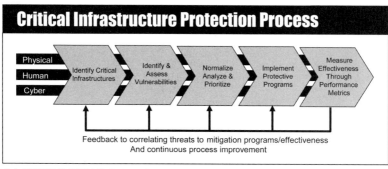

## Critical Infrastructure Protection Process

Ref: DCSINT HNDBK 1.02 Critical Infrastructure, flowchart, p. III-4.

On the following two pages is a flow chart designed to assist in the understanding of what is critical and the weaknesses within those systems. The flow chart was designed by NORTHCOM's J34, Assessments Branch, to assist units and organizations in looking at themselves, their missions and to identify weaknesses and single points of failure within the infrastructures.

The process starts with identifying all of the missions the higher headquarters has directed the unit to perform as well as those functions the higher headquarters perform that are located within the unit's area of responsibility. The staff works their way through the process identifying missions and requirements at their own level, their higher's level as well as those they support, and decide if each are critical. When the staff reaches the end of the process they must conduct a Dependency Analysis in an effort to identify Single Points of Failure (SPOF). These SPOFs are the likely targets of attack as they will result in most damage for the least expenditure.

# I. CIP Assessment Flow Chart

*Ref: DCSINT Handbook No. 1.02, Critical Infrastructure (Aug '06), pp. III-1 to III-6.*

The process is designed to help garrisons and staffs to determine what are their critical infrastructures and where are they vulnerable. These vulnerabilities are above and beyond those single points of failure that a higher office or headquarters may already have identified as critical to their operations but the physical asset is located on the lower headquarters facility or post. The list of critical infrastructures and their vulnerabilities, those of each level of command, must be nested together so that the individuals responsible for the security of the installation know the entire lists of assets that must be secured. Simply put, what is critical to one person or level of command might not be critical to another, but those responsible for the security where the critical asset resides must know it is critical in order to protect and secure it. The nesting of these various layers can only be insured through coordination and synchronization between all levels of command. Once a list of assets and single points of failure exists it must be updated as plans and priorities change.

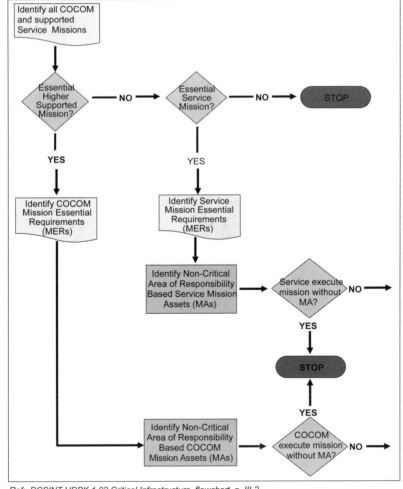

Ref: DCSINT HDBK 1.02 Critical Infrastructure. flowchart. p. III-2.

Critical
Infrastructure

Critical infrastructures are composed of physical, personal, and cyber components, and as any of those three portions change so does the list of critical assets requiring security. If a plan or mission changes the need to review a CIP list is often obvious, but a change in personnel, a piece of equipment or even software can also require a review. Periodic reviews of all CIP plans is necessary to ensure that missions are updated, information from higher and lower is incorporated and changes within organizations are included.

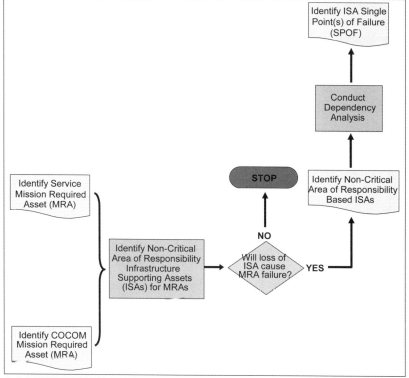

Ref: DCSINT HDBK 1.02 Critical Infrastructure, flowchart, p. III-3.

# II. Defense Critical Infrastructure Program (DCIP) Procedures

The Department of Defense Directive 3020.40, dated 19 August 2005 established the Defense Critical Infrastructure Program (DCIP). The directive requires the Army to establish, resource and execute an organizational critical infrastructure program. The directive set responsibilities for each of the different sectors of the DCIP:

| DEFENSE SECTOR | LEAD AGENT |
| --- | --- |
| Defense Industrial Base (DIB) | Director, Defense Contract Management Agency |
| Financial Services | Director, Defense Finance & Accounting Service |
| Global Information Grid (GIG) | Director, Defense Information Systems Agency |
| Health Affairs | Assistant Secretary of Defense of Health Affairs |
| Intelligence, Surveillance, and Reconnaissance (ISR) | Director, Defense Intelligence Agency |
| Logistics | Director, Defense Logistics Agency |
| Personnel | Director, DoD Human Resources Activity |
| Public Works | Chief, U.S. Army Corps of Engineers |
| Space | Commander, U.S. Strategic Command |
| Transportation | Commander, U.S. Transportation Command |

Enclosure #3 of the DCIP Interim Implementation Guidance dated July 2006 outlines the DoD DCIP risk management procedures for all critical infrastructures. The purpose of the DCIP is to ensure the availability of assets critical to all DoD missions.

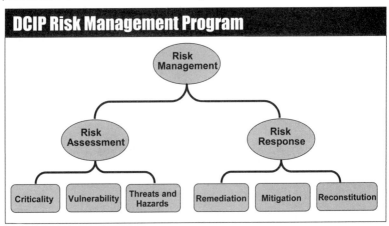

Ref: DCSINT HNDBK 1.02 Critical Infrastructure, p. III-5.

Once risks are assessed in all tasks and missions then possible responses can be reviewed and emplaced to ensure all missions will be accomplished no matter what actions are taken against an infrastructure. The DCIP Interim Implementation Guidance stresses that Risk management is cyclical, as changes are constantly made to systems and personnel are replaced, risks to infrastructures must be re-assessed.

*See pp. 5-18 to 5-21 for related discussion of Risk Management for DoD Installations.*

# III. Critical Infrastructure Protection Five-Step Process

*Ref: DCSINT Handbook No. 1.02, Critical Infrastructure (Aug '06), pp. III-4 to III-5.*

The national CIP program is based on a risk management framework. It is continuously influenced by the ever changing threat environment, both physical and natural. The goal is to reduce the vulnerabilities to our nation's assets from attack and natural disaster. The same methodology used at the national level can be used by garrison, installation, and command staffs as part of the ongoing process of narrowing down the list or set of assets that are critical. The five steps are explained below:

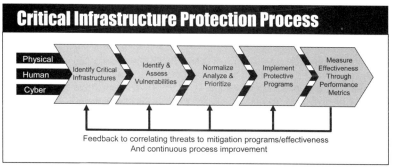

**Critical Infrastructure Protection Process**

Physical / Human / Cyber → Identify Critical Infrastructures → Identify & Assess Vulnerabilities → Normalize Analyze & Prioritize → Implement Protective Programs → Measure Effectiveness Through Performance Metrics

Feedback to correlating threats to mitigation programs/effectiveness
And continuous process improvement

*Ref: DCSINT HNDBK 1.02 Critical Infrastructure, flowchart, p. III-4.*

## 1. Identify Critical Assets

The first step will be to identify the critical assets located within your area of responsibility. The process should be an ongoing with constant review of unit missions, higher headquarters missions and requirements, as well as the overall operations within your location. The information collected should be used as the base for further discussion.

## 2. Identify and Assess Vulnerabilities

Vulnerability assessments should be conducted on those items identified in step 1. Potential areas of weakness need to be identified as well as protective measures that need to be undertaken to mitigate those vulnerabilities. Interdependencies within and between infrastructures need to be identified to minimize cascading effects. The vulnerability assessment needs to take into account effects which might cascade into other organizations.

## 3. Normalize, Analyze, and Prioritize

The staff or group accumulating the vulnerability assessments needs to normalize the information from each subordinate section or staff, and then prioritize against all of the assets the higher organization is responsible for. This step will identify which areas offer the greatest risk and the best benefit from protective measures.

## 4. Implement Protective Programs

The information gathered during the process will assist in developing and executing programs to protect or minimize damage to infrastructures. The staff or organization can find assistance in developing programs from their higher headquarters or through various federal agencies such as the Department of Homeland Security (DHS).

## 5. Measure Performance

Metrics need to be established for each protective measure to ensure they are being performed consistently, are sustainable and are effective. Continuous review of the metrics will result in improvements to the framework and the protection plan.

**Critical Infrastructure**

# Human Attacks

Ref: DCSINT Handbook No. 1.02, Critical Infrastructure (Aug '06), pp. V-1 to V-2.

The safety and security of personnel is discussed in several Force Protection manuals and handbooks. The purpose of this section is not to provide ways to protect personnel, but to explain ways to ensure infrastructures are protected from loss of personnel. The human links of a critical infrastructure are all too often the overlooked potential points of failure.

The loss of an individual within a military unit rarely results in the unit failing to accomplish its mission. The military trains and prepares for losses within its personnel structure so that no matter what the cause, natural or man-made, the system continues to function with little or no interruption. Unfortunately, this often is not the case within many organizations that do not practice and train for the loss of individuals responsible for issuing instructions or experts in procedures or special equipment.

The loss of the Information Management Officer (IMO) during critical computer operations, the absence of a specialized technician if the water treatment plant's or electrical grid's systems fail or a multi-situational event resulting in a shortage of health or emergency personnel. Military units train everyday for the loss of a leader, member of the chain of command or special systems operator, but this contingency planning does not always extend to everyday operations or crisis planning. Even those organizations that plan for replacement of individuals rarely train for their loss which can result in delay or lack of coordination.

As an organization's critical infrastructures are identified the weaknesses and single points of failure are identified. If personnel are identified as one of the weaknesses or single points of failure, due to training, numbers of personnel, or responsibilities, a plan must be developed and trained against to ensure their absence will not result in the breakdown of the infrastructure.

Different methods of protection against damaging critical infrastructures from absence of "key personnel":

- Designate a sequence of personnel to cover the missing key personnel, and conduct training to ensure the echelon of replacements understands the specific function of the key person to the critical infrastructure.

- Reconfigure the infrastructure to negate the single point of failure or reduce the damage to the infrastructure if key personnel are absent.

- Ensure the key personnel have redundant communications available in order to provide guidance or instructions if needed.

- Ensure the key personnel have created readily available files covering situations where their importance to the infrastructure is understood to the point other could fulfill their purpose.

Too often key personnel's input into a critical infrastructure is forgotten until the crisis is at hand. Rehearsals that include the loss of certain individuals can easily identify problems early and result in reduction of risk to the critical infrastructure.

# II. Critical Infrastructure Risk Management

*Ref: NIPP 2013, National Infrastructure Protection Plan: Partnering for Critical Infrastructure Security and Resilience, Dept of Homeland Security (2013), pp. 15-20.*

The national effort to strengthen critical infrastructure security and resilience depends on the ability of public and private sector critical infrastructure owners and operators to make risk-informed decisions on the most effective solutions available when allocating limited resources in both steady-state and crisis operations.

Risk management enables the critical infrastructure community to focus on those threats and hazards that are likely to cause harm, and employ approaches that are designed to prevent or mitigate the effects of those incidents. It also increases security and strengthens resilience by identifying and prioritizing actions to ensure continuity of essential functions and services and support enhanced response and restoration.

*RM, as it is discussed in terms of critical infrastructure, is not to be confused with Operational Risk Management (ORM). ORM methods are applied during the course of military operations and are focused on improving safety for personnel engaged in those operations. RM is focused on reducing risks to the installation and its critical assets.*

# I. CI Risk Management Framework

Critical infrastructure partners manage risks based on diverse commitments to community, focus on customer welfare, and corporate governance structures. Risk tolerances will vary from organization to organization, as well as sector to sector, depending on business plans, resources, operating structure, and regulatory environments. They also differ between the private sector and the government based on underlying constraints. Different entities are likely to have different priorities with respect to security investment as well as potentially differing judgments as to what the appropriate point of risk tolerance may be. Private sector organizations generally can increase investments to meet their risk tolerances and provide for their community of stakeholders, but investments in security and resilience have legitimate limits. The government must provide for national security and public safety and operates with a different set of limits in doing so.

## Critical Infrastructure Risk Management Framework

*Ref: NIPP 2013, National Infrastructure Protection Plan (2013), fig. 3, p. 15.*

The critical infrastructure risk management framework supports a decision-making process that critical infrastructure partners collaboratively undertake to inform the selection of risk management actions. This framework is not binding and many organizations have risk management models that have proved effective and should be maintained. It does, however, provide an organizing construct for those models.

# A. Set Infrastructure Goals and Objectives

This National Plan establishes a set of broad national goals for critical infrastructure security and resilience. These national goals are supported by objectives and priorities developed at the sector level, which may be articulated in Sector-Specific Plans (SSPs) and serve as targets for collaborative planning among SSAs and their sector partners in government and the private sector.

A set of national multi-year priorities, developed with input from all levels of the partnership, will complement these goals. These priorities might focus on particular goals or cross-sector issues where attention and resources could be applied within the critical infrastructure community with the most significant impact. Critical infrastructure owners and operators, as well as SLTT and regional entities, can identify objectives and priorities for critical infrastructure that align to these national priorities, national goals, and sector objectives, but are tailored and scaled to their operational and risk environments and available resources.

# B. Identify Infrastructure

To manage critical infrastructure risk effectively, partners must identify the assets, systems, and networks that are essential to their continued operation, considering associated dependencies and interdependencies. This aspect of the risk management process also should identify information and communications technologies that facilitate the provision of essential services.

Critical infrastructure partners view criticality differently, based on their unique situations, operating models, and associated risks. The Federal Government identifies and prioritizes nationally significant critical infrastructure based upon statutory definition and national considerations. SLTT governments identify and prioritize infrastructure according to their business and operating environments and associated risks. Infrastructure owners and operators identify assets, systems, and networks that are essential to their continued operations and delivery of products and services to customers. At the sector level, many SSAs collaborate with owners and operators and SLTT entities to develop lists of infrastructure that are significant at the national, regional, and local levels.

Effective risk management requires an understanding of criticality as well as the associated interdependencies of infrastructure. This National Plan identifies certain lifeline functions that are essential to the operation of most critical infrastructure sectors. These lifeline functions include communications, energy, transportation, and water. Critical infrastructure partners should identify essential functions and resources that impact their businesses and communities. The identification of these lifeline functions can support preparedness planning and capability development.

# C. Assess and Analyze Risks

Critical infrastructure risks can be assessed in terms of the following:

- **Threat** – natural or man-made occurrence, individual, entity, or action that has or indicates the potential to harm life, information, operations, the environment, and/or property.

- **Vulnerability** – physical feature or operational attribute that renders an entity open to exploitation or susceptible to a given hazard.

- **Consequence** – effect of an event, incident, or occurrence.

Risk assessments are conducted by many critical infrastructure partners to inform their own decision making, using a broad range of methodologies. These assessments allow critical infrastructure community leaders to understand the most likely and severe incidents that could affect their operations and communities and use this information to support planning and resource allocation in a coordinated manner.

# II. National Preparedness Mission Areas

Ref: NIPP 2013, National Infrastructure Protection Plan (2013), p. 19.

Prevention activities are most closely associated with efforts to address threats; protection efforts generally address vulnerabilities; and response and recovery efforts help minimize consequences. Mitigation efforts transcend the entire threat, vulnerability, and consequence spectrum. These five mission areas -- Prevent, Protect, Mitigate, Respond, Recover -- as described in the National Preparedness Goal and System, provide a useful framework for considering risk management investments. Figure 4 illustrates the relationship of the national preparedness mission areas to the elements of risk.

## CI Risk in the Context of National Preparedness

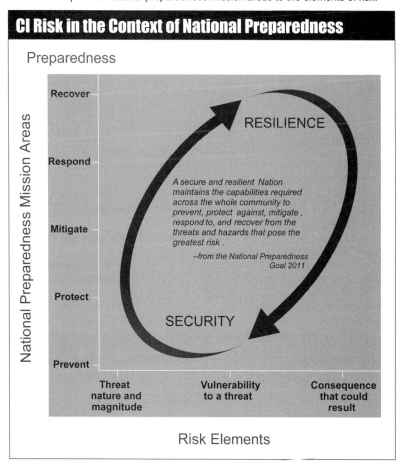

Ref: NIPP 2013, National Infrastructure Protection Plan (2013), fig. 4, p. 19.

The National Preparedness Goal also establishes 31 core capabilities that support the five national preparedness mission areas. The development of many of these core capabilities contributes to the achievement of critical infrastructure security and resilience and communities and owners and operators can apply these capabilities to identified activities to manage risk. Such efforts are enhanced when critical infrastructure risks are considered as part of setting capability targets

# III. Risk Management for DoD Installations (Overview)

*Ref: DODI 6055.17, DOD Installation Emergency Management; DODI 2000.16, DOD Antiterrorism Standards; DODI 3020.45, Defense Critical Infrastructure Program; and DODM 3020.45, Vol. 1, Defense Critical Infrastructure Program, DOD Mission-Based Critical Asset Identification Process (Contributed by Paul Beach, R4A LLC.)*

Critical infrastructure in the DOD is strategically viewed as a sub-set of elements that contribute to overall mission assurance. DOD installation commanders must identify their emergency management (EM) priorities based upon what Mission Essential Functions (MEFs) are conducted or supported at the installation. MEFs have four key components at risk:

- **Mission Essential Personnel (MEP)** – The sub-set of installation personnel that actually perform MEFs or protect the MEPs (first responders, etc.).
- **Critical Mission Facilities (CMFs)** – The physical location/building/facility where the MEF is conducted or supported from (wharf, hangar, air operations tower, EOC, etc.).
- **Critical Assets** – Those assets used while conducting MEFs (ships, planes, IT servers, etc.).
- **Critical Infrastructure** – The systems and public works that enable the CMFs and critical assets to function (energy grid, fuel systems, communications, water, sanitation, etc.).

**Risk** is a condition that DOD installations must manage continuously. In the context of DOD Critical Infrastructure, risk can be defined as "the potential for a negative outcome as a consequence of the occurrence of a hazard or threat".

**Hazard** can be defined as "any phenomenon (other than terrorism) that has the potential to disrupt or disable an installation's MEFs".

**Threat** can be defined as "the potential for attack, either by a known adversary or terrorist entity, using unconventional warfare tactics, with the intent to disrupt or disable an installation's MEFs".

The following steps depict a broad overview of the RM process. Refer to local installation instructions for specific details regarding the conduct of an RA.

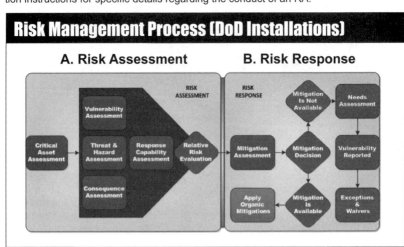

## Risk Management Process (DoD Installations)

### A. Risk Assessment          B. Risk Response

The risk management (RM) process depicted above involves identifying and assessing mission critical assets for hazards and threats, and then determining what mitigation measures are necessary to reduce the asset's overall risk to an acceptable level. An asset's risk profile is determined by conducting a series of internal or external installation assessments collectively referred to as the asset's Risk Assessment (RA). After all pertinent assessment data is collected, the installation EM staff responds to each identified risk by removing, preventing or mitigating the hazard or threat. Many hazards and threats cannot be prevented, thus, the risk to the asset cannot be eliminated. The best time to apply mitigation measure is before the hazard or threat strikes. However, an unknown hazard or threat that occurs and produces serious damage must also be assessed and mitigated after the fact during the recovery phase of an incident.

*RM, as it is discussed in terms of DOD critical infrastructure, is not to be confused with Operational Risk Management (ORM). ORM methods are applied during the course of military operations and focused on improving safety for personnel engaged in those operations. Installation RM is focused on improving the all hazards resiliency of the installation and its critical assets.*

Continued on next page

# A. Risk Assessment

## Risk Assessment Components

- **Criticality Assessment (CA)**
- **Vulnerability Assessment (VA)**
- **Threat Assessment (TA)**
- **Hazard Assessment (HA)**
- **Consequence Assessment**
- **Response Capability Assessment**
- **Relative Risk Evaluation**

*For related discussion of risk assessment components, see pp. 6-24 to 6-29.*

### Criticality Assessment (CA)
DODI 3020.45, Defense Critical Infrastructure Program (DCIP), requires the DCIP assessment team to conduct a triennial CA for Installation. The DOD installation Antiterrorism Officer (ATO) conducts an internal CA annually during off-cycle years. This assessment is where critical assets, infrastructure, and personnel essential to sustaining DOD and installation MEFs are identified.

### Vulnerability Assessment (VA)
DODI 2000.16, (DOD Antiterrorism Standards), requires the Joint Mission Assurance Assessment (JMAA) team, or equivalent MAA team to conduct a higher headquarters (HHQ) VA for all DOD installations on a triennial basis. The installation ATO will normally conduct an internal VA annually during off-cycle years. A VA is a measure of the effectiveness of safeguards taken to protect the installation and if certain assets are vulnerable to terrorism. The installation EM staff will assess each critical asset for vulnerabilities to natural, technological, and terrorism hazards/threats. Vulnerabilities

Continued on next page

# III. Risk Management for DoD Installations (Cont.)

Continued from previous page

identified during the VA process are normally reported up the installation commander's reporting chain, where they are tracked for situational awareness and mitigation planning. A vulnerability is deemed to exist after a critical asset is identified, assessed, and a determination is made that the risks to that asset cannot be mitigated within the installation's capabilities.

## Threat Assessment (TA)
DODI 2000.16 requires the Heads of the DoD Components to establish an antiterrorism RM process that includes annual TAs for all DOD installations. This is normally accomplished by the service department's criminal investigative agency. This assessment focuses on the full range of known or estimated terrorist capabilities within the installation's area of interest, including weapons of mass destruction (WMD), toxic industrial chemicals (TICs), and toxic industrial materials (TIMs).

## Hazard Assessment (HA)
DODI 6055.17, (DOD Installation Emergency Management), requires all DOD installations to conduct an assessment of all natural, technological, and terrorism related hazards that threaten the installation and its critical assets prior to the annual update of the installation's EM plan. The HA must assess each potential hazard for its threat value towards all installation personnel, critical assets, critical infrastructure, and MEFs performed on the installation. A thorough HA enables the installation's EM staff to develop hazard specific plans providing detailed preparedness, response, and recovery actions and informs what mitigation response is appropriate to protect the asset.

## Consequence Assessment
The installation EM staff conducts the Consequence Assessment annually. The Consequence Assessment is an analysis of the potential impacts of each threat or hazard occurring at the installation's current level of preparedness/response capability. Installation hazard consequences to consider are:

- Death or injuries to all installation personnel
- Damage or destruction of critical infrastructure, facilities, or assets
- Disruption of MEFs or critical missions

## Response Capability Assessment
The installation EM staff conducts a Response Capability Assessment to calculate the hazard mitigating effects of existing emergency response manpower, procedures, training, equipment, and exercises. The assessment is considered a baseline look using the installation's assigned emergency response capabilities.

Continued from previous page

## Relative Risk Evaluation
The installation EM staff conducts a comparative analysis of all assets and hazards. This Relative Risk Evaluation uses the data derived from the previously described assessments to identify hazards and threats that pose the greatest risk to the installation. Once completed, all hazards, threats, and critical assets are compared relative to each other to provide the installation commander a prioritized list of vulnerable assets. The

asset list, ranked in order of highest to lowest relative risk factors (RRFs), supports the installation commander's and EM staff's risk response decision making.

# B. Risk Response

## Mitigation Assessment

After completing the RA for all critical assets, the installation EM staff considers all available risk mitigation options for those critical assets with the highest RRFs. The overall risk mitigation strategy must reduce the probability and consequences of hazards and threats with the highest RRFs in the most cost effective manner. Options to consider are:

- Improved procedures
- Enhanced construction techniques
- Improving drainage
- Redundant systems (generators, lighting, etc.)
- Targeted training and public awareness campaigns
- Random Anti-Terrorism Measures (RAMs)
- Specialized response equipment
- Measures that improve or hasten recovery efforts
- Multiple layers of protection (defense in depth)

The installation EM staff should document all mitigation options required to reduce the risks for critical assets. Mitigation options that are currently available to the installation are applied immediately. Required mitigation options that are not available to the installation must be identified in a Needs Assessment and reported as a vulnerability to the installation commander's chain of command. A vulnerability that cannot be mitigated should have a waiver or exception granted. Requests for waivers or exceptions must be routed to the HHQ organization that created the asset protection requirement, normally an Echelon 1 command.

## Additional Risk Response

The RM process culminates in the application of mitigation measures for the installation's critical assets. Developing controls and supervising their application are essential follow-through actions of the RM process. The installation EM staff and all stakeholders involved in the RM process should evaluate the effectiveness of applied controls, under simulated or real world conditions, and capture lessons learned.

To assess risk effectively, critical infrastructure partners—including owners and operators, sector councils, and government agencies—need timely, reliable, and actionable information regarding threats, vulnerabilities, and consequences. Non¬governmental entities must be involved in the development and dissemination of products regarding threats, vulnerabilities, and potential consequences and provide risk information in a trusted environment. Partners should understand intelligence and information requirements and conduct joint analysis where appropriate. Critical infrastructure partnerships can bring great value in improving the understanding of risk to both cyber and physical systems and assets. Neither public nor private sector entities can fully understand risk without this integration of wide-ranging knowledge and analysis.

Supporting information-sharing initiatives exist both at the national and regional level. Information-sharing activities can protect privacy by applying the FIPPs and protect civil liberties by complying with applicable laws and policies. It is equally crucial to ensure adequate protection of sensitive business and security information that could cause serious adverse impacts to private businesses, the economy, and public or private enterprise security through unauthorized disclosure, access, or use. The Federal Government has a statutory responsibility to safeguard critical infrastructure information. DHS and other agencies use the Protected Critical Infrastructure Information (PCII) program and other protocols such as Classified National Security Information, Law Enforcement Sensitive Information, and Federal Security Classification Guidelines. The PCII program, authorized by the Critical Infrastructure Information (CII) Act of 2002 and its implementing regulations (Title 6 of the Code of Federal Regulations Part 29), defines both the requirements for submitting CII and those that government agencies must follow for accessing and safeguarding CII.

# D. Implement Risk Management Activities

Decision makers prioritize activities to manage critical infrastructure risk based on the criticality of the affected infrastructure, the costs of such activities, and the potential for risk reduction. Some risk management activities address multiple aspects of risk, while others are more targeted to address specific threats, vulnerabilities, or potential consequences. These activities can be divided into the following approaches:

## Identify, Deter, Detect, Disrupt, and Prepare for Threats and Hazards

- Establish and implement joint plans and processes to evaluate needed increases in security and resilience measures, based on hazard warnings and threat reports.
- Conduct continuous monitoring of cyber systems.
- Employ security protection systems to detect or delay an attack or intrusion.
- Detect malicious activities that threaten critical infrastructure and related operational activities across the sectors.
- Implement intrusion detection or intrusion protection systems on sensitive or mission-critical networks and facilities to identify and prevent unauthorized access and exploitation.
- Monitor critical infrastructure facilities and systems potentially targeted for attack (e.g., through local law enforcement and public utilities).

## Reduce Vulnerabilities

- Build security and resilience into the design and operation of assets, systems, and networks.
- Employ siting considerations when locating new infrastructure, such as avoiding floodplains, seismic zones, and other risk-prone locations.

- Develop and conduct training and exercise programs to enhance awareness and understanding of common vulnerabilities and possible mitigation strategies.
- Leverage lessons learned and apply corrective actions from incidents and exercises to enhance protective measures.
- Establish and execute business and government emergency action and continuity plans at the local and regional levels to facilitate the continued performance of critical functions during an emergency.
- Address cyber vulnerabilities through continuous diagnostics and prioritization of high-risk vulnerabilities.
- Undertake research and development efforts to reduce known cyber and physical vulnerabilities that have proved difficult or expensive to address.

## Mitigate Consequences

- Share information to support situational awareness and damage assessments of cyber and physical critical infrastructure during and after an incident, including the nature and extent of the threat, cascading effects, and the status of the response.
- Work to restore critical infrastructure operations following an incident.
- Support the provision of essential services such as: emergency power to critical facilities; fuel supplies for emergency responders; and potable water, mobile communications, and food and pharmaceuticals for the affected community.
- Ensure that essential information is backed up on remote servers and that redundant processes are implemented for key functions, reducing the potential consequences of a cybersecurity incident.
- Remove key operational functions from the Internet-connected business network, reducing the likelihood that a cybersecurity incident will result in compromise of essential services.
- Ensure that incidents affecting cyber systems are fully contained; that asset, system, or network functionality is restored to pre-incident status; and that affected information is available in an uncompromised and secure state.
- Recognize and account for interdependencies in response and recovery/restoration plans.
- Repair or replace damaged infrastructure with cost-effective designs that are more secure and resilient.
- Utilize and ensure the reliability of emergency communications capabilities.
- Contribute to the development and execution of private sector, SLTT, and regional priorities for both near- and long-term recovery.

The above activities are examples of risk management activities that are being undertaken to support the overall achievement of security and resilience, whether at an organizational, community, sector, or national level. Prevention activities are most closely associated with efforts to address threats; protection efforts generally address vulnerabilities; and response and recovery efforts help minimize consequences. Mitigation efforts transcend the entire threat, vulnerability, and consequence spectrum. These five mission areas, as described in the National Preparedness Goal and System, provide a useful framework for considering risk management investments.

# E. Measure Effectiveness

The critical infrastructure community evaluates the effectiveness of risk management efforts within sectors and at national, State, local, and regional levels by developing metrics for both direct and indirect indicator measurement. SSAs work with SCCs through the sector-specific planning process to develop attributes that support the national goals and national priorities as well as other sector-specific priorities. Such measures inform the risk management efforts of partners throughout the critical infrastructure community and help build a national picture of progress toward the vision of this National Plan as well as the National Preparedness Goal.

At a national level, the National Plan articulates broad area goals to achieve the Plan's vision that will be complemented by a set of multi-year national priorities. The critical infrastructure community will subsequently evaluate its collective progress in accomplishing the goals and priorities.

This evaluation process functions as an integrated and continuing cycle:

- Articulate the vision and national goals;
- Define national priorities;
- Identify high-level outputs or outcomes associated with the national goals and national priorities;
- Collect performance data to assess progress in achieving identified outputs and outcomes;
- Evaluate progress toward achievement of the national priorities, national goals, and vision;
- Update the national priorities and adapt risk management activities accordingly; and
- Revisit the national goals and vision on a periodic basis.

Just as regular evaluation of progress toward the national goals informs the ongoing evolution of security and resilience practices, planned exercises and real-world incidents also provide opportunities for learning and adaptation. For example, fuel shortages after Hurricane Sandy illustrated the interdependencies and complexities of infrastructure systems, the challenges in achieving shared situational awareness during large events, and the need for improved information collection and sharing among government and private sector partners to support restoration activities. The critical infrastructure and national preparedness communities also conduct exercises on an ongoing basis through the National Exercise Program and other mechanisms to assess and validate the capabilities of organizations, agencies, and jurisdictions. During and after such planned and unplanned operations, partners identify individual and group weaknesses, implement and evaluate corrective actions, and share best practices with the wider critical infrastructure and emergency management communities. Such learning and adaptation inform future plans, activities, technical assistance, training, and education.

# III. Cyber Threats & Cyber-Terrorism

*Ref: JP 3-12 (Redacted), Cyberspace Operations (Feb 13); DCSINT Handbook No. 1.02, Critical Infrastructure (Aug '06), section VII; and US Air Force Doctrine, Annex 3-12, Cyberspace Operations, updated 30 Nov 2011. (Compiled by Jay Martin.)*

Civilian, commercial and government networks are probed millions of times per day and are routinely the victims of intrusion, exploitation, and low-level computer attack. Often, hackers gain and maintain access to systems, even those thought to be off the network, for periods of more than a year before the victims even realize their systems have been compromised. This access provides the potential for damaging and even catastrophic attacks.

*(Shutterstock.com)*

## I. Cyberspace Attacks

Cyberspace attacks come in many forms and can range from obvious to non-obvious. Cyber attacks that clearly deny (degrade, disrupt, or destroy) a network are obvious. The most troublesome attacks, however are not obvious and may involve the manipulation of data. When these attacks are detected, they can cast doubt on the integrity of the entire network. Still, other attacks involve the exfiltration and exploitation of data, sometimes revealing plans or capabilities and undermining mission success.

A cyber attacker possesses inherent advantages over a defender. In contrast to land warfare, in cyberspace the concept of a culminating point does not apply. The cyber attacker does not tire nor expend resources. His lines of communication do not require sustainment or protection, and he usually has multiple avenues of approach. In fact the cyber attacker may get stronger as he penetrates defenses and finds it easier to sustain the attack. The more cyber attackers the enemy employs, both human and machine, the greater their chances of success.

Several studies examining the cyber threat have shown that critical infrastructures are potential targets of cyber terrorists. These infrastructures make extensive use of computer hardware, software, and communications systems. However, the same systems that have enhanced their performance potentially make them more vulnerable to disruption by both physical and cyber attacks to these IT systems. These infrastructures include:

- Energy systems
- Emergency services
- Telecommunication
- Banking and finance
- Transportation
- Water system

A quick review of the automation used in the electric power industry demonstrates the potential vulnerabilities to our critical infrastructures. The electrical industry has capitalized on computer technology for improved communication and automation of control centers, substations and remote protection equipment. They use a host of computer-based equipment including SCADA systems; substation controllers consisting of programmable logic controllers, remote terminal units, data processing units and communication processors; and intelligent electronic devices consisting of microprocessor-controlled meters, relays, circuit breakers, and circuit reclosers.

Although there have been no major terrorist attacks to these critical infrastructure systems to date, there is evidence that terrorist groups have been conducting surveillance on them. As stated earlier in this section under "Research," police have found a pattern of surveillance by unknown browsers located in the Middle East and South Asia against emergency telephone systems, electrical generation and transmission facilities, water storage and distribution systems, nuclear power plants, and gas facilities.

Although these systems fall within the civilian sector, the military is highly dependent on all of these critical functions and would be directly impacted if they were successfully attacked. Consider the impact on unit deployment if a successful cyber attack, or a combination of cyber and physical attack, is conducted against our critical infrastructure during movement—

- Disruption of the rail system could severely impact movement of equipment to a port of embarkation
- A successful attack against a power substation could halt loading operations at the port
- A successful attack against the telecommunications systems would directly impact the command and control of the operations

# II. Cyber-Terrorism

Cyber-terrorism is a development of terrorist capabilities provided by new technologies and networked organizations, which allows terrorists to conduct their operations with little or no physical risk to themselves. Cyber-terrorism is a new and somewhat nebulous concept, with debate as to whether it is a separate phenomenon, or just a facet of information warfare practiced by terrorists. Even for those that believe cyber-terrorism is a separate phenomenon; the boundaries often become blurred between information warfare, computer crime, online social activism, and cyber-terrorism.

Cyber-terrorism differs from other improvements in terrorist technology because it involves offensive information technology capabilities, either alone or in combination with other forms of attack. Some examinations of cyber-terrorism focus on the physi-

# A. Cyber Threat Capabilities, Methods, and Indicators

The following table lists capabilities and methods used by cyber attackers and links them to indicators that show a network user that an attack may have occurred.

## Sample Cyberspace Threat Capabilities

| Capability | Methods | Indicators |
|---|---|---|
| Denial of Service Attack | Phishing to obtain network access leads to other attacks (botnet, attacks, land attacks, cyber nukes), that deny access | Abnormal network performance, inability to navigate web and access sites, uncontrolled spam, and system reboots |
| Network penetration | Man-in-the-middle attacks, phishing, poisoning, stolen certificates, exploiting unencrypted messages and homepages with poor security features | Unfamiliar emails, official looking addresses requiring urgent reply, IP packets replaced, non- legitimate pages with the look of legitimate sites, directed moves from site to site, requests to upgrade and validate information, and unknown links |
| Emplaced malware (virus, worms spyware, and root-kits) | Phishing, spear-phishing, pharming, insider threat introduction, open source automation services, victim activated through drive-by downloads and victim emplaced data storage devices | Pop-ups, erroneous error reports, planted USB drives, CDs, & DVDs, unknown e-mail attachments, changed passwords without user knowledge, automatic downloads, unknown apps, and degraded network |
| Interrupt and/or blind information systems, digital downlinks in the electromagnetic spectrum | Commercially available high- powered lasers, high powered micro-waves, and repurposed or re- engineered communications systems | Symptoms may not be evident if passive; may manifest as interference with microwave reception on command and control networks, software or hardware malfunctions, or inability to transmit data |

# B. Cyber Threat Categories

*Ref: US Air Force Doctrine, Annex 3-12, Cyberspace Operations (Nov '11), pp. 13 to 16.*

Threats are combinations of actors, entities, and forces that have the capability and intent to harm United States forces, national interests, or the homeland. Information technology infrastructures are inherently vulnerable to malfunction and exploitation (intended or unintended). Cyber-attacks and network intrusions result in disruption, neutralization, and exploitation of data from information technology networks. Cyber-attacks often exploit vulnerabilities within friendly force networks and can be difficult to detect and counter.

The four major categories of cyber threats that have implications for military operations are as follows:

- Nation state threat
- Transnational actor threat
- Criminal organization threat
- Individual actor threat

## Nation State Threat

This threat is potentially the most dangerous because of access to resources, personnel, and time that may not be available to other actors. Other nations may employ cyberspace to either attack or conduct espionage against the US. Nation state threats involve traditional adversaries and sometimes, in the case of espionage, even traditional allies. Nation states may conduct operations directly or may outsource them to third parties to achieve their goals.

## Transnational Actor Threat

Transnational actors are formal and informal organizations that are not bound by national borders. These actors use cyberspace to raise funds, communicate with target audiences and each other, recruit, plan operations, destabilize confidence in governments, and conduct direct terrorist actions within cyberspace.

## Criminal Organization Threat

Criminal organizations may be national or transnational in nature. Criminal organizations steal information for their own use or, in turn, to sell to raise capital. They also may be used as surrogates by nation states or transnational actors to conduct attacks or espionage through CO.

## Individual Actors or Small Group Threat

Individual actors or small groups of people can illegally disrupt or gain access to networks or computer systems. Their intentions are as varied as the number of groups and individuals. These actors gain access into systems to discover vulnerabilities, sometimes sharing the information with the owners; however, they also may have malicious intent. Political motivations often drive their operations, and they use cyberspace to spread their message. They may also create and then install malware on commercial or government systems. These actors can be exploited by others, such as criminal organizations or nation states, in order to execute concealed operations against targets in order to preserve their identity or create plausible deniability.

# Additional Categories

Cyberspace threats can also be categorized as traditional, irregular, catastrophic, accidental, natural, or insider.

## Traditional Threat

Traditional threats typically arise from states employing recognized military capabilities and forces in well-understood forms of military conflict. Within cyberspace, these threats may be less understood due to the continuing evolution of technologies and methods. Traditional threats are generally focused against the cyberspace capabilities that enable our air, land, maritime, special operations, and space forces and are focused to deny the US military freedom of action and use of cyberspace.

## Irregular Threat

Irregular threats can use cyberspace as an unconventional asymmetric means to counter traditional advantages. These threats could also manifest through an adversary's selective targeting of US cyberspace capabilities and infrastructure. They attempt to shield themselves from US law enforcement, intelligence, and military operations through use of commercial security products and services readily available in cyberspace. Irregular threats from criminal elements and advocates of radical political agendas seek to use cyberspace for their own ends to challenge government, corporate, or societal interests.

## Catastrophic Threat

Catastrophic threats involve the acquisition, possession, and use of weapons of mass destruction (WMD) or methods producing WMD-like effects. While WMD attacks are physical (kinetic) events, they may have profound effects within the cyberspace domain by degrading or destroying key cyber-based systems vital to infrastructure like supervisory control and data acquisition (SCADA) systems. Well-planned attacks on key nodes of the cyberspace infrastructure have the potential to produce network collapse and cascading effects that can severely affect critical infrastructures locally, nationally, or possibly even globally.

## Disruptive Threat

Disruptive threats are breakthrough technologies that may negate or reduce current US advantages in warfighting domains. Global research, investment, development, and industrial processes provide an environment conducive to the creation of technological advances.

## Natural Threat

Natural threats that can damage and disrupt cyberspace include events such as floods, hurricanes, solar flares, lightning, and tornados. These types of events often produce highly destructive effects requiring the DOD to maintain or restore key cyberspace systems. These events also provide adversaries the opportunity to capitalize on infrastructure degradation and diversion of attention and resources.

## Accidental Threat

Accidental threats are unpredictable and can take many forms. From a backhoe cutting a fiber optic cable of a key cyberspace node, to inadvertent introduction of viruses, accidental threats unintentionally disrupt the operation of cyberspace.

## Insider Threat

The "insider" is an individual currently or at one time authorized to access an organization's information system, data, or network. Such authorization implies a degree of trust in the individual. The insider threat refers to harmful acts that trusted insiders might carry out; for example, something that causes harm to the organization, or an unauthorized act that benefits the individual.

**Critical Infrastructure**

# C. Tools of Cyber Attacks

Ref: DCSINT Handbook No. 1.02, Critical Infrastructure (Aug '06), pp. IV-9 to IV-11.

## Backdoor

This is used to describe a back way, hidden method, or other type of method of by passing normal security in order to obtain access to a secure area. It is also referred to as a trapdoor. Sometimes backdoors are surreptitiously planted on a network element; however, there are some cases where they are purposely installed on a system.

## Denial of Service Attacks (DOS)

A DOS attack is designed to disrupt network service, typically by overwhelming the system with millions of requests every second causing the network to slow down or crash. An even more effective DOS is the distributed denial of service attack (DDOS). This involves the use of numerous computers flooding the target simultaneously. Not only does this overload the target with more requests, but having the DOS from multiple paths makes backtracking the attack extremely difficult, if not impossible. Many times worms are planted on computers to create zombies that allow the attacker to use these machines as unknowing participants in the attack. To highlight the impact of these type attacks, in February 2000, DOS attacks against Yahoo, CNN, eBay and other e-commerce sites were estimated to have caused over a billion dollars in losses. DOS attacks have also been directed against the military. In 1999, NATO computers were hit with DOS attacks by hactivists protesting the NATO bombing in Kosovo.

## E-mail Spoofing

E-mail spoofing is a method of sending e-mail to a user that appears to have originated from one source when it actually was sent from another source. This method is often an attempt to trick the user into making a damaging statement or releasing sensitive information (such as passwords). For example, e-mail could be sent claiming to be from a person in authority requesting users to send them a copy of a password file or other sensitive information.

## IP Address Spoofing

A method that creates Transmission Control Protocol/Internet Protocol (TCP/IP) packets using somebody else's IP address. Routers use the "destination IP" address to forward packets through the Internet, but ignore the "source IP" address. This method is often used in DDOS attacks in order to hide the true identity of the attacker.

## Keylogger

A software program or hardware device that is used to monitor and log each of the keys a user types into a computer keyboard. The user who installed the    program or hardware device can then view all keys typed in by that user. Because these programs and hardware devices monitor the actual keys being typed, a user can easily obtain passwords and other information the computer operator may not wish others to know.

## Logic Bomb

A program routine that destroys data by reformatting the hard disk or randomly inserting garbage into data files. It may be brought into a computer by downloading a public-domain program that has been tampered with. Once it is executed, it does its damage immediately, whereas a virus keeps on destroying.

## Physical Attacks

This involves the actual physical destruction of a computer system and/ or network. This includes destroying transport networks as well as the terminal equipment.

## Sniffer

A program and/or device that monitors data traveling over a network. Although sniffers are used for legitimate network management functions, they also are used during cyber attacks for stealing information, including passwords, off a network. Once emplaced, they are very difficult to detect and can be inserted almost anywhere through different means.

## Trojan Horse

A program or utility that falsely appears to be a useful program or utility such as a screen saver. However, once installed performs a function in the background such as allowing other users to have access to your computer or sending information from your computer to other computers.

## Viruses

A software program, script, or macro that has been designed to infect, destroy, modify, or cause other problems with a computer or software program. There are different types of viruses. Some of these are:

- **Boot Sector Virus:** Infects the first or first few sectors of a computer hard drive or diskette drive allowing the virus to activate as the drive or diskette boots.

- **Companion Virus:** Stores itself in a file that is named similar to another program file that is commonly executed. When that file is executed the virus will infect the computer and/or perform malicious steps such as deleting your computer hard disk drive.

- **Executable Virus:** Stores itself in an executable file and infects other files each time the file is run. The majority of all computer viruses are spread when a file is executed or opened.

- **Overwrite Virus:** Overwrites a file with its own code, helping spread the virus to other files and computers.

- **Polymorphic Virus:** Has the capability of changing its own code allowing the virus to have hundreds or thousands of different variants making it much more difficult to notice and/or detect.

- **Resident Virus:** Stores itself within memory allowing it to infect files instantaneously and does not require the user to run the "execute a file" to infect files.

- **Stealth Virus:** Hides its tracks after infecting the computer. Once the computer has been infected the virus can make modifications to allow the computer to appear that it has not lost any memory and or that the file size has not changed.

## Worms

A destructive software program containing code capable of gaining access to computers or networks and once within the computer or network causing that computer or network harm by deleting, modifying, distributing, or otherwise manipulating the data.

## Zombie

A computer or server that has been basically hijacked using some form of malicious software to help a hacker perform a Distributed Denial of Service attack (DDOS).

cal destruction of information hardware and software, or physical damage to person-nel or equipment using information technology as the medium. Examples of this ap-proach would include the chaos and destruction caused by disrupting a nation's air traffic control system, crashing two trains together by overriding the railroad signal and switching system, interfering with the control systems for water or electricity, or blocking and falsifying commercial communications to cause economic disruption.

One common aspect is that organizations trying to attack using information tech-nology will more than likely want to keep the information network up, or at least limit their destruction or disruptions to discrete portions of the network. For a true "cyber-terrorist," the network is the method of attack. It is the weapon, or at the least, the medium through which an attack is delivered. Information warfare of this sort re-quires that messages and computer commands are transmitted, programs and mali-cious software be emplaced, fraudulent transactions take place, and information be available for exploitation. Defacing websites, crashing portions of a target network, accessing enemy information, denying network access to other groups, manipulating financial confidence and causing panic exemplify this warfare. Still, they require that the target network remain more or less intact.

# III. Cyber Support to Terrorism

> Al-Qaeda "was using the Internet to do at least reconnaissance of American utilities and American facilities. If you put all the unclassified information together, sometimes it adds up to something that ought to be classified."
>
> Richard Clark, Former Chairman, President's Critical Infrastructure Protection Board, February 13, 2002

Terrorists recognize the benefit of cyber operations and continue to exploit informa-tion technology in every function of their operations. Macro-functions include:

## A. Planning

Terrorists use the cyber infrastructure to plan attacks, communicate with each other, and posture for future exploitation. Employing easy-to-use encryption programs that they can easily download from the Internet, terrorists are able to communicate in a secure environment. Using steganography, they hide instructions, plans and pictures for their attacks in pictures and posted comments in chat rooms. The images and instructions can only be opened using a "private key" or code known only to the recipients. Additionally, encryption programs can scramble telephone conversations.

## B. Recruitment

Recruitment is the life-blood of a terrorist organization and they use multiple methods to entice new members. In addition to traditional methods, such as written publications, local prayer leaders, audio-video cassettes and CDs promoting their cause; terrorist groups also use their own websites to recruit new members. This is accomplished by providing their view of the history of their organization, its cause, and additional information to encourage potential members to join. Additionally, they often have hyperlinks to other material to encourage membership. They also use these sites to collect "donations" for their cause.

## C. Research

Using the Internet, terrorists can tap into thousands of databases, libraries and newsgroups around the world to gather information on any subjects that they need to research. The information can be in the form of text, maps, satellite images, pictures or even video material. The use of search engines, such as Google, have made searching the Internet very easy and allows terrorists to obtain critical information located in the public domain using very simple resources. For example, by typing "Bombs" in the Google search engine, 2,870,000 references were found in 0.17 seconds. To narrow this list, typing "Bombs AND Homemade," resulted in 47,200 references being found in 0.08 seconds. Although most of these are harmless references that may just refer to news articles, many provide detailed information on how to manufacture bombs. One site not only provided information on bombs, but also provided additional references on subjects such as drugs, fake IDs, fraud, lock picking, and weapons.

To highlight the importance terrorists place on research over the Internet, an al Qaeda training manual recovered in Afghanistan states: "Using public sources openly and without resorting to illegal means, it is possible to gather at least 80% of information about the enemy." After finding this manual, Secretary of Defense Donald Rumsfeld disseminated a memo to the armed services stating: "One must conclude our enemies access DoD Web sites on a regular basis." The memo directed the military to purge their websites of information that could benefit our potential enemies.

Although the military has tightened up security on their sites, terrorists can still conduct research on military units. Using a search engine, they simply type in a specific organization and the search engine will provide the links if they exist. For example, typing in "Army AND Fort Hood" resulted in the Fort Hood home page being displayed. This site provided the entire list of units assigned to III Corps simply by opening the web page. Looking at a Fort Bragg web site, available references included a map of the installation, the schedule for the installation shuttle bus, and a copy of the official telephone directory, which provides all of the units on the installation. Other critical information is available on the military, such as every Army and Air Force airfield in the United States, and the location of military ammunition depots throughout CONUS.

Terrorists can also use the Internet to research information on the critical infrastructure of the United States. Unfortunately, using the convenience of the Internet, terrorists can virtually research any subject, to include information on potential targets, without ever leaving the safety of their locales overseas or within the United States.

# D. Propaganda

Terrorist organizations depend on the backing of a broad base of support for both recruiting and funding. They use propaganda to discredit their enemy while making themselves look good. Earlier terrorist groups published newspapers and leaflets to spread their propaganda. Although this form of media is still widely used, terrorist groups are now using the Internet.

Most radical groups of international significance operate Internet sites. These groups post articles supporting their agendas on these sites, which make them instantly available to the worldwide cyber community. Radical Islam in particular makes use of propaganda to enlist the support of their own public for jihad and to demoralize the enemy. The statement from the Hizballah website is an example of some of their propaganda.

Critical Infrastructure

# National Cyber Investigative Joint Task Force

*Ref: https://www.fbi.gov/about-us/investigate/cyber/ncijtf*

Communication, commerce, and government are just a few aspects of our daily lives that have been forever changed and, in many ways, made more convenient by the Internet. Unfortunately, these same advancements also have introduced a new breed of technologically-savvy criminal. Such crimes as terrorism, espionage, financial fraud, and identity theft have long existed in the physical realm, but are now being perpetrated in the cyber domain. As criminals more effectively exploit this new frontier, their use of the Internet and technology adds a layer of complexity that cannot be overcome through the efforts of any one agency.

To address this evolving cyber challenge, the National Cyber Investigative Joint Task Force (NCIJTF) was officially established in 2008. The NCIJTF is comprised of over 20 partnering agencies from across law enforcement, the intelligence community, and the Department of Defense, with representatives who are co-located and work jointly to accomplish the organization's mission from a whole-of-government perspective.

As a unique multi-agency cyber center, the NCIJTF has the primary responsibility to coordinate, integrate, and share information to support cyber threat investigations, supply and support intelligence analysis for community decision-makers, and provide value to other ongoing efforts in the fight against the cyber threat to the nation.

The NCIJTF also synchronizes joint efforts that focus on identifying, pursuing, and defeating the actual terrorists, spies, and criminals who seek to exploit our nation's systems. To accomplish this, the task force leverages the collective authorities and capabilities of its members and collaborates with international and private sector partners to bring all available resources to bear against domestic cyber threats and their perpetrators.

Through the coordination, collaboration, and sharing that occurs at the NCIJTF, members across the U.S. Government work toward placing cyber criminals behind bars and removing them from the nation's networks.

## Cyber Task Forces

The 2008 Comprehensive National Cybersecurity Initiative (CNCI) created the foundation for a whole-of-government approach to protecting the nation from cybersecurity threats. As part of the CNCI, the National Cyber Investigative Joint Task Force (NCIJTF) was established under Presidential Directive as one of the country's national cybersecurity centers. Located in the Washington, D.C. area, the FBI-led NCIJTF serves as the national focal point for coordinating cyber threat investigations. In its role as a headquarters-level task force environment, the NCIJTF enhances collaboration and integrates operations among the represented U.S. Intelligence Community and federal law enforcement partners against:

- Cyber terrorists exploiting vulnerabilities in critical infrastructure control systems;
- Nation-state theft of intellectual property and trade secrets;
- Financially-motivated criminals stealing money or identities or committing cyber extortion;
- Hactivists illegally targeting businesses and government services;
- Insiders conducting theft and sabotage.

Chap 6

# I. Protection Warfighting Function

Ref: ADP 3-37, Protection (Aug '12) and ADRP 3-0, Unified Land Operations (May '12), pp. 3-5 to 3-6. See also p. 1-41.

Protection is the preservation of the effectiveness and survivability of mission-related military and nonmilitary personnel, equipment, facilities, information, and infrastructure deployed or located within or outside the boundaries of a given operational area. (JP 3-0).

Commanders and staffs synchronize, integrate, and organize capabilities and resources throughout the operations process to preserve combat power and the freedom of action and to mitigate the effects of threats and hazards. Protection safeguards the force, personnel (combatants and noncombatants), systems, and physical assets of the United States and unified action partners. Survivability refers to the capacity, fitness, or tendency to remain alive or in existence. For the military, survivability is about much more than mere survival—it is also about remaining effective. Military forces are composed of personnel and physical assets, each having their own inherent survivability qualities or capabilities that permit them to avoid or withstand hostile actions or environmental conditions while retaining the ability to fulfill their primary mission.

## I. The Protection Warfighting Function

The protection warfighting function is the related tasks and systems that preserve the force so that commanders can apply maximum combat power to accomplish the mission (ADRP 3-0). Preserving the force includes protecting personnel (combatants and noncombatants), systems, and physical assets of the United States and unified action partners. The protection warfighting function enables commanders to preserve force integrity and combat power by integrating protection capabilities to safeguard bases/base camps, secure routes, and protect forces. Commanders incorporate protection when they understand and visualize capabilities available for protection. Some of these actions or effects may be achieved through the combined integration of the eight elements of combat power, resulting in an increasingly effective and efficient scheme of protection.

The supporting tasks of the protection warfighting function are—

- Conduct operational area security
- Employ safety techniques (including fratricide avoidance)
- Implement operations security
- Provide intelligence support to protection
- Implement physical security procedures
- Apply antiterrorism measures
- Conduct law and order
- Conduct survivability operations
- Provide force health protection
- Conduct chemical, biological, radiological, and nuclear operations
- Provide explosive ordnance disposal and protection support
- Coordinate air and missile defense
- Conduct personnel recovery operations
- Conduct internment and resettlement

Refer to JP 3-0 for more information on joint protection tasks.

Protection

# II. The Role of Protection

Ref: ADP 3-37, Protection (Aug '12), pp. 1 to 2.

Protection is the preservation of the effectiveness and survivability of mission-related military and nonmilitary personnel, equipment, facilities, information, and infrastructure deployed or located within or outside the boundaries of a given operational area (Joint Publication [JP] 3-0). Commanders and staffs synchronize, integrate, and organize capabilities and resources throughout the operations process to preserve combat power and mitigate the effects of threats and hazards. Protection is a continuing activity; it integrates all protection capabilities to safeguard the force, personnel (combatants and noncombatants), systems, and physical assets of the United States and unified action partners.

Operational environments are uncertain, marked by rapid change and a wide range of threats and hazards. These evolving operational environments will provide significant challenges for commanders and staffs who are integrating protection capabilities. Protection preserves the combat power potential of the force by providing capabilities to identify and prevent threats and hazards and to mitigate their effects. Army units may also be required to provide protection for civilians in order to support mission objectives. This may include protecting civilians from widespread violence (such as mass atrocities), mitigating civilian casualties, and ensuring a secure environment for the population and nonmilitary partners.

Protection can be maximized by integrating the elements of combat power to reinforce protection or to achieve complementary protective effects. The goal of protection integration is to balance protection with the freedom of action throughout the duration of military operations. This is accomplished by integrating reinforcing or complementary protection capabilities into operations until all significant vulnerabilities have been mitigated, have been eliminated, or become assumed risks. The employment of synchronized and integrated reinforcing and complementary protection capabilities preserves combat power and provides flexibility across the range of military operations. The collaboration, integration, and synchronization between the warfighting functions assist in identifying and preventing threats and hazards and in mitigating their effects.

Army leaders are responsible for clearly articulating their visualization of operations in time, space, purpose, and resources. The commander's inherent responsibility to protect and preserve the force and secure the area of operations is vital in seizing, retaining, and exploiting the initiative. Protection must be considered throughout the operations process to—

- Identify threats and hazards
- Implement control measures to prevent or mitigate enemy or adversary actions
- Manage capabilities to mitigate the effects and time to react or maneuver on the adversary to gain superiority and retain the initiative

A shared understanding and purpose of the joint protection function (see JP 3-0) allows Army leaders to integrate actions within the unified action and to synchronize operations. The joint protection function focuses on preserving the joint force fighting potential in four primary ways:

- **Active defensive measures** to protect the joint force, its information, its bases/base camps, critical infrastructure, and lines of communications from an enemy or adversary attack
- **Passive defensive measures** to make friendly forces, systems, and facilities difficult to locate, strike, and destroy
- The application of technology and procedures to **reduce the risk of fratricide**
- **Emergency management and response** to reduce the loss of personnel and capabilities due to accidents, health threats, and natural disasters

# Protection Logic Map

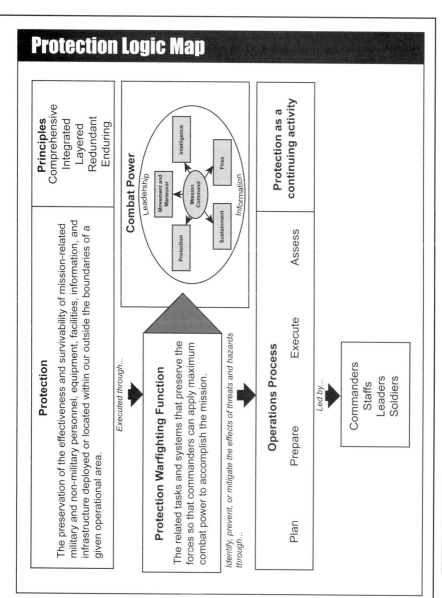

*Ref: ADP 3-37, Protection, fig. 1, p. iii.*

Army Doctrine Publication (ADP) 3-37 provides guidance on protection and the protection warfighting function. It also provides the guiding protection principles for commanders and staffs who are responsible for planning and executing protection in support of unified land operations. ADP 3-37 corresponds with the Army operations doctrine introduced in ADP 3-0.

Protection

# IV. Protection Integration in the Operations Process

*Ref: ADP 3-37, Protection (Aug '12), pp. 3 to 7.*

Protection is integrated throughout the operations process to provide a synchronization of efforts and an integration of capabilities. The protection warfighting function tasks are incorporated into the process in a layered and redundant approach to complement and reinforce actions to achieve force protection.

## Protection within the Operations Process

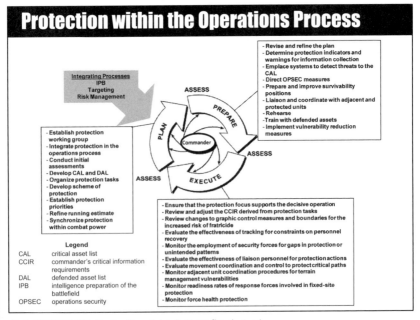

*Ref: ADRP 3-37, Protection, introductory fig. 1, p. vi.*

## A. Plan

Planning is the first step toward effective protection. Commanders consider the most likely threats and hazards and decide which personnel, physical assets, and information to protect. They set protection priorities for each phase or critical event of an operation. The military decisionmaking process and troop leading procedures provide a deliberate process to develop and examine information for use in the various continuing activities and integrating processes that comprise the operations process. Effective protection schemes and risk decisions are developed based on information that flows from mission analysis, allowing a thorough understanding of the environment (operational and mission variables). The integrating processes provide a context to identify and analyze threats and hazards, to develop a situational understanding of the operational environment, and to develop a scheme of protection. Staffs assess threats, hazards, criticality, vulnerability, and capability to help commanders determine protection priorities, task organizations, and protection task integration.

Commanders and staffs apply protection considerations in relation to the mission and the operational environment throughout the operations process. They discern hazards that are preventable and divide threats into those that may be deterred and those that may require the application of security or defensive measures to achieve protection. Commanders provide risk guidance, critical information requirements, essential elements of friendly information, and asset or capability criticality to help focus staffs and subordinate leaders. Commanders direct staffs to conduct the necessary tasks to protect the force, secure the area, and mitigate the effects of current and potential threats and hazards.

The keys to protection planning are identifying the threats and hazards, assessing the threats and hazards to determine the risks, developing preventive measures, and integrating protection tasks Into a comprehensive scheme of protection that includes mitigating measures. The warfighting functions are synchronized throughout the operations process to assist in the development of an enduring scheme of protection. The critical asset list and the defended asset are developed and revised during this process.

During planning, the protection cell/working group—
- Establishes a protection working group
- Conducts initial assessments
- Develops a critical asset list and a defended asset list
- Integrates and layers protection tasks
- Develops a scheme of protection.
- Recommends protection priorities
- Refines the running estimate
- Synchronizes protection within the elements of combat power
- Identifies communication channels among key personnel within protection and leadership
- Develops and publishes personnel recovery guidance
- Establishes personnel recovery that is related to the commander's critical information requirements

Continued on next page

# B. Prepare

During the preparation phase, protection focuses on deterring and preventing the enemy or adversary from actions that would affect combat power and the freedom of action. The implementation of protection tasks with ongoing preparation activities assists in the prevention of negative effects. Commanders ensure the integration of protection warfighting function tasks and systems to safeguard bases/base camps, secure routes, and protect the force while it prepares for operations. Active defense measures assist in denying the initiative to the enemy or adversary, while the execution of passive defense measures prepares the force against the threat and hazard effects and speeds the mitigation of those effects.

Assessment occurs during preparation and includes activities required to maintain situational understanding; monitor and evaluate running estimates and tasks, methods of evaluation, and measures of performance; and identify variances for decision support. These assessments generally provide commanders with a composite estimate of preoperational force readiness or status in time to make adjustments.

Preparation includes increased application and emphasis on protection measures. During preparation, the protection cell/working group—
- Revises and refines the plan
- Determines protection indicators and warnings for information collection
- Emplaces systems to detect threats to the critical assets
- Directs operations security measures
- Prepares and improves survivability positions
- Conducts liaison and coordinates with adjacent and protected units
- Rehearses
- Trains with defended assets
- Reviews the personnel recovery readiness of subordinate units
- Establishes personnel recovery architecture
- Implements vulnerability reduction measures

Continued on next page

**Protection**

# IV. Protection Integration in the Operations Process (Cont.)

Ref: ADP 3-37, Protection (Aug '12), pp. 3 to 7.

## C. Execute

Continued from previous page

Commanders who exercise mission command decide, direct, lead, access, and provide leadership to organizations and Soldiers during execution. As operations develop and progress, the commander interprets information that flows from systems for indicators and warnings that signal the need for execution or adjustment of decisions. Commanders may direct and redirect the way that combat power is applied or preserved, and they may adjust the tempo of operations through synchronization. The continuous and enduring character of protection makes the continuity of protection tasks and systems essential during execution. Commanders implement control measures and allocate resources that are sufficient to ensure protection continuity and restoration.

Commanders and leaders must be flexible and adaptive as they seek opportunities to seize, retain, and exploit the initiative. Leaders must have situational understanding during simultaneous operations due to the diversity of threats, the proximity to civilians, and the impact of information during operations. The changing nature of operations may require the surge of certain capabilities, such as protection, to effectively link decisive operations to shaping or stabilizing activities in the area of operations.

Commanders must accept prudent risk to exploit time-sensitive opportunities by acting before enemies or adversaries discover vulnerabilities, take evasive or defensive action, and implement countermeasures. Commanders and leaders can continue to act on operational and individual initiative by making prudent risk decisions faster than the enemy or adversary, ultimately breaking their will and morale through relentless pressure. Commanders can leverage technological advancements or processes that minimize fratricide and increase the probability of mission accomplishment.

An accurate assessment is essential for effective decisionmaking and the assignment of combat power to protection tasks. The staff monitors the conduct of operations during execution, looking for variances from the scheme of maneuver and protection. When variances exceed a threshold value, adjustments are made to prevent a developing vulnerability or to mitigate the effects of the unforecasted threat or hazard. The status of protection assets is tracked and evaluated on the effectiveness of the protection systems as they are employed. Commanders maintain protection by applying comprehensive protection capabilities, from main and supporting efforts to decisive and shaping operations. Protection can be derived as a by-product or a complementary result of some combat operations (such as security operations), or it can be deliberately applied as commanders integrate and synchronize tasks that comprise the protection warfighting function.

Continued from previous page

The force continues to identify and prevent threats and hazards. The effects of a threat or hazard are identified to verify the presence of adversary action, qualifying and quantifying the specific hazard and collecting and preserving forensic evidence. Once a threat or hazard is known, it is imperative that the force is warned and begins responding to the action. Response actions save lives, protect property, and continue essential services, mitigating the effects of the threat or hazard and allowing the force to retain the initiative and deny it to the enemy or adversary. Restoring mission readiness and implementing measures from assessments prepare the force to continue operations and prepare for future operations.

The protection cell/working group monitors and evaluates several critical ongoing functions associated with execution for operational actions or changes that impact protection cell proponents, which include—

- Ensuring that the protection focus supports the commander's intent and concept of the operation
- Reviewing and recommending adjustment to the commander's critical information requirements and essential elements of friendly information derived from protection tasks
- Reviewing changes to graphic control measures and boundaries for the increased risk of fratricide
- Monitoring and evaluating personnel recovery operations
- Monitoring the employment of security forces for gaps in protection or unintended patterns
- Evaluating the effectiveness of liaison personnel for protection activities
- Evaluating movement coordination and control to protect critical paths
- Monitoring adjacent unit coordination procedures for terrain management vulnerabilities
- Monitoring the readiness rates of response forces involved in fixed-site protection
- Monitoring force health protection
- Coordinating continuously with unified action partners
- Coordinating with the Mission Management Center, U.S. Army Space and Missile Defense Command, on personnel recovery operations

# D. Assess

Assessing protection is an essential, continuous activity that occurs throughout the operations process. While a failure in protection is typically easy to detect, the successful application of protection may be difficult to assess and quantify.

Assessment is the determination of the progress toward accomplishing a task, creating a condition, or achieving an objective (JP 3-0). Commanders typically base assessments on their situational understanding, which is generally a composite of several informational sources and intuition. Assessments help the commander determine progress toward attaining the desired end state, achieving objectives, and performing tasks. It also involves continuously monitoring and evaluating an operational environment to determine what changes might affect the conduct of operations.

Staff members develop running estimates that illustrate the significant aspects of a particular activity or function over time. These estimates are used by commanders to maintain situational understanding and direct adjustments. Significant changes or variances among or within running estimates can signal a threat or an opportunity, alerting commanders to take action.

Staffs monitor and evaluate variances in threats and hazards, vulnerabilities, capabilities, risks, and priorities. They also track the status of protection assets and evaluate the effectiveness of the protection systems as they are employed. If an action appears to be failing in its desired effect, it may be attributed to personnel or equipment system failure, insufficient resource allocation at vulnerable points, or a variance in anticipated threat combat power ratio. This can result in an increased risk or ineffective supporting efforts and can lead to a cumulative failure of more critical elements. The staff then recommends adjustments to protection priorities, posture, resource allocation, systems, or the scheme of protection.

# V. Protection in Support of Unified Land Operations

*Ref: ADRP 3-37 (FM 3-37), Protection (Aug '12), p. 1-1.*

The synchronization, integration, and organization of capabilities and resources to preserve combat power from the effects of threats and hazards are essential. The ability to protect and preserve the force and secure the area of operations is vital in seizing, retaining, and exploiting the initiative. Protection emphasizes the importance of planning and expanding our protection priorities, to include protecting unified action partners, civilian populations, equipment, resources, infrastructure, and cultural landmarks across the range of military operations. It focuses on adapting our force to better leverage, integrate, and synchronize unified action capabilities and better understand operational environments. It emphasizes the need for Soldiers, leaders, and organizations to identify, prevent, or mitigate threats and hazards. Mutually supporting and overlapping protection capabilities through operational and tactical level actions better position forces to defend, respond, and recover from threat and hazard effects and to deter, counterattack, neutralize, and defeat the threats.

## Protection Principles

The following principles of protection provide military professionals with a context for implementing protection efforts, developing schemes of protection, and allocating resources:

### Comprehensive

Protection is an all-inclusive utilization of complementary and reinforcing protection tasks and systems available to commanders, incorporated into the plan, to preserve the force.

### Integrated

Protection is integrated with other activities, systems, efforts, and capabilities associated with unified land operations to provide strength and structure to the overall effort. Integration must occur vertically and horizontally with unified action partners throughout the operations process.

### Layered

Protection capabilities are arranged using a layered approach to provide strength and depth. Layering reduces the destructive effect of a threat or hazard through the dispersion of energy or the culmination of the force.

### Redundant

Protection efforts are often redundant anywhere that a vulnerability or a critical point of failure is identified. Redundancy ensures that specific activities, systems, efforts, and capabilities that are critical for the success of the overall protection effort have a secondary or auxiliary effort of equal or greater capability.

### Enduring

Protection capabilities are ongoing activities for maintaining the objectives of preserving combat power, populations, partners, essential equipment, resources, and critical infrastructure in every phase of an operation.

# II. Protection Supporting Tasks

Ref: ADRP 3-37 (FM 3-37), Protection (Aug '12), chap. 1.

Commanders and staffs synchronize, integrate, and organize capabilities and resources throughout the operations process to preserve combat power and the freedom of action and to mitigate the effects of threats and hazards. Protection safeguards the force, personnel (combatants and noncombatants), systems, and physical assets of the United States and unified action partners. Survivability refers to the capacity, fitness, or tendency to remain alive or in existence. For the military, survivability is about much more than mere survival—it is also about remaining effective. Military forces are composed of personnel and physical assets, each having their own inherent survivability qualities or capabilities that permit them to avoid or withstand hostile actions or environmental conditions while retaining the ability to fulfill their primary mission. These inherent qualities or capabilities are affected by various factors (dispersion, redundancy, morale, leadership, discipline, mobility, situational understanding, terrain and weather conditions) and can be enhanced by tasks within the protection warfighting function.

# I. Supporting Tasks

Supporting task of the protection warfighting function include:

## Protection Supporting Tasks

| | |
|---|---|
| **A** Conduct Operational Area Security | **H** Conduct Survivability Operations |
| **B** Employ Safety Techniques (including Fratricide Avoidance) | **I** Provide Force Health Protection |
| **C** Implement OPSEC | **J** Provide Explosive Ordnance Disposal (EOD) and Protection Support |
| **D** Provide Intelligence Support to Protection | **K** Conduct Chemical, Biological, Radiological, and Nuclear (CBRN) Operations |
| **E** Apply Antiterrorism Measures | **L** Coordinate Air and Missile Defense |
| **F** Implement Physical Security Procedures | **M** Conduct Personnel Recovery |
| **G** Conduct Law and Order | **N** Conduct Internment and Resettlement |

Ref: ADRP 3-37 (FM 3-37), Protection (Aug '12), p. 1-3.

Protection

# A. Conduct Operational Area Security

The task of conducting operational area security is a form of security operations conducted to protect friendly forces, installations, routes, and actions within an area of operations. Forces engaged in operational area security protect the force, installation, route, area, or asset. Although vital to the success of military operations, operational area security is normally an economy-of-force mission, often designed to ensure the continued conduct of sustainment operations and to support decisive and shaping operations by generating and maintaining combat power.

Operational area security may be the predominant method of protecting support areas that are necessary to facilitate the positioning, employment, and protection of resources required to sustain, enable, and control forces. Operational area security is often an effective method of providing civil security and control during some stability operations. Forces engaged in operational area security can saturate an area or position on key terrain to provide protection through early warning, reconnaissance, or surveillance and to guard against unexpected enemy or adversary attack with an active response. This early warning, reconnaissance or surveillance may come from ground- and space-based sensors. Operational area security often focuses on named areas of interest in an effort to answer commander's critical information requirements, aiding in tactical decisionmaking and confirming or denying threat intentions. Forces engaged in operational area security are typically organized in a manner that emphasizes their mobility, lethality, and communications capabilities. The maneuver enhancement brigade and some military police units are specifically equipped and trained to conduct operational area security and may constitute the only available force during some phases of an operation. However, operational area security takes advantage of the local security measures performed by all units, regardless of their location in the area of operations.

All commanders apportion combat power and dedicate assets to protection tasks and systems based on an analysis of the operational environment, the likelihood of threat action, and the relative value of friendly resources and populations. Based on their assessments, joint force commanders may designate the Army to provide a joint security coordinator to be responsible for designated joint security areas. Although all resources have value, the mission variables of METT-TC make some resources, assets, or locations more significant to successful mission accomplishment from enemy or adversary and friendly perspectives. Commanders rely on the risk management process and other specific assessment methods to facilitate decisionmaking, issue guidance, and allocate resources. Criticality, vulnerability, and recoverability are some of the most significant considerations in determining protection priorities that become the subject of commander guidance and the focus of operational area security.

*See facing page for further discussion.*

# B. Employ Safety Techniques (Including Fratricide Avoidance)

Safety techniques are used to identify and assess hazards to the force and make recommendations on ways to prevent or mitigate the effects of those hazards. Commanders have the inherent responsibility to analyze the risks and implement control measures to mitigate them. All staffs understand and factor into their analysis how their execution recommendations could adversely affect Soldiers. Incorporating protection within the risk management integrating process is key. It ensures a thorough analysis of risks and implements controls to mitigate their effects. All commands develop and implement a command safety program that includes fratricide avoidance, occupational health, risk management, fire prevention and suppression, and accident prevention programs focused on minimizing safety risks.

# Operational Area Security

*Ref: ADRP 3-37 (FM 3-37), Protection (Aug '12), pp. 1-4 to 1-5.*

## Base/Base Camp Defense

Base defense is the local military measures, both normal and emergency, required to nullify or reduce the effectiveness of enemy attacks on, or sabotage of, a base to ensure that the maximum capacity of its facilities is available to U.S. forces (JP 3-10).

## Critical Asset Security

Critical asset security is the protection and security of personnel and physical assets or information that is analyzed and deemed essential to the operation and success of the mission and to resources required for protection.

## Node Protection

Command posts and operations centers are often protected through area security techniques that involve the employment of protection and security assets in a layered, integrated, and redundant manner.

## High-Risk Personnel Security

High-risk personnel are personnel who, by their grade, assignment, symbolic value, or relative isolation, are likely to be attractive or accessible terrorist targets (JP 3-07.2).

## Response Force Operations

Response force operations expediently reinforce unit organic protection capabilities or complement that protection with maneuver capabilities based on the threat. Response force operations include planning for the defeat of Level I and II threats and the shaping of Level III threats until a designated combined arms tactical combat force arrives for decisive operations. *Refer to FM 3-39 for more information.*

## Lines of Communications Security

The security and protection of lines of communications and supply routes are critical to military operations since most support traffic moves along these routes. The security of lines of communications and supply routes (rail, pipeline, highway, and waterway) presents one of the greatest security challenges in an area of operations. Route security operations are defensive in nature and are terrain-oriented (see FM 3-90).

## Checkpoints and Combat Outposts

It is often necessary to control the freedom of movement in an area of operations for a specific period of time or as a long-term operation. This may be accomplished by placing checkpoints and combat outposts along designated avenues and roadways or on key terrain identified through METT-TC. *Refer to ATTP 3-90.4 for more information.*

## Convoy Security

A convoy security operation is a specialized kind of area security operations conducted to protect convoys (FM 3-90). Units conduct convoy security operations anytime there are insufficient friendly forces to continuously secure routes in an area of operations and there is a significant danger of enemy or adversary ground action directed against the convoy. *Refer to FM 4-01.45 for more information.*

## Port Area and Pier Security

Ground forces may typically provide area security for port and pier areas. The joint force commander and subordinate joint force commanders ensure that port security plans and responsibilities are clearly delineated and assigned. *Refer to JP 3-10 for more information.*

## Area Damage Control

Commanders conduct area damage control when the damage and scope of the attack are limited and they can respond and recover with local assets and resources. Optimally, commanders aim to recover immediately.

Protection

# Fratricide

Fratricide is the unintentional killing or wounding of friendly or neutral personnel by friendly firepower. The destructive power and range of modern weapons, coupled with the high intensity and rapid tempo of combat, increase the potential for fratricide. Tactical maneuvers, terrain, and weather conditions may also increase the danger of fratricide.

Fratricide is accidental and is usually the end product of an error by a leader or Soldier. Accurate information about locations and activities of friendly and hostile forces and an aggressive airspace management plan help commanders avoid fratricide. The U.S. Army Space and Missile Defense Command Mission Management Center provides joint friendly force tracking for all Services, which improves the situational awareness and helps prevent fratricide. Liaison officers increase situational understanding and enhance interoperability. Commanders, leaders, and Soldiers must know the range and blast characteristics of their weapons systems and munitions to prevent ricochet, penetration, and other unintended effects.

Commanders, leaders and Soldiers are responsible for preventing fratricide. They must lower the probability of fratricide without discouraging boldness and audacity. Good leadership that results in positive weapons control, the control of troop movements, and disciplined operational procedures contribute to achieving this goal. Situational understanding, friendly personnel identification methods, and combat identification methods also help. Soldiers must be confident that the probability of misdirected friendly fire is low. Contractors authorized to accompany the force; local, national day laborers; and nongovernmental organization personnel who support Army operations face the same risks as U.S. forces. Since these personnel work and often live in and among U.S. forces, commanders must include them in protection and combat identification plans.

The potential for fratricide may increase with the fluid nature of the noncontiguous battlefield and the changing disposition of attacking and defending forces. The presence of noncombatants in the area of operations further complicates the scheme of maneuver. Simplicity and clarity are often more important than a complex, detailed plan when developing fratricide avoidance methods.

The effects of fratricide can be devastating to unit moral and confidence and can quickly diminish the mission effectiveness of a unit. Known postfratricide events have resulted in the following unit behavior:

- Hesitation to conduct limited visibility operations
- Loss of confidence in unit leadership
- Increase of leadership self-doubt
- Hesitation to use supporting combat systems
- Oversupervision of units
- Loss of initiative
- General degradation of unit cohesiveness, morale, and combat power

*See facing page for discussion of risk mitigation and fratricide prevention.*

# Fire Prevention, Fire suppression, and Firefighting

Fire prevention, fire suppression, and firefighting encompass all efforts aimed at preventing or stopping fires. Fire prevention programs exist at all levels, and all levels of command are responsible for the Army fire protection plan. Commanders and supervisors are responsible for fire safety policies and plans in their organizations. Army firefighting capabilities consist of general firefighting and tactical firefighting:

*Refer to FM 5-415 for more information on fire prevention, fire suppression, and firefighting.*

# Risk Mitigation and Fratricide Prevention

*Ref: ADRP 3-37 (FM 3-37), Protection (Aug '12), p. 1-8.*

Commanders ensure that risk mitigation strategies and fratricide prevention methods are employed and trained to lessen the risk of fratricide on the battlefield. Prevention methods include fratricide prevention training, weapons control measures, rules of engagement training, assembly area procedures, reconnaissance, rehearsals, back-briefs, unexploded ordnance training and reporting procedures, field discipline, friendly troop marking procedures and, most importantly, awareness at all levels.

In any situation involving the risk of fratricide due to friendly fire, leaders must be prepared to take immediate actions to prevent casualties, equipment damage, and equipment destruction. The recommended actions in fratricide situations include—

- Identify the incident and order all parties involved to cease fire
- Conduct an in-stride risk assessment
- Identify and implement controls to prevent the incident from recurring

Fratricide may be more prevalent during joint and multinational operations when communications and interoperability challenges are not fully resolved. Fratricide avoidance is normally accomplished through a scheme of protection that emphasizes prevention and is centered on awareness and target identification:

## Awareness

Awareness is the immediate knowledge of the conditions of the operation, constrained geographically and in time. It includes the real-time, accurate knowledge of one's own location and orientation and the locations, activities, and intentions of other friendly, enemy, adversary, neutral, or noncombatant elements in the area of operations, sector, zone, or immediate vicinity. As previously mentioned, the U.S. Army Space and Missile Defense Command joint friendly force tracking mission aids in the overall awareness of personnel location in the operational environment.

## Target Identification

Target identification is the accurate and timely characterization of a detected object on the battlefield as friend, neutral, or enemy. This aspect of combat identification is time sensitive and directly supports a combatant's shoot or don't-shoot decision for detected objects on the battlefield (FM 3-20.15). Unknown objects should not be engaged; rather, the target identification process should continue until positive identification is made. An exception to this is a weapons-free zone where units can fire at anything that is not positively identified as friendly.

Protection

# C. Implement Operations Security (OPSEC)

Operations security is a process of identifying critical information and subsequently analyzing friendly actions attendant to military operations and other activities (JP 3-13.3). OPSEC may also be used to—

- Identify actions that can be observed by enemy or adversary intelligence systems
- Determine indicators of hostile intelligence that systems might obtain which could be interpreted or pieced together to derive critical information in time to be useful to adversaries or enemies
- Execute measures that eliminate or reduce (to an acceptable level) the vulnerabilities of friendly actions to enemy or adversary exploitation

OPSEC applies to all operations. All units conduct OPSEC to preserve essential secrecy. Commanders establish routine OPSEC measures in unit standing operating procedures. The unit OPSEC officer coordinates additional OPSEC measures with other staff and command elements and synchronizes with adjacent units. The OPSEC officer develops OPSEC measures during the military decisionmaking process. The assistant chief of staff, intelligence, assists the OPSEC process by comparing friendly OPSEC indicators with enemy or adversary intelligence collection capabilities.

*Refer to JP 3-13.3 for additional OPSEC information.*

# D. Provide Intelligence Support to Protection

This is an intelligence warfighting function task that supports the protection warfighting function. It includes providing intelligence that supports measures which the command takes to remain viable and functional by protecting itself from the effects of threat activities. It also provides intelligence that supports recovery from threat actions. It includes analyzing the threats, hazards, and other aspects of an operational environment and utilizing the intelligence preparation of the battlefield process to describe the operational environment and identify threats and hazards that may impact protection. Intelligence support develops and sustains an understanding of the enemy, terrain and weather, and civil considerations that affect the operational environment. Information collection is an activity that synchronizes and integrates the planning and employment of sensors and assets as well as the processing, exploitation, and dissemination of systems in direct support of current and future operations (FM 3-55). Information collection can complement or supplement protection tasks. Through information collection, commanders and staffs continuously plan, task, and employ collection assets and forces. These forces collect, process, and disseminate timely and accurate information to satisfy the commander's critical information requirements and other intelligence requirements. When necessary, information collection assets (ground- and space-based reconnaissance and surveillance activities) focus on special requirements, such as personnel recovery.

*Refer to ADRP 2-0 for additional intelligence information.*

# E. Apply Antiterrorism (AT) Measures

AT consists of defensive measures that are used to reduce the vulnerability of individuals and property to terrorist acts, including limited response and containment by local military and civilian forces. AT is a consideration for all forces during all military operations.

AT is an integral part of Army efforts to defeat terrorism. Terrorists can target Army elements at any time and in any location. By effectively preventing and, if necessary, responding to terrorist attacks, commanders protect all activities and people so that Army missions can proceed unimpeded. AT is neither a discrete task nor the sole responsibility of a single branch; all bear responsibility. AT must be integrated into all Army operations and considered at all times. Awareness must be built into every mission, every Soldier, and every leader. Integrating AT represents the foundation that is crucial for Army success.

# F. Implement Physical Security Procedures
*Ref: ADRP 3-37 (FM 3-37), Protection (Aug '12), p. 1-8.*

Physical security consists of physical measures that are designed to safeguard personnel; to prevent unauthorized access to equipment, installations, material, and documents; and to safeguard them against espionage, sabotage, damage, and theft. The Army employs physical security measures in depth to protect personnel, information, and critical resources in all locations and situations against various threats through effective security policies and procedures. This total system approach is based on the continuing analysis and employment of protective measures, including physical barriers, clear zones, lighting, access and key control, intrusion detection devices, defensive positions, and nonlethal capabilities.

The goal of physical security systems is to employ security in depth to preclude or reduce the potential for sabotage, theft, trespass, terrorism, espionage, or other criminal activity. To achieve this goal, each security system component has a function and related measures that provide an integrated capability for—

## Deterrence
A potential aggressor who perceives a risk of being caught may be deterred from attacking an asset. The effectiveness of deterrence varies with the aggressor's sophistication, the attractiveness of the asset, and the aggressor's objective.

## Detection
A detection measure senses an act of aggression, assesses the validity of the detection, and communicates the appropriate information to a response force.

## Assessment
Assessment—through the use of alarm systems, video surveillance systems, other types of detection systems, patrols, or fixed posts—assists in localizing and determining the size and intent of an unauthorized intrusion or activity.

## Delay
Delay measures protect an asset from aggression by delaying or preventing an aggressor's movement toward the asset or by shielding the asset from weapons and explosives.

## Response
Most protective measures depend on response personnel to assess unauthorized acts, report detailed information, and defeat an aggressor.

*Refer to ATTP 3-39.32 for additional information on physical security procedures.*

**Protection**

Typical Army AT programs are composed of several adjunct and information programs, including tasks for specialized, nonprotection military occupational specialties. AT includes the following areas at a minimum:

- Risk management (threat, critical asset, and vulnerability assessments of units, installations, facilities, and bases/base camps)
- AT planning (units, installations, facilities, and bases)
- AT awareness training and command information programs
- The integration of various vulnerability assessments of units, installations, facilities, bases/base camps, personnel, and activities
- AT protection measures to protect individual personnel, high-risk personnel, physical assets (physical security), and designated critical assets and information
- Resource application
- Civil and military partnerships
- Force protection condition systems to support terrorist threat and incident response plans
- Comprehensive AT program review

*Refer to FM 3-37.2 for additional information on AT measures.*

# G. Conduct Law and Order Operations

Law and order operations encompass policing and the associated law enforcement activities to control and protect populations and resources and to facilitate the existence of a lawful and orderly environment. Law and order operations and the associated skills and capabilities inherent in that function provide the fundamental base on which all other military police functions are framed and conducted.

Law and order operations are conducted across the range of military operations. As the operation transitions and the operational environment stabilizes, civil control efforts are implemented and the rule of law is established. The closer the operational environment moves toward stability and full implementation of host nation governance under the rule of law, the more general policing activities transition to law enforcement activities.

The ultimate goal is to maintain order while protecting personnel and assets. Military police Soldiers and leaders apply this policing approach when conducting all operations. The military police view shares a common general understanding of the operational environment, while adding a degree of focus on those aspects that are necessary to maintain order and enforce laws. Care should be taken to eliminate jurisdictional overlap and under lap. Law and order operations include—

- Performing law enforcement
- Conducting criminal investigations
- Conducting traffic management and enforcement
- Employing forensics capabilities
- Conducting police engagement
- Providing customs support
- Providing host nation police development
- Supporting civil law enforcement
- Supporting border control, boundary security, and the freedom of movement

*Refer to ATTP 3-39.10 for additional information on law and order operations.*

# H. Conduct Survivability Operations

Personnel and physical assets have inherent survivability qualities or capabilities that can be enhanced through various means and methods. When existing terrain features offer insufficient cover and concealment, survivability can be enhanced by altering the physical environment to provide or improve cover and concealment. Similarly, natural or artificial materials may be used as camouflage to confuse, mislead, or evade the enemy or adversary. Together, these are called survivability operations—those military activities that alter the physical environment to provide or improve cover, concealment, and camouflage. By providing or improving cover, concealment, and camouflage, survivability operations help military forces avoid or withstand hostile actions. Although such activities often have the added benefit of providing shelter from the elements, survivability operations focus on providing cover, concealment, and camouflage. All units conduct survivability operations within the limits of their capabilities. Engineer and CBRN personnel and units have additional capabilities to support survivability operations.

Survivability operations enhance the ability to avoid or withstand hostile actions by altering the physical environment. They accomplish this by providing or improving cover, concealment, and camouflage in four areas:

- Fighting positions
- Protective positions
- Hardened facilities
- Camouflage and concealment

The first three areas focus on providing cover (although not excluding camouflage and concealment). The fourth area focuses on providing protection from observation and surveillance. All four areas, but especially the first three, often have the added benefit of providing some degree of shelter from the elements. The areas of survivability operations are often addressed in combination. For example, fighting positions and protective positions usually require camouflage and concealment also. Camouflage and concealment activities often accompany activities to harden facilities.

*Refer to FM 5-103 for more information on survivability and survivability operations. Refer to FM 3-34.400 for information on base camps. Refer to FM 90-7 for information on obstacle integration.*

# I. Provide Force Health Protection

Force health protection encompasses measures to promote, improve, or conserve the mental and physical well-being of Soldiers. These measures enable a healthy and fit force, prevent injury and illness, protect the force from health hazards, and include the prevention aspects of a number of Army Medical Department functions:

- Preventive medicine (medical surveillance, occupational and environmental health surveillance)
- Veterinary services (food inspection, animal care missions, prevention of zoonotic disease transmissible to man)
- Combat and operational stress control
- Dental services (preventive dentistry)
- Laboratory services (area medical laboratory support)

Army personnel must be physically and behaviorally fit. This requirement demands programs that promote and improve the capacity of personnel to perform military tasks at high levels, under extreme conditions, and for extended periods of time. These preventive and protective capabilities include physical exercise, nutritional diets, dental hygiene and restorative treatment, combat and operational stress management, rest, recreation, and relaxation that are geared to individuals and organizations.

Protection

Methods to prevent disease are best applied synergistically. Sanitation practices, waste management, and pest and vector control are crucial to disease prevention. Regional spraying and insect repellent application to guard against hazardous flora and fauna are examples of prevention methods. Prophylactic measures can encompass human and animal immunizations, dental chemoprophylaxis and treatment, epidemiology, optometry, counseling on specific health threats, and protective clothing and equipment.

The key to preventive and protective care is information—the capacity to anticipate the current and true health environment and the proper delivery of information to the affected human population. Derived from robust health surveillance and medical intelligence, this information addresses occupational, local environmental, and enemy- or adversary-induced threats from industrial hazards, air and water pollution, endemic or epidemic disease, CBRN threats or hazards, and directed-energy device weapons (high-powered microwaves, particle beams, lasers). Health service support must be capable of acquiring, storing, moving, and providing information that is timely, relevant, accurate, concise, and applicable to individuals. In summary, this information capability is crucial to force health protection. Force health protection includes—

- Preventing and controlling diseases
- Assessing environmental and occupational health
- Determining force health activities protection
- Employing preventive medicine toxicology and laboratory services
- Performing health risk assessments
- Disseminating health information

*Refer to ATTP 4-02 for more information on force health protection.*

# J. Provide Explosive Ordnance Disposal and Protection Support

The role of EOD is to eliminate or reduce the effects of explosive ordnance and hazards to protect combat power and the freedom of action. Explosive ordnance and hazards are ever-present dangers in most areas of operation. They limit mobility, deny the use of critical assets, and potentially injure or kill Soldiers and civilians. The U.S. and multinational use of munitions that disperse submunitions across a wide area has led to increased amounts of unexploded ordnance on the battlefield. EOD forces have the capability to render-safe and destroy explosive ordnance and hazards across the range of military operations. EOD units are specifically trained in render-safe procedures and the disposal of explosive ordnance, explosive hazards, and CBRN munitions. While other forces may have the ability to destroy limited explosive ordnance by detonation, they are not properly equipped, trained, or authorized to perform render-safe procedures or other disposal procedures. EOD elements normally—

- Identify and collect information on explosive ordnance and hazards.
  - Perform an initial assessment of found munitions, which include single munitions discovered or captured during military operations (patrols, raids, maneuvers) and those obtained through buyback or amnesty programs
  - Assist commanders with AT, including intelligence support, electronic-warfare defense plans, bomb threat and search procedures, facility site surveys, and the development and implementation of EOD emergency response and AT plans
  - Collect weapons technical intelligence on explosive ordnance and hazards, including first-seen items of interest

# K. Conduct Chemical, Biological, Radiological, and Nuclear (CBRN) Operations

*Ref: ADRP 3-37 (FM 3-37), Protection (Aug '12), pp. 1-11 to 1-12.*

CBRN threats and hazards include WMD, improvised weapons and devices, and toxic industrial material. All of these can potentially cause mass casualties and large-scale destruction. Many state and nonstate actors (including terrorists and criminals) possess or have the capability to possess, develop, or proliferate WMD.

CBRN operations include the employment of tactical capabilities that counter the entire range of CBRN threats and hazards through—

- Weapons of mass destruction (WMD) proliferation prevention (security cooperation and partner activities and threat reduction cooperation)
- WMD counterforce (interdiction, offensive operations, and elimination)
- CBRN defense (active and passive defense)
- CBRN consequence management

CBRN operations support operational and strategic objectives to combat WMD and operate safely in a CBRN environment. They include—

- **Providing WMD security cooperation and partner activities support.** WMD security cooperation and partner activities improve or promote defense relationships and the capacity of allied and partner nations to execute or support other military mission areas to combat WMD through military-to-military contact, burden-sharing arrangements, combined military activities, and support to international activities.

- **Providing WMD threat reduction cooperation support.** WMD threat reduction cooperation activities are undertaken with the consent and cooperation of host nation authorities in a permissive environment to enhance physical security and to reduce, dismantle, redirect, and/or improve the protection of an existing state WMD program, stockpiles, and capabilities.

- **Conducting WMD interdiction operations**. WMD interdiction operations track, intercept, search, divert, seize, or otherwise stop the transit of WMD, WMD delivery systems, or WMD-related materials, technologies, and expertise.

- **Conducting WMD offensive operations.** WMD offensive operations disrupt, neutralize, or destroy a WMD threat before it can be used; or they deter the subsequent use of a WMD.

- **Conducting WMD elimination operations.** WMD elimination operations are conducted in a hostile or uncertain environment to systematically locate, characterize, secure, disable, or destroy WMD programs and related capabilities. *Refer to ATTP 3-11.23 for more information.*

- **Conducting CBRN active defense.** CBRN active defense includes measures to defeat an attack with CBRN weapons by employing actions to divert, neutralize, or destroy those weapons or their means of delivery while en route to their target.

- **Conducting CBRN passive defense.** CBRN passive defense includes measures taken to minimize or negate the vulnerability to, and effects of, CBRN incidents. This mission area focuses on maintaining force ability to continue military operations in a CBRN environment. *Refer to FM 3-11.3 to 3-11.5.*

- **Conducting CBRN consequence management operations.** CBRN consequence management consists of actions taken to plan, prepare, respond to, and recover from a CBRN incident that requires forces and resource allocation beyond passive defense capabilities. *Refer to FM 3-11 and FM 3-11.21*

*Refer to FM 3-11 for additional information on CBRN operations.*

- Render-safe and dispose of explosive ordnance and hazards
  - Assist commanders with the implementation of protective works and consequence management
  - Provide technical advice and assistance to combat engineers during route, area, and minefield clearance operations
  - Support responses to nuclear and chemical accidents and incidents, including technical advice and procedures to mitigate hazards associated with such items
  - Provide EOD Soldiers in support of humanitarian assistance efforts that involve explosive ordnance and hazards

EOD is the only force equipped, manned, and trained to positively identify, render-safe, and dispose of U.S. and foreign explosive ordnance and improvised explosive devices.

*Refer to ATTP 4-32 for additional EOD information.*

# L. Coordinate Air and Missile Defense

Air and missile defense protects the force from missile attack, air attack, and aerial surveillance by ballistic missiles, cruise missiles, conventional fixed- and rotary-wing aircraft, and unmanned aerial systems. It prevents enemies from interdicting friendly forces, while freeing commanders to synchronize movement and firepower. All members of the combined arms team perform air defense tasks; however, ground-based air defense artillery units execute most Army air and missile defense operations. Air and missile defense elements coordinate and synchronize defensive fires to protect installations and personnel from over-the-horizon strikes. Army air and missile defense capabilities increase airspace situational understanding and complement the area air defense commander.

Indirect-fire protection systems protect forces from threats that are largely immune to air defense artillery systems. The indirect-fire protection intercept capability is designed to detect and destroy incoming rocket, artillery, and mortar fires. This capability assesses the threat to maintain friendly protection and destroys the incoming projectile at a safe distance from the intended target.

The air and missile defense task consists of active and passive measures that protect personnel and physical assets from an air or missile attack. Passive measures include camouflage, cover, concealment, hardening, and OPSEC. Active measures are taken to destroy, neutralize, or reduce the effectiveness of hostile air and missile threats. The early warning of in-bound missile threats is provided in theater by the globally located, joint tactical ground stations.

Protection cell planners coordinate with the Air Defense Airspace Management Cell for Air and Missile Defense for the protection of the critical asset list (CAL) and defended asset list (DAL) and for other air and missile defense protection as required. There is continuous coordination to refine the CAL and DAL throughout operations, ensuring the protection of critical assets and forces from air and missile attack and surveillance.

The air and missile defense assets integrate protective systems by using the six employment guidelines—mutual support, overlapping fires, balanced fires, weighted coverage, early engagement, and defense in depth—and additional considerations necessary to mass and mix air and missile defense capabilities. These employment guidelines enable air defense artillery forces to successfully accomplish combat missions and support overall force objectives.

*Refer to ADRP 3-09 for more information on air and missile defense operations and airspace control.*

# M. Conduct Personnel Recovery

*Ref: ADRP 3-37 (FM 3-37), Protection (Aug '12), pp. 1-13 to 1-14.*

Army personnel recovery is the sum of military, diplomatic, and civil efforts to prevent isolation incidents and to return isolated persons to safety or friendly control. Personnel recovery is the overarching term for operations that focus on recovering isolated or missing personnel before they become detained or captured.

Personnel recovery operations are conducted to recover and return personnel who are isolated, missing, detained, or captured in an operational area. These personnel consist of U.S. forces, Army civilians, or other personnel (as designated by the President or the Secretary of Defense) who are in an operational environment beyond the Army's positive or procedural control, requiring them to survive, evade, resist, or escape. Every unit must have procedures in place to recover personnel.

Commanders must understand the operational environment and the impact of PMESII-PT to ensure that personnel recovery is incorporated into and supports each mission. This includes the characteristics of the particular operational environment and how aspects of the environment become essential elements in shaping the way that Army forces conduct operations. Threats to isolated Soldiers will vary based on the operational environment.

Personnel recovery is not a stand-alone mission; it is incorporated into mission planning. Personnel recovery operations are supported through joint friendly force tracking activities. Personnel recovery guidance must synchronize the actions of commanders and staffs, recovery forces, and isolated individuals. In order to synchronize the actions of all three, commanders develop personnel recovery guidance based on command capabilities to conduct recovery operations. By knowing what actions they have dictated to potential isolated Soldiers, commanders develop situational understanding and provide guidance to their staffs and recovery forces to synchronize their actions with those of isolated personnel.

Commanders must integrate personnel recovery throughout operations. This requires an understanding of the complex, dynamic relationships between friendly forces and enemies and the other aspects of the operational environment (including the populace). This understanding helps commanders visualize and describe their intent for personnel recovery and helps them develop focused planning guidance. As commanders develop personnel recovery guidance for subordinate units, they must ensure that subordinates have adequate combat power for personnel recovery. Commanders must also provide resources and define command relationships with the requisite flexibility to plan and execute personnel recovery operations.

Commanders provide personnel recovery planning guidance within their initial guidance. Personnel recovery guidance provides a framework for how the unit and subordinates will synchronize the actions of isolated personnel and the recovery force. Effective personnel recovery planning guidance accounts for the operational environment and the execution of operations. Personnel recovery guidance is addressed in the synchronization of each warfighting function. It broadly describes how the commander intends to employ combat power to accomplish personnel recovery tasks within the higher commander's intent.

*Refer to FM 3-50.1 for additional information on personnel recovery operations.*

CBRN threats and hazards include WMD, improvised weapons and devices, and toxic industrial material. All of these can potentially cause mass casualties and large-scale destruction. Many state and nonstate actors (including terrorists and criminals) possess or have the capability to possess, develop, or proliferate WMD.

*Refer to FM 3-11 for additional information on CBRN operations.*

**Protection**

## N. Conduct Internment and Resettlement

Internment and resettlement operations are conducted by military police to shelter, sustain, guard, protect, and account for populations (detainees, dislocated civilians, and U.S. military prisoners) as a result of military or civil conflict and natural or man-made disasters or to facilitate criminal prosecution:

### Internment

Internment involves the detainment of a population or group that pose some level of threat to military operations.

### Resettlement

Resettlement involves the quartering of a population or group for their protection.

These operations inherently control the movement and activities of their specific population for imperative reasons of security, safety, or intelligence gathering. The Army is the DOD executive agent for all detainee operations and for the long-term confinement of U.S. military prisoners.

Internment and resettlement operations include—

- Performing internment
- Interning U.S. military prisoners
- Supporting host nation corrections reform
- Conducting resettlement operations
- Conducting enemy prisoner of war operations
- Conducting detainee operations

*Refer to FM 3-39.40 for more information on internment and resettlement operations.*

# II. Tasks and Systems Integration

In order to achieve protection and preserve combat power across the range of military operations, the scheme of protection must be comprehensive, integrated, layered, redundant, and enduring.

The protection warfighting function tasks and systems, when integrated throughout the operations process, help establish control measures against potential threats and hazards. The layering of protection tasks and systems, some even redundant, ensures a comprehensive scheme of protection. The layered approach of protection provides strength and depth. Units utilize their available capabilities to defend the protection priorities and a layering of capabilities reduces the destructive effect of threats and hazards.

Individuals are protected at the lowest level by awareness, personal protective equipment, an understanding of the rules of engagement, and fratricide avoidance measures. By implementing additional protection measures in the area surrounding an individual (fighting positions, vehicles, collective protection, and force health protection measures taken against accidents and disease), the force then provides a layering of protection. Implementing AT and physical security measures, enhancing survivability measures, and applying active and passive defense operations add to the next layer of a comprehensive, integrated, layered scheme of protection. Implementing the protection tasks and utilizing protection systems in a comprehensive, layered scheme of protection preserves the critical assets throughout the range of military operations in any operational environment.

# III. Protection Planning

*Ref: ADRP 3-37 (FM 3-37), Protection (Aug '12), chap. 2. See also p. 7-6.*

Planning is the first step toward effective protection. Commanders consider the most likely threats and hazards and then decide which personnel, physical assets, and information to protect. They set protection priorities for each phase or critical event of an operation. The military decisionmaking process or troop leading procedures provide a deliberate process and context to develop and examine information for use in the various continuing activities and integrating processes that comprise the operations process. An effective scheme of protection and risk decisions are developed based on the information that flows from mission analysis, allowing a thorough understanding of the situation, mission, and environment. Mission analysis provides a context to identify and analyze threats and hazards, the situational understanding of the operational environment, and the development of the scheme of protection.

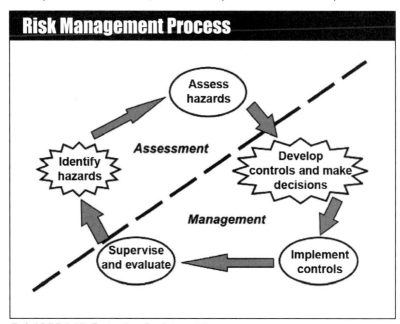

## Risk Management Process

*Ref: ADRP 3-37, Protection, fig. 2-1, p. 2-2.*

# I. Initial Assessments

Initial protection planning requires various assessments to support protection prioritization; namely, threat, hazard, vulnerability, criticality, and capability. These assessments are used to determine which assets can be protected given no constraints (critical assets) and which assets can be protected with available resources (defended assets). Commanders make decisions on acceptable risks and provide guidance to the staff so that they can employ protection capabilities based on the CAL and DAL. All forms of protection are utilized and employed during preparation and continue through execution to reduce friendly vulnerability.

Protection

## Initial Assessments (Protection)

 **Threat and Hazard Assessment** *(p. 6-26)*

 **Vulnerability Assessment** *(p. 6-28)*

 **Criticality Assessement** *(p. 6-28)*

 **Capability Assessement** *(p. 6-29)*

*Ref: ADRP 3-37, Protection, chap. 2.*

# II. Integrating Processes

The integrating processes of intelligence preparation of the battlefield, targeting, and risk management are essential in providing assessments or key information to assessments. They are a vital part of integrating protection within the other warfighting functions and throughout the operations process.

## Intelligence Preparation of the Battlefield (IPB)

The intelligence preparation of the battlefield is a systematic process of analyzing and visualizing the mission variables of threat, terrain, weather, and civil considerations in a specific area of interest and for a specific mission. By applying the intelligence preparation of the battlefield, commanders gain the information necessary to selectively apply and maximize operation effectiveness at critical points in time and space.

## Targeting

The targeting process integrates commander guidance and priorities to determine which targets to engage and how, when, and where to engage them in order to assign friendly capabilities to achieve the desired effect. The staff then assigns friendly capabilities that are best suited to produce the desired effect on each target. An important part of targeting is identifying possibilities for fratricide and collateral damage. Commanders establish control measures, including the consideration for restraint, that are necessary to minimize the chance of these events. The protection priorities must be integrated within the targeting process to achieve the desired effects while ensuring the preservation of combat power.

## Risk Management

Risk management is the process of identifying, assessing, and controlling risks that arise from operational factors and making decisions that balance risk cost with mission benefits. Threat, hazard, capability, vulnerability, and criticality assessments are utilized to evaluate the risk to the force, determine the critical assets, ascertain available resources, and apply security or defensive measures to achieve protection. Risk management helps commanders preserve lives and resources, avoid or mitigate unnecessary risk, identify and implement feasible and effective control measures where specific standards do not exist, and develop valid courses of action (COAs). Risk management integration during operations process activities is the primary responsibility of the unit protection officer or operations officer.

*See fig. 2-1 on previous page for an overview of the risk management process.*

# Threats and Hazards

Ref: ADRP 3-37 (FM 3-37), Protection (Aug '12), p. 2-3.

The protection warfighting function preserves the combat power potential and survivability of the force by providing protection from threats and hazards. Threats and hazards have the potential to cause personal injury, illness, or death; equipment or property damage or loss; or mission degradation.

- **Hostile actions.** Threats from hostile actions include any capability that forces or criminal elements have to inflict damage upon personnel, physical assets, or information. These threats may include improvised explosive devices, suicide bombings, network attacks, mortars, asset theft, air attacks, or CBRN weapons.
- **Nonhostile activities.** Nonhostile activities include hazards associated with Soldier duties within their occupational specialty, Soldier activity while off duty, and unintentional actions that cause harm. Examples include on- and off-duty accidents, OPSEC violations, network compromises, equipment malfunctions, or accidental CBRN incidents.
- **Environmental conditions.** Environmental hazards associated with the surrounding environment could potentially degrade readiness or mission accomplishment. Weather, natural disasters, and diseases are common examples. The staff also considers how military operations may affect noncombatants in the area of operations. Such considerations prevent unnecessary collateral damage and regard how civilians will affect the mission. Heavy civilian vehicle or pedestrian traffic adversely affects convoys and other operations.

## Threats

The various actors in any area of operations can qualify as a threat, enemy, adversary, neutral, or friendly. Land operations often prove complex because actors intermix, often with no easy means to distinguish one from another.

- A **threat** is any combination of actors, entities, or forces that have the capability and intent to harm United States forces, United States national interests, or the homeland (ADRP 3-0). Threats may include individuals, groups of individuals (organized or not organized), paramilitary or military forces, nation-states, or national alliances.
- An **enemy** is a party identified as hostile against which the use of force is authorized (ADRP 3-0). An enemy is also called a **combatant** and is treated as such under the law of war.
- An **adversary** is a party acknowledged as potentially hostile to a friendly party and against which the use of force may be envisaged (JP 3-0)
- A **neutral** is a party identified as neither supporting nor opposing friendly or enemy forces (ADRP 3-0)
- A **friendly** is a contact positively identified as friendly (JP 3-01)
- A **hybrid threat** is the diverse and dynamic combination of regular forces, irregular forces, terrorist forces, and/or criminal elements unified to achieve mutually benefitting effects (ADRP 3-0).

## Hazards

A hazard is a condition with the potential to cause injury, illness, or death of personnel; damage to or loss of equipment or property; or mission degradation (JP 3-33). Hazards are usually predictable and preventable and can be reduced through effective risk management efforts. Commanders differentiate hazards from threats and develop focused schemes of protection and priorities that match protection capabilities with the corresponding threat or hazard, while synchronizing those efforts in space and time. However, hazards can be enabled by the tempo or friction or by the complacency that sometimes develops during extended military operations.

# A. Threat and Hazard Assessment

*Ref: ADRP 3-37 (FM 3-37), Protection (Aug '12), pp. 2-3 to 2-5.*

Personnel from all staff sections and warfighting functions help conduct threat and hazard analysis. This analysis comprises a thorough, in-depth compilation and examination of information and intelligence that address potential threats and hazards in the area of operations. The integrating processes (intelligence preparation of the battlefield, targeting, and risk management) provide an avenue to obtain the threats and hazards that are reviewed and refined. Threat and hazard assessments are continuously reviewed and updated as the operational environment changes.

Considerations for the threat and hazard assessment include—

- Enemy and adversary threats
  - Operational capabilities
  - Intentions
  - Activities
- Foreign intelligence and security service threats
- Crimes
- Civil disturbances
- Medical and safety hazards
- CBRN weapons and toxic industrial material
- Other relevant aspects of the operational environment
- Incident reporting and feedback points of contact

The threat and hazard assessment results in a comprehensive list of threats and hazards and determines the likelihood or probability of occurrence of each threat or hazard. Table 2-1 shows examples of potential threats and hazards in an area of operations. In the context of assessing risk, the higher the probability or likelihood of a threat or hazard occurring, the higher the risk of asset loss.

# Potential Threats and Hazards

| Area of Concern | Potential Threats and Hazards |
|---|---|
| **Area security** | • Assassination of, or attacks on, important personnel<br>• Enemy, adversary or terrorist attacks on facilities<br>• Ambushes or attacks on convoys<br>• Enemy or adversary attacks on convoy routes |
| **Safety** | • Hazards associated with enemy or adversary activity<br>• Accident potential<br>• Weather or environmental conditions<br>• Equipment |
| **Fratricide avoidance** | • Poor or reduced awareness<br>• Inexperienced or poorly equipped or disciplined personnel<br>• Complex or poorly defined mission against an experienced enemy or adversary |
| **OPSEC** | • Accidental friendly release of essential elements of friendly information<br>• Enemy or adversary collection and exploitation of essential elements of friendly information<br>• Enemy or adversary capture of unclassified friendly information<br>• Physical security violations<br>• Enemy or adversary intelligence gathering |
| **AT** | • Improvised explosive devices<br>• Suicide bombs<br>• Mail bombs<br>• Snipers<br>• Standoff weapons<br>• WMD<br>• Active shooters<br>• Insider threats |
| **Survivability** | • Environmental conditions<br>• Capabilities of threat weapons and sensors |
| **Force health protection** | • Endemic and epidemic diseases<br>• Environmental factors<br>• Diseases from animal bites, poisonous plants, animals, or insects<br>• Risks associated with the health, sanitation, or behavior of the local populace |
| **CBRN** | • CBRN weapons<br>• Toxic industrial materials |
| **EOD** | • Explosive ordnance and hazards (friendly and enemy)<br>• Adversary attacks on personnel, vehicles, or infrastructure |
| **Air and missile defense** | • Artillery<br>• Mortars<br>• Rockets<br>• Ballistic and cruise missiles<br>• Fixed- and rotary-wing aircraft<br>• Unmanned aerial systems |
| **Personnel recovery** | • Events that separate or isolate individuals or small groups of friendly forces from the main force |

Legend:
AT    antiterrorism
CBRN   chemical, biological, radiological, and nuclear
EOD    explosive ordnance disposal
OPSEC   operations security
WMD    weapons of mass destruction

*Ref: ADRP 3-37, Protection, table 2-1, pp. 2-4 to 2-5.*

Protection

# B. Vulnerability Assessment

A vulnerability assessment is an evaluation (assessment) to determine the magnitude of a threat or hazard effect against an installation, personnel, unit, exercise, port, ship, residence, facility, or other site. It identifies the areas of improvement necessary to withstand, mitigate, or deter acts of violence or terrorism. The staff addresses who or what is vulnerable and how it is vulnerable. The vulnerability assessment identifies physical characteristics or procedures that render critical assets, areas, infrastructures, or special events vulnerable to known or potential threats and hazards. Vulnerability is the component of risk over which the commander has the most control and greatest influence. The general sequence of a vulnerability assessment is—

**Step 1.** List assets and capabilities and the threats against them

**Step 2.** Determine the common criteria for assessing vulnerabilities

**Step 3.** Evaluate the vulnerability of assets and capabilities

Vulnerability evaluation criteria may include the degree to which an asset may be disrupted, quantity available (if replacement is required due to loss), dispersion (geographic proximity), and key physical characteristics.

DOD has created several decision support tools to perform criticality assessments in support of the vulnerability assessment process, including—

## MSHARPP (mission, symbolism, history, accessibility, recognizability, population, and proximity)

MSHARPP is a targeting analysis tool that is geared toward assessing personnel vulnerabilities, but it also has application in conducting a broader analysis. The purpose of the MSHARPP matrix is to analyze likely terrorist targets and to assess their vulnerabilities from the inside out.

## CARVER (criticality, accessibility, recuperability, vulnerability, effect, and recognizability)

The CARVER matrix is a valuable tool in determining criticality and vulnerability. For criticality purposes, CARVER helps assessment teams and commanders (and the assets that they are responsible for) determine assets that are more critical to the success of the mission.

*Refer to FM 3-37.2 for more information on MSHARPP and CARVER.*

# C. Criticality Assessment

A criticality assessment identifies key assets that are required to accomplish a mission. It addresses the impact of a temporary or permanent loss of key assets or the unit ability to conduct a mission. A criticality assessment should also include high-population facilities (recreational centers, theaters, sports venues) which may not be mission-essential. It examines the costs of recovery and reconstitution, including time, expense, capability, and infrastructure support. The staff gauges how quickly a lost capability can be replaced before giving an accurate status to the commander. The general sequence for a criticality assessment is—

**Step 1.** List the key assets and capabilities.

**Step 2.** Determine if critical functions or combat power can be substantially duplicated with other elements of the command or an external resource.

**Step 3.** Determine the time required to substantially duplicate key assets and capabilities in the event of temporary or permanent loss.

**Step 4.** Set priorities for the response to threats toward personnel, physical assets, and information.

The protection cell staff continuously updates the criticality assessment during the operations process. As the staff develops or modifies a friendly COA, information collection efforts confirm or deny information requirements. As the mission or threat changes, initial criticality assessments may also change, increasing or decreasing the subsequent force vulnerability. The protection cell monitors and evaluates these changes and begins coordination among the staff to implement modifications to the protection concept or recommends new protection priorities. Priority intelligence requirements, running estimates, measures of effectiveness (MOEs), and measures of performance (MOPs) are continually updated and adjusted to reflect the current and anticipated risks associated with the operational environment.

## D. Capability Assessment

A capability assessment of an organization determines its current capacity to perform protection tasks based on the integrated material and nonmaterial readiness of the assets. A capability assessment considers the mitigating effects of existing manpower, procedures, and equipment. It is especially important in identifying capability gaps, which may be addressed to reduce the consequences of a specific threat or hazard. A capability assessment—

- Considers the range of identified and projected response capabilities necessary for responding to any type of hazard or threat
- Lists force resources, by type, and corresponding protection tasks
- Determines which assets are necessary to defend key areas

# III. Protection Priorities

Criticality, vulnerability, and recuperability are some of the most significant considerations in determining protection priorities that become the subject of commander guidance and the focus of area security operations. The scheme of protection is based on the mission variables and should include protection priorities by area, unit, activity, or resource.

Although all military assets are important and all resources have value, the capabilities they represent are not equal in their contribution to decisive operations or overall mission accomplishment. Determining and directing protection priorities may be the most important decisions that commanders make and that staffs support. There are seldom sufficient resources to simultaneously provide the same level of protection to all assets. For this reason, commanders use risk management to identify increasingly risky activities and events, while other decision support tools assist in prioritizing protection resources.

Most prioritization methodologies assist in differentiating what is important from what is urgent. In protection planning, the challenge is to differentiate between critical assets and important assets and to further determine what protection is possible with available protection capabilities. Event-driven operations may be short in duration, enabling a formidable protection posture for a short time; while condition-driven operations may be open-ended and long-term, requiring an enduring and sustainable scheme of protection. In either situation, commanders must provide guidance on prioritizing protection capabilities and categorizing important assets.

# IV. Critical and Defended Asset Lists

Ref: ADRP 3-37 (FM 3-37), Protection (Aug '12), pp. 2-6 to 2-7.

Initial assessments identify threats and hazards to the force, determine the criticality of systems and assets, and assess protection capabilities to mitigate vulnerabilities. The CAL and DAL are key protection products developed during initial assessments; they are dynamic lists that are continuously revised.

## A. Critical Asset List (CAL)

The critical asset list is a prioritized list of assets, normally identified by phase of the operation and approved by the joint force commander, that should be defended against air and missile threats (JP 3-01). Once the threat, criticality, and vulnerability assessments are complete, the staff presents the prioritized CAL to the commander for approval. Commanders typically operate in a resource-constrained environment and have a finite amount of combat power for protecting assets. The protection cell/ working group determines which assets are critical for mission success and recommends protection priorities based on the available resources. The CAL will vary depending on the mission variables.

During threat assessment, members of the protection cell/working group identify and prioritize the commander's critical assets using the vulnerability assessment, criticality assessment, and plan or order. Critical assets are generally specific assets of such extraordinary importance that their loss or degradation would have a significant and debilitating effect on operations or the mission. They represent what should be protected. The protection cell/working group uses information derived from command guidance, the intelligence preparation of the battlefield, targeting, risk management, warning orders, and the restated mission to nominate critical assets from their particular protection functional area. Vulnerability and criticality assessments are generally intended to be sequential. However, the criticality assessment can be conducted before, after, or concurrent with threat assessments. The vulnerability assessment should be conducted after the threat and criticality assessments to orient protection efforts on the most important assets. These assessments provide the staff with data to develop benchmarks, running estimates, commander's critical information requirements, change indicators, variances, MOEs, and MOPs.

CAL development may require the establishment of evaluation criteria, such as—

- Value (impact of loss)
- Depth (proximity in distance and time)
- Replacement impact (degree of effort, cost, or time)
- Capability (function and capacity for current and future operations)

The lack of a replacement may cause a critical asset to become the first priority for protection. Not all assets listed on the CAL will receive protection from continuously applied combat power. Critical assets with some protection from applied combat power become part of the DAL.

## B. Defended Asset List (DAL)

The defended asset list is a listing of those assets from the critical asset list prioritized by the joint force commander to be defended with the resources available (JP 3-01). Critical assets that are reinforced with additional protection capabilities or capabilities from other combat power elements become part of the DAL. It represents what can be protected, by priority. The DAL allows commanders to apply finite protection capabilities to the most valuable assets. The combat power applied may be a weapons system, electronic sensor, obstacle, or combination.

# V. Scheme of Protection Development
*Ref: ADRP 3-37 (FM 3-37), Protection (Aug '12), pp. 2-7 to 2.8.*

The scheme of protection describes how protection tasks support the commander's intent and concept of operations, and it uses the commander's guidance to establish the priorities of support to units for each phase of the operation. A commander's initial protection guidance may include protection priorities, civil considerations, protection task considerations, potential protection decisive points, high-risk considerations, and prudent risk.

Planners receive guidance as commanders describe their visualization of the operational concept and intent. This guidance generally focuses on the COA development by identifying decisive and supporting efforts, massing effects, and stating priorities. Effective planning guidance provides a broad perspective of the commander's visualization, with the latitude to explore additional options.

The scheme of protection is developed after receiving guidance and considering the principles of protection in relation to the mission variables, the incorporation of efforts, and the tasks that comprise the protection warfighting function. The scheme of protection is based on the mission variables, thus includes protection priorities by area, unit, activity, or resource. It addresses how protection is applied and derived during the conduct of operations. For example, the security for routes, bases/base camps, and critical infrastructure is accomplished by applying protection assets in dedicated, fixed, or local security roles; or it may be derived from economy-of-force protection measures such as area security techniques. It also identifies areas and conditions where forces may become fixed or static and unable to derive protection from their ability to maneuver and press the offensive. These conditions, areas, or situations are anticipated; and the associated risks are mitigated by describing and planning for the use of response forces. The staff considers the following items, at a minimum:

- Protection priorities
- Work priorities for survivability assets
- Air and missile defense positioning guidance
- Specific terrain and weather factors
- Intelligence focus and limitations for security efforts
- Areas or events where risk is acceptable
- Protected targets and areas
- Civilians and noncombatants in the area of operations
- Vehicle and equipment safety or security constraints
- Personnel recovery actions and control measures
- Force protection condition status
- Force health protection measures
- Mission-oriented protective posture guidance
- Environmental guidance
- Information operations condition
- Explosive ordnance and hazard guidance
- Ordnance order of battle
- OPSEC risk tolerance
- Fratricide avoidance measures
- Rules of engagement, standing rules for the use of force, and rules of interaction
- Escalation of force and nonlethal weapons guidance
- Operational scheme of maneuver
- Military deception
- Obscuration

# VI. Protection Cell and Working Group

Commands utilize a protection cell and protection working group to integrate and synchronize protection tasks and systems for each phase of an operation or major activity.

## A. Protection Cell

At division level and higher, the integration of the protection function and tasks is conducted by a designated protection cell and the chief of protection. At brigade level and below, the integration occurs more informally, with the designation of a protection coordinator from among the brigade staff or as an integrating staff function assigned to a senior leader. Chiefs of protection and protection coordinators participate in various forums to facilitate the continuous integration of protection tasks into the operations process. This occurs through protection working groups, staff planning teams, and staffs conducting integrating processes.

## B. Protection Working Group

The protection cell forms the core membership of the protection working group, which includes other agencies as required. Protection cell and protection working group members differ in that additional staff officers are brought into the working group. These additional officers meet operational requirements for threat assessments, vulnerability assessments, and protection priority recommendations. The protection working group calls upon existing resources across the staff.

The protection working group is led by the chief of protection and normally consists of the following:

- Air and missile defense officer
- AT officer
- CBRN officer
- Engineer officer
- Electronic warfare element representative
- EOD officer
- Fire support representative
- OPSEC officer
- Provost marshal
- Safety officer
- Intelligence representative
- Civil affairs officer
- Personnel recovery officer
- Public affairs officer
- Staff judge advocate
- Surgeon
- Medical representative
- Veterinary representative
- Subordinate unit liaison officers
- Operations representative
- Area contracting officer

Commanders augment the team with other unit specialties and unified action partners depending on the operational environment and the unit mission. The protection officer determines the working group agenda, meeting frequency, composition, input, and expected output.

# I. Countering Weapons of Mass Destruction

Ref: JP 3-40, Countering Weapons of Mass Destruction (Oct '14), chap. 1.

## I. General

Weapons of mass destruction (WMD) are chemical, biological, radiological, or nuclear weapons or devices capable of a high order of destruction and/or causing mass casualties. This does not include the means of transporting or propelling the weapon where such means is a separable and divisible part of the weapon. WMD does not include high-yield explosives. The existence of chemical, biological, radiological, and nuclear (CBRN) materials and the potential for use by actors of concern precipitates the need to plan, prepare for, and counter their use.

(FBI.GOV)

Countering weapons of mass destruction (CWMD) entails activities across the United States Government (USG) to ensure the US, its Armed Forces, allies, partners, and interests are not attacked or coerced by actors of concern possessing WMD. CWMD is a national security priority.

*"The gravest danger to the American people and global security continues to come from weapons of mass destruction, particularly nuclear weapons."*

National Security Strategy, May 2010

### Actors of Concern

Actors of concern are those state or non-state actors that carry out activities that, left unaddressed, pose a clear threat to the strategic objectives of the USG. Actor of concern's possession of WMD, proliferation of WMD, and the pursuit of WMD by extremists present grave threats to the American people. Actors of concern with WMD possess an asymmetric advantage capable of significantly neutralizing the superior technology, military, and economic strength of the US and its allies. CWMD is a continuous campaign that requires a coordinated, whole-of-government effort to curtail the conceptualization, development, possession, proliferation, use, and effects of WMD-related expertise, materials, and technologies.

The Department of Defense (DOD) contributes to this whole-of-government effort by providing joint forces that plan and execute tasks to ensure that the US, its forces, allies, partners, and interests are neither coerced nor attacked with WMD. These joint forces also prepare for the execution of contingency responses to WMD-related crises. The world events that define the WMD problem have evolved over time. With the advent of US conventional military preeminence and continued improvements in US missile defenses and capabilities to counter and mitigate the effects of WMD, the role of US nuclear weapons in deterring nonnuclear attacks—conventional, biological, or chemical—has declined. To that end, US declaratory policy is not to use or threaten to use nuclear weapons against nonnuclear weapons states that are party to the Treaty on the Nonproliferation of Nuclear Weapons (NPT) and in compliance with their nuclear nonproliferation obligations. In making this declaration, the US affirms that any state eligible for the assurance that uses chemical or biological weapons against the US or its allies and partners would face a devastating conventional military response. Given the catastrophic potential of biological weapons and the rapid pace of biotechnology development, the US reserves the right to make any adjustment in the assurance that may be warranted by the evolution and proliferation of the biological weapons threat and US capacities to counter that threat. In the case of states that possess nuclear weapons and states not in compliance with nuclear nonproliferation obligations there remains a narrow range of contingencies in which US nuclear weapons may be employed in deterring a conventional or WMD attack.

# II. National Strategy and Guidance

National guidance provides the foundation for the development of DOD CWMD strategy and guidance documents. Top-level strategy and general guidance for CWMD is derived from the National Security Strategy (NSS) and WMD-specific Presidential decision directives (e.g., national security Presidential directives [NSPDs] and Presidential policy directives [PPDs]). b. Unified Command Plan (UCP). The UCP is Presidential-level guidance establishing responsibilities of both geographic and functional combatant commanders (CCDRs), to include specific responsibilities for CWMD as well as other mission areas such as counterterrorism (CT), pandemic influenza and infectious disease (PI&ID), and homeland defense (HD). Various aspects of these responsibilities complement and overlap with the CWMD mission set.

# III. DoD Strategy and Guidance

## A. Defense Strategic Guidance

In January 2012, the Secretary of Defense (SecDef) released strategic guidance for DOD. Sustaining US Global Leadership: Priorities for 21st Century Defense reflects the President's strategic direction and recognizes that CWMD is one of ten primary missions of the US Armed Forces. This guidance emphasizes the threat posed by the proliferation of CBRN weapons technology to additional state actors and nonstate actors access to WMD. The guidance also recognizes that military forces conduct a range of activities to prevent the proliferation and use of WMD and states that, "in partnership with other elements of the USG, DOD will continue to invest in capabilities to detect, protect against, and respond to WMD use, should preventive measures fail."

## B. Nuclear Posture Review

In April 2010, SecDef released the Nuclear Posture Review report, which described five objectives of nuclear weapons policies and posture: preventing nuclear proliferation and nuclear terrorism; reducing the role of US nuclear weapons in US NSS; maintaining strategic deterrence and stability at reduced nuclear force levels; strengthening regional deterrence and reassuring US allies and partners; and sustaining a safe, secure, and effective nuclear arsenal.

# DODS-CWMD Strategic Approach

*Ref: JP 3-40, Countering Weapons of Mass Destruction (Oct '14), pp. I-3 to I-4.*

The objectives outlined in the DODS-CWMD are advanced through three CWMD lines of effort (LOEs): prevent acquisition, contain and reduce threats, and respond to crises. These three LOEs are supported by one strategic enabler; prepare. Together, the three LOEs and this strategic enabler comprise DOD's revised strategic approach for CWMD:

## Strategy for Countering WMD

Department of Defense Strategy for Countering Weapons of Mass Destruction Strategic Approach

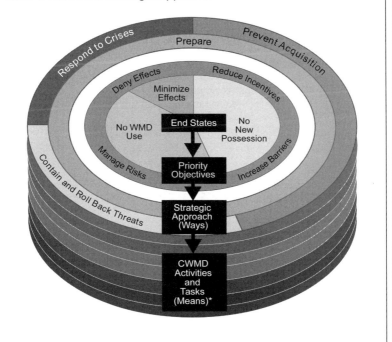

*Ref: JP 3-40, Countering WMD, fig. I-1, p. I-4.*

- **Prepare** is the continuous cycle that ensures DOD's set of enabling, foundational, and specialized activities, tasks, and capabilities support the CWMD LOEs
- **Prevent acquisition** focuses on actions to ensure that those not possessing WMD do not obtain them.
- **Contain and reduce threats** focuses on actions to reduce risks posed by extant WMD
- **Respond to crises** focuses on activities and operations to manage and resolve complex WMD crises

*See following page for further discussion.*

# C. Department of Defense Strategy for Countering Weapons of Mass Destruction (DODS-CWMD)

The DODS-CWMD seeks to ensure that the US and its allies and partners are neither attacked nor coerced by actors with WMD. It outlines three departmental CWMD end states, establishes priority objectives, defines a strategic approach, and identifies essential activities and tasks.

*See previous page for further discussion.*

## End States

The DODS-CWMD identifies three overarching end states that all departmental CWMD efforts should pursue:

- No new WMD possession
- No WMD use
- Minimization of WMD effects

## DODS-CWMD Priority Objectives

Priority objectives are derived from the end states and take into account general trends in the strategic environment. Strategic priorities will typically shift with changes in national and defense leadership. Planning priorities are also dynamic, and reflect the nature of the WMD challenge across the strategic environment. Planning priorities may be revised more frequently than JPs. CWMD priority objectives identified in the DODS-CWMD are:

- Reduce incentives to pursue, possess, and employ WMD
- Increase barriers to the acquisition, proliferation, and use of WMD
- Manage WMD risks emanating from hostile, fragile, or failed states and safe havens
- Deny the effects of current and emerging WMD threats through layered, integrated defenses

# D. DOD Planning Guidance

The Guidance for Employment of the Force (GEF) and the Joint Strategic Capabilities Plan (JSCP) provide primary guidance for joint planning at the strategic and operational levels:

## Guidance for Employment of the Force (GEF)

The GEF provides two-year direction to combatant commands (CCMDs) for operational planning, force management, security cooperation (SC), and posture planning. The GEF is the method through which the Office of the Secretary of Defense (OSD) translates strategic priorities set in the NSS and National Defense Strategy into implementable direction for operational activities. The GEF identifies specific CWMD planning requirements and establishes the priority of CWMD planning within DOD.

## Joint Strategic Capabilities Plan (JSCP)

The JSCP refines the guidance in the GEF and assigns specific responsibilities for planning to individual CCMDs. Additionally, the JSCP describes the relationship between the various global planning efforts and between them and theater planning and contingency plans. The JSCP assigns CWMD planning requirements to specific CCMDs based on functional and regional responsibilities. United States Strategic Command (USSTRATCOM) is designated the DOD synchronizer for CWMD planning and leads the effort for the DOD CWMD campaign plan. All geographic CCMDs regional CWMD planning is guided by and synchronized with DOD global CWMD planning and nested under their theater campaign plans (TCPs). The JSCP also reinforces that CWMD planning should be coordinated with interagency partners for unity of effort.

# IV. CWMD Activities and Tasks

*Ref: JP 3-40, Countering Weapons of Mass Destruction (Oct '14), pp. I-4 to I-6.*

The means to counter WMD include the forces, equipment, training, and systems employed to address DOD's strategic priorities. The DODS-CWMD organizes capabilities in three categories based upon the CWMD activities and tasks with which they are associated: synchronizing, foundational, or specialized activities and tasks.

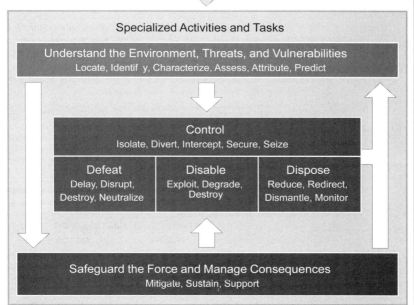

The objectives, approach, activities, and supporting tasks described by the DODS-CW-MD provide the strategic construct for the development of the DOD Global Campaign Plan for Combating Weapons of Mass Destruction (GCP-CWMD) and geographic combatant commanders' (GCCs') supporting CWMD campaign plans. The construct of the GCP-CWMD promotes unified action by providing a strategy and approach for joint force commanders (JFCs) to organize their CWMD effort that is scalable and tailorable.

DOD policy and planning guidance influences CWMD doctrine. CWMD doctrine provides the scope and context in which these responsibilities, objectives, and planning requirements can be addressed and executed.

# V. Coordinating CWMD with Other Efforts

## A. Counterterrorism (CT)

The global campaign to counter WMD and the goals outlined in the National Strategy for CT are separate, yet mutually supportive efforts; both address keeping dangerous weapons out of the hands of dangerous actors. To prevent terrorists from acquiring WMD, the global campaign to counter WMD includes efforts to identify and monitor state weapons programs and program elements; improve site and stockpile security; and encourage states to be responsible stewards of their WMD in order to prevent proliferation of weapons, technology, materials, and expertise to non-state actors of concern. The global CT strategy contributes to the CWMD effort by addressing overall national CT goals in general and addressing the non-state actor component of the WMD problem specifically by stating that the US will actively seek to deny acquisition and/or use of WMD by actors of concern. Coordination of these two efforts also includes sharing intelligence, integrating plans, and synchronizing operations.

*See chapter 4 for further discussion.*

## B. Global Campaign for PI&ID

The global campaign to counter WMD is mutually supportive of the global campaign for PI&ID. Both campaigns conduct bio-surveillance and enable DOD's response to the initial stages of a potential outbreak or incident. Regardless of whether the event is naturally occurring or the result of an accident or deliberate attack, numerous response activities concern both global efforts. CWMD activities include understanding the operational environment (OE), threats, and vulnerabilities associated with all biological weapons programs and civilian biological laboratories. Additional CWMD tasks relevant to PI&ID are to mitigate the effects of a biological incident and support the civilian response. Coordination of these two efforts also includes the analysis of threat and medical intelligence, forensics, and hazard modeling.

*For further guidance on PI&ID, refer to the National Strategy for Pandemic Influenza.*

## C. Homeland Defense (HD)

HD is the protection of US sovereignty, territory, domestic population, and critical infrastructure against external threats and aggression, or other threats, as directed by the President. These include transnational threats—defined in Title 50, United States Code(USC), Section 3021, as "any transnational activity (including international terrorism,narcotics trafficking, the proliferation of WMD and the delivery systems for such weapons,and organized crime) that threatens the national security of the US." United States Northern Command (USNORTHCOM) and United States Pacific Command (USPACOM) have been assigned the responsibility to plan, organize, and, as directed, execute HD operations within their respective areas of responsibility (AORs). CWMD as a part of HD is a global mission that crosses AOR boundaries and requires an integrated and synchronized effort among interagency and multinational partners for mission accomplishment. USNORTHCOM and USPACOM integrate the CWMD related aspects of their HD plans and synchronize related operations and activities in collaboration with USSTRATCOM, the other CCMDs, and the Services. Additionally, HD operations require pre-event and ongoing coordination with interagency and multinational partners to integrate capabilities and facilitate unified action. CWMD contributes to HD by protecting the US through an active, layered defense in depth. DOD plays an essential role in HD by providing a full range of operational capabilities to protect against the threat of, or the actual use of WMD. DOD, as directed by the President,

# CBRN Consequence Management

Ref: JP 3-40, Countering Weapons of Mass Destruction (Oct '14), pp. I-8 to I-9.

DOD's role in CBRN CM is described in multiple DOD policy documents. CBRN CM is the overarching USG capability and the strategic national direction taken to plan, prepare, respond to, and recover from CBRN incidents at home or abroad, whether or not they are attributed to an attack using WMD. The CBRN CM mission highlights the complexity of the various laws, agreements, and differing lexicons to describe and conduct CBRN CM with interagency, multinational, intergovernmental organization (IGO), and nongovernmental organization (NGO) partners. DOD CBRN CM operations include actions to respond to the effects of a WMD attack or inadvertent release of CBRN materials in order to maintain or restore essential services and manage and mitigate problems. CBRN CM operations allow the JFC to plan and execute incident management, sustainment, and the support that may be required to be given to outside agencies or nations. There are three types of CBRN CM the JFC should consider dependent on incident location and authorities; domestic, foreign, and DOD-led.

For further guidance on CBRN CM, refer to JP 3-41, Chemical, Biological, Radiological, and Nuclear Consequence Management.

## Domestic CBRN CM

The Department of Homeland Security (DHS) is the USG lead for domestic CBRN incident management. DHS coordination is outlined in the NRF, unless the incident occurs on a DOD installation. DHS will establish a national operations center as the primary, multiagency, national hub for situational awareness, operations, and resource coordination. When civil authorities, up to, and including the federal level, lack necessary capabilities to mitigate the effects of a CBRN incident, or they anticipate being overwhelmed, they typically request military support.

## Foreign Consequence Management (FCM)

The Department of State (DOS) is the USG lead for FCM. FCM is a USG activity that assists foreign governments in responding to the effects from an intentional or accidental chemical, biological, radiological, or nuclear incident on foreign territory in order to maximize preservation of life.

## DOD-Led CBRN CM

In most domestic and foreign environments, CBRN CM actions conducted by DOD are in support of the lead federal agency, DHS for domestic and DOS for foreign CBRN CM actions. If directed by the President or SecDef, DOD forces may be directed to lead CBRN CM operations as a direct result of US military operations in a foreign country, where DOS does not have an established diplomatic presence, or on a DOD installation.

*See chap. 8, Consequence Management, for further discussion.*

Countering WMD

may conduct preemptive HD actions in support of CWMD operations and activities in accordance with international and domestic law, national policy, and directives.

## D. Defense Support of Civil Authorities (DSCA)

DOD provides support to civil authorities for domestic emergencies and for designated law enforcement and other activities. Joint forces supporting civil authorities in response to a domestic CBRN incident also contribute to the overall CWMD effort through preparations to respond and mitigate damage or effects of the damage. These forces are incorporated into the domestic incident management effort and operate in accordance with the National Response Framework (NRF). The National Incident Management System forms the foundation for conducting domestic response operations. The NRF is the USG's comprehensive approach to domestic incident management built on the template of the National Incident Management System. As part of a comprehensive national response, DOD supports a primary federal agency to prevent or to respond to an emergency, to include a CBRN incident or WMD attack. The NRF provides the structure and mechanisms for national-level policy and operational direction for managing this national response.

## F. Strategic Deterrence

Strategic deterrence figures prominently in the attainment of the CWMD end states of "no new WMD possession" and "no WMD use." A structured method to conduct deterrence operations begins with clear and concise deterrence objective(s). Deterrence objectives should specify who is being deterred from doing what, and under what conditions. Tailored deterrence objectives allow analysts to assess key decision factors that motivate an actor of concern. These objectives provide the JFC with a framework to develop activities and operations that increase an actor of concern's perception of the costs of action and benefits of restraint.

*For further guidance on deterrence, refer to JP 3-0, Joint Operations.*

An effective WMD deterrence strategy rests on a credible declaratory deterrence policy, possessing credible capabilities to hold at risk an actor of concern strategic centers of gravity, political will to face down the actor of concern, and effective means to defend against the use and effects of WMD.

Overall USG deterrence goals are supported by a credible capability to intercept WMD in transit; destroy critical nodes, links, and sources; defend against WMD attack; attribute WMD attacks; and dismantle WMD programs.

JFC deterrence efforts should be part of a long-term sustained effort with potential application across all operational phases and should include synchronized communications for maximum effectiveness. Deterrence activities should be integrated into campaign plans in order to enhance strategic stability and prevent future threats. This methodology remains valid and assures deterrence objectives are supported in crisis or conflict.

## G. Counter Threat Finance (CTF)

CTF is the means to detect, counter, contain, disrupt, deter, or dismantle the transnational financing of state and non-state actors of concern threatening US national security. Actions to monitor, assess, analyze, and exploit financial information are key support functions of CTF activities. CTF is not operational area specific, it is a whole-of-government and international effort that applies to stemming the flow of funds involving multiple operational areas. DOD works with other USG departments and agencies and with partner nations (PNs) to deny, disrupt, degrade, or defeat actor of concern's ability to use global licit and illicit financial networks to negatively affect US interests.

Countering WMD

# II. Weapons (WMD) & Associated Concerns

Ref: JP 3-40, Countering Weapons of Mass Destruction (Oct '14), chap. 2.

> "Actors of concern pose a threat of developing, acquiring, proliferating, or employing weapons of mass destruction (WMD) and related capabilities– expertise, materials, technologies, and means of delivery. These activities present a clear potential threat to the strategic objectives of the United States."
>
> Department of Defense Strategy for Countering Weapons of Mass Destruction, June 2014

Actors of concern that seek or possess WMD to enhance their influence and achieve greater strategic leverage against US advantages pose an enduring challenge to peace and stability worldwide. Increased access to technology, materials, and expertise heightens the risk that actors of concern will develop, proliferate, and use WMD to achieve their goals. The evolution of the WMD threat has created new challenges for JFCs beyond dealing with actors of concern WMD use, including the following challenges:

- The varied nature of WMD, including the emergence of nontraditional threats
- The dual-use applicability of related facilities, technology, and expertise
- The diversity of threats and actors
- The complex and dynamic WMD proliferation continuum
- The increasing complexity and number of WMD proliferation networks
- The psychological impact of WMD use

This chapter provides a general overview of the CBRN threat. Actors of concern may use these weapons to conduct an attack on US citizens, infrastructure, or vital interests; to exploit US power projection, sustainment, and force protection vulnerabilities; to deny access to an area, limiting the ability of the US to respond to urgent threats; or to undermine support by key regional partners for US vital interests through intimidation. The topics covered in this chapter include nuclear and radiological weapons, biological weapons, chemical weapons, delivery systems, WMD actors of concern, WMD pathways, and the issue of dual-use technologies.

# I. Types of Weapons of Mass Destruction (WMD)

A. Nuclear and Radiological Weapons *(see pp. 7-10 to 7-11)*

B. Biological Weapons *(see pp. 7-12 to 7-13)*

C. Chemical Weapons *(see pp. 7-14 to 7-15)*

D. Cruise and Ballistic Missiles *(see p. 7-16)*

E. Improvised Weapons *(see p. 7-16)*

F. Dirty Bombs *(see p. 7-17)*

**Countering WMD**

# A. Nuclear and Radiological Weapons

*Ref: JP 3-40, Countering Weapons of Mass Destruction (Oct '14), pp. II-1 to II-4.*

## Nuclear Weapons

Nuclear weapons derive their explosive power from the energy released during either fission or a combination of fission and fusion nuclear reactions. Fission is a process in which the nucleus of an atom splits into two or more nuclei and releases energy, fission products, and neutrons. The neutrons released by fission can, in turn, cause the fission of other fissile isotopes. Fissile material is composed of nuclides for which fission is possible with neutrons of any energy level. Fissile materials in a nuclear weapon—highly enriched uranium or plutonium—must achieve a supercritical state for a nuclear detonation to occur. Fusion is a process in which nuclei (generally light nuclei such as tritium and deuterium), combine and release energy, helium nuclei, and neutrons.

### Single Stage Fission Weapons

- **Gun-assembled**. A gun-assembled device contains two or more pieces of fissile material, each a subcritical mass, brought together very rapidly to form a supercritical mass. A nuclear detonation results from a self-sustaining chain reaction of exponentially increasing numbers of fission events within that mass.

- **Implosion-assembled**. A spherical device in which a quantity of fission material normally at a density constituting a subcritical mass at ordinary pressure, can have its volume reduced suddenly by compression (a step typically accomplished by the use of chemical explosives) to form a supercritical mass at a much higher density. A nuclear detonation results from a supercritical chain reaction of exponentially increasing numbers of fission events within that mass.

- **Boosted Weapons**. A boosted weapon is an implosion-assembled weapon whose fission output is increased by thermonuclear neutrons from the fusion of deuterium and tritium gas introduced into the pit. This increases its explosive yield through fusion reactions that serve to increase the efficiency of the fission bomb.

### Thermonuclear Weapons

A thermonuclear weapon is a device where radiation from a fission primary is used to transfer energy to compress and ignite a physically separate component containing thermonuclear fuel referred to as the secondary, resulting in nuclear fusion.

### Improvised Nuclear Device

A device intended to produce a nuclear yield using fissile or fissionable material that is not developed and produced by a nation for military purposes. An improvised nuclear device may be fabricated from components developed by a state program or may be an improvised modification to a US or foreign weapon design.

### Delivery Options

Nuclear weapons have been adapted for delivery by mortar, artillery shell, land mine, depth charge, torpedo, and missile. However, significant weapon design understanding is needed to produce a nuclear device that is both small enough and light enough to be delivered by such systems with reduced payload capacity. Given their significant destructive power, nuclear weapons need not be optimally employed to cause a mass casualty event. While nuclear weapons have been designed for stand-off delivery at specific altitudes and other conditions, they could simply be loaded onto a ship or truck, transported to the target, and detonated.

### Nuclear Weapons Effects

When detonated, a nuclear weapon will release its energy as blast, thermal radiation, and nuclear radiation (alpha and beta particles, gamma rays, and neutrons). The interaction of the X-rays with surrounding air molecules can produce a secondary effect known as electromagnetic pulse (EMP). EMP is the electromagnetic radiation from a strong electronic pulse produced by a nuclear explosion. The pulse can couple with electrical or electronic systems to produce damaging current and voltage surges. The EMP fields are dependent upon the yield of the weapon and the height of burst. Nuclear generated EMP is a potential threat to unshielded electronics and electrical systems. High-altitude EMP, in particular, can briefly cover many thousands of square kilometers of the earth's surface with a potentially damaging electromagnetic field. The primary hazards for unshielded personnel are prompt radiation and thermal radiation, which are dependent on the size of the weapon, the proportion of energy released due to fission instead of fusion, the height of the detonation, and atmospheric conditions. When the detonation occurs as an air burst high enough that the fireball does not touch the ground, the fission products are scattered widely from the point of detonation. When the detonation occurs under, at, or near the surface, the fission products mix with surface materials, such as dirt and soil, and settle in a pattern commonly known as fallout around the area of detonation in the direction of the prevailing winds. This produces the preponderance of the radiation hazard and casualties beyond the immediate point of detonation. The effects from a nuclear weapon will extend hundreds of meters to hundreds of kilometers depending on the weapon characteristics and method of delivery.

*For further information on EMP, refer to JP 3-13.1, Electronic Warfare; and JP 3-11, Operations in Chemical, Biological, Radiological, and Nuclear Environments.*

# Radiological Weapons

Radiological weapons include radiological dispersal devices (RDDs) and radiological exposure devices (REDs). An RDD, other than a nuclear explosive device, is designed to disseminate radioactive material in order to cause panic, chaos, and fear. A RED is a highly radioactive source which is placed in a location where people could be exposed. Radiological weapons are not considered to be militarily useful for a state-sponsored military, but may be desirable for non-state actors and terrorist organizations wishing to inflict psychological and economic damage. Radiological weapons are considered a serious threat due to the availability of radiological sources. These sources are used throughout the medical, research and industrial communities with minimal security precautions.

**RDD.** RDDs contaminate the environment with radioactive materials and threaten populations with exposure. Their use may also result in area denial and costly cleanup or decontamination. An RDD is a possible terrorist weapon given the prevalent commercial use of radioactive source material and the relatively easy way this material could be dispersed through conventional explosives.

**RED.** REDs are radioactive sources that may produce adverse physiological effects to those within a given proximity of the source, which could be hidden in lobbies, arenas or stadiums, elevators, public transit, or other areas where people congregate.

## Delivery

Several options exist for the delivery of radiological weapons. A conventional high-explosive bomb placed near a radioactive source, sometimes called a dirty bomb, could be used to disperse radioactive particles. A commercial mobile sprayer such as crop-dusting aircraft could be used to spread radioactive particles. Radioactive contamination could also be spread via a food chain, water sources, or ventilation systems, relying on a vector (an insect, animal, etc., that carries germs that cause disease) rather than a weapons system. A RED might simply consist of a radioactive source placed in a public area to expose people passing by it and could be placed in any area where a target population is present. Due to the nature of such weapons, radiological material would not necessarily have to be effectively disseminated to cause significant casualties and panic.

*For further guidance on improvised explosive devices, refer to JP 3-15.1, Counter-Improvised Explosive Device Operations. (See p. 7-17 for dirty bombs.)*

# B. Biological Weapons

Ref: JP 3-40, Countering Weapons of Mass Destruction (Oct '14), pp. II-4 to II-6.

A biological agent, either natural or man-made, is a microorganism that causes disease in personnel, plants, or animals or causes the deterioration of material. The knowledge to develop a biological capability has become increasingly widespread with the evolution of biotechnology and has become readily obtainable by both state and non-state actors. In the wrong hands, this knowledge can lead to the development of biological weapons. Biological weapons differ from chemical, nuclear, and radiological threats in that small amounts of infectious agents are self-replicating and capable of spreading from person to person. Deliberately or accidentally released biological weapons against an unprotected population without biosurveillance or efficient epidemiologic investigative capability can have as much effect as weapons designed to create mass casualties.

## Categories

Biological agents are categorized as pathogens or toxins. A thorough discussion of the effects of these agents, as well as transmissibility, viability, lethality, and dissemination methods is contained in JP 3-11, Operations in Chemical, Biological, Radiological, and Nuclear Environments.

- **Pathogens**. Pathogens are disease producing microorganisms (e.g., bacteria, viruses, prions, and fungi) that directly attack human tissue and biological processes. Pathogens are further divided into noncontagious and contagious. When biological threats are contagious, planning needs to account for possible restrictions of movement to include quarantine and isolation. In addition to known threats, the JFC should be alert for emerging or novel threats.

- **Toxins**. Toxins are nonliving poisonous substances that are produced naturally by living organisms (e.g., plants, animals, insects, bacteria, fungi) but may also be synthetically manufactured.

## Novel or Emerging Threats

Current changes in science and technology may contribute to actors of concern finding ways to employ irregular, disruptive, and potentially catastrophic agents as threats in the future. The exploitation of bioregulators and modulators (peptides), which can potentially cause physiological effects (disrupt or damage nervous system, alter moods), represents a potential vector for development of novel threats. Emerging disease outbreaks such as severe acute respiratory syndrome and hantavirus pulmonary syndrome may be difficult to distinguish from the intentional introduction of infectious diseases by terrorist groups. Other pathogens such as prions that can cause fatal diseases in humans and animals could be used to create panic within the civilian populace.

*For more information on biological agents, refer to JP 3-11, Operations in Chemical, Biological, Radiological, and Nuclear Environments.*

## Employment

Because the primary route of infection for most biological warfare agents is inhalation, various systems and techniques have been developed to disseminate solid or liquid biological agents as an aerosol. Such systems have included spray tanks attached to aircraft or cruise missiles and bombs with bomblets that can explosively disseminate biological warfare agents. Ventilation systems could be contaminated and mass gathering locations could be targeted for an aerosol attack.

Due to their nature as living organisms, biological agents, other than those in spore form, need to be employed shortly after production in order to be a viable weapon. Bacillus anthracis, the causative agent of anthrax, is unique in producing spores that can be desiccated, milled to a roughly five micrometer diameter particulate powder, and then loaded in weapons for dispersal. Once desiccated, anthrax spores remain viable for years under the right conditions. Loss of accountability of frozen aliquots of an amount of bacterial or viral agents can pose significant hazards as small samples can be cultured to produce amounts large enough to cause mass casualties.

There are numerous unconventional means of disseminating biological warfare agents—from human vectors to remotely piloted aircraft. In 2001, anthrax deliberately mailed to media offices and the US Congress killed five people and infected 22. Other means of dispersing biological agents include contamination of food or water supplies, contaminated object (e.g., dish or clothing), injection of animals, or through vectors.

## Determining Deliberate Use

Disease outbreaks must be aggressively addressed to save lives, but it is also imperative to discern whether an outbreak is deliberate, accidental, or naturally occurring. Forensics provides attribution, to identify those responsible. Following a disease outbreak, a case definition needs to be constructed to determine the number of cases and the attack rate. If the attack rate deviates from the norm, an outbreak is more likely. Potential epidemiological clues to a biological attack include highly unusual events with large numbers of casualties; higher morbidity or mortality than expected for a given disease; unprecedented antibiotic resistance for a given pathogen; uncommon disease in a geographical area; point-source outbreak with shorter incubation time than usual (due to an increased amount of inoculum); multiple disease outbreaks; lower attack rates in protected individuals; dead animals; reverse spread (i.e., from humans to animals or disease observation in animals and people concurrently); unusual disease manifestation (e.g., inhalation and cutaneous anthrax in multiple regions concurrently); downwind plume pattern; and direct evidence.

Information critical for intelligent decisions concerning prevention and response is listed below:

---

### Biological Weapons Critical Information

- Ability to detect the agent (sensitivity)
- Distinction of the agent from similar species (specificity)
- Diagnosis from clinical samples
- Identification of the animal reservoir, when applicable
- Knowledge of the collection, packaging, storage, and transport of specimens
- Vaccines to prevent the disease caused by the pathogen
- Post-exposure prophylaxis before development of clinical signs
- Treatment of disease
- Control of disease spread
- Triage and quarantine of suspected exposed individuals
- Knowledge of appropriate personal protective equipment for that agent and when to use it
- Transmission of the agent (aerosol, contaminated food, water, insect vectors)
- Routes of exposure (inhalation, ingestion, percutaneous routes [absorption or injection] personal contact, infected fluids, inanimate objects like bedding
- Survival of the agent on fomites and in the environment
- Disinfection, sterilization requirements

---

# C. Chemical Weapons

*Ref: JP 3-40, Countering Weapons of Mass Destruction (Oct '14), pp. II-6 to II-9.*

A chemical agent is a chemical substance that is intended for use in military operations to kill, seriously injure, or incapacitate mainly through its physiological effects. The term excludes riot control agents when used for law enforcement purposes, herbicides, smoke, and flames. The knowledge required to develop a chemical weapons capability is obtainable by both state and non-state actors. When the intent and capability to develop chemical weapons are combined they become a threat. The acquisition and development of chemical weapons encapsulates several activities that would culminate in an ability to use or proliferate. Due to the ubiquitous and dual-use nature of chemical production capabilities, the expertise, materials, technology, infrastructure, facilities, and means of delivery may be difficult to attribute to actors of concern or link to an intent to develop chemical weapons.

(Shutterstock)

## Categories of Chemicals

### 1. Traditional Agents

These chemical weapons include blister (H and L series), nerve (G and V series), blood, and choking agents. Many traditional blood and choking agents (e.g., hydrogen cyanide and phosgene) have common industrial uses and are not defined as chemical weapons by the Chemical Weapons Convention (CWC) when used for those purposes.

### 2. Nontraditional Agents (NTAs)

NTAs are chemicals and biochemicals researched or developed with potential application or intent as chemical warfare agents, but which do not fall in the category of traditional chemical agents per the CWC. NTAs differ from traditional blister and nerve agents on which the US previously focused its defensive efforts. NTAs exist in four primary forms: solid, dusty, liquid, and aerosol. Each class of NTA has its own set of distinguishing characteristics. While NTAs possess some of the same properties as traditional chemical agents (i.e., nerve agents), typically these properties are enhanced when compared to traditional chemical agents; increased toxicity, garment penetration, and extremely low volatility.

*For more information on NTAs, refer to Chairman of the Joint Chiefs of Staff (CJCS) Guide 3215, CJCS Guide to Non-traditional Agents.*

## 3. Toxic Industrial Chemicals (TICs)

TICs are toxic substances typically found in solid, liquid, or gaseous form that are manufactured, used, transported, or stored for industrial, medical, or commercial purposes. Some TICs, such as particular pesticides, are highly toxic. Others are routinely transported and stored in very large quantities (e.g., anhydrous ammonia and chlorine), making them a pervasive threat in theaters of operation. Potential releases can occur through industrial or transportation accidents and can have significant impacts on joint operations. Additionally, releases can occur collaterally or result from a malevolent act. Some TICs can be turned into improvised weapons.

## 4. Riot Control Agents and Incapacitants

A riot control agent is any chemical that can produce sensory irritation or disabling physical effects rapidly in humans which disappear within a short time following termination of exposure. Riot control agents are normally extremely irritating and in wide use by law enforcement. Incapacitants are substances that affect the higher regulatory functions of the central nervous system and are often abused drugs. The effects of these substances may be quite severe depending on the amount of exposure an individual receives. Certain riot control agents are lethal when used at higher concentration. These riot control agents fit into a special class of NTA.

*For more information concerning employment of riot control agents, refer to CJCSI 3110.07, Guidance Concerning Employment of Riot Control Agents and Herbicides, as well as standing and supplemental rules of engagement.*

# Employment

Chemical agents are traditionally employed in artillery shells, rockets, missiles, bombs, mines, and spray tanks to produce vapors and aerosols or spread toxic liquids. Chemical agents can be incorporated into improvised explosive devices or other improvised dispersing devices. Because many chemical agents pose both an inhalational hazard and a percutaneous hazard (they can be absorbed through the skin), they do not need to be aerosolized to inflict casualties and contaminate areas. Targeting to produce widespread immediate lethal effects requires a high concentration and desired rate of action of agent in the target area. Targeting of this nature is enhanced by favorable weather factors (wind, air stability, temperature, humidity, and precipitation) and confined spaces (e.g., transportation terminals and building interiors). Persistent chemical weapons can be employed for denial of terrain, facilities, material, and logistics to reduce operations tempo and degrade the mission. Nontraditional employment (e.g., contamination of food or water supplies or aerosol generation at a mass gathering location) is possible and could be used to target particular populations.

# Chemical Agent Effects

Most chemical agents are extremely lethal and rapidly produce mass causalities among unprotected personnel. The burden posed by implementing protective measures and measures to mitigate the spread of contamination will likely negatively affect operations tempo. Mass causalities could overwhelm medical facilities or spread contamination denying continued use of those facilities. Command and control (C2) assets can become overwhelmed with managing effects of the chemical weapon attack, which would adversely impact awareness of other activities. Additionally, contaminated ports and airfields could hamper the flow of logistics and reduce sortie generation.

*For further information on chemical weapons, refer to JP 3-11, Operations in Chemical, Biological, Radiological, and Nuclear Environments.*

**Countering WMD**

## D. Cruise and Ballistic Missiles

The mating of chemical, biological, or nuclear weapons with long-range cruise or ballistic missiles is a critical aspect of WMD risk. Cruise missiles are capable of delivering large payloads long distances. Cruise missiles present a significant challenge to early warning and air defense systems because they are self-navigating and can fly at low altitude.

Ballistic missiles are capable of carrying large payloads even greater distances and are likewise difficult to defeat. During their boost phase, ballistic missiles present large radar and infrared signatures. Ballistic missiles typically become smaller (as stages separate) and unpowered as they enter free fall. When cruise or ballistic missiles are launched from a mobile platform—such as an aircraft or submarine—their range and ability to evade detection and interception are further magnified.

Cruise and ballistic missile defense interceptors largely use "hit-to-kill" technology, which relies on the kinetic energy of physical impact to destroy the ballistic missile warhead. Planning teams rely on analysis from locally deployed technical support teams or technical reachback to model the potential consequence of intercept effects. Subcritical nuclear detonations, radiological dispersion, survival of persistent chemical and biological agents, and missile debris, may present hazards to infrastructure, populations, lines of communications, or other strategically vital areas. Missile defense interceptors which use close proximity blast fragmentary warheads to intercept cruise and ballistic missiles face a higher risk of residual effects from intercept.

*For further information on cruise and ballistic missiles, refer to JP 3-01, Countering Air and Missile Threats.*

## E. Improvised Weapons

Improvised weapons include modified weapons and munitions, IEDs, and improvised CBRN, and are typically employed by non-state actors, and can include chemical, biological, or radiological enhancements. These weapons incorporate destructive payloads and fillers designed to kill, destroy, incapacitate, harass, or distract. Improvised weapons can incorporate military ordnance, but are normally made from a combination of military ordnance and nonmilitary components.

*For further information on improvised weapons, refer to JP 3-15.1, Counter-Improvised Explosive Device Operations, and the Weapons Technical Intelligence Handbook.*

## F. Dirty Bombs

A "dirty bomb" is one type of a radiological dispersal device (RDD) that combines conventional explosives, such as dynamite, with radioactive material. The terms dirty bomb and RDD are often used interchangeably in the media. Most RDDs would not release enough radiation to kill people or cause severe illness - the conventional explosive itself would be more harmful to individuals than the radioactive material. However, depending on the situation, an RDD explosion could create fear and panic, contaminate property, and require potentially costly cleanup. Making prompt, accurate information available to the public may prevent the panic sought by terrorists.

*See facing page for an overview and further discussion.*

# II. Weapons of Mass Destruction Pathways

Globalization has enabled the creation of new, innovative and sophisticated pathways that enable both development and proliferation efforts. WMD pathways consist of networks or links among individuals, groups, organizations, governmental entities, etc., that promote or enable the development, possession, and/or prolifera-

# Dirty Bombs (RDD)

Ref: http://www.nrc.gov/reading-rm/doc-collections/fact-sheets/fs-dirty-bombs.htm

A "dirty bomb" is one type of a radiological dispersal device (RDD) that combines conventional explosives, such as dynamite, with radioactive material. The terms dirty bomb and RDD are often used interchangeably in the media. Most RDDs would not release enough radiation to kill people or cause severe illness - the conventional explosive itself would be more harmful to individuals than the radioactive material. However, depending on the situation, an RDD explosion could create fear and panic, contaminate property, and require potentially costly cleanup. Making prompt, accurate information available to the public may prevent the panic sought by terrorists.

A dirty bomb is in no way similar to a nuclear weapon or nuclear bomb. A nuclear bomb creates an explosion that is millions of times more powerful than that of a dirty bomb. The cloud of radiation from a nuclear bomb could spread tens to hundreds of square miles, whereas a dirty bomb's radiation could be dispersed within a few blocks or miles of the explosion. A dirty bomb is not a "Weapon of Mass Destruction" but a "Weapon of Mass Disruption," where contamination and anxiety are the terrorists' major objectives.

## Impact of a Dirty Bomb

The extent of local contamination would depend on a number of factors, including the size of the explosive, the amount and type of radioactive material used, the means of dispersal, and weather conditions. Those closest to the RDD would be the most likely to sustain injuries due to the explosion. As radioactive material spreads, it becomes less concentrated and less harmful. Prompt detection of the type of radioactive material used will greatly assist local authorities in advising the community on protective measures, such as sheltering in place, or quickly leaving the immediate area. Radiation can be readily detected with equipment already carried by many emergency responders. Subsequent decontamination of the affected area may involve considerable time and expense.

Immediate health effects from exposure to the low radiation levels expected from an RDD would likely be minimal. The effects of radiation exposure would be determined by:

- the amount of radiation absorbed by the body;
- the type of radiation (gamma, beta, or alpha);
- the distance from the radiation to an individual;
- the means of exposure-external or internal (absorbed by the skin, inhaled, or ingested); and the length of time exposed.
- The health effects of radiation tend to be directly proportional to radiation dose. In other words, the higher the radiation dose, the higher the risk of injury.

## Protective Actions

In general, protection from radiation is afforded by:

- minimizing the time exposed to radioactive materials;
- maximizing the distance from the source of radiation; and
- shielding from external exposure and inhaling radioactive material.

## Sources of Radioactive Material

Radioactive materials are routinely used at hospitals, research facilities, industrial activities, and construction sites. These radioactive materials are used for such purposes as diagnosing and treating illnesses, sterilizing equipment, and inspecting welding seams. The Nuclear Regulatory Commission together with 37 "Agreement" States, which also regulate radioactive material, administers more than 22,000 licenses of such materials. The vast majority of these materials are not useful as an RDD.

tion of WMD and related capabilities. These pathways encompass ideas, materials, technologies, facilities, processes, products, and events. The evolution of weapons, materials, and technology, combined with the spread of knowledge and access to critical components, makes both detection and dissuasion more difficult. Also of significant concern are the dangers that arise from the potential convergence of violent extremism, political instability, and inadequate WMD security. Monitoring and controlling WMD pathways is essential in denying actors of concern access to WMD technology, knowledge, materials, expertise, and weapons. DOD will continue to enhance its capabilities, acting with an array of interagency and international partners, to conduct effective operations to counter the proliferation of WMD.

# A. Acquisition

WMD technologies and capabilities may be acquired by state or nonstate actors through systematic development, theft, barter, or purchase to accelerate the WMD development process. Due to geopolitical instability (e.g., states with WMD capabilities that are in civil war or susceptible to potential collapse), WMD technologies, materials, and expertise may be vulnerable. This increases the risk of proliferation through loss of control, security, and accountability. Actors of concern may seek to capitalize on geopolitical instability to circumvent the development process by directly acquiring WMD technologies, capabilities, and expertise. Individuals with key WMD technical or network knowledge may seek sanctuary from the dangers of geo-political instability through other state or non-state actors in exchange for their cooperation.

# B. Development

WMD development involves a range of processes that lead to weapons possession and includes critical human resources, logistics, C2, research efforts, production infrastructure, equipment, materials, financial networks, and other supporting networks.

# C. Proliferation

WMD proliferation is the transfer of WMD or related materials, technologies, and expertise from suppliers to state or non-state actors.

## Transfer Between States

States that were once recipients of WMD related technologies and materials may begin to indigenously produce and export these same technologies to other countries of proliferation concern. The ability and willingness of these states to export WMD-related expertise, technologies, and materials to other states outside of, or in noncompliance with, international nonproliferation rules are a serious threat.

## Non-State Actors

Non-state actors (e.g., terrorists, criminals, scientists, businesses, facilitators) and their networks may be involved in the intentional or unintentional proliferation of WMD-related technologies and materials. This compounds the risks of acquisition of WMD by actors of concern. Non-state actors who operate outside of international and state controls, while difficult to detect, should remain a JFC concern.

**Proliferation networks** are the supporting infrastructure that a state or non-state actor uses to gain or transfer access to weapons, material, technology, and expertise. A proliferation network is one form of WMD pathway. It is important to note that many of these networks are not organized specifically for the proliferation of WMD.

# III. WMD Activity Continuum

*Ref: JP 3-40, Countering Weapons of Mass Destruction (Oct '14), pp. II-11 to II-12.*

## WMD Activity Continuum

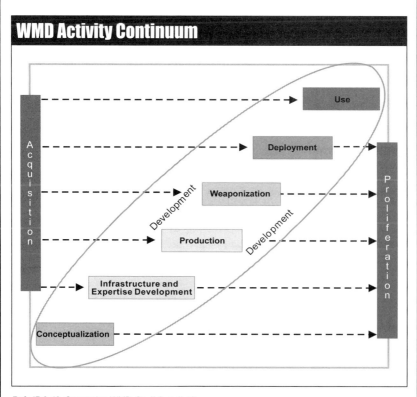

*Ref: JP 3-40, Countering WMD, fig. II-3, p. II-12.*

The WMD activity continuum is a complex but identifiable process with several generic activities that together constitute the progression from conceptualization to use. This continuum represents key decision points by an actor to acquire, develop, proliferate, or use WMD. Generic WMD continuum activities include: conceptualization; infra-structure and expertise development; production; weaponization; deployment; and use. In some cases, infrastructure and expertise development, facility preparation, and production may be concealed within industrial or agricultural production (dual-use facilities, equipment, expertise, technologies, and materials), academic institutions, or within concealed facilities, making intelligence collection efforts more difficult. Further-more, JFCs should bear in mind that Article IV of the NPT guarantees its signatories the right to develop nuclear energy for peaceful purposes, which may also mask the development of fissile material for weapons. WMD actors may, at any point along the proliferation continuum, effectively bypass one of the steps by acquiring (by theft, bar-ter, or purchase) the capability, thereby accelerating the WMD development process. A JFC should be prepared to counter these activities at every stage of the continuum to minimize WMD risk.

Countering WMD

# IV. Actors

## Actors of Concern

Actors of concern may have the intent to use or proliferate WMD capabilities against US interests. These actors may also perceive WMD destructive capabilities as a highly desirable means to counter more technologically advantaged nations and alliances. State or non-state actors that carry out activities that, left unaddressed, pose a clear potential threat to the strategic objectives of the USG. In the WMD context, an actor of concern poses a threat of developing, acquiring, proliferating, or employing WMD, related expertise, materials, technologies, and means of delivery. These actors also have the intent to use or proliferate this capability against US interests. They may perceive WMD destructive capabilities as highly desirable means to counter military and technologically advantaged adversaries and to threaten US and PNs interests.

## State Actors

States may view WMD possession as a source of strategic leverage, international prestige, regional dominance, deterrence, or as a means to counter US and Western powers. This may be accomplished through the threat or actual use of a weapon. For a state to employ WMD, it must possess one or more weapons, a delivery capability to put a weapon on target, and the infrastructure necessary for command and control of the weapon system. Those states lacking a conventional delivery capability or seeking to avoid attribution may use asymmetric means or proxies (state or non-state) to deliver weapons. JFCs use joint intelligence preparation of the operational environment (JIPOE) to assess an actor of concern's capability to employ CBRN weapons.

If state and regional instability increases in or around WMD possessor states, full control of weapons or critical weapons components may be jeopardized. JFCs should partner with other USG and multinational partners to advocate for responsible stewardship.

## Non-State Actors

Non-state actors may seek to acquire or use WMD in order to increase their influence or impose their will. JFCs should include CWMD considerations as part of the JIPOE, coordinate plans, and synchronize operations with USG and international partners to deter or prevent non-state actors from acquiring WMD. If acquired, use of WMD by non-state actors is more likely than an established state and thus requires due diligence to prevent access and acquisition to WMD and related components.

# V. Dual-Use Challenges

JFCs should understand the implications associated with dual-use technologies, materials, equipment, and expertise, which can provide the capability to develop WMD. Many CBRN-associated resources have a range of legitimate applications in industry, the public health sector, academia, and research. Even though they are normally used for civilian purposes, they may be exploited for military or nefarious applications. These dual-use items present state and non-state actors of concern a means to covertly acquire or develop CBRN weapon capabilities. The legitimate appearance of these activities and facilities complicates the JFC's ability to detect, track, and target these capabilities.

Countering WMD

# III. CWMD Planning

Ref: JP 3-40, Countering Weapons of Mass Destruction (Oct '14), chap. 4.

# I. General CWMD Planning Considerations

This section provides JFCs with planning constructs and considerations to assist them in translating strategic CWMD guidance into an operational approach and supporting plans. This chapter discusses CWMD integration into joint campaign and operation planning, the integration of military CWMD planning with the other instruments of national power in the accomplishment of USG strategic objectives, and general CWMD planning considerations. CWMD planning is not conducted in isolation nor as a separate process; it is the integration of WMD-specific knowledge, experience, and capabilities into the JFC's joint planning efforts.

> "Countering WMD [weapons of mass destruction] efforts often occur as part of larger US Government activities or military operations. Consequently, they must be fully integrated into other plans and activities rather than isolated as separate efforts."
>
> Department of Defense Strategy for Countering Weapons of Mass Destruction
> June 2014

CWMD planning includes the development of global and regional campaign plans to shape the environment to prevent the US and multinational partners from being attacked or coerced by actors possessing WMD. Campaign plans focus on ongoing operations, military engagement, SC, deterrence, and other shaping or preventive activities. Regional CWMD planning can either be written into stand-alone plans or incorporated into a command's TCP. Although a key aspect of campaign plans is shaping to prevent conflict and preparation of the environment in support of CWMD, they also set the conditions for potential contingency operations. Contingency plans are conceptually considered branches of campaign plans. Activities to respond to WMD aggression, instability or failure of a possessor state, and other WMD-related threats are typically contained in contingency plans.

## A. CWMD Planning Characteristics

While conducting their regional campaign and contingency planning, GCCs should integrate their plans within the global DOD CWMD approach. JFCs need to integrate their CWMD planning with their respective TCP. All plans should be coordinated with relevant USG and multinational partners to the extent circumstances allow.

### Strategic Approach

All CWMD plans should support achievement of DOD's strategic CWMD objectives, namely reducing incentives to pursuing, possessing, and employing WMD; increasing barriers to acquisition, proliferation, and use of WMD; managing WMD risks and denying the effects of WMD threats through layered, integrated defenses. GCC planning also needs to account for the regional, as well as the transregional and global, implications of their CWMD-related efforts. CWMD planning should be coordinated with bordering and functional CCMDs to support achievement of common regional and global objectives. GCCs should maintain awareness of CWMD operations and activities occurring outside their AOR to avoid negatively impacting or being impacted by other GCC decisions and/or activities. Additionally, Services and CSAs resource the majority of strategic CWMD programs and activities. GCCs should therefore coordinate their plans with these organizations to ensure alignment with current resources and capability development.

## Strategic Implications

Commanders at every level need to be aware of the strategic implications associated with any WMD threat and adapt their CWMD planning efforts accordingly. The three levels of warfare–strategic, operational, and tactical–are all applicable to CWMD efforts and help clarify the links between national strategic objectives and tactical actions. In a world of constant, immediate communications, any single action may have consequences at all levels. Nowhere is this more evident than in joint operations involving WMD, where action or inaction at the tactical level can have profound strategic repercussions.

## Interagency Coordination

USG departments and agencies planning and acting together can generate effects that cannot be created by DOD alone due to differing authorities, responsibilities, and capabilities. The nature and complexity of a CWMD mission often places DOD in a supporting role to another USG department or agency. GCCs should consider command relationships, integration of resources, and synchronization of activity as they develop any CWMD-related plans.

## Domestic and International Partnerships

DOD CWMD efforts have a greater likelihood of success if planned in cooperation with domestic and international security partners. CWMD shaping activities planned and executed in cooperation with partners may prevent or disrupt actor of concern acquisition, development, or employment of WMD, and alleviate the need for more aggressive and costly action later. In addition, collaborative action is effective at building partner capabilities and creating stronger security relationships with international partners, which enhance the GCC's ability to respond to all types of crises.

# B. Review of Strategic Guidance

CCDRs integrate strategic direction into their CWMD plans. The three strategic CWMD end states are: no new WMD possession; no WMD use; and minimization of WMD effects. The GEF and the JSCP translate strategic guidance into CWMD-specific end states and mandate the integration of CWMD-related planning tasks into CCMD planning. Finally, USSTRATCOM, as the global synchronizer for DOD CWMD planning, conducts comprehensive campaign planning that puts into effect a global strategy and provides directive guidance for CWMD planning to align global and regional CWMD objectives with strategic guidance.

# C. Understanding the Operational Environment (OE)

Progress in the effort to counter WMD depends on understanding the environment as it is, recognizing the change desired, identifying activities to bring about that change, assessing whether that change has occurred, and determining whether the change is a result of those activities or some external factor. Assessing the conditions in the OE will determine where DOD resources and efforts can be focused to achieve a more acceptable set of conditions (i.e., responsible state behavior). This understanding provides planners and operators a better perspective of the actor of concern by accounting for issues such as aggressive state behavior, lack of WMD program transparency, and poor stockpile security. The JFC is then enabled with this understanding to support preparation of the environment activities for any possible CWMD operation.

## JIPOE

JIPOE supports characterization of networks enabling WMD proliferation and use, and assessment of network vulnerabilities to facilitate development of the operational design elements and effective targeting. Identity intelligence products support an in-depth understanding of WMD threats and their potential effect on the OE. JIPOE supports the JFC by characterizing the WMD OE as a system of networks, actors, resources, and capabilities. This approach is holistic in its methodology–identifying state and non-state actors (individuals, extremist organizations, and nongovernmental entities) in a comprehensive fashion, not as singular entities operating independent from one another. Additionally, analysis of potential transformational events, such as the rise of new actors of concern and the impact of technology breakthroughs, facilitates national-level determination of end states, objectives, and priorities.

*For further guidance on JIPOE, refer to JP 2-01.3, Joint Intelligence Preparation of the Operational Environment.*

## Understanding Baseline Conditions

As part of the JIPOE process, the GCCs develop an understanding of baseline conditions within the AORs. Establishing baseline conditions is essential to generating effects, achieving objectives, and measuring progress toward attaining end states. Analysis of baseline conditions enables the JFC to identify where desired change is possible and to assess whether change has occurred. Baseline conditions are critical to identifying anomalies that may indicate the presence of a WMD threat. Many potential WMD threats may not be readily apparent without an understanding of historical conditions. For instance, identifying biological anomalies that are potential indicators of WMD usage requires an understanding of current and historical disease patterns, since many potential biological weapons are the intentional use of naturally occurring pathogens. Another consideration is the toxic industrial materials that may be manufactured, stored, and/or transported within the AOR which may cause WMD-like effects.

## Systems Perspective

A JFC's ability to characterize and monitor proliferation networks and state WMD programs as holistic systems is essential to affecting that system. One of the primary challenges facing the JFC is the proliferation of WMD technology and products. This proliferation takes place through systems. The JFC strives to understand the continuous and complex interaction of friendly, enemy, adversary, and neutral systems.

*For further guidance on intelligence support to joint operations, refer to the JP 2-0 series. For further guidance on JIPOE, refer to JP 2-01.3, Joint Intelligence Preparation of the Operational Environment.*

---

# D. Defining the Problem and Developing an Operational Approach

Once the GCC and staff have reviewed and analyzed the strategic guidance for CWMD together with the OE in their AOR, they should be able to articulate current and desired conditions relevant to countering WMD proliferation. Understanding the underlying factors associated with existing conditions enables planners to clearly define the WMD proliferation problem. Once the problem has been defined, the GCC and staff develop their operational approach to describe the commander's vision of where and how resources and effort can be applied to create effects to achieve objectives. The GCC's operational approach for CWMD should be consistent with the strategic approach. However, it needs to be specific to the GCC's understanding of the OE and definition of the problem. It should not be a simple repetition of the DODS-CWMD strategic approach. The CWMD operational approach reflects the JFC's visualization for attaining desired conditions and provides the necessary foundation for detailed planning, including both deliberate and crisis action planning. During development of the operational approach, the GCC and staff use the CWMD considerations outlined in the following sections.

### End State and Objectives

Although WMD may be one of many threats addressed in most plans, JFCs need to consider whether each situation warrants inclusion of CWMD considerations as part of the end state or the supporting objectives of their plan. Based on the type of planning, the process for developing end states and objectives will vary.

The GEF prescribes broad global, theater, and functional end states. Based on the OE, CCDRs develop concrete and achievable military objectives to support progress towards designated end states. Based on strategic guidance and the OE, development of CWMD-specific military objectives may be appropriate.

For deliberate planning, the GEF prescribes end states for which JFCs develop supporting strategic and operational objectives. Based on the strategic guidance and the OE, inclusion of CWMD-specific strategic and/or operational level objectives may be appropriate.

For crisis action planning, JFCs develop the military end states based on termination criteria, likely to be provided by the President or SecDef. Following Presidential or SecDef approval of the military end state, JFCs develop supporting strategic and operational objectives. Based on the strategic guidance and the OE, inclusion of CWMD-specific criteria in the military end state or inclusion of CWMD-specific strategic and/or operational level objectives may be appropriate.

### Effects

An effect is a physical and/or behavioral state of a system that results from an action, a set of actions, or another effect. A desired effect can also be thought of as a condition that can support achieving an associated objective, while an undesired effect is a condition that can inhibit progress toward an objective. When campaigns or operations include CWMD activities, the JFC and staff identify CWMD-related desired and undesired effects that either support or inhibit achievement of the commander's objectives.

### Lines of Effort (LOE)

The range of tasks and missions required to achieve CWMD objectives and attain end states, along with the number of nonmilitary factors, make LOEs a valuable construct for focusing efforts and achieving unity of effort. For a campaign or operation encompassing efforts beyond CWMD, it may be appropriate to consolidate CWMD activities and tasks into a single LOE as part of a larger operational approach. Use of well-designed LOEs can provide a clear and logical explanation of the JFC's concept and how it will result in achievement of objectives.

# II. Deliberate and Crisis Action Planning

CWMD planning encompasses the full range of plans and orders, including global campaign plans, TCPs, contingency plans, and operation orders. While some of these plans are CWMD specific, a CWMD planning effort is more commonly part of a larger planning effort and must be integrated with other strategies, plans, and operations at the global, theater, and JTF levels. CWMD planning supports and informs overarching global, theater, and JTF strategies and plans.

## A. Adaptive Planning and Execution (APEX) and Joint Operation Planning Process (JOPP)

Planning for joint operations uses two closely related, integrated, collaborative, and adaptive processes—APEX and JOPP. The majority of APEX activities and products occur prior to SecDef approval and the CJCS transmittal of an execute order.

While there is a distinct location for CWMD considerations within the structure of a plan– planners must fully integrate CWMD tasks and required resources throughout all pertinent annexes of a plan or order. In addition, planning for CWMD operations must be integrated in JOPP. Including WMD considerations throughout the seven steps of JOPP–the most crucial of which is mission analysis–is critical for a successful operation or campaign.

*For further guidance on APEX and JOPP, refer to JP 5-0, Joint Operation Planning, and Chairman of the Joint Chiefs of Staff Manual (CJCSM) 3130.03, Adaptive Planning and Execution (APEX) Planning Formats and Guidance.*

# B. CWMD Plans Integration

Integrating DOD CWMD planning efforts is intended to achieve the integrated, yet decentralized, execution of global activities and operations. As the DOD global synchronizer for CWMD, USSTRATCOM develops and maintains the global CWMD plan for DOD. GCCs align regional CWMD efforts with the global CWMD plan either by developing regional CWMD plans, or incorporating their directed CWMD efforts into their TCPs. The UCP task to synchronize planning pertains specifically to planning efforts only and does not, by itself, convey authority to execute operations or direct execution of operations. The DOD GCP-CWMD provides directive guidance for CWMD planning and prioritization, which informs the development and execution of operations and activities through theater campaign and contingency plans. GCCs develop regional CWMD campaign plans that nest under their TCPs as subordinate campaign plans, or incorporate directed CWMD planning directly into the TCPs. Contingency plans are considered branches to an overarching campaign plan. Contingency plans may be developed for specific WMD scenarios; however, many contingency plans with a broader focus often contain significant CWMD activities and tasks.

## GCP-CWMD

The GCP-CWMD operationalizes the CWMD strategy and is maintained in accordance with strategic planning guidance in the GEF, the JSCP, and other directives. The GCP-CWMD provides the CCMDs, the Services, and CSAs with a common strategy and framework to synchronize planning on a regional, transregional, and global basis. The GCP-CWMD is a comprehensive campaign plan focused on steady-state activities to prevent WMD crises and is an executable plan within this context. The GCPCWMD integrates DOD CWMD planning by linking CWMD end states to military objectives and campaign tasks through the three CWMD LOEs. The GCP-CWMD delineates responsibilities and specified campaign tasks to guide the GCCs' efforts in their respective AORs.

- **Prioritized Risks.** The GCP-CWMD identifies and prioritizes global strategic WMD risks. GCCs prioritize the risks differently based on their assessment of the OE and theater strategies. GCCs should coordinate with adjacent commanders to mitigate prioritized risks that span the operational gaps and seams between AORs.

- **Military Objectives.** The GCP-CWMD military objectives are intended to be achievable and measurable within a specific time-frame, provide linkages between global and theater-level campaigns, allow for plan synchronization and GCC development of subordinate tasks, and inform the assessment process. GCCs consider the GCP-CWMD military objectives while developing theater objectives to maintain the relationship between theater-level and global objectives.

- **Lines of Effort (LOE).** The GCP-CWMD LOEs provide the foundation of the objective to task linkage required to operationalize CWMD efforts and accommodate the range of activities required to counter WMD globally.

## Relationship between Global Campaign Plans

The GCP-CWMD is only one of DOD's global campaign plans. The GCPCWMD is coordinated with the global campaign plans for PI&ID, CT, and global distribution to address activity along mission seams and eliminate potential gaps. The coordination among global campaign plans is carried into GCC's theater and subordinate campaign plans.

## TCPs and Subordinate Campaign Plans

TCPs are the centerpiece of the GCC's family of plans. Each GCC's regional CWMD campaign planning is synchronized with the DOD CWMD campaign plan and is nested under their TCP as a subordinate campaign plan or fully incorporated into the TCP. Regional CWMD planning contains the GCC's strategy and overall approach for achieving CWMD objectives within their AOR. CWMD planning, whether written into regional stand-alone plans or integrated into their TCP, becomes part of the command's day-to-day operational approach to shape the environment to prevent crises or prepare for contingencies. Within their TCPs, GCCs integrate and prioritize operations and activities associated with each of their subordinate campaign plans. Collectively, TCPs and subordinate campaign plans contain the day-to-day activities executed by a GCC.

## Deliberate and Crisis Action Planning

Products from both deliberate and crisis action planning are typically thought of as branch plans to an overarching campaign plan. Contingencies and crises represent a departure from the shaping activities, which are the primary focus of the DOD CWMD campaign plan and TCPs. Although the GCPCWMD and TCPs encompass certain phase 0 activities associated with a GCC's contingency plans, developing additional plans and orders extends beyond phase 0 and includes the other phases of the phasing model. JFCs will often need to incorporate CWMD considerations into termination criteria, and end states and subsequently throughout their planning processes.

# C. Plan Levels

In accordance with the GEF, contingency plans are developed to one of four levels of planning detail: level 1 (Commander's Estimate), level 2 (Base Plan), level 3 (Concept Plan), and level 4 (Operation Plan). While crisis action planning does not formally use these four levels, planning begins at the conceptual level with a commander's estimate and additional levels of detail are added until an operations order is completed. There is a risk that significant CWMD tasks and activities will not be adequately addressed in less detailed contingency plans and in the earlier stages of crisis action planning. To mitigate this concern, JFCs and staffs are advised to evaluate CWMD objectives during mission analysis and integrate critical CWMD elements into level 2 base planning products, rather than waiting for annex development. CWMD planning should not be executed in isolation.

# D. CWMD Objectives
*Ref: JP 3-40, Countering Weapons of Mass Destruction (Oct '14), pp. IV-7 to IV-8.*

Global objectives should be integrated into the objectives contained in theater plans. The objectives within the DOD CWMD campaign plan are incorporated into regional CWMD campaign plans or TCPs and adjusted in accordance with prioritized theater WMD risks. The regional CWMD objectives are integrated into TCPs, reflected in the CCDR's operational approach, and support attainment of GEF-directed theater strategic end states. Additionally, CWMD objectives should be coordinated across geographic and functional boundaries to ensure they are mutually supportive and aligned with the broader DOD strategic CWMD end states. The following outlines CWMD planning considerations that have application across all phases.

## Cooperate with and Support Partners
These activities include DOD interaction with partners to build relationships that promote specific US security interests, develop allied and friendly capabilities for self-defense and multinational operations, and provide US forces with access to HNs. The importance of effectively planning CWMD activities with partners and allies cannot be emphasized enough, as they are a critical means for furthering progress towards CWMD strategic end states and encouraging future cooperation in case of a crisis or WMD event. CWMD planning conducted in cooperation with allied and PNs reduces WMD risks by improving or promoting defense relationships and capacity of allied and PNs to conduct CWMD operations. Mutually beneficial improved CWMD capabilities are achieved through SC arrangements, military-to-military contact, burden-sharing agreements, combined military activities, and support to international institutions. These activities also support cooperation with NGOs and diplomatic efforts such as treaties, agreements, and control regimes.

## Dissuasion, Deterrence, and Assurance
Campaign and contingency plans provide granularity on options and specific activities, before, during and after conflict, to dissuade or deter potential state and non-state adversaries and to assure friends and allies. Preventing instability or conflict is a combination of assuring partners through cooperative security agreements, dissuading potential actors of concern from making adverse geopolitical choices, and deterring known actors of concern from challenging global norms. CCMDs may use dissuasion, deterrence, and assurance to prevent those not possessing WMD from obtaining them or to contain and reduce existing threats. These activities, including demonstrating US resolve and increased capabilities to respond to, recover from, mitigate the effects of, and attribute the source of WMD may preclude the need to directly employ offensive capabilities against actors of concern.

## Shaping the Theater
JFCs should consider CWMD-related activities necessary to shape the theater for potential contingencies. TCPs should include objectives and activities to posture and prepare US forces for designated contingencies. Potential activities may include enhancing physical security of existing WMD programs, stockpiles, or capabilities; adapting force footprints and supporting agreements; or collecting WMD-related information requirements.

# E. Plan Phases

Ref: JP 3-40, Countering Weapons of Mass Destruction (Oct '14), pp. IV-9 to IV-11.

## Notional Operation Plan Phases

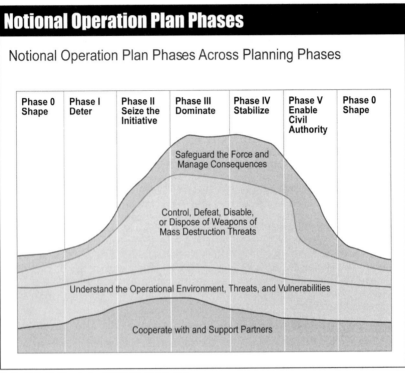

Notional Operation Plan Phases Across Planning Phases

| Phase 0 Shape | Phase I Deter | Phase II Seize the Initiative | Phase III Dominate | Phase IV Stabilize | Phase V Enable Civil Authority | Phase 0 Shape |

Safeguard the Force and Manage Consequences

Control, Defeat, Disable, or Dispose of Weapons of Mass Destruction Threats

Understand the Operational Environment, Threats, and Vulnerabilities

Cooperate with and Support Partners

Ref: JP 3-40, Countering WMD, fig. V-1, p. V-2.

## Phase 0 (Shape)

The intent of this phase is to shape the OE to dissuade or deter potential actors of concern from developing, acquiring, proliferating, or using WMD; assure international partners; and increase partner CWMD capability and capacity. CWMD-related phase 0 operations and activities typically occur in the context of day-to-day military engagement and SC programs. Such CWMD activity would identify persons of interest and map actors of concern activities and networks; through information sharing, develop working relationships through cooperative defense initiatives; and conduct bilateral and multilateral exercises containing CWMD activity to build partnership capacity and support for global initiatives like the Proliferation Security Initiative (PSI). Within their TCPs, CCMDs integrate and prioritize phase 0 activities associated with their contingency plans and day-today activities associated with their CWMD mission set to shape the environment to influence and to respond to WMD crises.

## Phase I (Deter)

The intent of this phase is to deter undesirable actions of actors of concern by demonstrating capabilities and resolve. JFCs plan carefully tailored flexible deterrent options (FDOs) to bring an issue to early resolution without armed conflict. FDOs can be used individually, in packages, sequentially, or concurrently. FDOs are developed for each instrument of national power—diplomatic, informational, military, and economic—but they are most effective when used in combination to increase the influence on an actor of concern. Examples of CWMD-focused FDOs include: demonstrating international resolve to stand against WMD threats; publicizing violations of international law by actors of concern; forward basing assets capable of striking or interdicting WMD capabilities; and enacting restrictions on WMD-related technology transfers. The GCPCWMD contains some objectives and tasks that apply to this phase, and it may provide a starting point for deliberate and crisis action planning.

## Phase II (Seize the Initiative)

JFCs seize the initiative through the application of appropriate joint force capabilities to force actors of concern action and to set the conditions for decisive operations. Actor of concern's use of WMD can quickly change an operation or campaign, as the use or threat of use of these weapons can cause an immediate shift in initiative and reprioritization of strategic and operational objectives. Multinational operations also become more complicated with the threat of WMD employment. An actor of concern may use WMD against partners, especially those with little or no defense against these weapons, to defeat an alliance or coalition. Accordingly, planning for this phase should include CBRN defensive and offensive actions employing lethal or nonlethal means to prevent an actor of concern from attaining its desired goal. The employment of forensics to characterize and contribute to the attribution of WMD materials and precursors is particularly useful in supporting both defensive and potential offensive operations. JFCs need to consider national and strategic objectives before conducting such operations against WMD-related targets, as there are intelligence exploitation and collateral damage considerations.

*For further guidance on CBRN defense, refer to JP 3-11, Operations in Chemical, Biological, Radiological, and Nuclear Environments. For further guidance on active defense measures against WMD, refer to JP 3-01, Countering Air and Missile Threats. For further guidance on offensive actions against WMD-related targets, refer to JP 3-05, Special Operations, JP 3-09, Joint Fire Support, JP 3-60, Joint Targeting, and DODD S-2060.04, DOD Support to the National Technical Nuclear Forensics (NTNF) Program.*

## Phase III (Dominate)

The dominate phase focuses on breaking the enemy's will for organized resistance or, in noncombat situations, control of the OE. During this phase, JFCs will continue to plan a combination of defensive and offensive CWMD activities. As friendly control in the operational area increases, JFCs may also need to plan for control, defeat, disable, and dispose activities to prevent future use or transfer of WMD. Dependent on the scale and scope of the WMD threat, this may require significant combat power and specialized expertise and equipment.

## Phase IV (Stabilize)

The stabilize phase is typically characterized by a shift in focus from sustained combat operations to stability operations. During this phase, JFC plans should include activities to conduct or set conditions for long-term systematic disposition of a WMD program, the transition of responsibility from DOD, facilitation of interagency or international WMD verification activities, and/or FCM.

*For further guidance on FCM operations, refer to JP 3-41, Chemical, Biological, Radiological, and Nuclear Consequence Management, DODI 2000.21, Foreign Consequence Management (FCM), or CJCSI 3214.01, Defense Support for Chemical, Biological, Radiological, and Nuclear Incidents on Foreign Territory.*

## Phase V (Enable Civil Authority)

This phase is predominately characterized by joint force support to legitimate civil governance in theater. During this phase, the JFC may need to support the transition of WMD disposition operations to defense agency, international, or HN forces, transition FCM activities to international or HN forces, or engage in SC activities to build the HN's CWMD capabilities.

# III. Additional Planning Considerations

## A. Legal Guidance

The complexity of CWMD and associated laws, policies, treaties, and agreements requires continuous involvement of the staff judge advocate (SJA) or appropriate legal advisor with the planning, oversight, and assessment of operations.

The SJA should be involved throughout the planning process, including mission analysis and course of action development, to make the JFC aware of potential CWMD-related legal issues. For instance, multinational partners, allies, and HNs will have their own treaty obligations and laws that may significantly differ from our own and restrict or prohibit their participation in CWMD operations or the transit of CBRN materials through an AOR. SJA involvement in WMD targeting and rules for the use of force or rules of engagement development is essential. The SJA can advise the JFC and the staff of potential associated issues, such as consequences of execution and harmful environmental impacts, collateral damage, or other WMD-related legal issues that should be considered in the targeting process.

The SJA should develop a legal staff estimate during mission analysis that accounts for WMD-related legal issues associated with joint operations. The legal staff estimate should reflect the description of legal support required for the mission as developed during the planning process.

## B. International Law and Agreements

International law, policies, treaties, and agreements to which the US is a signatory identify certain rights and obligations that impact joint operations. These legal requirements may pose constraints and restraints. Treaties and control regimes establish global norms against the proliferation of WMD precursors, weapons, their means of delivery, dual-use goods, and weapons manufacturing equipment. The US and its partners and allies also participate in a variety of nonbinding working groups and activities to counter the threat of WMD, particularly the proliferation of CBRN materials. JFCs should account for these agreements and activities that seek to strengthen international norms and common values and serve as capacity building activities through information-sharing and exercises.

# IV. Cooperative Threat Reduction (CTR) Program

In coordination with appropriate military organizations, other USG departments and agencies, and global partners, the CTR Program works cooperatively with partner governments to reduce the threat to the US and its allies from WMD, and related materials, technologies, and expertise, including associated delivery systems and infrastructure. The objectives of the CTR Program are: dismantle and destroy stockpiles of nuclear, chemical, or biological weapons, equipment, or means of delivery that partner countries own, possess, or that is in their control; account for, safeguard, and secure nuclear, chemical, and biological materials, equipment, or expertise which, if vulnerable to theft or diversion, could result in WMD threats; and prevent and detect acquisition, proliferation, and use of nuclear, chemical, or biological weapons, weapons-usable and related materials, equipment, or means of delivery and knowledge. The CTR Program was originally established and authorized to conduct threat reduction activities in the countries of the former Soviet Union. In 2010, in accordance with the authorities of the National Defense Authorization Act for 2008, the CTR Program began expanding to address emerging security challenges and urgent threats in regions of the world beyond the former Soviet Union. The CTR Program is currently authorized to operate in Asia, Africa, and the Middle East on an array of activities to include chemical weapons destruction, bio-engagement, nuclear security projects, and proliferation prevention.

# IV. CWMD Execution

Ref: JP 3-40, Countering Weapons of Mass Destruction (Oct '14), chap. 5.

> "US forces conduct a range of activities aimed at preventing the proliferation and use of nuclear, biological, and chemical weapons."
> Sustaining US Global Leadership: Priorities for 21st Century Defense, January 2012

This section provides details on the recommended specific activities and associated tasks that will need to be employed to achieve DOD's priority objectives associated with its strategy for CWMD.

# I. CWMD Activities Construct

The CWMD activities construct serves as a method for logically grouping tasks to counter specific WMD threats. Typically, tasks are categorized within activities: understand the OE, threats, and vulnerabilities; cooperate with and support partners; control, defeat, disable, and/or dispose of WMD threats; and safeguard the force and manage consequences. While CWMD tasks within these activities may be conducted individually or concurrently during an operation, collectively they support JFC operations.

## A. CWMD Activities and Phasing

CWMD activities can be accomplished during any phase (0-V) of an operation. However, the level of effort in each of these activities varies depending on the phase. The level of effort required for the "understand the environment, threats, and vulnerabilities" and "cooperate with and support partners" activities will likely remain constant throughout each phase of an operation. While the control, defeat, disable, and dispose of WMD threats, safeguard the force, and manage consequences activities occur in all phases of an operation, efforts activities will likely peak during higher intensity phases (III and IV).

## B. Tasks and Enabling Capabilities

The CWMD activity and task construct leverages specialized and non-CWMD specific activities. The tasks and associated capabilities discussed in this document support the end states and objectives, and are employed across all LOEs. When performing CWMD tasks the JFC will employ DOD and interorganizational capabilities to respond to a range of other threats, meet other requirements, and are the responsibility of organizations with missions that extend beyond CWMD. These capabilities include DOD-specific capabilities, such as ballistic missile defense, materials analysis conducted by national laboratories, and port security conducted by PNs. These tasks and capabilities promote common threat awareness, CWMD self-sufficiency, military and civilian preparedness, and CBRN risk reduction. The JFC and staff need to understand that CWMD tasks and activities are not linear, nor strictly confined to a single LOE, and may span all operational phases.

Notional Operation Plan Phases Across Planning Phases

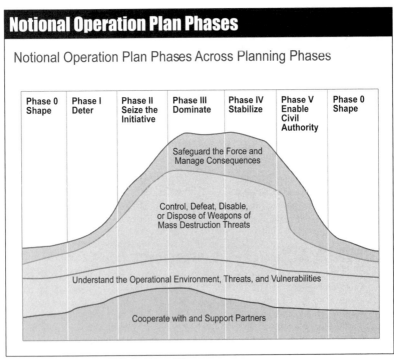

| Phase 0 Shape | Phase I Deter | Phase II Seize the Initiative | Phase III Dominate | Phase IV Stabilize | Phase V Enable Civil Authority | Phase 0 Shape |
|---|---|---|---|---|---|---|

Safeguard the Force and Manage Consequences

Control, Defeat, Disable, or Dispose of Weapons of Mass Destruction Threats

Understand the Operational Environment, Threats, and Vulnerabilities

Cooperate with and Support Partners

Ref: JP 3-40, Countering WMD, fig. V-1, p. V-2.

# II. Specialized CWMD Activities and Tasks

Effective execution of CWMD operations requires a deep understanding of CWMD activities and their supporting tasks. The following sections discuss the purpose and a general approach for joint force execution of CWMD activities during any military operation. Depending on the mission and OE, joint forces may also need to execute actions beyond those discussed in this chapter.

## A. CWMD Activity 1: Understand the Environment, Threats, and Vulnerabilities

This activity aids the JFC in developing and maintaining a more comprehensive understanding of both the actors and materials that affect the OE. To accomplish this, the JFC needs to locate, identify, characterize, assess, and predict threats against US and partner vulnerabilities. Attribution is a task that provides a dissuade and deterrence value if properly signaled to actors of concern, but as a capability is focused on response activities. Capabilities that support these tasks include detection, modeling, identity intelligence, detailed operational planning, and analysis of materials, precursors, and agents related to WMD proliferation, development, or use. The JFC may use a combination of assets and resources such as surveillance, reconnaissance, intelligence specialists, interorganizational experts, conventional forces, and SOF in support of this activity. This activity is an iterative process undertaken continually throughout the planning process and during execution of operations and activities. As a result, it is an essential enabler to planning, preparing, and executing the other three CWMD activities.

*See following page for an overview and further discussion.*

# Application of Countering WMD Activity Construct

*Ref: JP 3-40, Countering Weapons of Mass Destruction (Oct '14), fig. V-2, p. V-4.*

| Countering Weapons of Mass Destruction Lines of Effort | Notional Tasks Performed in Typical Operations and Missions | Countering Weapons of Mass Destruction Activity Categories: Understand the Environment | Cooperate with and Support Partners | Control, Defeat, Disable or Dispose of Weapons of Mass Destruction Threats | Safeguard the Force and Manage Consequences |
|---|---|---|---|---|---|
| Prevent Acquisition | | Locate, Identify, Characterize, Assess, Predict<br>Intelligence, surveillance, and reconnaissance; medical planning and logistics | Partner, Coordinate<br>Security cooperation; unified action; communication synchronization; interdiction; target planning; civil-military cooperation; border security | Divert and Intercept, Seize, Delay or Disrupt, Neutralize, and Destroy<br>Targeting; interdiction; information operations; ntelligence, surveillance, and reconnaissance; communication synchronization | Mitigate and Sustain<br>Force protection |
| Contain, Reduce Threats | | Locate, Identify, Characterize, Assess, Predict<br>Intelligence, surveillance, and reconnaissance; weapons technical intelligence; medical planning and logistics; meteorological and oceanographic operations | Partner, Coordinate<br>Security cooperation; unified action; bio-surveillance; strategic communications; targeting; information operations | Divert and Intercept, Isolate, Secure, Seize, Delay or Disrupt, Neutralize, Destroy, Exploit, Degrade, Reduce, Dismantle, Redirect, and Monitor<br>Targeting; interdiction; site security; site exploitation; special forces and unified action; cooperative threat reduction; cooperation; civil-military cooperation; sanctions enforcement | Mitigate, Sustain, Support<br>Force protection; health services; route reconnaissance |
| Respond to Crises | | Locate, Identify, Characterize, Assess, Attribute, and Predict<br>Intelligence, surveillance, and reconnaissance; force posturing; bio-surveillance; forensics and evidence collection; hazard modeling | Partner, Coordinate<br>Security cooperation; unified action; civil-military cooperation; communication synchronization; force protection; logistics | Divert and Intercept, Isolate, Secure, Seize, Delay or Disrupt, Neutralize, Destroy, Exploit, Degrade, Mitigate, Sustain, Support<br>Targeting; interdiction; site security; information operations; special forces and unified action; force protection | Mitigate, Sustain, Support<br>Force protection; health services; decontamination operations; contamination avoidance |

# Understand the Environment, Threats, and Vulnerabilities

*Ref: JP 3-40, Countering Weapons of Mass Destruction (Oct '14), pp. V-5 to V-6.*

## 1. Locate Task

The JFC uses SOF, and intelligence collection assets to locate WMD-associated system nodes and program elements, to include production facilities, storage/stockpile sites, and key program personnel. Developing robust information sharing relationships with interorganizational partners, particularly related to identity data, is an essential component to this task.

## 2. Identify Task

Once a WMD-related element and capability is located, the JFC's intelligence staff, in coordination with interorganizational experts, scope, categorize, and prioritize the posed threat. Confirmation of a threat will lead to further analysis to characterize and then assess specific elements of the program more effectively. During conflict, initial identification of CBRN materials will most likely be performed by conventional forces.

## 3. Characterize Task

Prior to conflict, the JFC gains understanding of an actor of concern's WMD program by mapping its individual components, its internal linkages, and its external associations through a variety of intelligence collection and analysis capabilities. This includes the types of weapons and the related materials, technology, and expertise associated with each WMD capability. The JFC staff uses characterization to inform assessment, attribution, and predictive analysis. During and after conflict, characterization occurs when the joint force has access to and can fully examine WMD facilities, stockpiles, weapons, and/or personnel.

## 4. Assess Task

Analysis conducted in conjunction with larger DOD, civilian, USG, and international partners interorganizational effort helps the JFC determine the threat posed by an actor of concern's WMD program. This includes an assessment by the JFC staff of US and PN vulnerabilities in relation to a specific actor's WMD capability. The JFC may use hazard estimation, measurement, and modeling systems, as well as multinational exercises to assess the level of threat that an actor of concern's WMD poses to US and friendly forces.

## 5. Attribute Task

Attribution is an effort to determine the origin of the material or weapon as well as those responsible for a CBRN event. The process derives forensics conclusions from the definitive analysis of samples collected, law enforcement, and intelligence information. Forensic-enabled intelligence collection, processing, exploitation, and analysis capabilities support the identification of CBRN sourcing and attribution. Joint forces directly support the attribution process through intelligence (e.g., site exploitation), sample collection and transfer, and technical analysis. These forces require training, certification, and specialized equipment and expertise, and in some cases, unique authorities that must be requested by the JFC prior to execution. These forces must be identified early in the planning process.

## 6. Predict Task

Specialized, technical capabilities are used to construct a common operational picture presenting current and forecasted information on the actors of concern, friendly forces, neutral elements, the environment, and geospatial information. JFCs use modeling, diagnostics, intelligence, and analysis capabilities to understand the current environment, detecting anomalies, and continually assessing the WMD threat and related networks to extrapolate possible future threats.

# B. CWMD Activity 2: Cooperate with and Support Partners

This activity promotes common threat awareness, builds CWMD self-sufficiency, improves military interoperability, enhances military and civilian preparedness, deterrence, and in some cases facilitates security of dual-use and CBRN materials. JFCs should plan to perform tasks associated with this activity in full cooperation with state and local authorities, USG interagency partners in a variety of departments and agencies, multinational partners, and NGOs. The JFC will coordinate with state and local authorities, interagency partners, multinational partners, and NGOs to ensure the partner and coordinate tasks associated with this activity are successfully conducted, to various degrees, within military engagement, SC, CTR, and deterrence operations and activities during all military operational phases. The JFC should seek to strengthen existing partner relationships and support programs to build the foundation for future partnering opportunities. Whenever conducting this activity, CCMDs coordinate with DOS to make contact with international counterparts in PNs. JFCs need to include partners in planning and execution processes as early as possible. GCCs can then leverage existing activities, such as interorganizational and multinational training and exercises to strengthen relationships and improve regional capabilities and capacity to achieve CWMD objectives. As part of this activity, CCMDs should coordinate with DOS to make contact with international counterparts.

## Partner Task

Domestic and foreign security partnerships support the collective capability to respond to and defeat WMD threats and manage the consequences of an attack. Existing partnerships must be maintained and new relationships sought out, building partner capacity in key areas that support deterrence and all operational phases.

## Coordinate Task

Promote and improve common threat awareness, interoperability, response preparedness, and WMD risk reduction. Actions that support this task include operational planning with partners and SC efforts that synchronize counterproliferation activities such as interception.

# C. CWMD Activity 3: Control, Defeat, Disable, and/or Dispose of WMD Threats

The purpose of the control, defeat, disable, and/or dispose of WMD threats activity is to reduce WMD-related threats. DOD has developed specialized capabilities and units to address the tasks associated with this CWMD activity. When conducted on a small scale, this activity may constitute part or all of a crisis response or limited contingency operation. For major operations and campaigns, which balance offensive, defensive, and stability operations, this activity supports the joint force's offensive actions. Typically, JFCs control, defeat, disable, or dispose of individual WMD threats, as appropriate. These tasks may be conducted utilizing lethal and/or nonlethal capabilities that require specialized equipment and expertise. The JFC should focus on controlling an actor of concern's program elements and then transitioning control to a competent authority for final disposition as the situation/mission dictates.

*See following pages (pp. 7-36 to 7-37) for an overview and further discussion.*

# Control, Defeat, Disable and/or Dispose of WMD Threats

Ref: JP 3-40, Countering Weapons of Mass Destruction (Oct '14), pp. V-9 to V-13.

## 1. Control Supporting Tasks

Control supporting tasks are accomplished with capabilities to divert, intercept, isolate, seize, and secure WMD, including related technology, materials, expertise, and means of delivery.

**Divert Task.** This task involves efforts and resources to change the intended course or destination of shipments of WMD, related technologies, materials, expertise, and/or means of delivery either willingly or by force. The JFC may use a combination of operations to accomplish this task. In some cases this may not require direct action, rather a show of force, the demonstration of a US presence, or a formal communication of US Government concern will render the desired effect.

**Intercept Task.** Conventional forces and SOF capabilities may be necessary to stop the movement of CBRN materials, WMD components, means of delivery, WMD-related personnel, or functional weapons into or out of specified areas or nations. Such actions may require boardings and search and detection capabilities to secure and seize shipments. Intercept operations will likely involve interagency or multinational partners.

**Isolate Task.** This task includes conducting critical factors analyses of WMD programs to identify capabilities, requirements, and vulnerabilities that can be acted upon. Isolating and denying access to critical WMD program components is intended to prevent actors of concern from furthering WMD acquisition, development, proliferation, or utilization.

**Seize Task.** This task involves taking possession of WMD capabilities (e.g., a designated area, building, transport, materials, or personnel) to deny an actor of concern's access to WMD capabilities. Seizing differs from securing because it requires offensive action to obtain control of the designated area or objective.

**Secure Task.** Preventing unauthorized access to sites or the removal of WMD-related technologies, materials, or personnel may be necessary to prevent use, proliferation, looting, or compromising integrity of physical evidence. The secure task may allow characterization and exploitation operations to begin. The requirement to secure sites is a crucial mission analysis consideration due to the potentially large force requirements and the balance of competing JFC priorities.

## 2. Defeat Supporting Tasks

Pathway and WMD defeat activities cover the spectrum of offensive activity, from conventional to cyberspace and special operations, that addresses an actor of concern's development and use of WMD. Pathway defeat activities focus on actions to delay, disrupt, destroy, or otherwise complicate conceptualization, development, possession, and proliferation of WMD. After an actor of concern has obtained WMD critical requirements (e.g., expertise, technology, components, materials, delivery systems, facilities), WMD defeat efforts target critical vulnerabilities (e.g., the ability to assemble, stockpile, deliver, transfer, or employ WMD) and seek to neutralize or destroy them.

**Delay Task.** JFC efforts to hinder an actor of concern's development, acquisition, proliferation, or use of WMD include lethal and nonlethal capabilities employed directly against the actor of concern or in support of another lead agency. This can include direct action against specific nodes in a WMD network or program such as production facilities, computer networks, and transportation or financial nodes. Efforts to delay key actors may include financial sanctions, legal actions, or restriction of travel (e.g., national watch list).

**Disrupt Task.** The JFC may choose to disrupt an actor of concern's development, acquisition, or proliferation of WMD. This may be done with direct action interdicting material en route. Disruption is particularly well suited to targeting key nodes in an actor of concern's network, such as transportation, leadership, logistics, or financial nodes.

**Neutralize Task**. Neutralization includes efforts to render WMD capabilities ineffective or unusable. Examples include making CBRN agents and materials harmless or making delivery systems unusable. When assigning tasks to neutralize WMD, commanders specify the actor of concern's capability or material and the duration it should be rendered ineffective or unusable.

**Destroy Task**. This task involved destroying WMD capabilities so they cannot perform their intended function without being entirely rebuilt. Such actions require a significant amount of pre-strike planning and authorization prior to execution. Typically the capability cannot be reconstituted. Proper weaponeering and hazard modeling help the JFC employ the proper resources, understand the potential consequences of execution, and minimize collateral damage.

## 3. Disable Supporting Tasks

Disablement includes efforts to exploit and degrade or destroy critical and at-risk components of a WMD program. Critical components are those that pose a threat to friendly forces, while at-risk components are those components of a WMD program that are at risk of loss or proliferation. Disable tasks seek to ensure that these items are not used, lost, or proliferated. They also seek to reduce the risk of those capabilities being proliferated, lost, or stolen.

**Exploit Task**. WMD exploitation tasks seek to maximize the value of intelligence gained from personnel, data, information, and materials obtained during CWMD operations. Site exploitation should be integrated into CWMD operations due to the inherently strategic implications of WMD.

**Degrade Task.** Typically destruction and disposal of an actor's WMD capability are preferred to degradation, but factors such as time, resources, access, and security may necessitate only the most critical at-risk elements be degraded and/or destroyed. Whatever the reason, the JFC may need to accept that degradation is the best course of action given the circumstance.

## 4. Dispose Supporting Tasks

This task involves the systematic effort to get rid of the remnants (program elements, facilities, personnel, surplus, dual-use capacity, confiscated/seized cargo, equipment, delivery systems) of an actor's WMD program. This may include deliberate technical processes that reduce or dismantle production methods, materials, stockpiles, and technical infrastructure; establishment of protocols of reductions and compensation or agreements to return seized cargo; the redirection of WMD, related technologies, materials, or an actor's efforts and expertise towards peaceful productive activities; and monitoring to ensure expertise or program elements are not re-constituted or reused in any illicit capacity.

**Reduce Task**. This disposal task seeks to diminish a potential threat, improve the security of the remnants, reduce costs of sustaining the program elements, and eliminate excess capacity or capability. Reduction programs and operations may be led by another USG department or agency, or international partner or organization.

**Dismantle Task**. Dismantling a WMD facility, stockpile, or program is the process by which the program is systematically reduced to a level that it can no longer operate for its intended purpose. Depending on the operating environment, the lead for this effort may have already transitioned to another organization or PN.

**Redirect Task**. Redirection involves repurposing facilities, expertise, and material associated with an actor of concern's WMD program elements. This is especially acute when program elements have a dual-use nature. Redirection of expertise includes retaining personnel with WMD expertise (e.g., scientists and engineers) for new, legitimate employment.

**Monitor Task.** Monitoring is the disposal task action to continually review and inspect programs, personnel, and facilities to ensure that they are not producing WMD and that remnants are not being reconstituted or reused in any illicit capacity.

Countering
WMD

# D. CWMD Activity 4: Safeguard the Force and Manage Consequences

The purpose of this activity is to allow the joint force and other mission-critical personnel to sustain effective operations and support US and foreign civil authorities and their populations by responding to a CBRN incident and mitigating the hazards and the effects of their use. When conducted on a small scale, safeguard the force and manage consequences tasks may constitute part or all of a crisis response or limited contingency operation. For major operations and campaigns, which balance offensive, defensive, and stability operations, this activity supports the joint force's defensive and stability actions. Within the construct of such operations, the joint force needs to be prepared for a variety of WMD situations, such as an inadvertent release, release due to joint force action, or actor of concern's employment of CBRN materials.

*For more information to safeguard the force and manage consequences, refer to JP 3-11, Operations in Chemical, Biological, Radiological, and Nuclear Environments, and JP 3-41, Chemical, Biological, Radiological, and Nuclear Consequence Management, respectively.*

## 1. Mitigate Task
Mitigate is the ability to plan, prepare, respond to, and recover from CBRN incidents. This task focuses on maintaining the joint force's ability to continue military operations in a CBRN contaminated environment, and on minimizing or negating the vulnerability to, and effects of, CBRN attacks. These activities may support civil authorities and foreign governments.

## 2. Sustain Tasks
Sustain is the ability to maintain response, and recover operations from CBRN incidents. In reference to the joint force, sustainment is the ability to support operations in a CBRN environment and conduct recovery/reconstitution operations to regenerate unit combat readiness (e.g., detailed troop decontamination, detailed equipment decontamination, medical activities, and rest and relaxation). These activities may support civil authorities and foreign governments.

## 3. Support Task
In many scenarios DOD, and the JFC, will be directed to support another USG department or agency (e.g., DHS or DOS) in the conduct of operations initiated to provide assistance to civil authorities when their own capabilities are insufficient to save lives and maintain essential government services. In the event of a CBRN incident where HN support for local population and DOS does not have a presence, DOD may be directed by the President or SecDef to lead support operations. The JFC should be aware of any standing agreement that may provide a means to deliver this support as required.

# Consequence Management (CM)

*Ref: JP 3-41, Chemical, Biological, Radiological, and Nuclear Consequence Management (Jun '12), chap. 1 and ATP 3-11.41, Multi-Service TTPs for CBRN Consequence Management Operations (Jul '15).*

This chapter overviews response to disasters – both natural and man-made, and addresses issues related to consequence management of natural disasters or acts of terrorism, including weapons of mass destruction (WMD) events. Responding to terrorism involves instruments that provide crisis management and consequence management.

(Sgt. Melissa Parrish / U.S. Army)

## Crisis Management

"Crisis management" refers to measures to identify, acquire, and plan the use of resources needed to anticipate, prevent, and/or resolve a threat or act of terrorism. The Federal Government exercises primary authority to prevent, preempt, and terminate threats or acts of terrorism and to apprehend and prosecute the perpetrators; State and local governments provide assistance as required. Crisis management is predominantly a law enforcement response.

## Consequence Management

"Consequence management" refers to measures to protect public health and safety, restore essential government services, and provide emergency relief to governments, businesses, and individuals affected by the consequences of terrorism. State and local governments exercise primary authority to respond to the consequences of terrorism; the Federal Government provides assistance as required. Consequence management is generally a multifunction response coordinated by emergency management.

This chapter provides information on the National Response Framework (NRF) aligns federal coordination structures, capabilities, and resources into a unified, all-discipline, and all-hazards approach to domestic incident management. It includes and understanding of how local, state, and federal emergency agencies interact and discusses how to plan and construct consequence and contingency plans to meet both natural and man-made emergencies.

The National Incident Management System (NIMS) is a comprehensive approach to all aspects of incident management, regardless of size, complexity, or cause. The guidance for NIMS was published by the Department of Homeland Security (DHS) in March 2004, and the guidance continues to be refined and updated by the NIMS Integration Center. One of the six primary elements of NIMS is the use of a standardized command and management system for incident scene operations, the Incident Command System (ICS); and for supporting operations centers, the Multiagency Coordination System.

# I. United States Government (US) Approach to a CBRN Incident

The USG approach to managing the consequences of a CBRN incident is vested in chemical, biological, radiological, and nuclear consequence management (CBRN CM). CBRN CM can be described as the overarching USG capability and the strategic national direction, to prepare for, respond to, and recover from the effects of a CBRN incident at home or abroad, and whether or not it is attributed to an attack using weapons of mass destruction (WMD). When required, the USG will coordinate its response to a CBRN incident in one of three ways based on the geopolitical situation.

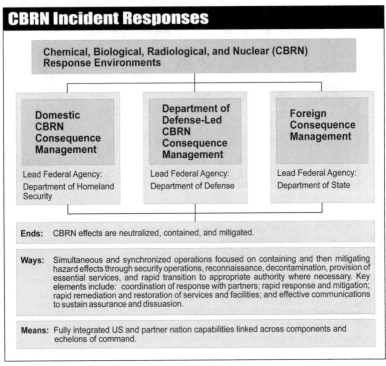

Ref: JP 3-41, CBRN Consequence Management, fig. I-1, p. I-3.

The Department of Homeland Security (DHS) is the USG lead agency for incident management that would include a domestic CBRN incident. Overseas, excluding homeland areas, the Department of State (DOS) is the USG lead for what is termed

# FBI Critical Incident Response Group (CIRG)

*Ref: https://www.fbi.gov/about-us/cirg/overview*

The FBI's Critical Incident Response Group (CIRG) was established in 1994 to integrate tactical, negotiations, behavioral analysis, and crisis management resources into one cohesive structure to facilitate the FBI's rapid response to critical incidents. As the Bureau's mission has expanded over the years, so have CIRG's responsibilities, but the premise behind its formation remains. Today, CIRG, which has a motto of Proventus Per Adparatus—Success Through Readiness—has grown into a "one-stop shop" that provides expertise in the following fields:

- Crisis management
- Hazardous devices disruption
- Crisis negotiations
- Behavioral analysis and assessments
- Strategic information dissemination
- Tactical and technical operations
- Ground and air surveillance
- Aviation support
- Special events management
- Rapid deployment logistics

*(FBI.GOV)*

CIRG personnel are on call around the clock, seven days a week, ready to assist FBI field divisions and law enforcement partners in pre-crisis planning and response to critical incidents, major investigations, and special events. Through the Strategic Information Operations Center (SIOC), CIRG also facilitates enterprise-wide situational awareness and maintains a platform for critical interface and the dissemination of strategic information. In addition, CIRG provides training programs to FBI field offices and federal, state, local, and international law enforcement partners. With aggressive training programs, state-of-the-art equipment, and expertise in a broad range of tactical and investigative techniques, CIRG is capable of fulfilling its overall mission of "Readiness, Response, and Resolution" to manage critical incidents.

# II. CBRN Technical Reachback

Ref: ATP 3-11.41, Multi-Service TTPs for CBRN Consequence Management Operations (Jul '15), pp. A-25 to A-26.

Technical reachback provides commanders with added expertise and knowledge when needed during the conduct of CBRN CM.

Technical reachback is the capability to contact technical subject matter experts when an information requirement exceeds the knowledge base of the responding ICS organization. A common situational awareness among all elements at the incident site, military and civilian, is imperative. Critical command decisions rely on multiple information sources that include technical reachback input.

(Shutterstock.com)

Reachback should be conducted using established protocols. Technical reachback can support the following representative requirements:

## Nonstandard Agent Identification of Chemical, Biological, Radiological, and Nuclear Warfare Agents and Toxic Industrial Material

Military responders are trained to detect and identify selected military warfare agents. If a TIM is used, or is suspected, ICS personnel should obtain additional technical information. This technical information may include persistency, medical effects, decontamination methods, and/or protection requirements.

### Modeling

During CBRN CM operations, the spread of contamination must be limited. Technical reachback can help support detailed analysis of an area to assist in determining downwind hazards; locating staging areas, operations centers, and decontamination sites; making shelter in place decisions; and conducting an evacuation.

## CBRN Agent Sample Analysis and Evacuation

Sample analysis and evacuation can use technical reachback to obtain critical information for patient treatment. Samples evacuated can also be used as forensic evidence.

## Hazard Prediction

Technical experts can use modeling to provide a better indication of where vapor, liquid, or aerosolized hazards may occur. Pre incident planning can identify technical reachback sources that may be used to provide verifiable, validated, and reliable information. The planning and execution process helps determine the operational value of those capabilities. Other planning considerations include the following:

- Is technical reachback available at the incident site or at a remote site?
- Do communication requirements include secure or nonsecure capabilities and/or audio or video capabilities?
- Does resourcing support technical reachback 24 hours a day, 7 days a week?

# Technical Reachback Contact Information

| | | Capability | | | |
|---|---|:---:|:---:|:---:|:---:|
| | | C | B | R | N |
| **Department of Defense** | | | | | |
| Armed Forces Radiobiology Research Institute | (301) 295-0316/0530 | | | X | X |
| Defense Threat Reduction Agency | (877) 240-1187 | X | X | X | X |
| Edgewood Chemical-Biological Center | (800) 831-4408 | X | X | | |
| U.S. Army Medical Research Institute of Infectious Diseases | (888) 872-7443 | | X | | |
| U.S. Army Medical Research Institute for Chemical Defense | (410) 436-3277 | X | | | |
| U.S. Army Center for Health Promotion and Preventive Medicine | (800) 222-9698 | X | X | X | X |
| **Department of Homeland Security** | | | | | |
| National Response Center, Chemical Terrorism/chemical-biological Hot Line | (800) 424-8802 or (202) 267-2675 | X | X | | |
| Federal Emergency Management Agency | (800) 621-FEMA (3362) | X | X | X | X |
| **Other Federal Agencies** | | | | | |
| Centers for Disease Control and Prevention | (800) CDC-INFO (232-4636) | X | X | | |
| Department of Energy, Radiation Emergency Assistance Center | (865) 576-3131 | | | X | X |
| Environmental Protection Agency, Environmental Response Team | (732) 321-6743 | X | X | X | X |
| National Institute for Occupational Safety and Health | (800)-35-NIOSH (356-4674) | X | | | |
| National Atmospheric Release Advisory Center | (202) 586-8100 | X | X | X | X |
| **State Agencies** | | | | | |
| State Emergency Management Agencies | (202) 646-2500 | X | X | X | X |

Legend:
B          biological
C          chemical
N          nuclear
R          radiological
U.S.      United States

*Ref: ATP 3-11.41, Multi-Service TTPs for CBRN Consequence Management Operations (Jul '15), table A-2, p. A-26.*

Consequence
Management

# III. Pandemic Influenza (PI) and Other Infectious Diseases

*Ref: JP 3-41, Chemical, Biological, Radiological, and Nuclear Consequence Management (Jun '12), pp. I-8 to I-10 (Contributor: Dr. Thomas Hennefer).*

A pandemic is an outbreak of an infectious disease that may be of natural, accidental, or deliberate origin, occurring over a wide geographic area. It is unique in that it is not a discrete event but a prolonged environment in which military operations, including any CBRN response, may continue.

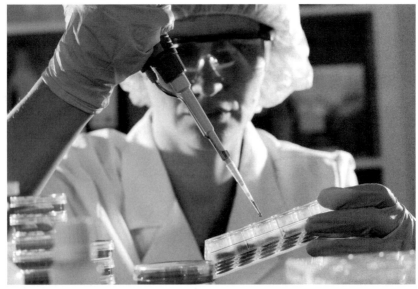

*(Shutterstock)*

The National Strategy for Pandemic Influenza (NSPI) uses a three-pillar construct for preparation and response that can be extended to other pandemics as well. These three pillars are: EP, surveillance and detection, and response and containment. DOD plays a major role in the USG effort to contain, mitigate, and reduce the spread of PI or infectious diseases. Such actions also help preserve US combat capabilities and readiness, support USG efforts to save lives, reduce human suffering, and mitigate the spread of infection. Due to the ability of infected people to cross the globe at will, the possibility of another pandemic is a higher probability then in was when the Spanish Flue decimated many countries. The global mortality rate from the 1918-19 pandemic is not known, but an estimated 10% to 20% of those infected died with about a third of the world population being infected. Considering that the current world population was estimated at 7.349 billion in 2015 a death rate of 10-20% even with a short-lived pandemic could easily overwhelm even the most modern and well-prepared country.

Throughout a PI or infectious disease outbreak, US military forces strive to preserve combat capabilities, accomplish assigned missions, and achieve strategic objectives. This force protection and preventive action may require units to isolate themselves from the general civilian population up to an including so that resources and response capabilities remain intact for future contingency missions. While this seems harsh to ignore the needs of a population the military has sworn to protect, certain events such as a CBRN event or pandemic would greatly strain limited military resources and render them unable to effectively intervene especially if a CBRN or pandemic event becomes long-term.

## EP Within DOD for PI and Infectious Diseases

Throughout a PI or infectious disease outbreak, US military forces strive to preserve combat capabilities, accomplish assigned missions, and achieve strategic objectives. This force protection and preventive action may require units to isolate themselves from the general civilian population up to an including so that resources and response capabilities remain intact for future contingency missions. While this seems harsh to ignore the needs of a population the military has sworn to protect, certain events such as a CBRN event or pandemic would greatly strain limited military resources and render them unable to effectively intervene especially if a CBRN or pandemic event becomes long-term. Implementation of force health protection measures is the primary focus throughout the entire spectrum of PI and infectious disease preparation, planning, and operations regardless of whether the virus was natural, accidental, or of deliberate origin.

## Health Surveillance

Detecting and tracking the spread of an infectious disease is key to its containment. The same assets used to detect and track a biological threat or hazard are used to detect a PI or infectious disease outbreak. A major focus by the World Health Organization (WHO) is as follows " One of the major means of addressing the concerns about communicable diseases in both industrialized and developing countries is through the development of strong surveillance systems. However, in view of the disparity among national surveillance systems, partnerships in global surveillance are a logical starting point in this area of common commitment." A major obstacle to tracking infectious diseases across international boundaries has a lot to due with social, religious and culture conventions that may reduce or restrict the collection of data to an effective level that will support early detection and prevention. While WHO members have a legal obligation to report contagious outbreaks, the inability or refusal of NGO (non-government organization) to participate can allow the global transportation of an infected person(s) to bypass established regulations and bring a contagion to a country or region with little if any warning.

## Response and Containment

CBRN forces should be prepared to respond to CBRN incidents during a pandemic. While containment of infected person(s) or those exposed to a commutable disease such as smallpox seems like a prudent response since placing those infected in a single location makes treatment, disposal and reduction of the disease from spreading into the general population, legal considerations must also be evaluated since placing infected person(s) in some type of contained area such as an interment camp represents a historically negative image and will often find that extended public support for camps may become problematic since those in a camps cannot be denied their Constitution rights.

Containment will manifest in several forms of restriction of movement: Limitations on travel to reduce the likelihood of disease migration, isolation or quarantine to contain infection within a known area or population, and entry limitations to keep infected people from entering areas where the infection has not yet migrated.

*For further doctrinal guidance on epidemics and medical procedures, refer to JP 4-02, Health Service Support.*

*Refer to Disaster Response SMARTbook 3 – Disaster Preparedness for further discussion of outbreaks, epidemics and pandemics. Chapters 10 and 11 provide extensive discussion of natural and man-made disasters to include: hurricanes, earthquakes, wildfiros, floods, volcanoes, tsunamis, tornadoes, drought & famine, blizzards & ice storms, outbreaks, epidemics & pandemics, nuclear events, civil disturbances, explosions & chemical spills.*

Consequence Management

foreign consequence management (FCM). In either of those situations, and when directed, Department of Defense (DOD) typically supports the USG lead. A third scenario could require DOD to lead the USG effort during military operations when the host nation (HN) is unable to respond properly, or DOS is unable to lead the USG response. Also, a USG response is not necessarily triggered by recognition of a CBRN hazard or environment.

## CBRN Hazards

CBRN hazards are CBRN materials that, if released, could create an adverse effect within the environment. If the size and scope of a CBRN hazard and/or environment exceeds established parameters, civil authorities may declare an emergency and the situation may be deemed a CBRN incident. However, only when local, tribal, or state authorities are overwhelmed by the situation would a USG response normally be required. Subsequently, if there are shortfalls in federal and state CBRN capabilities, the USG approach would likely require a request for DOD assistance in the form of CBRN CM.

## CBRN Incidents

A CBRN incident is any occurrence resulting from the use of CBRN weapons or devices, or the release of CBRN hazards, to include toxic industrial materials (TIMs) from any source. This may include the emergence of CBRN hazards arising from counterforce targeting during military operations. Domestically, an incident may result in the President declaring an emergency or a major disaster. For CBRN incidents occurring on foreign soil, either an HN or intergovernmental organization (IGO) could request a USG response, or if it is likely to create a deleterious domestic effect, such as the spread of infectious disease or radioactivity across borders into the US, that may require the President to declare an emergency under the National Emergencies Act. Outside of certain response requirements discussed in DOD issuances, an order from the President/Secretary of Defense (SecDef) is typically required for DOD CBRN response.

## CBRN CM

CBRN CM considers the capabilities and limitations of the affected civil authorities, from the local first responders, up through the state response, to the federal (national) level. When the civil authorities up to and including the federal level lack necessary capabilities to mitigate the situation, or they anticipate being overwhelmed, military support typically is requested. For all domestic incidents (including a CBRN incident), the National Response Framework (NRF) and the National Disaster Recovery Framework provide national guidance for incident management and acknowledges the DOD as a full partner in the federal response when tasked. DOD and Chairman of the Joint Chiefs of Staff (CJCS) issuances frame US military support of a USG response for foreign and domestic CBRN incidents.

## CBRN Response

DOD installation commanders develop CBRN responses for the installation as part of their installation emergency action plan in accordance with (IAW) Department of Defense Instruction (DODI) 2000.18, Department of Defense Installation Chemical, Biological, Radiological, Nuclear, and High-Yield Explosive Emergency Response Guidelines, and DODI 6055.17, DOD Installation Emergency Management (IEM) Program.

*"CBRN response" is captured in the NRF and in Presidential Policy Directive (PPD)-8, National Preparedness. Domestically, DOD conducts CBRN response in support of the broader USG activities to prepare for, respond to, and provide a foundation to recover from CBRN effects as a result of natural or man-made disasters. The term FCM still applies to foreign support through DOS to an HN and is a valid term when used accordingly.*

# I. All Hazards Response

Ref: JP 3-28, Defense Support of Civil Authorities (Jul '14), chap. 2.

## I. The Nature of a Catastrophic Incident

A catastrophic incident, as defined by the NRF, is "any natural or man-made incident, including terrorism, that results in extraordinary levels of mass casualties, damage, or disruption severely affecting the population, infrastructure, environment, economy, national morale, and/or government functions." Catastrophic incident is the same as catastrophic event as defined by DOD. A catastrophic event could result in significant nationwide impacts over a prolonged period of time. It almost immediately exceeds resources normally available to state, territory, tribal, local, and private-sector authorities in the impacted area, and it significantly interrupts governmental operations and emergency services to such an extent that national security could be threatened.

---

**Complex Catastrophe**

*Any natural or man-made incident, including cyberspace attack, power grid failure, and terrorism, which results in cascading failures of multiple, interdependent, critical, life-sustaining infrastructure sectors and causes extraordinary levels of mass casualties, damage or disruption severely affecting the population, environment, economy, public health, national morale, response efforts, and/or government functions.*

*Deputy Secretary of Defense Memorandum, 19 February 2013*

---

The catastrophic event becomes complex (complex catastrophe) when it causes cascading failures of multiple, interdependent, critical life-sustaining infrastructure, in which disruption of one infrastructure component (such as the electric power grid) disrupts other infrastructure components (such as transportation and communications).

Recognizing that federal or national resources are required to augment overwhelmed state, interstate, territory, tribal, and local response efforts, the NRF—Catastrophic Incident Annex establishes protocols to pre-identify and rapidly deploy key essential resources (e.g., medical teams, search and rescue [SAR] teams, transportable shelters, medical and equipment caches, and emergency communications) required to save lives and contain incidents.

When a situation is beyond the capability of an affected state or territory, the governor may request federal assistance from the President. The President may also proactively direct the federal government to provide supplemental assistance to state, territorial, tribal, and local governments to alleviate the suffering and damage resulting from disasters or emergencies.

---

*Refer to The Homeland Defense & DSCA SMARTbook (Protecting the Homeland / Defense Support to Civil Authority) for further discussion. Topics and references include homeland defense (JP 3-28), defense support of civil authorities (JP 3-28), Army support of civil authorities (ADRP 3-28), multi-service DSCA TTPs (ATP 3-28.1/MCWP 3-36.2), DSCA liaison officer toolkit (GTA 90-01-020), key legal and policy documents, and specific hazard and planning guidance.*

# II. National Incident Management System (NIMS) & the National Response Framework (NRF)

The NRF and NIMS are two parts of a combined effort with the NRF providing the framework for the goals of response and NIMS providing the active development of systems to meet these goals within standardized response efforts. The goals and the systems are interlocked and one program is not "over" the other.

The National Response Framework (NRF) is a guide to how the Nation conducts all-hazards response. It builds upon the NIMS coordinating structures to align key roles and responsibilities across the Nation, linking all levels of government, nongovernmental organizations, and the private sector.

The National Incident Management System (NIMS) provides the incident management basis for the National Response Framework (NRF) and defines standard command and management structures. Standardizing national response doctrine on NIMS provides a consistent, nationwide template to enable the whole community to work together to prevent, protect against, mitigate, respond to, and recover from the effects of incidents regardless of cause, size, location, or complexity.

| National Directives | HSPD-7 HSPD-8 |
|---|---|

The NRF and NIMS are the bridge from national strategy to operational response where the priorities of life safety, stabilization, & preservation are the focus of the coordination.

| National Response Framework (NRF) | National Incident Management System (NIMS) |
|---|---|
| **Guidance and Goals** | **Methods & Best Practices** |
| ❑ Prevention | ❑ Preparedness |
| ❑ Protection | ❑ Communications and |
| ❑ Mitigation | Information Management |
| ❑ Response | ❑ Resource Management |
| ❑ Recovery | ❑ Command and Management |
| | ❑ Ongoing Management and Maintenance |

National Directives, Laws, and Presidential Orders provide the strategic goals of national response and frame concepts like preservation of our way of government and what essential services and functions the government must perform in order to provide the people with the requirements of governance: security, essential services, Rule of Law, and economic opportunity. These things are provided by government in order to maintain an environment of stability within the social construct the nation. These goals are strategic. Response to disaster is a subset of this greater design for stability.

The function of the NRF and NIMS is to take those strategic concepts and convert them from strategic national goals to a standardized system of operational response methodologies that can be used at the state and local level. This is still a wide scope and the methods described are general application and can be used in most situations. This is call an All Hazards approach.

The significant aspect of the All Hazards approach is that it is the first level of coordination where the priorities of life saving, stabilization of the incident, and preservation of property, infrastructure and the environment are the major focus. Plans above this level are focused on protecting resources, infrastructure, and government function as well as providing authority, resources, and essential support functions.

The National Response Framework outlines the first set of broad goals for response by identifying goals for preparation and response before, during, and after an incident.

- **Prevention**: The capabilities necessary to prevent imminent threats.

- **Protection**: The capabilities necessary to secure the homeland against any incident.

- **Mitigation**: The capabilities necessary to lessen the impact of disasters.

- **Response**: The capabilities necessary to protect and provide after an incident has occurred.

- **Recovery**: The capabilities necessary to assist communities to recover effectively.

NIMS represents a core set of doctrines, concepts, principles, terminology, and organizational processes that enables effective, efficient, and collaborative incident management to meet the requirements as listed in the NRF. By building on the foundation provided by existing emergency management and incident response systems used by jurisdictions, organizations, and functional disciplines at all levels, NIMS integrates best practices into a comprehensive framework. These best practices lay the groundwork for the components of NIMS and provide the mechanisms for the further development and refinement of supporting national standards, guidelines, protocols, systems, and technologies.

Understand that NIMS is not an operational incident management or resource allocation plan, but rather the methods that will be used in incident management. These are still very general areas but the specifics found within these concepts provide the detail required to make the system work in All Hazards and responses. They are:

- **Preparedness**: Preparedness involves an integrated combination of planning, procedures and protocols, training and exercises, personnel qualifications and certification, and equipment certification.

- **Communications and Information Management**: NIMS promotes the concepts of interoperability, reliability, scalability, portability, and the resiliency and redundancy of communications and information systems.

- **Resource Management**: Resources such as personnel, equipment, and/or supplies.

- **Command and Management**: Provides methods and standards for state and local response via the Incident Command System, Multiagency Coordination Systems, and Public Information.

- **Ongoing Management and Maintenance**: Preservation of capacity via two components: the National Integration Center (NIC) and Supporting Technologies.

Together the NRF and NIMS provide the basic structure of standardized goals and methods in order to develop and maintain a response capacity that is flexible and responsive to the needs of the nation and its people by promoting these capabilities at the regional, state, tribal, and local level.

*Refer to Disaster-Response SMARTbook 1 - National Incident Management System (NIMS and National Preparedness) for further discussion of NIMS and the National Response Framework. Topics include national-level plans, elements of national authority, national response framework (NRF), national incident management system (NIMS), national- and regional-level resource management, the role of FEMA/regional-to-state connections, and training requirements.*

# III. Incident Command System (ICS)

The Incident Command System (ICS) is a sub-component of NIMS and provides specific instruction as to the methods of incident response at the regional, state, tribal, and local level. The importance of ICS is that it provides for consistency of method and coordination of effort so that all responders are using the same standardized terminology, interoperable technologies, organizational structure, and management techniques. This allows any responder to have a common understanding and expectation of how agencies and departments will organize when working together to response to an incident. This commonality of knowledge, structure, and function provides a level of functionality that can expand and interact as the needs of the situation demand.

The need for, and development of, a standardized method of incident response was based upon the lessons learned following a series of catastrophic fires in California in the 1970s. Property damage ran into the millions, and many people died or were injured. The personnel assigned to determine the causes of these disasters studied the available records and discovered that response problems could rarely be attributed to lack of resources or failure of tactics. The failures that caused death and destruction was specifically found in the lack of effective communication and the lack of coordination of effort.

The development and application of ICS enabled responders to avoid these weaknesses in all types of incident responses. ICS was so effective it's now required by law. The use of ICS is mandated by the National Incident Management System (NIMS).

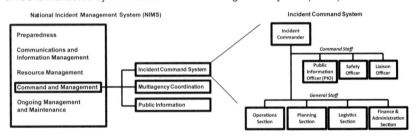

The Incident Command system is not a "stand alone" program. It is coordinated with other national initiatives designed to provide for the safety and security of everyone within its jurisdictions. Examples of other interlocking laws that are integrated into ICS are National Incident Management System (NIMS), Superfund Amendments and Reauthorization Act (SARA) – 1986, Occupational Safety and Health Administration (OSHA) Rule 1910.120, and State and local regulations.

ICS can be used to manage multiple simultaneous situations that require coordination of effort. Understand that ICS is not just about disasters. ICS can provide coordination of effort for any situation that requires agencies and departments to work together towards a common goal. These can include natural hazards, technological hazards, human-caused hazards, and planned events. This means ICS can be practiced every day. By using ICS principles in coordination of planning for events and activities an agency can become very proficient at ICS before ever having to use it in response to a disaster.

## ICS Benefits

These "best practices" provide some very important advantages. ICS allows for the efficient use of resources which leads to the achievement of response objectives in the shortest time frame and at the lowest cost (in both lives and resources). These efficiencies help to ensure the safety of everyone in the incident area of effect. This has two major impacts; first, it provides the greatest opportunity for minimizing the loss of life, property, and infrastructure. And second, it minimizes the loss or injury of responding personnel, equipment, and materials thus preserving operational capacity.

Consequence Management

# ICS Essential Functions

ICS is made up of two kinds of tools; essential functions which make up the working parts of the system and management principles which express uniform methodology for how those functions are to be use. These are expressed in the essential functions list of ICS Features. They are called essential because they are common to every ICS response and are a basic requirement for successful ICS implementation. A short introduction is provided here but a review of the detailed components of ICS in Book 2 of this series provide an in depth explanation of these functions and principles. The essential functions are listed here. The management principles are found as components within the essential functions.

## Standardization
This includes the use of common terminology for clear communications as well as standards for training, accreditation, and certification of skills.

## Command
This provides a method to establish a clear Chain of Command.

## Planning/Organization Structure
These methods provides for the standardization of methods for establishing objectives, making an Incident Action Plan (IAP), developing flexibility with modular organization, and promoting manageable command and control as well as span of control.

## Facilities and Resources
This standardized the naming and purposes of incident locations and facilities as well as designating a comprehensive resource management program to ensure resources, materials, and equipment are available during and incident response.

## Communication/Information Management
This established the development of integrated communications and interoperable technologies. It also addressed methods of information and intelligence management in the scene of managing situational awareness.

## Professionalism
This standardized the expectations for, and methods of, accountability at all levels; command, fiscal, and logistics. The standardization of dispatch and deployment ensures more accurate accountability of personnel and equipment.

ICS provides the operational and tactical aspects of incident response. Military personnel will recognize much within the system but should not assume it operates the same as military ground operations. There are significant differences that should be understood before civil-military operations are conducted.

*Refer to Disaster Response SMARTbook 2 – Incident Command System (ICS) (On-Scene, All-Hazards Incident Management) for further discussion. Topics include incident command system (ICS) purpose, features, and principles; command and staff functions; leadership and management; unified command, area command, and multiagency coordination; planning; ICS briefings and meetings; organizational flexibility; incident/ event management; resource management; and demobilization.*

Consequence Management

# IV. Department of Defense Immediate Response and Emergency Authority

## A. Immediate Response Authority (IRA)

Under DODD 3025.18, Defense Support of Civil Authorities (DSCA), federal military commanders, heads of DOD components, and responsible DOD civilian officials have immediate response authority. In response to an RFA from a civil authority, under imminently serious conditions and if time does not permit approval from higher authority, DOD officials may provide an immediate response by temporarily employing the resources under their control, subject to any supplemental direction provided by higher headquarters, to save lives, prevent human suffering, or mitigate great property damage within the US. Immediate response authority is not an exception to the PCA, nor does it permit actions that would subject civilians to the use of military power that is regulatory, prescriptive, proscriptive, or compulsory.

IAW DODD 3025.18, Defense Support of Civil Authorities (DSCA), a DOD official directing immediate response authority shall notify, through the chain of command, the National Joint Operations and Intelligence Center (NJOIC) as soon as practical. The NJOIC will inform United States Northern Command (USNORTHCOM) and/or United States Pacific Command (USPACOM) and the appropriate DOD components.

Immediate response ends when DOD assistance is no longer required (e.g., when there are sufficient resources and capabilities available from state, local, and other federal agencies to respond adequately) or when a DOD authority directs an end to the response. The DOD official directing a response under immediate response authority makes an assessment, no later than 72 hours after receipt of request for DOD assistance, as to whether there remains a need for the continued DOD support.

Support provided under immediate response authority should be provided on an incremental, cost-reimbursable basis, where appropriate or legally required, but will not be delayed or denied based on the inability or unwillingness of the requester to make a commitment to reimburse DOD.

State officials have the authority to direct state-level or local-level immediate response authority using NG personnel serving in state active duty or Title 32, USC, status if this is IAW the laws of that state. As not all state officials have immediate response authority, there may be delays in obtaining approval from the governor.

The distance from the incident to the DOD office or installation is not a limiting factor for the provision of support under immediate response authority. However, DOD officials should use the distance and the travel time to provide support as a factor in determining DOD's ability to support the request for immediate response.

The scale of the event should also be a determining factor for whether or not to provide support to incidents that are several miles or hundreds of miles away from the installation under immediate response authority. In some cases of a catastrophic incident, the demands for life-saving and life-sustaining capabilities may exceed both the state's and USG's ability to mobilize sufficient resources to meet the demand. In these circumstances, installations and facilities that are not directly impacted should be prepared to provide immediate response support if they are able to save lives, prevent human suffering, or prevent great property damage..

## B. Emergency Authority

In extraordinary emergency circumstances, where authorization by the President is impossible and duly constituted local authorities are unable to control the situation, involved federal military commanders are granted "emergency authority." Emergency authority enables the involved military commander to engage in temporary actions to quell large-scale, unexpected civil disturbances to prevent significant loss of life or wanton destruction of property and to restore governmental function and public order. When duly constituted federal, state, territorial, or local authorities are unable or decline to provide adequate protection for federal property or federal governmental functions, federal action, including the use of federal military forces, is authorized when necessary to protect the federal property or functions. Responsible DOD officials and commanders will use all available means to seek presidential authorization through the chain of command while applying their emergency authority.

*Refer to DODI 3025.21, Defense Support of Civilian Law Enforcement Agencies, and DODD 3025.18, Defense Support of Civil Authorities (DSCA), for more information on emergency authority.*

# V. Interorganizational (IGO) Coordination

When the overall coordination of federal response activities is required, it is implemented through the Secretary of Homeland Security consistent with HSPD-5, Management of Domestic Incidents. Other federal departments and agencies carry out their response authorities and responsibilities within this overarching construct. Nothing in the NRF alters or impedes the ability of federal, state, territory, tribal, or local departments and agencies to carry out their specific authorities or perform their responsibilities under all applicable laws, EOs, and directives. Additionally, nothing in the NRF is intended to impact or impede the ability of any federal department or agency to take an issue of concern directly to the President or any member of the President's staff.

## Planning Considerations for IGO Coordination

DOD works closely with other federal agencies, in particular DHS and its subordinate organizations, when planning for DSCA. DSCA plans shall be compatible with the NRF, NIMS, and DOD issuances. DSCA planning should consider C2 options that emphasize unity of effort. DOD organizations and agencies provide numerous LNOs to DHS and DHS components. DOD LNOs may represent organizations and specialties such as the Office of the Secretary of Defense (OSD), combatant commands (CCMDs), intelligence organizations, or engineers.

Commander, United States Northern Command (CDRUSNORTHCOM) and Commander, United States Pacific Command (CDRUSPACOM), the supported geographic combatant commanders (GCCs), are DOD's principal planning agents for DSCA, and have the responsibility to provide joint planning and execution directives for peacetime assistance rendered by DOD within their assigned areas of responsibility (AOR). In addition to participating in interagency steering groups and councils, DOD has responsibilities under the NRF.

To ensure DOD planning supports the needs of those requiring DSCA, DOD coordinates with interagency partners through the Chief, National Guard Bureau (CNGB) to states/territories on all matters pertaining to the NG. Coordination will align with the NRF, NIMS, and interagency coordination guidelines provided in the Guidance for Employment of the Force (GEF).

The domestic operating environment for DSCA presents unique challenges to the joint force commander (JFC). It is imperative that commanders and staffs at all levels understand the relationships, both statutory and operational, among all USG departments and agencies involved in the operation. Moreover, it is equally important to understand DOD's role in supporting other USG departments and agencies. DOD provides assistance to the primary agency upon request by the appropriate authority and approval by the President or SecDef. There are also specific USNORTHCOM and USPACOM domestic plans (e.g., DSCA, civil disturbance operations) where the responsibilities of various USG entities are described in detail.

Consequence Management

# VI. Emergency Support Functions (ESFs)

Following a catastrophic event, segments of state, tribal, and local governments as well as NGOs and the private sector may be severely compromised. The federal government should be prepared to fill potential gaps to ensure continuity of government and public- and private-sector operations. The incident may cause significant disruption of the impacted area's critical infrastructure/key resources, such as energy, transportation, telecommunications, law enforcement, and public health and health care systems.

The USG and many state governments organize much of their resources and capabilities as well as those of certain private-sector and NGOs under 15 emergency support functions (ESFs). ESFs align categories of resources and provide strategic objectives for their use. ESFs utilize standardized resource management concepts such as typing, inventorying, and tracking to facilitate the dispatch, deployment, and recovery of resources before, during, and after an incident. ESF coordinators and primary agencies are identified on the basis of authorities and resources. Support agencies are assigned based on the availability of resources in a given functional area. ESFs provide the greatest possible access to USG department and agency resources regardless of which organization has those resources.

*See facing page for an overview of ESFs.*

# VII. Unity of Effort

The diplomatic, informational, military, and economic power of the US are applied in unified action to attain desired end states.

## Responsibilities

Incidents are managed at the lowest level possible. Federal support is provided in response to requests from state or local officials through the state coordinating officer to the federal coordinating officer (FCO). The FCO coordinates for DOD support through the defense coordinating officer (DCO) in the JFO. DOD may provide support to the LFA, which has the lead in managing the federal response to a domestic incident. DHS is responsible for domestic incident management and the framework for federal interaction with state, local, and tribal governments; the private sector; and NGOs in the context of incident preparedness, response, and recovery activities. DOD support to this response will be initiated through a formal RFA or mission assignment process, or provided as directed by the President or SecDef.

## Domestic Incident Management

HSPD-5, Management of Domestic Incidents, states that to prevent, prepare for, respond to, and recover from terrorist attacks, major disasters, and other emergencies, the USG shall establish a single, comprehensive approach to domestic incident management. The objective of the USG is to ensure that all levels of government across the nation have the capability to work efficiently and effectively together, using a national approach to domestic incident management. In these efforts, with regard to domestic incidents, the USG treats crisis management (CrM) and consequence management as a single, integrated function, rather than as two separate functions. DOD categorizes such support domestically as DSCA. Within DOD, there is also the use of the term "crisis management" and the use of other terminology that may be specific to the actual type of operation, such as chemical, biological, radiological, and nuclear (CBRN) consequence management (CBRN CM).

Non-DOD actors, including local civil authorities and first responders, are frequently not familiar with US military terms, definitions, and doctrine. When working with non-DOD actors/partners, especially in an emergency situation, clear, effective, and mutually understandable communication is essential. DOD elements will be able to work much more seamlessly, efficiently, and productively by employing operational

# Emergency Support Functions (ESFs)

*Ref: ATP 3-28.1, Multi-Service TTP for DSCA (Feb '13), table 1, pp. 4-5 .*

## Emergency Support Functions (ESFs)

| ESFs | Coordinator |
|------|-------------|
| #1 Transportation | Department of Transportation |
| #2 Communications | Department of Homeland Security (DHS) – National Communications System |
| #3 Public Works and Engineering | Department of Defense (DOD) – US Army Corps of Engineers |
| #4 Firefighting | United States Department of Agriculture (USDA ) – US Forest Service |
| #5 Emergency Management | DHS – Federal Emergency Management Agency(FEMA) |
| #6. Mass Care, Emergency Assistance, Housing, and Human Services | DHS – FEMA |
| #7 Logistics Management and Resource Support | General Services Administration and DHS – FEMA |
| #8 Public Health and Medical Services | Department of Health and Human Services |
| #9 Search and Rescue | DHS – FEMA |
| #10 Oil and Hazardous Materials Response | Environmental Protection Agency |
| #11 Agriculture and Natural Resources | USDA |
| #12 Energy | Department of Energy |
| #13 Public Safety and Security | Department of Justice |
| #14 Long-Term Community Recovery | DHS – FEMA |
| #15 External Affairs | DHS |

*Note: DOD is a supporting agency for all ESFs except ESF #3, Public Works and Engineering. Although the Army Corps of Engineers is the Coordinator for #3, it does so based upon its congressionally mandated status and not as a subordinate part of a federal military joint task force.*

Refer to Disaster-Response SMARTbook 2 – Incident Command System (ICS) (On-Scene, All-Hazards Incident Management) for further discussion. Topics include incident command system (ICS) purpose, features, and principles; command and staff functions; leadership and management; unified command, area command, and multiagency coordination; planning; ICS briefings and meetings; organizational flexibility; incident/event management; resource management; and demobilization.

Consequence Management

concepts and terms that other departments, agencies, and authorities already under-stand. The main sources of these concepts and language include the NRF and NIMS.

CrM is predominantly a law-enforcement response, normally executed under federal law.

(The NRF defines incident management as how incidents are managed across all homeland security activities, including prevention, protection, and response and re-covery. This is consistent with the DOD view that incident management is a national comprehensive approach to preventing, preparing for, responding to, and recovering from terrorist attacks, major disasters, and other emergencies. The NRF further de-fines emergency management as a subset of incident management, the coordination and integration of all activities necessary to build, sustain, and improve the capability to prepare for, protect against, respond to, recover from, or mitigate against threat-ened or actual natural disasters, acts of terrorism, or other man-made disasters.

Historically, much of DOD's DSCA mission set has involved operations responding to the consequences of natural or man-made incidents. This is due to legal restrictions that preclude DOD from participating in certain CrM law enforcement investigations and operations. Responses to Hurricanes Ike and Katrina included a joint task force (JTF) for DOD DSCA operations in support of another agency.

# VIII. Department of Defense and Emergencies in the Homeland

DSCA is initiated by a request for DOD assistance from civil authorities or qualifying entities or is authorized by the President or SecDef.

Title 32, USC, Section 101(a)(13)(B), 12304a states DSC-led JTFs are the usual and customary C2 arrangement established in response to an emergency or major disaster within the US when both federal and state military forces are supporting the response.

Requests for DSCA should be written and include a commitment to reimburse DOD IAW Title 42, USC, Section 5121 (also known as The Stafford Act), Title 31, USC, Section b. Title 32, USC, Section 101(a)(13)(B), 12304a states DSC-led JTFs are the usual and customary C2 arrangement established in response to an emergency or major disaster within the US when both federal and state military forces are sup-porting the response.

Requests for DSCA should be written and include a commitment to reimburse DOD IAW Title 42, USC, Section 5121 (also known as The Stafford Act), Title 31, USC, Section 1535 (also known as The Economy Act), or other authorities except requests for support for immediate response, and mutual or automatic aid, IAW DODD 3025.18, Defense Support of Civil Authorities (DSCA). Unless approval authority is otherwise delegated by SecDef, all DSCA requests shall be submitted to the office of the Executive Secretary of DOD.

Civil authorities shall be informed that verbal requests for DOD assistance during emergency circumstances must be followed by a formal written RFA, which includes intent to reimburse DOD, at the earliest opportunity. DSCA may be provided on a nonreimbursable basis when required by law or when otherwise approved by SecDef.

Per DODD 3025.18, Defense Support of Civil Authorities (DSCA), civil authority requests for DOD assistance are evaluated for:

- Legality (compliance with laws)
- Lethality (potential use of lethal force by or against DOD forces)
- Risk (safety of DOD forces)
- Cost (including the source of funding and the effect on the DOD budget)
- Appropriateness (whether providing the requested support is in the interest and within the capability of DOD)

• Readiness (impact on DOD's ability to perform its primary mission)

DSCA plans will be compatible with the NRF, NIMS, and DOD issuances. DSCA planning will consider C2 options that emphasize unity of effort.

With limited exceptions (e.g., local requests for immediate and emergency response), initial RFAs will be directed to the OSD, Executive Secretariat. SecDef-approved RFAs are assigned to the appropriate CCDR. The supported CCDR determines the appropriate level of C2 for each response and usually directs a senior military officer to deploy to the incident site. However, in the USPACOM AOR, CDRUSPACOM has delegated this responsibility to Commander, Joint Task Force (CJTF)-Homeland Defense. The DCO serves as DOD's single point of contact in the JFO. Requests will be coordinated and processed through the DCO with the exception of requests for United States Army Corps of Engineers (USACE) support, NG forces operating in state active duty or Title 32, USC, status (i.e., not in federal service), or, in some circumstances, DOD forces in support of the Federal Bureau of Investigation (FBI) or the United States Secret Service (USSS).

*Refer to The Homeland Defense & DSCA SMARTbook (Protecting the Homeland / Defense Support to Civil Authority) for further discussion. Topics and references include homeland defense (JP 3-28), defense support of civil authorities (JP 3-28), Army support of civil authorities (ADRP 3-28), multi-service DSCA TTPs (ATP 3-28.1/MCWP 3-36.2), DSCA liaison officer toolkit (GTA 90-01-020), key legal and policy documents, and specific hazard and planning guidance.*

# IX. Phases of Disaster Response

(ADRP 3-28) Commanders conducting DSCA planning should be familiar with the phases of disaster response operations, as used in the NRF and in USNORTHCOM plans for DSCA. USNORTHCOM planners use six operational phases, which are similar to the flexible phasing model described in JP 3-0 but somewhat modified for DSCA: shape, anticipate, respond, operate, stabilize, and transition. The NRF uses three phases: prepare, respond, and recover. The figure below illustrates the relationship between the NRF phases and the USNORTHCOM phases.

*Army doctrine does not specify operational phases. Refer to ADRP 3-0, chapter 2.*

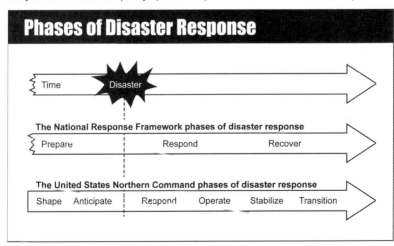

*Ref: ADRP 3-28 DSCA, fig. 1-10, p. 1-29.*

*See following page for further discussion of the five operational phases.*

# Operation Phases of Defense Support of Civil Authorities

Ref: JP 3-28, Defense Support of Civil Authorities (Jul '14), p. II-15 to II-16.

DSCA operations are generally conducted in six phases: shape, anticipate, respond, operate, stabilize, and transition. During planning, the JFC establishes conditions, objectives, or events for transitioning from one phase to another. Phases are designed to be conducted sequentially, but some activities from a phase may begin in a previous phase and continue into subsequent phases. A DSCA operation may be conducted in multiple phases simultaneously if the JOA has widely varying conditions.

## Phase 0 (Shape)

Phase 0 is continuous situational awareness and preparedness. Actions in this phase include interagency coordination, planning, identification of gaps, exercises, and public affairs (PA) outreach. These activities continue through all phases. Shaping operations are inclusive of normal and routine military activities and various interagency activities to assure or solidify relationships with partners, friends, and allies. This phase sets the conditions for expanded interoperability and cooperation with interagency partners via active engagements in planning, conferences, training programs and exercises, and coordination and interaction.

## Phase I (Anticipate)

Phase I begins with the identification of a potential DSCA mission, a no-notice event, or when directed by the President or SecDef. The phase ends with assigned response forces deployed or when the determination is made that there is no event requiring DSCA response. Phase I success is achieved when deployment of a DCO, EPLO, and other selected response forces is accomplished. These forces are postured to facilitate quick response after coordination with the primary agency PFO/JFO and coordination with state, local, and tribal officials.

## Phase II (Respond)

Phase II begins with the deployment of initial response capabilities. The phase ends when response forces are ready to conduct operations in the JOA. Phase II success is achieved when forces are deployed with sufficient capability to support civil authorities in accomplishment of the mission. DSCA operations are based on RFAs, which will be made at different times, and for missions that will be completed at different times. Consequently, forces will likely deploy into and out of the JOA during the entire DSCA operation.

## Phase III (Operate)

Phase III begins when DSCA response operations commence. Phase III ends when Title 10, USC, forces begin to complete mission assignments and no further requests for DOD assistance are anticipated from civil authorities. Phase III success is achieved when currently deployed DOD capabilities are sufficient to support civil authorities.

## Phase IV (Stabilize)

Phase IV begins when military and civil authorities decide that DOD support will scale down. Phase IV ends when DOD support is no longer required by civil authorities and transition criteria are established. Phase IV success is achieved when all operational aspects of mission assignments are complete.

## Phase V (Transition)

Phase V begins with the redeployment of remaining DOD forces. The phase ends when response forces have been relieved, redeployed, and OPCON is transferred to their respective commands. Phase V success is achieved when DOD forces have transitioned all operations back to civil authorities.

# II. DoD Perspective of CBRN CM

*Ref: JP 3-41, Chemical, Biological, Radiological, and Nuclear Consequence Management (Jun '12), chap. 1 and ATP 3-11.41, Multi-Service TTPs for CBRN Consequence Management Operations (Jul '15).*

Incidents involving CBRN material produce a chaotic and hazardous environment requiring immediate response to minimize pain and suffering, reduce casualties, and restore essential infrastructure. Responders at the local, state, and federal levels may be overwhelmed by the magnitude of the incident, and U.S. DOD forces may be requested to provide additional support through the NRF.

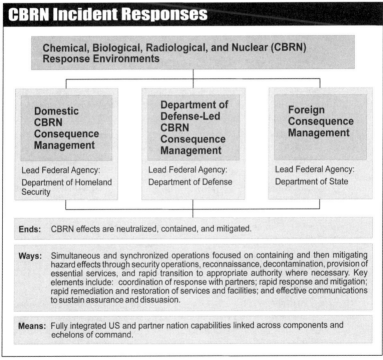

## CBRN Incident Responses

**Chemical, Biological, Radiological, and Nuclear (CBRN) Response Environments**

| Domestic CBRN Consequence Management | Department of Defense-Led CBRN Consequence Management | Foreign Consequence Management |
|---|---|---|
| Lead Federal Agency: Department of Homeland Security | Lead Federal Agency: Department of Defense | Lead Federal Agency: Department of State |

**Ends:** CBRN effects are neutralized, contained, and mitigated.

**Ways:** Simultaneous and synchronized operations focused on containing and then mitigating hazard effects through security operations, reconnaissance, decontamination, provision of essential services, and rapid transition to appropriate authority where necessary. Key elements include: coordination of response with partners; rapid response and mitigation; rapid remediation and restoration of services and facilities; and effective communications to sustain assurance and dissuasion.

**Means:** Fully integrated US and partner nation capabilities linked across components and echelons of command.

*Ref. JP 3-41, CBRN Consequence Management, fig. I-1, p. I-3.*

The strategic national direction leads to the characterization of CBRN CM as DOD support of the overarching USG response to a CBRN incident at home or abroad. As such, a CBRN incident may be managed at the national level (USG or HN government), with DOD providing support as directed. During military operations, the USG would typically have DOD lead the response. Examples of CBRN incidents related to military operations include those that result from the execution of US military operations (e.g., offensive operations against WMD facilities); and a CBRN attack or inadvertent release affecting civilians in areas in which the US military is responsible for civilian security, safety, public health, etc., as determined by the President.

Ideally, each CBRN response may include a whole-of-government approach as required by the President or lawful directives. While NRF incident management includes operations to "prevent, protect, prepare, respond, and recover" from an incident, and FCM includes operations to "prepare US forces to provide requested assistance," CBRN CM addresses only the common areas of "prepare" and "respond" within the USG overarching response to reduce the effects of a CBRN incident.

## Domestic, Foreign, and Military Situations

CBRN CM operations occur in foreign and domestic settings. DOD must be prepared to conduct CBRN CM operations when called on.

An operational environment is a composite of the conditions, circumstances, and influences that affect the employment of capabilities and bear on the decisions of the commander. DOD conducts CM operations in three types of operational environments:

- **DSCA during a domestic response**. This response includes assisting federal agencies within the United States, territories, and possessions according to guidance in the NRF. DOD supports operations within its capabilities through liaison with the incident commander (IC).

- **DOD-led operations.** DOD leads the operational response for an incident involving U.S. forces and allies across the range of military operations. This also includes responding on a DOD-installation.

- **Defense support to a foreign request.** DOD supports the Department of State (DOS) with operations originating from a foreign request. Tasks originate from the HN through the DOS. However, DOD commanders may take appropriate action in life-threatening situations while awaiting DOD or DOS tasking.

DOD forces tasked to support civil authorities during domestic CM and FCM operations will use the level of protection as determined by the IC. However, in a DOD-led CM response, the senior DOD official will make risk-based decisions, to include decisions on the level of protection.

A domestic CM response will normally be led by the DHS, and the DOS will normally lead a foreign response. In the first two environments, DOD will normally operate in support of the DHS or the DOS. However, DOD will likely have full control in the third operational environment. In each of the three response elements, DOD retains C2 of all DOD assets.

# I. Chemical, Biological, Radiological, and Nuclear Response

Domestic CBRN CM is the USG effort to prepare for and respond to a CBRN incident within the US and its territories IAW the NRF. Domestic CBRN response (with DOD and/or National Guard [NG] in Title 10 or Title 32, United States Code (USC), status or state active duty) is a form of civil support (CS)/defense support of civil authorities (DSCA) (with DHS as the lead for coordinating the USG response). Domestic CBRN response leverages the total force capabilities of the Active Component (AC) and Reserve Component (RC) (NG, and reserves) in the homeland. The DOD CBRN Response Enterprise is an integrated AC and RC approach to CBRN response. As such, different elements of the DOD CBRN Response Enterprise may be in direct support of different entities at any given time. For example, NG forces may be under the command and control (C2) of a state governor while Title 10, USC, forces are under the C2 of Commander, United States Northern Command (CDRUSNORTHCOM) in support of the lead federal agency (LFA).

FCM encompasses the overall USG effort to prepare for and respond to a CBRN incident on foreign territory in which an impacted nation has primary responsibility, and DOS is the lead USG agency responsible for coordinating the USG response.

# II. CBRN CM Goals

Ref: ATP 3-11.41, Multi-Service TTPs for CBRN Consequence Management Operations (Jul '15), pp. 1-3 to 1-4.

Incidents involving CBRN material produce a chaotic and hazardous environment requiring immediate response to minimize pain and suffering, reduce casualties, and restore essential infrastructure. Responders at the local, state, and federal levels may be overwhelmed by the magnitude of the incident, and U.S. DOD forces may be requested to provide additional support through the NRF.

The primary goals of CBRN CM are to save lives; prevent injury; provide temporary critical life support; protect critical property, infrastructure, and the environment; restore essential operations; contain the event; and preserve national security.

The CBRN defense principles of contamination avoidance, protection, and decontamination support these same goals. For example—

## Saving Lives
Saving lives is the greatest priority during CM operations. This includes immediate life saving measures given by first responders, life-sustaining techniques (emergency decontamination, MCD), and prophylaxis to ensure long-term casualty care, treatment, and safety.

## Preventing Injury
Protection-related measures help prevent or mitigate exposure to hazards that cause injury or illness. These measures include setting up a security perimeter and establishing hazard control zones.

## Providing Temporary Critical Life Support
Response-related measures are conducted to assist civil authorities in the provision of medical services to injured personnel.

## Protecting Critical Property, Infrastructure, and the Environment
The protection of critical property, infrastructure, and the environment occurs through the rapid application of decontamination efforts, early warning, reporting of incidents, and protection of key personnel. Command decisions to shelter in place or evacuate also support the protection of resources.

## Restoring Essential Operations
Following a CBRN event, a likely consequence is the loss of one or more essential services or operations. The rapid restoration of power, water, communication nodes, and transportation routes accompanied by decontamination efforts are vital to continuing critical command missions.

## Containing the Event
Controlling access to an incident site and conducting proper decontamination procedures limit the spread of contamination. Establishing hazard control zones(cold, warm, and hot) helps to ensure safe work areas for emergency responders and supporting resources.

## Preserving National Security
CBRN defense principles contribute to the preservation of national security by protecting critical infrastructure

Consequence Management

DOD provides support as requested by the impacted nation, coordinated through DOS, and approved by SecDef. The USG may provide FCM to an affected nation either at the request of the affected nation or upon affected nation acceptance of a USG offer of assistance.

Domestic and FCM responses formally begin when support is requested by either domestic or foreign civilian authorities, and continues until either those civilian authorities have determined that DOD support is no longer required or otherwise directed by SecDef. The final phase of USG operations will almost always be addressed and coordinated by civilian authorities in both the domestic and foreign situations. This final recovery phase may or may not require continued DOD assistance, depending upon the hazard and the circumstances.

In DOD-led CBRN CM, DOD serves as the lead USG agency, although it may be supported by other organizations. DOD-led CBRN CM would typically occur during military operations (e.g., WMD offensive operations), or in other situations in which DOS lacks sufficient local authority or presence to lead the USG effort.

# A. The Joint Force in CBRN Response

Due to the potentially catastrophic nature of a CBRN incident, a DOD joint force may be called upon to assist with a civilian CBRN incident prior to civilian resources being overwhelmed or depleted. A joint task force (JTF) may be established, or an existing one tasked, to provide or facilitate the provision of a variety of response capabilities to mitigate the incident. Even prior to being formally tasked to assist, the joint force commander (JFC) should strive to develop full situational awareness with respect to the incident's cause to better understand the impact and to prevent further injury or harm to the civilian populace or the responding joint force. Situational awareness is especially important in suspected or known adversary attacks for force protection considerations.

SecDef designated supported JFC is ultimately responsible for the DOD CBRN response and its role in providing resources to mitigate the consequences of the CBRN incident.

Many DOD strategies, activities, and programs support preparation for a CBRN response. Examples include unit training, local, regional, and national and international level planning, and national and command exercises in both the domestic and foreign environments. Security cooperation and partner activities (e.g., multinational exercises, exchanges, experimentation, and counterproliferation and nonproliferation activities), while not a part of FCM, still serve to foster positive working relationships and build partner capacity to prepare for and respond to CBRN incidents, which may reduce the need for US forces in FCM operations.

# B. Assessment

A thorough assessment of the employed CBRN material and/or its effects provides feedback such as protection requirements, hazard levels, areas of contamination, expected duration of hazards, etc. This information contributes to the commander's situational awareness and technical assessment capability throughout any response. Objectives may include providing temporary critical life support; protecting critical infrastructure, preventing great property damage, protecting the environment; containing the incident and enabling community recovery. In addition, it is advantageous to respond in such a manner that the effects of the incident are minimal and serve as a deterrent for future domestic and international terrorist attacks. Every incident will be different, but the underlying concepts remain constant.

Immediately after a CBRN incident, initial assessments determine the scope and magnitude of the incident and ultimately determine the need for DOD and joint force participation. Assessments should be done as quickly as possible to avoid additional lives being lost.

*See facing page for further discussion.*

# Assessments

*Ref: JP 3-41, Chemical, Biological, Radiological, and Nuclear Consequence Management (Jun '12), pp. IV-9 to IV-10.*

There are several assessments available to a commander to assist with overall planning. These include:

## Operational Environment Assessment

An operational environment assessment provides the commander information on the threat, the physical environment, and the political environment. Decision support tools may be used in conjunction with this information to assist predictive modeling.

The threat assessment identifies what enemy or adversary the force may face during a DOD-led CBRN CM operation, if in a hostile environment. The threat assessment also addresses the types of agents and hazards and includes occupational and environmental health assessments.

The physical environment includes terrain, weather, and characteristics of the geographical area. Characteristics include critical infrastructure, hazard sites, and zone analysis considerations. Analysis of urban areas within the JOA can facilitate the complex transition from combat operations to CBRN CM when required.

The political environment includes applicable impacted nation agreements, SOFAs, and other sovereignty issues that may apply.

## Capabilities Assessment

Capabilities assessment provides an assessment of the JFC's ability to conduct DOD-led CBRN CM and includes plans, organization, manpower, equipment, logistics, medical, training, leadership, and readiness.

## Vulnerability Assessment

A vulnerability assessment is an evaluation of the organization's strengths and weaknesses compared with the operational environment and CBRN threat. Vulnerability analyses of key APOD, SPOD, and JRSOI sites, to include proximity of TIM storage facilities or sites, are used to develop measures to reduce the organization's vulnerability to identified CBRN threats. The ultimate purpose of a vulnerability assessment is to help ensure that adequate defensive and CBRN CM assets are available.

## Risk Assessment

These assessments attempt to quantify the level of risk that exists in the conduct of DOD-led CBRN CM operations. In certain incidents, such as high radiation hazards, the risk may preclude mission accomplishment.

## Criticality Assessment

The criticality assessment evaluates a command's missions and functions/capabilities and determines mission impact or consequence of loss of assets that support execution of the command's missions.

## Threat Assessment

The threat assessment provides an assessment on the adversary's CBRN capability. This threat can come from nation states and non-state actors alike, sometimes simultaneously, and may occur in a variety of forms. These include deliberate attacks or accidental releases.

Consequence Management

# III. CBRN CM Operations Process

Ref: ATP 3-11.41, Multi-Service TTPs for CBRN Consequence Management Operations (Jul '15), pp. 1-6 to 1-8 (fig. 1-4).

The operations process consists of four primary activities—plan, prepare, execute, and continually assess. CBRN CM follows this model.

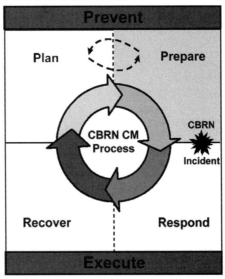

Ref: ATP 3-11.41 (Jul '15), fig. 1-4, p. 1-7.

*Within the CBRN CM process, the execution activity is further expanded into two subordinate activities—response and recovery. This expansion is necessary to address the graduated level of effort from immediate actions to full restoration. Assessments are continuous throughout pre incident and post-incident activities. The planning and preparation activities support the NRF prevention efforts, while the response and recovery actions support the NRF mitigation efforts.*

## Plan

Planning involves the assessment of the operational environment and enables commanders to identify minimum standards for training, organizing, equipping, and protecting resources. The response unit planning process determines preparation and facilitates response and recovery operations.

## Prepare

Preparation implements the approved plan and relevant agreements to increase readiness through training, exercises, and certification. Vulnerability reduction measures are initiated by the response unit to support prevention and mitigation functions.

## Respond

The response process addresses the short-term, direct effects of an incident. Response measures initiated by the response unit include those actions taken to save lives, protect property, and establish control.

## Recover

The response unit initiates the recovery process, focusing on restoring mission capability and essential public and government services interrupted by the incident. The recovery phase also includes completing the mitigation of the immediate hazard.

# Joint Operational Phases

*Ref: ATP 3-11.41, Multi-Service TTPs for CBRN Consequence Management Operations (Jul '15), pp. 1-8 to 1-9 (fig. 1-5).*

During domestic or foreign response operations, response elements follow a multi phase operational approach that is similar to the approach taken for other military deployment operations.

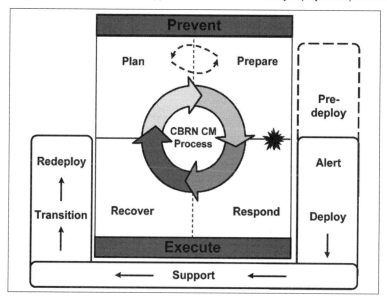

*Ref: ATP 3-11.41 (Jul '15), fig. 1-5, p. 1-8.*

The operational phases are—

## Alert, preparation, and situation assessment
Response elements take actions such as alerting unit personnel, assessing the incident and preparing for deployment. The advanced echelon travels to the incident site.

## Deployment
Upon receipt of the appropriate directive, the unit moves to the designated location within the time frame specified.

## Support to U.S., Civil, or HN authorities
Response elements (remaining under DOD C2) support coordinated actions to accomplish the CM goals.

## Transition
This phase outlines the remaining tasks for the response element to complete before redeployment, following coordination between the DOD C2 element and the applicable HN or domestic authority.

## Redeployment
The response unit begins redeployment when directed. This phase is complete when the unit has reached its designated home station.

# IV. CBRN CM Tasks

Ref: ATP 3-11.41, Multi-Service TTPs for CBRN Consequence Management Operations (Jul '15), pp. 1-5 to 1-6 and 2-5 to 2-6.

CBRN CM tasks are conducted during the operations process. The components are—

## Assess the Situation

Response units continually collect and analyze information before, during, and after each mission to enable the confirmation, correction, or refutation of existing analyses. Assessment activities provide the ability to predict future requirements to make necessary planning and operational adjustments. Assessment activities include threat, readiness, plans and TTP, detection and analysis, and surveillance. At the tactical level, the response element (a decontamination or survey team) assesses information on the hazard (such as agent flammability, reactivity, explosiveness, and physical properties; protective clothing requirements; weather information; and site drawings).

## Coordinate Operations

Response units coordinate the full range of activities across the spectrum of the mission. Coordination activities include exercise, warning, and reporting; C2 and synchronization; security and control; forensics; sample collection and packaging; and public and civil affairs activities. At the tactical level, the response element (the CBRN survey team) conducts coordination within the military task force (or with other supporting activities) to coordinate linkup times and locations for staging area operations or operational updates. Responding units report to the incident command post and are assigned tasks according to its level of training and incident requirements.

## Conduct Logistics

Response units plan and conduct the movement and sustainment of forces for CBRN CM operations. Logistic activities that may be conducted by response elements include pre-positioning materials; transporting casualties, remains, and samples; deploying personnel and material; and maintaining facilities and material.

## Provide Health Service Support

Response units provide health service support (HSS) during CBRN CM operations. HSS addresses services performed, provided, or arranged to promote, improve, conserve, or restore the mental or physical well-being of personnel. These services include the management of health services resources (manpower, monies, facilities); preventive and curative health measures; evacuation of the wounded, injured, or sick; selection of the medically fit and disposition of the medically unfit; blood management; medical supplies and equipment and maintenance thereof; combat stress control; and medical, dental, veterinary, laboratory, optometric, nutrition therapy, and medical intelligence services. The term force health protection will be used, according to JP 1-02, when the following definition applies: measures to promote, improve, or conserve the behavioral and physical well-being of a Service member to enable a healthy and fit force, prevent injury and illness, and protect the force from health hazards.

## Decontaminate

Response units remove contamination from personnel, equipment, and facilities. Decontamination activities include emergency, responder, mass casualty, and patient decontamination.

Representative tactical-level CM tasks include the following:
- Provide logistic and engineering support of operations
- Handle, process, store, and transport contaminated equipment, material, samples, residues,and animal remains
- Handle, process, store, and transport contaminated human remains
- Protect against exposure and effects of chemical agents
- Protect against exposure and effects of biological agents
- Protect against exposure and effects of nuclear and radiological agents
- Provide large-scale medical services
- Conduct tactical CM crisis action planning
- Assess the operational environment
- Conduct tactical CM C2
- Perform incident/hazard risk assessment
- Establish and maintain access/egress controls and hazard zone perimeter
- Conduct victim and casualty search, rescue, and extraction
- Establish temporary housing and processing operations and evacuate the affected population
- Conduct decontamination operations
- Isolate, quarantine, and manage potentially contaminated or infectious human and animal populations
- Perform medical surveillance

# V. Joint Task Force-Consequence Management (JTF-CM) Notional Structure

*Ref: JP 3-41, Chemical, Biological, Radiological, and Nuclear Consequence Management (Jun '12), pp. I-6 to I-8 (Contributor: Dr. Thomas Hennefer).*

A joint task force (JTF) may be established, or an existing one tasked, to provide or facilitate the provision of a variety of response capabilities to mitigate the incident.

These capabilities may be located within the current force or they may have to be requested from other DOD sources and attached temporarily to the JTF. The capabilities may be CBRN specific (e.g., CBRN reconnaissance, decontamination) or general (e.g., security, transportation) capable of functioning in CBRN environment. For example, some tasks, associated with CBRN CM technical rescue, require the rescuers to function in personal protective equipment (PPE), a specific capability that all rescue units may not possess. The exact composition of each element will be based on incident type and severity.

## 1. CBRN CM Command and Control Element

This element focuses on the overall management of the incident as well as the interim intrateam communications, interagency communications, and ability to provide situational awareness to adjacent agencies and supported higher headquarters. The CBRN CM C2 element should provide:

- Secure encrypted digital voice and data communications via Nonsecure Internet
- Protocol Router Network (NIPRNET)/ SECRET Internet Protocol Router
- Network (SIPRNET)/Global Command and Control System
- High-speed secure multimedia communications with Reachback capability
- Warning reporting services
- Functionality to conduct incident simulation and projection exercises
- Assistance in dealing with displaced civilians (civil affairs)
- Assistance in transitioning support to civilian authority

## 2. CBRN Reconnaissance and Surveillance Element

This element provides capabilities to locate, detect, identify, quantify, collect samples, survey, observe, monitor, report, and mark contaminated areas. This type of reconnaissance is best managed, planned and executed by first responders well-trained and well-equipped to handle areas of contamination due to the inability of most first responders to quickly and accurately identify contaminates and the knowledge of proper safety and management techniques. Due to the long-term impact on both the physical area, inhabitants and future generations, proper management of contaminates and contaminated area must not be assigned to units unprepared for long-term contingency implementation.

## 3. CBRN CM Decontamination Element

This element supports methods and technologies required to neutralize or remove hazardous materials (HAZMAT) including chemical warfare (CW) agents, TIMs, biological warfare agents, and radiological contamination. As stated previously, this type of assignment needs to be managed by those organizations (both military and civilian) trained in the identification, classification and treatment of CBRN disposal since unlike traditional ordinance can appear benign to the casual observer but result in devastating long-term effects, illness and death, and can without proper management enlarge the contaminated area or population either directly or indirectly.

The capabilities needed for decontamination include:

- Rapid assembly and dissemination of the decontamination capability at multiple sites
- Decontamination of personnel, ambulatory and non-ambulatory

## 4. CBRN CM Medical Element

This element supports force health protection and all capabilities required for the transport, tracking, diagnosis, and treatment of casualties involved in a CBRN incident CBRN incident. Medical assistance and treatment of CBRN casualties is unlike what most traditional trauma centers are equipped or trained to deal with primarily because close and unprotected exposure by medial professionals to those exposed to CBRN elements can themselves be both casualties and disseminators of CBRN after-effects to a wider population.

## 5. CBRN CM Force Protection Element

This element supports the protection of DOD personnel attending to a CBRN CM incident. Separate security elements may be required to provide convoy, airport, military aircraft, seaport, and ship security, as appropriate to the mission being performed. Additionally, coordination with USG crime scene investigators may be necessary. Due to the nature of CBRN attacks or accidental exposure to the general military or civilian population, Force Protection units are the first, best choice to manage any CBRN event due to the training an resources available to the military and the ability of interagency support.

The force protection element may be called upon for:

- Implementing appropriate antiterrorism (AT) measures
- Establishing early warning systems within the JTF operational area
- Providing convoy and patient transport security
- Incident site control, to include entry and exit management

## 6. Search and Rescue Element

This element supports all capabilities necessary to search for and rescue casualties from a contaminated or hazardous environment. Casualties are usually decontaminated prior to transit from the incident site to reduce the spread of contaminates and to protect both first responders working in post event critical care units as well as those participating in search, rescue and recovery efforts. This element requires specialized technical rescue training to support the rescue of personnel and equipment from a CBRN environment using unique equipment for structural collapse (urban) search and rescue.

A consideration in theses efforts is the probability that the recovery process will include fatalities whose remains cannot be returned in the usual manner after applicable identification, but decontaminated prior to release to family members, and in some sever cases, those remains may not be candidates for return. Due to the nature of CBRN casualties, separate and highly controlled grave identification morgues must be established, then after a CBRN event has been resolved, the morgue itself must be decontaminate since some radioactive elements can have a shelf-life of hundreds of years and biological contaminates and become dormant but still virile and deadly long after the primary CBRN event has been declared resolved.

## 7. General Support Element

This element supports all capabilities necoessary to provide the general support to all the other mission areas and maintain force readiness. This includes providIng the transportation, maintenance, engineering, and personnel support services to enable the effective employment of the other mission areas.

# VI. Operational Planning Considerations (Site Assessments)

*Ref: JP 3-41, Chemical, Biological, Radiological, and Nuclear Consequence Management (Jun '12), pp. I-17 to I-19.*

The CCDR, at the request of federal and state/territory or supported nation authorities, sends a site assessment team to conduct assessments to gain early situational awareness in response to a CBRN incident. Common assessment requirements are provided below:

**Damage and Injury Reports**. Examine initial damage and injury reports for information on specific CBRN effects. Reports should be scanned for details including contamination control measures initiated and the number of contaminated casualties. Each CBRN incident has unique characteristics requiring appropriate follow-on response measures.

**Nature of the Incident**. Examine the effect on the population and infrastructure to identify response capabilities required to address the incident. This includes assessing risk to responders in order to determine force protection requirements.

**Force Protection**. Plan for and implement force protection measures. Force protection considerations are a top priority during any CBRN response operation and include providing proper protective equipment to personnel, planning for site safety, security, individual awareness of hazards and dangers, protection from contamination through proper marking and avoidance of contaminated areas, air monitoring, and health service support (HSS). Force protection efforts must include consideration of secondary incidents/devices that may target first responders or be designed to intentionally spread contamination. While these factors are primarily CBRN-oriented, the force may also be vulnerable to multiple types of opportunistic threats by adversaries, so the threat assessment must not be focused solely on CBRN.

**Duration and Geographical Extent of the Incident**. Assess the number of jurisdictions affected by the incident and the likelihood of the scope expanding significantly due to population migration and weather/terrain.

**Weather and Terrain**. Examine the effects weather and terrain may have on the CBRN material to include dispersion of chemical, biological, or radiological agents or toxic material by wind or water (e.g., stream/river flows).

**Public Reaction**. Gauge public reaction to the incident as it can affect response requirements, particularly if the level of fear is high or likely to grow, or if massive population movement is under way or expected.

**Mission Duration**. Assess mission duration, as it drives sustainment requirements. Extenuating circumstances may prolong CBRN response in the event civilian capability is lacking or inadequate. However, transition back to local responders should occur as soon as practical.

**CBRN Reconnaissance and Surveillance Tasks**. Plan for the conduct of locating, detecting, identifying, quantifying, sample collecting, surveying, observing, monitoring, reporting, and marking contaminated areas. Military forces generally have only basic sampling and detection capabilities, so specialized military units may be required.

**Identification of Supporting DOD Forces**. Local authorities may have some DOD forces assisting within their area under immediate response authority. The GCC should coordinate through the Services to identify Title 10, USC, units that are providing support either under immediate response or under local authority prior to the execute order (EXORD) and JTF establishment.

# III. Domestic Consequence Management (CM)

Ref: JP 3-41, Chemical, Biological, Radiological, and Nuclear Consequence Management (Jun '12), chap. 2.

CBRN CM conducted by DOD in the homeland in support of civil authorities is conducted as a DSCA operation. The capability and capacity to effectively respond to domestic CBRN incidents and sustain operations in CBRN environments require properly trained and equipped forces that follow the parameters set forth in this section.

## Domestic CBRN Consequence Management

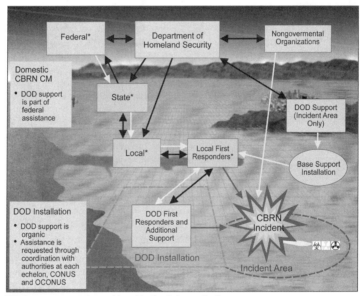

*Tribal response may require special consideration during coordination.

Legend

| | |
|---|---|
| CBRN | chemical, biological, radiological, and nuclear |
| CBRN CM | chemical, biological, radiological, and nuclear consequence management |
| CONUS | continental United States |
| DOD | Department of Defense |
| OCONUS | outside the continental United States |

◄────► request for assistance/coordination
───── provision of assistance
◄────► response to incident

Ref: JP 3-41, CBRN Consequence Management, fig. II-1, p. II-2.

A description of DOD's participation in the whole-of-government response to a domestic CBRN incident is provided in the NRF. It further details the authorities that delineate the roles and limits for DOD in a domestic response. In conducting DSCA to include CBRN response, a distinction is made between the different chains of command for active DOD, Title 10, USC, federal forces providing support to civil authorities and for NG forces commanded by the state governor under Title 32, USC,

# I. Domestic Consequence Management

Ref: JP 3-41, Chemical, Biological, Radiological, and Nuclear Consequence Management (Jun '12), pp. II-2 to II-3 and II-17 to II-19.

DOD provides assistance upon request by an appropriate authority and after approval of SecDef. When conducting CBRN response IAW the NRF, DOD is in support of an NRF ESF primary agency or NRF incident annex coordinating agency. As a practical matter, DOD prefers a single source for mission assignments and generally identifies DHS FEMA as the primary agency in its EXORD, operation plan, or operation order (OPORD) authorizing federal military assistance. In any case, DOD may provide assistance that has been approved by the appropriate authorities.

For more information on ESFs, refer to the NRF and JP 3-28, Defense Support of Civil Authorities.

The domestic environment for DSCA presents many challenges to the JFC and more so when responding to a CBRN incident. It is imperative that commanders and staffs at all levels understand the statutory and operational relationships among all federal departments and agencies involved in the operation. NIMS provides a consistent nationwide template to enable federal, state, tribal, and local governments, the private sector, and NGOs to work together to prepare for, prevent, respond to, recover from, and mitigate the effects of incidents regardless of cause, size, location, or complexity. NIMS can be utilized for all incidents, ranging from daily occurrences to incidents requiring a coordinated federal response.

Commanders and their staffs at all levels should be knowledgeable about the NRF and NIMS and how their commands fit in to the overall national response framework. The NRF is a guide to how the US conducts all-hazard responses. It is built upon scalable, flexible, and adaptable coordinating structures to align key roles and responsibilities across the Nation. It describes specific authorities and best practices for managing domestic incidents that range from the serious but purely local, to large-scale terrorist attacks or catastrophic natural disasters. The NRF contains a number of incident annexes that apply to CBRN incidents. Each annex lists the coordinating agency or agencies and cooperating agencies involved in the response and provides information on applicable policies, authorities, planning assumptions, concept of operations, actions, and responsibilities of cooperating agencies for the particular incident described.

For more information on the NRF and NIMS, refer to the NRF Resource Center: http://www.fema.gov/NRF and the NIMS Resource Center: www.fema.gov/NIMS. These online resources are routinely updated and evolving.

## DOD Roles and Responsibilities

Domestic CBRN CM is managed at the lowest possible level, with DOD providing support as directed. When SecDef approves a request for DSCA during a CBRN incident, CDRUSNORTHCOM and Commander, United States Pacific Command (CDRUSPACOM) are the supported GCCs for CBRN responses within their respective AORs as designated in the Unified Command Plan (UCP) for a federal response. DOD supports the NRF primary and coordinating agencies during domestic CBRN CM operations. The operational chain of command for federal forces remains with the GCC; the operational chain of command for state controlled NG forces remains with the governor.

## The Joint Force in a CBRN CM Environment

Overarching requirements for a joint force in a CBRN environment are two-fold: the joint force shapes the composition of the response through proactive planning and interagency, intergovernmental, and nongovernmental coordination. The joint force is also responsible for protecting each member of DOD in support of civil authorities. The CBRN environment causes joint forces to plan in a unique way and recognize the primary reason for employment of the joint force is to support civil authorities and mitigate the consequences of a CBRN incident. Planning considerations are significantly different for the joint force conducting CBRN response as the primary mission than for the joint force conducting other missions. Requirements for protecting joint forces remain a constant priority for the JFC, especially when operating in a contaminated environment. Supporting civil authorities also may entail unique legal implications that need to be considered through all phases of planning and operations.

## Layered CBRN Response

The NRF describes a tiered response and emphasizes that response to incidents should be handled at the lowest jurisdictional level capable of handling the work. The response to a CBRN incident requires the integration and synchronization of capabilities from the local, state, tribal, and federal level. Federal agency teams respond on their agency's authority, if the problem exceeds the capabilities of lower tiers. From the DOD perspective, the layered response will likely begin within hours with employment of NG WMD-CSTs, HRFs, and CERFPs in Title 32, USC, or state active duty in addition to local Title 10, USC, commanders providing assistance under immediate response authority. When directed by SecDef, USNORTHCOM responds within hours with JTF-CS and the first DCRF and C2CRE echelons. These layered capabilities build quickly.

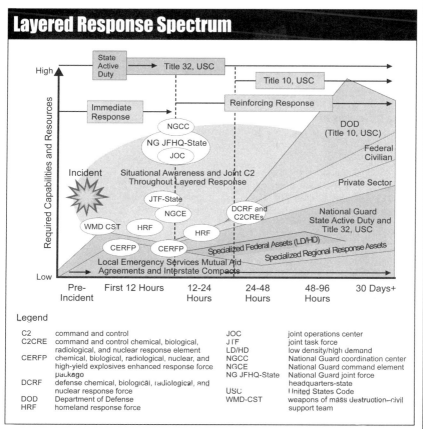

Ref: JP 3-41, CBRN Consequence Management, fig. II-3, p. II-18.

Consequence Management

and state active duty. State and local governments are closest to those affected by incidents, and have a lead role in response and recovery.

For a federal response to a CBRN incident, DOD support is tailored to the scope and magnitude of the incident. DOD assets are employed with a focus on response requirements beyond the resources of state and federal civil authorities. The DOD CBRN response is typically conducted via a JTF that provides C2 of forces trained and equipped for this mission, as well as contingency sourced conventional forces. Using a six-phased approach, the JFC leads the response forces from steady state through CBRN response operations. During phase 0, the CCDR sustains subordinate response force readiness through exercises, training, and rehearsal activities.

### Defense Support of Civil Authorities

DSCA policy and procedures guide DOD support provided by federal military forces, NG forces performing duty IAW Title 10 and Title 32, USC, DOD civilian, military contract personnel, and DOD component assets in a domestic response. It includes immediate response and response to approved RFAs during domestic CBRN incidents. This DSCA response includes support to federal departments and agencies that assist local, state, and tribal authorities within the US territories for CBRN CM operations. Figure II-1 illustrates the basic relationships of CBRN CM. It includes support provided by NG forces performing duty conducted as state-directed actions when approved by SecDef IAW Title 10 and Title 32, USC, or when NG forces are in state active duty status. SecDef policy and Joint Staff instructions provide guidance for the operational framework that serves as the foundation for a joint force's relationship with local, state, tribal, other federal, or nongovernmental entities.

# II. Command Relationships

Domestic CBRN CM may engage the full spectrum of government, NGOs, and the private sector. The efficient coordination of military and civil capabilities and activities within a stricken operating environment requires a unifying command structure to achieve unity of effort. Military forces always remain under the control of the chain of command as established by Title 10, USC, Title 14, USC, Title 32, USC, or state active duty.

NG Soldiers and Airmen may serve either in a federal status like other reserve soldiers, or in a state status (state active duty or Title 32, USC), under the command of the governor. The state governors, through TAGs, control NG forces when those forces are performing active duty in their state role and when performing active duty under Title 32, USC.

### Dual-Status Command

Legislation allows for a dual-status commander to have command authority over both federal and state forces. A dual-status commander provides a means for providing unity of effort for military forces operating in Title 32, USC, and Title 10, USC. A dual-status commander must be duly appointed and can be an active duty officer who accepts an additional state commission or can be a federalized state NG officer. Dual-status command can leverage military leadership that has local situational awareness and existing relationships with local civil agencies; provide continuity as federal forces are integrated into the response effort; and provide for continuity in response (same JTF C2 prior to and after federal response). Dual-status authority is vested in an individual commander, not the organization. Therefore, a dual-status commander should have a Title 10, USC, deputy and a Title 32, USC, deputy, as well as a joint staff manned by Title 10, USC, and state active duty/Title 32, USC, personnel. This augmented staff is particularly important should a dual-status JTF-State have to control naval forces since few states have naval militias from which to draw maritime expertise. The primary shared DOD and state interests are unity of effort and effective execution.

# III. CBRN Response Phases

Ref: JP 3-41, Chemical, Biological, Radiological, and Nuclear Consequence Management (Jun '12), pp. II-21 to II-27.

The JP 5-0, Joint Operation Planning, phasing model is adapted for domestic CBRN response operations as described below.

## CBRN Response Activities by Operational Phase

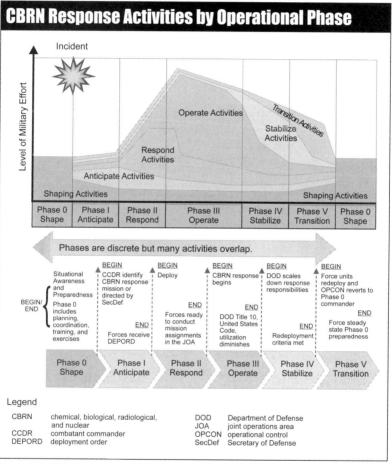

Ref: JP 3-41, CBRN Consequence Management, fig. II-4, p. II-22.

**Phase 0—Shape (Shape)**

**Phase I—Deter (Anticipate)**

**Phase II—Seize the Initiative (Respond)**

**Phase III—Dominate (Operate)**

**Phase IV—Stabilize (Stabilize)**

**Phase V—Enable Civil Authorities (Transition)**

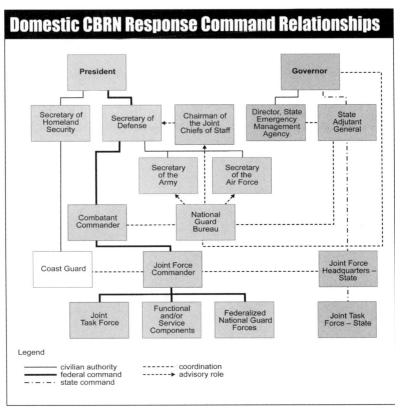

**Domestic CBRN Response Command Relationships**

Legend
— civilian authority
━━ federal command
—·—·— state command
------ coordination
------▸ advisory role

Ref: JP 3-41, CBRN Consequence Management, fig. II-2, p. II-13.

*For more information on dual authority under Title 10, USC, and Title 32, USC, refer to JP 3-27, Homeland Defense, and JP 3-28, Defense Support of Civil Authorities.*

# IV. Unique Planning Considerations in the Domestic Operational Environment

## A. Base Support Installation

A BSI is a military installation within the US or its territories controlled by any military Service or agency, in or near an actual or projected domestic emergency operational area, designated by DOD to provide military support for DOD and federal agency disaster response operation efforts.

Resources provided by a designated BSI may include, but are not limited to marshalling and lay down areas, security forces, personnel and equipment reception and staging areas and facilities, personnel support, billeting, transportation, material handling equipment, maintenance, general supply and subsistence support, contracting support, communications support, and medical services.

Logistic planners should consider appropriate Service and RC installations as potential BSIs that will facilitate JRSOI and sustainment of CBRN response units. Although the Services, when directed by SecDef, designate the appropriate BSI, locations for potential BSI should be based on previous site surveys, assessments, and mission analysis.

# V. CBRN Response Considerations

Ref: JP 3-41, Chemical, Biological, Radiological, and Nuclear Consequence Management (Jun '12), pp. II-17 to II-19..

## Strategic

During a CBRN incident, DHS coordinates the federal government's incident management efforts in support of the civil authorities. However, it is likely that the major elements of operational framework will have already been established IAW strategic decisions made by state and local responders in the initial hours of the response effort. A major decision is the determination of controls for the employment of first responders (police, fire, and emergency medical services) into the incident area to ensure that significant portions of the first responder community do not themselves become casualties. Another major decision concerns the ability of local civil government to control the evacuation out of the incident area. If the local government can control the evacuation through public information and rapid establishment of traffic control points, then operational conditions are favorable for the deliberate application of local, state, and federal resources at designated evacuee processing centers and urban search and rescue, decontamination, and medical triage and emergency medical sites at points upwind or crosswind from the incident area. If the local civil government is unable to control the evacuation of the civil population, then evacuation centers are established at resulting choke points either on major roads or near hospitals and will result in a less deliberate approach to application of local, state, and federal resources.

## 2. Operational

The WMD-CST arrives in the vicinity of the incident site within the first 6 hours. The WMD-CST is able to provide the initial assessment to the NG JFHQ State, JTF-State, and the incident commander, which forward the assessment to the NGCC and to USNORTHCOM. It is important the NGCC and USNORTHCOM joint operations center (JOC) forward the initial assessment and characterization of the threat to follow-on deploying NG WMD-CSTs, CERFPs, HRFs, and DCRF and C2CRE units, respectively, so these units can be better prepared for conditions they will face in the incident area. However, as discussed previously, much of the operational environment for CBRN response will be set based on early strategic decisions of the local authorities. If the evacuation of the population is controlled, CBRN response forces deploy to staging areas where they link up with local responders and are integrated into an existing network of evacuation processing centers. If the evacuation is uncontrolled, CBRN response forces may be required to establish evacuation centers at designated choke points or vicinity hospitals. For CBRN response forces, the most critical operational decision in the first 24 hours will be determination of how and where to employ life-saving (search and extraction, decontamination, and medical triage and emergency medical) capabilities.

## 3. Tactical

At the tactical level, the critical effort is rapid, and effective employment of reconnaissance capabilities is necessary to provide assessments on the effects in terms of casualties and medical treatment (detect and monitor). These assessments provide the necessary information to assist the incident commander in determining upwind and crosswind points and best locations for search and extraction, decontamination, medical triage and emergency medical services, and other sites. The next major effort is to increase the capability and capacity of local responders to perform search and extraction, decontamination, and medical triage and emergency medical care of casualties. DOD forces can reinforce evacuation centers to increase capacity and throughput or establish search and extraction, decontamination, medical triage and emergency medical—expanding the geographic distribution of response capability.

Consequence
Management

# VI. CBRN Control Zones

*Ref: JP 3-41, Chemical, Biological, Radiological, and Nuclear Consequence Management (Jun '12), pp. II-29 to II-31 (fig. II-5, p. II-30).*

In CBRN response, control zones are established to ensure the safety of all responders and control access into and out of a contaminated area. The three zones established at a chemical, radiological, nuclear, and some biological incident sites (where there is a contaminated area such as may be the case with anthrax) are often referred to as the hot zone, the warm zone, and the cold zone. Figure II-5 depicts these control zones. In nearly all cases, the control zones will decrease in size with time as CBRN hazards naturally decrease. Once the characteristics of the hazard are understood, the control zones can be effectively altered to allow more mission flexibility.

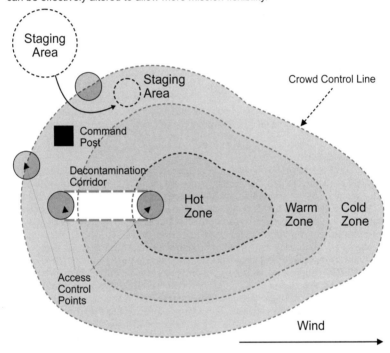

## 1. Hot Zone

The hot zone is an area immediately surrounding a hazardous material incident which extends far enough to prevent adverse effects from released contamination to personnel outside the zone. The level of risk and thus the included area is determined by the incident commander, accounting for characteristics of the hazards. The hot zone can also be referred to as the exclusion zone, red zone, or restricted zone and is the primary area of contamination. The hot zone is the area that the incident commander judges to be the most affected by the incident. This includes any area to which the contaminant has spread or is likely to spread. Primary contamination can occur when individuals enter this zone. Usually, no decontamination or patient care except evacuation is carried out in this zone. Access is only permitted to personnel who are properly trained and protected. The incident commander sets the perimeters of this zone after giving consideration to the type of agent, the volume released, the means of dissemination, the prevailing meteoro-logical conditions, and the potential of local topographic characteristics to channel agent dispersal. Priorities within the hot zone may include conducting search and rescue, performing hazard mitigation, and identifying CBRN hazards or other physical obstacles to the entry point.

## 2. Warm Zone

The warm zone includes control points for the access corridor and thus assists in reducing the spread of contamination. The warm zone can also be referred to as the decontamination zone, contamination-reduction zone, contamination-reduction corridor, yellow zone, or limited access zone. The warm zone is the area between the hot and cold zones where personnel and equipment decontamination and hot zone support take place. Management of the warm zone includes decontamination corridors where casual-ties, emergency responders, and equipment are decontaminated and where there is a risk of secondary contamination from objects or individuals brought from the hot zone. Maintaining access control points connecting the warm zone to the hot and cold zones and for the decontamination corridor assists in reducing the spread of contamination. Warm zone operation should be established in an area that is safe from downwind expo-sure and should include the bulk of the decontamination assets where survey teams are positioned and equipment decontamination is accomplished.

## Cold Zone

The cold zone is the area where the command post and support functions that are necessary to control the incident are located. It should be clean, meaning it is free of all contamination by HAZMAT, including discarded protective clothing and respiratory equipment. Contaminated casualties and emergency response personnel must be decontaminated before entering this zone. The cold zone is the area where the incident command post, staging areas for equipment, and other support functions that are neces-sary to control the incident are located upwind and uphill of the warm zone. The same basic considerations that are used for the hot and warm zones influence the extent of the cold zone. The cold zone must be readily accessible and provide the means for safety and rest. It must also be large enough to accommodate local, state, and federal CBRN response forces (if required) and to serve as the staging area for personnel and equipment. The operational priorities of the cold zone include providing C2 for opera-tions being conducted in the warm and hot zones and ensuring that there is an area of security for emergency personnel and response forces conducting operations. Access to the different zones should be tightly controlled and limited to as few people as possible. Communication between work areas should be face-to-face whenever possible, par-ticularly if the use of radios or other electronic devices (e.g., megaphones) is restricted because of the hazards involved.

### *Zone Control in Nuclear Detonations*

*DHS has worked with partner agencies and emergency response partners to establish standard guidance for emergency planners with nuclear detonation specific response recommendations to maximize the preservation of life in the event of an urban nuclear detonation. The planning guidance summarizes recommendations based on the effects of a 10 KT nuclear detonation in an urban environment. The nuclear explosion's observable phenomena, in the area around ground zero, are linked to an accumulation of the hazards from pressure (blast), heat (thermal), and radiation. These cumulative hazards make it more dangerous for rescue workers and less likely to find survivors the closer one moves toward the point of detonation. The observable phenomenon of damage to infrastructure and other objects provides a way to describe zones with rough approximation delineations that can assist planners and the initial emergency responders in managing risk before radiation levels have been measured and hazard areas marked.*

Consequence Management

# B. United States Army Corps of Engineers (USACE) Services

USACE is the designated ESF #3 (Public Works and Engineering) coordinator and a primary agency as directed by the NRF. USACE can provide water, ice, construction materials, and engineer services when activated under ESF#3 and ESF#6 (Mass Care, Emergency Assistance, Housing, and Human Services). If ESF#3 or ESF#6 have not been activated, the JTF or DCO may request engineering capabilities through the CCDR to the components.

# C. Mortuary Affairs

The joint force may aid federal and state agencies by providing mortuary affairs assistance. Any assistance provided will be IAW the NRF and existing civilian plans and local civilian direction.

The primary responsibility for responding to mortuary affairs issues rests with state and local authorities. A local or state medical examiner and/or coroner (ME/C) will have the responsibility for leading the response effort. DOD mortuary affairs assets are usually employed in support of the ME/C. Other important state and local stakeholders who may have significant operational involvement include Office of Emergency Management, Department of Public Health, NG, state law enforcement, EPA, and fire department and HAZMAT units.

Several conditions affect the ability of local and state officials to respond to mass fatality operations. Some of these factors include number of fatalities; quality and state of remains; the agent or agents (contaminated versus uncontaminated) present; location and size of the search and recovery area; conditions (weather, daylight, terrain); city and state resources available; and most important, public expectations. Within the construct of the civilian operation there are a number of different missions where joint forces may be asked to provide mortuary affairs assistance.

Expected DOD mortuary operations include advisory support, search and recovery, reception, remains storage, contamination mitigation of remains, photography, fingerprinting, forensic dentistry, forensic pathology, family assistance, disposition of remains and personal effects, administration and logistic support. Decedent identification is an ME/C responsibility; DOD mortuary affairs assets support the identification process through forensic recovery and preservation of decedent identification material.

For remains that cannot be decontaminated to a specified transportation level, protecting the health of Service members and the public takes precedence over rapid disposition. Temporary storage of remains in a refrigerated storage facility or interment of those contaminated remains that pose a threat to public health is recommended until remains can be safely handled.

A phased mortuary affairs plan may be required to assist civil authorities in augmenting ME/C. Not all mortuary affairs assets are deployed for each mass fatality incident; the mortuary affairs response will be tailored to meet the needs of the local jurisdiction.

*For additional information on mortuary affairs, refer to JP 4-06, Mortuary Affairs.*

# IV. Foreign Consequence Management (FCM)

*Ref: JP 3-41, Chemical, Biological, Radiological, and Nuclear Consequence Management (Jun '12), chap. 3.*

FCM is assistance provided by the USG to an impacted nation to mitigate the effects of a deliberate or inadvertent CBRN incident. From the national level, FCM encompasses USG efforts to assist partner nations to respond to incidents involving CBRN contaminants and the coordination of the US interagency response to a request from a partner nation following an incident involving CBRN contaminants. DOD's CBRN response includes efforts to protect its citizens and its Armed Forces abroad, as well as those of its friends and allies, in order to mitigate human casualties and to provide temporary associated essential services.

## Foreign Consequence Management

Legend

| | | |
|---|---|---|
| CBRN | chemical, biological, radiological, and nuclear | ◀──▶ request for assistance/coordination provision of assistance |
| DOD | Department of Defense | ◀── response to incident |

*Ref: JP 3-41, CBRN Consequence Management, fig. III-1, p. III-2.*

Primary responsibility for responding to a foreign CBRN incident resides with the impacted nation, unless otherwise stipulated under relevant international agreements. Unless otherwise directed by the President, DOS leads FCM operations and is responsible for coordinating the overall FCM response. When requested by DOS and directed by SecDef, DOD supports FCM operations by performing CBRN response activities to the extent allowed by law and subject to the availability of forces.

# I. Foreign Consequence Management (FCM)

*Ref: JP 3-41, Chemical, Biological, Radiological, and Nuclear Consequence Management (Jun '12), pp. III-2 to III-6 (fig. III-2, p. III-4).*

FCM applies to foreign incidents involving the deliberate or inadvertent release of CBRN materials, including TICs and TIMs. It does not apply to the following activities:

- Acts of nature or acts of man that do not involve CBRN materials. Response to such incidents is conducted as foreign DR or HA operations IAW DODD 5100.46, Foreign Disaster Relief.

- CBRN incidents that are the direct result of US military operations in a foreign country where DOS does not have an established presence.

- CBRN incidents that occur and are contained on DOD installations and facilities overseas for which DOD retains primary responsibility under relevant international agreements or arrangements IAW DODI 2000.18 and DODI 6055.17

## United States Government Offer of Assistance Process

The impacted nation's response may or may not be sufficient to mitigate the hazards from a CBRN incident. Support requests for foreign assistance may begin immediately after an incident. During this period, the US embassy in the country, the applicable GCC, and other USG entities need to begin to obtain situational awareness related to the nature and magnitude of effects from the CBRN incident. The USG may also begin considering whether to proactively offer assistance to the impacted nation.

## Request for Assistance Process

Figure III-2 depicts both the FCM request for assistance and FCM processes. Once the impacted nation determines additional capabilities are required, the impacted nation notifies the US embassy with a request for assistance and provides known information about the incident.

The COM, frequently the ambassador, notifies DOS in Washington, DC. DOS makes internal DOS and National Security Staff notifications and dispatches a foreign emergency support team (FEST) and/or a consequence management support team (CMST) to the US embassy. Additionally, DOS begins logistics, transportation, and other support coordination with the country team. It is expected that the country team will inform the relevant GCC, who will dispatch a liaison element to work with the country team to assess the situation, identify potential support requirements, and begin the flow of information through the combatant command to the NMCC.

The National Security Staff coordinates interagency deliberations to assess the request and determine whether the US will honor it; identify what specific support will be provided and which agencies will provide that support; and develop initial guidance for responding organizations.

Following interagency coordination, the National Security Staff provides guidance to executive departments and other organizations to initiate the formal USG response under FCM. The country team out of the US embassy increases coordination with the impacted nation regarding the specific support the US will provide and finalizes logistics, transportation, and legal negotiations.

Specific requests for DOD support are submitted to the OSD Executive Secretary or verbally through the NMCC with a follow-on formal request to the OSD Executive Secretary. Upon receipt of a request, DOD assesses it against specific request criteria, issues appropriate orders, and coordinates for the movement of tasked resources. DOD identifies command relationships, and the supporting commands coordinate the provision of identified resources. The supported combatant command identifies a TF organization, develops C2 guidance, and coordinates resource deployment with the country team.

# CBRN Affected State Coordination Process

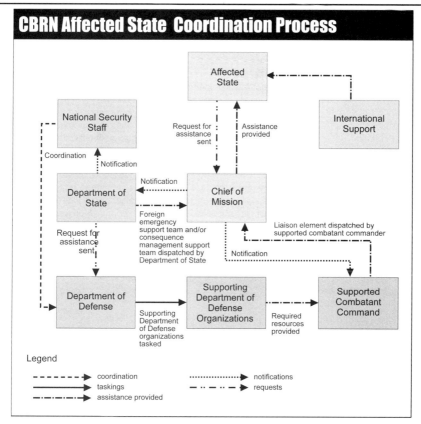

## Request for Assistance/Offer of Assistance Criteria

OSD and Joint Staff offices, in coordination with the supported GCC, will use the criteria outlined below to assess potential offers of, and requests for, assistance and provide a coordinated recommendation to SecDef.

- **Legality**—compliance with US and international laws and bilateral and multilateral agreements.
- **Lethality**—potential use of force by or against DOD assets.
- **Risk**—to national security (if the USG does or does not provide the requested assistance), the potential to effect US interests across national instruments of power, and to the health and safety of forces supporting FCM operations.
- **Cost and Reimbursement**—availability of funds, potential for reimbursement, and impact on DOD budget.
- **Readiness**—impact on DOD's ability to perform its primary mission and availability of appropriate forces.
- **Appropriateness**—whether or not DOD can and should perform the mission. Factors to be considered include the contributions provided by other USG departments or agencies, other nations, and international and private organizations.
- **CCDR input**—GCC issues regarding mission execution and impact of the mission on country-specific and regional policies, plans, and initiatives.
- **Timeliness**—ability to get requested capabilities where they are needed in a time frame that can make a positive difference.

# II. FCM Authorities and Assets

*Ref: JP 3-41, Chemical, Biological, Radiological, and Nuclear Consequence Management (Jun '12), pp. III-9 to III-11.*

In the event of a CBRN incident affecting foreign territory, various authorities exist to govern the response. The two major laws which govern US responses to foreign CBRN incidents are the International Disaster Assistance section of the Foreign Assistance Act (FAA) (Title 22, USC), and the military humanitarian response authorities set forth in Title 10, USC. In addition to a review of these authorizing laws, various restrictions on US foreign aid should be considered before any response or assistance is provided.

## The Foreign Assistance Act of 1961

The Foreign Assistance Act of 1961 provides authorization for USG foreign aid programs. Section 2292 of the FAA authorizes the President "to furnish assistance to any foreign country, international organization, or private voluntary organization, on such terms as he may determine, for international disaster relief and rehabilitation, including assistance relating to disaster preparedness, and to the prediction of, and contingency planning for, natural disasters abroad." Additionally it states, "In carrying out the provisions of this section the President shall insure that the assistance provided by the United States shall, to the greatest extent possible, reach those most in need of relief and rehabilitation as a result of natural and man-made disasters." The types of assistance that may be provided under this section are not enumerated; however, assistance relating to disaster prepared-ness is expressly approved.

## EO 12966

EO 12966 authorizes the military to respond to a CBRN incident in a foreign operational environment either at the direction of the President, with the concurrence of the Secre-tary of State, or on its own initiative to save human lives in emergency situations where there is insufficient time to consult with the Secretary of State. EO 12966 is analogous to the military's immediate response authority for domestic disasters. When conditions resulting from any emergency or attack in a foreign country require immediate action, local military commanders may take such actions as necessary to save lives. When such compelling conditions exist and time does not permit prior approval from higher head-quarters, commanders or officials acting under "immediate response authority" may take necessary action to respond to requests from local affected nation authorities or the US COM. Following their immediate response actions, commanders report to their higher headquarters of assistance being provided by the most expeditious means available, and seek approval or additional authorizations as needed. The GCC notifies the affected US COM at the time of higher headquarters notification.

## Assets

The following paragraphs identify organizations that could respond to an FCM incident:

- **Foreign Emergency Support Team**. The FEST is a DOS-led interagency support team that can be deployed immediately in support of the US embassy in response to actual or suspected terrorist incidents. The Office of the Coordinator for Coun-terterrorism exercises responsibility for the management of the FEST. The FEST is task-organized depending on the incident and may include DOD elements that pro-vide support to the US embassy, consulate, or mission for foreign emergency op-erations. The appropriate GCC provides liaison, and as required technical support to the FEST. A small FCM advisory component should be on the FEST whenever CBRN materials are involved. DOD provides additional support as required through the supported combatant command.

- **Consequence Management Support Team.** The CMST is a DOS-led interagency support team that can be deployed pre- or post-incident. The CMST provides CBRN CM advice, assistance, and support to a US embassy, consulate, or mission in country. It can be deployed in lieu of or as a subordinate element to the FEST. It is comprised of subject matter experts from DOS and other USG departments and agencies as required. The CMST provides FCM situation assessments to the USG and affected nation, as appropriate, and with the COM, coordinates the USG response for DOS. Upon approval by SecDef, DOD provides support to the CMST through the appropriate GCC as requested by DOS.

- **DTRA Consequence Management Advisory Team.** The CMAT deploys to provide joint technical support to the supported commander with expertise in CBRN response procedures, requirements, resources, C2, health physics, PA, legal affairs, and specialized technical information. The CMAT is able to task-organize and deploy to support commanders in the technical aspects of CBRN accidents or incidents. The incident tailored force has secure communications, trained technical experts, hazard prediction modeling capability, and rapid reachback capability.

- **The US Armed Forces Radiobiology Research Institute** can provide DOD technical support capability for nuclear and radiological incidents or accidents. An AFRRI medical radiobiology advisory team (MRAT) responds as part of the DTRA CMAT and is available at all times. The MRAT can provide on-site training to health professionals on the management of nuclear or radiological casualties. The team provides state-of-the-art expertise and advice to commanders and primary care providers following a nuclear or radiological accident (nuclear weapons, reactor, or radiological material). The MRAT provides access to biodosimetry and bioassay support to incident responders and local health authorities.

- **The United States Air Force Radiation Assessment Team (AFRAT)** is a globally responsive, specialty asset team that provides health physics and radiological support in response to radiation incidents and accidents. AFRAT provides subject matter experts to support planning, surveillance, analysis, and assessment to mitigate radiation and operational risks resulting from radiation/nuclear incidents. The team provides field radioanalytical support. It measures, analyzes, and interprets environmental and occupational samples for its radioactivity content, providing expert guidance on the type and degree of radiological hazards that face deployed forces. The AFRAT performs radioanalytical analysis on environmental samples (such as swipes, soil, water, air, and foodstuffs) and occupational samples (such as urine and feces). Analysis results are interpreted for the effect on deployed forces and noncombatants. The information is compiled for use by command and medical authorities on dose avoidance, dose reduction, and dose assessment; risk of communication; and additional requirements for effective CBRN CM.

- **US Marine Corps Chemical-Biological Incident Response Force.** CBIRF is a unit that was created to deploy on short notice in response to CBRN incidents. CBIRF consists of specially trained personnel and specialized equipment suited for operations in a wide range of contingencies. CBIRF is designed to minimize the effects of a CBRN incident through detection, identification, search and extraction, technical rescue, mass casualty decontamination, medical triage, and emergency medical support.

- **The United States Army 20th Support Command (CBRNE)** is the operational headquarters for Army CBRN specialized units. The 20th Support Command is the primary Army force provider of specialized CBRNE capabilities. It conducts CBRNE operations in support of the CCDR, JFC, Army, and provides support to federal agencies as required; provides C2 of assigned CBRN forces; provides CBRNE technical advice and assistance; and maintains a technical reachback assistance capability.

Any FCM response typically includes a number of USG departments and agencies in addition to DOD. In the case of a CBRN incident, the ability of the USG to assist an impacted nation government and its affected population is determined by the nature of the CBRN incident, the resources available to provide assistance, and the time required to deploy to the vicinity of the incident. FCM operations may be conducted concurrently with foreign DR and humanitarian assistance (HA) operations. FCM operations generally occur in a permissive environment, but the relevant GCC is responsible for force protection requirements for US military personnel.

> "Abroad, when requested by a host nation, the President may authorize and the Secretary of Defense may direct DOD support to US Government (USG) foreign consequence management (FCM) operations. For all consequence management activities, the military must be prepared either to support or lead consequence management operations, as directed."
>
> National Military Strategy to Combat Weapons of Mass Destruction, 13 February 2006

A foreign nation that endures a significant CBRN incident requiring external assistance may first request assistance from neighboring states, regional allies, and regional or international organizations that have the capacity to deliver that assistance in a timely manner. The USG may be asked to provide assistance, or the USG may offer assistance, as part of a bilateral or international response to the CBRN incident. It is unlikely that the USG would be the only foreign entity providing assistance.

For further guidance on foreign assistance, refer to JP 3-29, Foreign Humanitarian Assistance.

# III. Command Relationships

SecDef designates the supported and supporting combatant command relationships, and the supported CCDR establishes the command relationships of assigned forces for each specific CBRN response. The DOD supports the LFA during USG FCM operations unless otherwise directed by the President. DOD forces remain under the C2 of the supported CCDR. DOS retains responsibility for coordination among USG entities.

# IV. Affected Nation Considerations

An affected nation is one that has requested support to mitigate the effects of a CBRN incident. The affected nation has primary responsibility for responding to, managing, coordinating other nations' augmenting support, and mitigating the consequences of a CBRN incident within its borders. A major part of any FCM operation is augmenting affected nation operations, not replacing them. In order to avoid duplication of effort, affected nation capabilities need to be determined. In the aftermath of a CBRN incident, it may be difficult to determine which government ministry is performing certain functions. The US embassy within the country should be able to assist in identifying such details.

# V. Dept of Defense-led CBRN CM

Ref: *JP 3-41, Chemical, Biological, Radiological, and Nuclear Consequence Management (Jun '12), chap. 4.*

DOD conducts CBRN CM to mitigate hazards in support of operations or to support others in response/recovery (when required/as directed). All DOD CBRN CM capabilities are designed to be used in support of military operations. Like any other DOD capability, these military assets may be used in support of civilian operations or joint or multinational forces, as directed. Mitigating the hazard reduces the threat to personnel, facilitates freedom of action, and supports mission completion. In the majority of cases, DOD supports DOS in the conduct of FCM and DHS for domestic CBRN CM. However, during combat operations or in specific instances where DOS or DHS is unable or incapable of leading the USG effort, DOD could be given primary mission responsibility. DOD-led CBRN CM can occur in either domestic CBRN CM or FCM. DOD may be delegated or tasked with leading a USG CBRN CM effort.

## DOD [Department of Defense] Led CM [Consequence Management] Operations

In both domestic and foreign environments, CM actions are initiated at the national level with DOD providing support as directed by the President or SecDef [Secretary of Defense]. DOD forces may, however, be directed to lead [these] operations as a direct result of US military operations in a foreign country where DOS [Department of State] does not have an established presence.

Joint Publication 3-40, Combating Weapons of Mass Destruction, 10 June 2009

For DOD, the CBRN environment is hazard-focused and may involve deliberate, prolonged actions in and around the hazard area to support response and recovery efforts. While some hazard mitigation can be conducted by conventional forces, CBRN CM operations to address the source of the hazard often require specialized training and equipment.

DOD-led CBRN CM operations are generally conducted in one of two situations. DOD may be directed to coordinate the USG CBRN CM response in a permissive or uncertain environment where the DOS has no established diplomatic presence in the JOA to facilitate LFA activities, or there is no functioning HN government, to meet FCM requirements. The US military will lead CBRN CM operations conducted concurrently with military operations in hostile environments consistent with strategic planning guidance.

These unique conditions require the JFC to assume primary responsibility for planning, managing, and mitigating the incident until conditions permit transfer of responsibility as the lead USG agency for FCM to DOS or another authority. In these cases, the JFC becomes the de facto USG lead for the initial FCM response using available assets. The JFC requests additional support from the USG and other nations through DOS for follow-on operations. The conditions within the operational environment may range from active combat operations to crisis response in limited contingency in responding to or in mitigating the effects of, such an incident. DOD transitions DOD-led CBRN CM activities as soon as feasible to an appropriate civilian governmental authority.

# II. CBRN CM Planning Considerations during Military Operations

Ref: JP 3-41, Chemical, Biological, Radiological, and Nuclear Consequence Management (Jun '12), pp. IV-4 to IV-6.

GCC theater security cooperation activities (phase 0) support DOD-led CBRN CM operations by facilitating interaction with partner nation military forces to identify partner capabilities, build partner capacity, and increase interoperability. Planning for DOD-led CBRN CM should build on these activities and incorporate the experience gained in working with partner nations in operations.

DOD-led CBRN CM operations may be required to facilitate combat operations, and depending on the nature and purpose of the activities, may require coordination with response operations of multiple countries, partners, and a wide variety of international organizations and other NGOs. JFCs should be aware of the following planning considerations:

- Integration of specialized US military forces, USG departments and agencies, and contractors
- Integration of partner nation support and forces
- Support and integration of NGOs
- Development of a strategic communication plan

Coordination between DOD and other USG departments and agencies, NGOs, and IGOs will also be important aspects of any DOD-led CBRN CM operation. Regardless of the status of an impacted nation government or partner nations, IGOs and NGOs will have significant equities in the operation; therefore, JFCs should anticipate considerable interagency and intergovernmental coordination requirements.

Operations will likely be subject to monitoring by various government agencies or IGOs; therefore, planners should anticipate receiving specific US national level guidance. As DOD-led CBRN CM operations may involve significant interactions with foreign civilian authorities and IGOs that do not normally operate in a supporting role to DOD, the JFC should strongly consider forming a CMOC or supplementing an existing CMOC with appropriate FCM expertise. In addition to IGO participation, the CMOC often involves multinational partners that possess unique FCM capabilities.

For further guidance on CMOCs, refer to JP 3-57, Civil-Military Operations. For additional guidance on multinational operations refer to JP 3-16, Multinational Operations.

As with USG departments and agencies, NGOs and IGOs may have significant equities and capabilities; planning for their participation in a hostile or uncertain environment is challenging. Some of these agencies may demand to participate regardless of the risk, and others may not be willing to participate until a permissive environment exists.

DOD-led CBRN CM operations can occur at any point in a campaign; therefore, these operations should be considered as a branch to contingency operations. DOD-led CBRN CM-related activities are conducted in the following phases, which differ from traditional operational phases as found in JP 5-0, Joint Operation Planning:

## Phase 0 (Shape)
This is a continuous phase. The intent of this phase is to ensure DOD is organized, trained, equipped, and prepared to minimize the effects of CBRN incidents on foreign soil. Key tasks of this phase include planning response capabilities within the joint force, identifying possible partner nation FCM capabilities, incorporating DOD-led CBRN CM scenarios into training and exercises, and developing intelligence on friendly, neutral, and enemy CBRN threats in the operational area.

## Phase I - Deter (Situation Assessment and Preparation)
Transition to phase I occurs on reliable indications and warnings of a CBRN incident or upon notification that an incident has occurred. Phase I includes those actions required to conduct a timely and accurate assessment of the CBRN situation, preparation for deployment, and deployment of selected advance elements. Phase I ends when the nature and scope of the CBRN situation and initial response requirements are defined. The response spectrum may include technical expertise, specialized teams, or entire units. Conventional forces will also be needed to carry out non-CBRN tasks (medical, transportation, security, etc.). Any limited initial response to a CBRN incident conducted by DOD commanders operating under immediate response authority would likely occur during phase I. Plans should also include HA/DR considerations for those affected by the CBRN incident or its cause.

## Phase II - Seize the Initiative (Deployment)
Phase II begins with the deployment of designated forces and the establishment of formal command relationships between supported and supporting commanders. Depending on the nature and scope of the hazard, forces may continue to flow for some time (days, weeks, or even months). Commanders begin planning immediately for redeployment and transition to civilian agencies, including USG, other international governments, donors, and NGOs, and should identify the necessary or minimum conditions needed to effect the transition. Phase II ends when the first capability arrives and is operational.

## Phase III - Dominate (Mitigate Hazard Effects)
Phase III begins with the initialization of efforts to mitigate hazard effects. These efforts may include lifesaving operations, personnel and equipment decontamination, actions to stop or reduce the source of contamination, and actions to support associated HA/DR efforts as a result of the CBRN incident. Remediation (return to a pre-contaminated state) is usually not possible by DOD forces. Rather, the control of the hazard site and reduction to the threat to forces and any nearby civilians is the goal. When (due to operations) transition is not possible, the area will be marked to protect forces and any civilians in the area. Phase III ends when the on-scene commander determines that the incident site is under positive control.

## Phase IV - Stabilize (Transition to Close the Incident Site)
Phase IV begins initiation of the redeployment plan. The situation contained, the effort is now made to reduce the personnel needed to continue mitigation efforts. When possible, HN, NGO, or USG personnel may replace functions performed by DOD personnel. Otherwise, efforts will be made to mark the area to reduce any residual threat to personnel or civilians in the area. Phase IV ends when the mitigation of the incident is at such a point where it is determined that no or minimal personnel are needed to maintain security of the site.

## Phase V - Enable Civilian Authorities (Redeployment)
Phase V begins with the redeployment of the bulk US military forces involved in CBRN CM operations or the formal transition of those forces to a purely DR or HA mission. Phase V is complete when all forces have returned to their previous military posture or completed transition to other missions.

Consequence Management

Strategic and operational objectives drive the priority of DOD-led CBRN CM operations in relation to other ongoing military operations. JFC's should plan DOD-led CBRN CM operations as a complex contingency or branch operation executed in any environment to:

- Facilitate accomplishment of overall military objectives
- Reduce the effect of a CBRN incident on combat operations
- Provide assistance to civilian populace affected by a CBRN incident
- Facilitate transfer to stability operations

In general, DOD-led CBRN CM operations occur in one of the following two operational contexts:

- In response to CBRN incidents on foreign territory where DOS does not have an established diplomatic presence or there is no functioning HN government DOD may be required to act as the LFA for FCM requests to coordinate the USG response including in country activities and actions to minimize the effects of WMD use/CBRN hazards. Requested activities and actions will be assessed based on the following criteria: legality, lethality, risk, cost and reimbursement, readiness, appropriateness, GCC input, and timeliness to provide recommendations to SecDef and facilitate coordination of the USG response through DOS and interagency partners.

- CBRN CM operations conducted concurrently with military operations include:
  - CBRN CM assistance to the local populace within the operational area.
  - CBRN CM operations at APODs/SPODs to maintain force projection capacity.
  - Activities to minimize potential collateral effects from targeting adversary WMD capabilities.
  - CBRN CM activities as a result of US, allied, or adversary military operations that result in the release of CBRN or TIMs.

# III. Joint Force Considerations

In the context of DOD-led CBRN CM operations, the appropriate JFC assumes responsibility for the execution of operations within the JOA when a CBRN incident requiring a response occurs. The GCC approves end states for these operations by phase within the JOA. One major objective is to conduct DOD-led CBRN CM operations without jeopardizing critical military operations and objectives; however, commanders should plan for the diversion of combat forces and possible changes to overall end states and objectives due to the significance of a CBRN incident.

Providing assistance to civilian populace affected by a CBRN incident is an important aspect of these operations. Assistance may include, but is not limited to:

- Saving lives and preventing human suffering
- Providing support to displaced personnel
- Preventing/reducing additional damage
- Providing mortuary affairs support
- Providing emergency mitigation of CBRN hazards
- Providing minimum emergency restoration of life supporting services
- Conducting a noncombatant evacuation operation

# VI. Dept of Defense CBRN Response Assets

*Ref: JP 3-41, Chemical, Biological, Radiological, and Nuclear Consequence Management (Jun '12), app. C.*

The DOD CBRN Response Enterprise focuses on life-saving activities and includes AC and RC forces. The following forces constitute the DOD CBRN Response Enterprise. All elements described on the following page consist of assigned and allocated units, standardized to ensure they contain the required capabilities for that type element, and are trained and ready to deploy as a coherent element within prescribed timelines. WMD-CSTs, CERFPs, and HRFs are NG units in their respective states. The DCRF, C2CRE A, and C2CRE B are allocated to USNORTHCOM in the Global Force Management Allocation Plan.

## DoD CBRN Response Enterprise

**State Response** (Title 32, United States Code)

**Federal Response** (Title 10, United States Code)

National Guard assets may operate under state or federal control.

**DCRF** FP 1 FP 2

**C2CRE** A and B

- Command and control
- CBRN assessment
- Search and extraction
- Decontamination
- Emergency medical
- Level 2 and 3 medical with surgical capability
- Security
- Engineering
- Logistics
- Transportation
- Ground medical evacuation and casualty evacuation
- Aviation lift
- Aviation medical evacuation and casualty evacuation

+ Additional forces, if required

- Command and control
- CBRN assessment
- Search and extraction
- Decontamination
- Emergency medical
- Level 2 medical
- Security
- Engineering
- Logistics
- Transportation

+ Additional forces

**HRF** (10 Units)

- Command and control
- Search and extraction
- Decontamination
- Emergency medical
- Security

**CERFP** (17 Units)

- Search and extraction
- Decontamination
- Emergency medical

**WMD-CST** (57 Teams)

- Detection/ID
- Rapid assessment of HAZMAT

Prepared to deploy NLT N+3 hours

Prepared to deploy NLT N+6 hours

Prepared to deploy NLT N+6-12 hours

Prepared to deploy FP 1 NLT N+24 hours FP 2 NLT N+48 hours

Prepared to deploy NLT N+96 hours

← Allocated by SecDef to supported Governor →

← Allocated to USNORTHCOM/USPACOM →

### Legend

| | | | |
|---|---|---|---|
| C2CRE | command and control chemical, biological, radiological, and nuclear response element | HAZMAT | hazardous materials |
| CBRN | chemical, biological, radiological, and nuclear | HRF | homeland response force |
| CERFP | chemical, biological, radiological, nuclear, and high-yield explosives enhanced response force package | ID | identification |
| | | N+ | notification |
| | | NLT | not later than |
| | | SecDef | Secretary of Defense |
| DCRF | defense chemical, biological, radiological, and nuclear response force | USNORTHCOM | United States Northern Command |
| FP 1 | force package 1 | USPACOM | United States Pacific Command |
| FP 2 | force package 2 | WMD-CST | weapons of mass destruction–civil support team |

*Ref: JP 3-41, CBRN Consequence Management, fig. C-1, p. C-2.*

Consequence Management

# DoD Response Forces

*Ref: JP 3-41, Chemical, Biological, Radiological, and Nuclear Consequence Management (Jun '12), pp. C-1 to C-4.*

## A. National Guard WMD-CSTs

WMD-CSTs respond to a CBRN incident by providing a rapid response capability in the event of an intentional or unintentional release of CBRN threats and hazards. There are WMD-CSTs assigned to the NG. These are a high priority, rapid response unit made up of 22 full-time Title 32, USC, Active Guard and Reserve Army and ANG personnel as-signed. These units were established by Congress, certified by SecDef to Congress after they meet DOD certification guidelines. By statute, each WMD-CST operates under the control of the governor, in Title 32, USC, status, and can be employed as a state asset without DOD authorization. TAG will direct employment of the WMD-CST to support either a state response or to provide support to another state's response, if requested. Further, under Presidential mobilization, WMD-CST could be employed as part of the Title 10, USC, force package. The WMD-CST mission is to support civil authorities at a domestic incident site by identifying CBRN hazards/substances, assessing current or projected consequences, advising on response measures, and assisting with appropriate requests for state support to facilitate additional resources. This includes the intentional or unintentional release of CBRN and natural or man-made disasters in the US that result, or could result, in the catastrophic loss of life or property.

## B. National Guard CERFPs

The CERFP mission is, on order, to respond to a CBRNE incident or other catastrophic event and assist local, state, and federal departments and agencies in conducting CBRN CM by providing capabilities to conduct personnel decontamination, emergency medi-cal services, and casualty search and extraction. There are 17 CERFPs, consisting of 186 total personnel each, for a total of 3,162 personnel, to include 5 Active Guard and reserves and 5 full-time equivalents, per CERFP. (This number does not include the 11 ANG fatalities search and recovery team personnel.) They are a state and federal NG capability. Personnel who augment the CERFPs are not in a Title 32, USC, "operational status," which means they cannot assemble and deploy until the governor orders the unit members into state active duty. Units assigned to each of the 17 CERFPs remain under the control of the governor of the state in which they reside. Governors exercise their ex-ecutive authority through TAGs. Out-of-state CERFP support is requested from the state EOC IAW interstate agreements or EMACs. The NG JFHQ-State JOC may enter the governor's request into the Joint Information Exchange Environment (JIEE) for coordina-tion with the several states and NGB. Requests are coordinated with other states and NGB based on a supporting/supported relationship and operational or TACON provided by the gaining supported state IAW established MOAs or other agreements. In some circumstances, the President may federalize NG assets, to include HRFs, CERFPs, and WMD-CSTs. CERFP capabilities are casualty search and extraction, emergency medi-cal triage, treatment, and patient stabilization, and mass casualty decontamination, in a contaminated environment to support the incident commander's IAP objectives.

## C. National Guard HRFs

The HRF mission is, on order, alert, assemble, and deploy within 6–12 hours of noti-fication in response to a CBRN incident to save lives, mitigate human suffering, and prepare for follow-on forces in support of civil authorities. Capabilities include search and extraction, casualty decontamination, emergency medical triage and treatment, security element, and C2. There are 10 HRFs, one existing within each FEMA region, consisting of 566 personnel in each HRF with 25 percent full time manning in each, for a total of 5,660 personnel. The HRFs will be sourced from the existing Army and Air NG force. NG units that are selected as part of the HRF remain under the direction and control of the governor of the state in which they reside. Governors exercise their command, operational authority, or TACON of military forces through TAGs. Requests for out-of-state HRF support is requested from the state EOC IAW interstate agreements or EMAC (via a Requisition A) of which all states are signatories. The NG JFHQ-State JOC may enter the governor's request into the JIEE for coordination with other states and NGB. Requests are coordinated with other states and NGB based on a supporting/supported relationship and OPCON or TACON provided by the gaining/supported state IAW established MOAs or other agreements. The authority to notify, deploy, and employ an HRF, in almost all cases, is vested in the independent, sovereign state governors who control the NG capabilities with the understanding that HRFs are designed to be regional and national assets that support CBRN CM nationwide. In some circumstances, the President may federalize NG assets, to include HRFs, CERFPs, and WMD-CSTs. Capabilities include search and extraction, mass casualty decontamination, emergency medical triage and patient stabilization treatment, security, and C2 in a contaminated environment to support the incident commander's IAP objectives. The HRFs are the center of gravity for the DOD CBRN Response Enterprise integration in their respective FEMA region's states' planning.

## D. JTF-Civil Support

JTF-CS serves as the CBRN response headquarters for the DCRF. JTF-CS provides planning, training, and coordination for CBRN response operations. It serves as lead planning authority for development of operational JTF and tactical TF level CBRN response operation plans and develops projected CBRN response and DSCA force requirements and structures to support mission requirements for all CBRN national planning scenarios. JTF-CS is the C2 element responsible for executing domestic CBRN response by responding to federal request for assistance IAW the NRF and DOD policy to provide immediate actions to save lives, protect property and the environment, and meet basic human needs. The domestic CBRN response focuses on the operational to tactical levels in order to rapidly integrate and synchronize DOD capabilities in support of civil authorities.

## E. Defense Chemical, Biological, Radiological, and Nuclear Response Force (DCRF)

The DCRF includes approximately 5,200 personnel sourced primarily from the AC (multi-Service). DCRF capabilities include CBRN incident assessment, search and rescue, decontamination of DOD personnel and equipment, evacuee and casualty decontamination, emergency medical, Role 2 medical care (patient triage, along with trauma and emergency medical care), patient holding, ground and rotary-wing air patient movement, Role 3 medical care (surgical and intensive care), force health protection measures, military personnel and equipment operational security, site accessibility horizontal engineering, logistics, general support to enhance lifesaving and reduce human suffering, C2 aviation lift, mortuary affairs, and transportation. The DCRF is designed to employ these capabilities in multi-function packages in order to provide critical lifesaving capabilities in a synchronized manner. There are two force packages, Force Package 1 (2,100 personnel) and Force Package 2 (3,100 personnel). Commander, JTF-CS, has the flexibility to task organize the DCRF based on the situation and mission in order to provide the most effective support to a CBRN response.

## F. C2CRE A and B

The two C2CREs will include approximately 780 personnel each and be sourced from the AC and RC. C2CRE A and C2CRE B will contain much smaller elements of many of the capabilities contained in the DCRF. When directed, the C2CREs will begin initial operations, but must be quickly augmented with additional capabilities to sustain operations. These additional capabilities may include federalized NG assets (including WMD-CSTs, CERFPs, and HRFs) or forces from the AC and RC. Dedicated C2CRE capabilities include CBRN assessment, search and rescue, decontamination, emergency medical, Role 2 medical, engineering, C2, logistics, and transportation.

NG forces in the WMD-CSTs, CERFPs, or HRFs responding to an incident under state active duty or Title 32, USC, authorities, such as governor deployment, inter-state compact agreement, or EMACs request. Forces allocated to the DCRF and C2CRE A and B will conduct operations in Title 10, USC, status under federal control. The command and control structures in response to an incident are dependent on the nature and size of the incident.

## DOD CBRN Enterprise Mission

When directed (by SecDef for federal military forces and by the governor[s] concerned for NG forces under state C2), the DOD CBRN Response Enterprise conducts CBRN response operations within the US and its territories to support civil authorities in response to CBRN incidents in order to save lives and minimize human suffering.

## Unity of Effort

The DOD CBRN Response Enterprise is only a small part of the national response. An effective, unified national response requires layered, mutually supporting capabilities. The NRF systematically coordinates private sector and NGO capabilities with those of local, tribal, state, and federal for commitment in response to a CBRN incident. If requested, SecDef is responsible for assisting DHS and the NRF primary and coordinating agencies in CBRN response operations for a domestic CBRN incident. The synergistic construct of the DOD CBRN Response Enterprise supports unity of effort by facilitating a rapid and echeloned response providing redundancy of critical lifesaving capabilities and a layered integration of NG resources reinforced by federal capabilities.

**[CTS1]
Index**

# SMARTbooks
## INTELLECTUAL FUEL FOR THE MILITARY

Recognized as a "**whole of government**" doctrinal reference standard by military, national security and government professionals around the world, SMARTbooks comprise a **comprehensive professional library** designed with all levels of Soldiers, Sailors, Airmen, Marines and Civilians in mind.

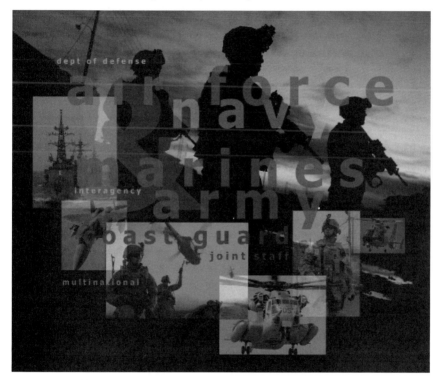

The SMARTbook reference series is used by **military, national security, and government professionals** around the world at the organizational/ institutional level; operational units and agencies across the full range of operations and activities; military/government education and professional development courses; combatant command and joint force headquarters; and allied, coalition and multinational partner support and training.

View, download FREE samples and purchase online:

# www.TheLightningPress.com

# Purchase/Order

**SMARTsavings on SMARTbooks!** Save big when you order our titles together in a SMARTset bundle. It's the most popular & least expensive way to buy, and a great way to build your professional library. If you need a quote or have special requests, please contact us by one of the methods below!

## View, download FREE samples and purchase online:
# www.TheLightningPress.com

### Order SECURE Online
**Web:** www.TheLightningPress.com
**Email:** SMARTbooks@TheLightningPress.com

### Phone Orders, Customer Service & Quotes
Live customer service and phone orders available
Mon - Fri 0900-1800 EST at (863) 409-8084

### 24-hour Voicemail/Fax/Order
Record or fax your order (or request a call back)
by voicemail at 1-800-997-8827

### Mail, Check & Money Order
2227 Arrowhead Blvd., Lakeland, FL 33813

## Government/Unit/Bulk Sales

The Lightning Press is a **service-disabled, veteran-owned small business**, DOD-approved vendor and federally registered—to include the SAM, WAWF, FBO, and FEDPAY.

We accept and process both **Government Purchase Cards** (GCPC/GPC) and **Purchase Orders** (PO/PR&Cs).

*The Lightning Press offers design, composition, printing and production services for units, schools and organizations wishing their own **tactical SOP, handbooks, and other doctrinal support materials**. We can start a project from scratch, or our SMARTbooks can be edited, custom-tailored and reproduced with unit-specific material for any unit, school or organization.*